The Psychology of Physical Activity

Albert V. Carron

University of Western Ontario

Heather A. Hausenblas

University of Florida

Paul A. Estabrooks

Kansas State University

Boston   Burr Ridge, IL   Dubuque, IA   Madison, WI   New York   San Francisco   St. Louis
Bangkok   Bogotá   Caracas   Kuala Lumpur   Lisbon   London   Madrid   Mexico City
Milan   Montreal   New Delhi   Santiago   Seoul   Singapore   Sydney   Taipei   Toronto

McGraw-Hill Higher Education &

*A Division of The **McGraw-Hill** Companies*

THE PSYCHOLOGY OF PHYSICAL ACTIVITY

Published by McGraw-Hill, a business unit of The McGraw-Hill Companies, Inc., 1221 Avenue of the Americas, New York, NY 10020. Copyright © 2003 by The McGraw-Hill Companies, Inc. All rights reserved. No part of this publication may be reproduced or distributed in any form or by any means, or stored in a database or retrieval system, without the prior written consent of The McGraw-Hill Companies, Inc., including but not limited to, in any network or other electronic storage or transmission, or broadcast for distance learning.

Some ancillaries, including electronic and print components, may not be available to customers outside the United States.

This book is printed on acid-free paper.

2 3 4 5 6 7 8 9 0 DOC/DOC 0 9 8 7 6 5 4 3

ISBN 0–07–248901–4

Vice president and editor-in-chief: *Thalia Dorwick*
Publisher: *Jane E. Karpacz*
Executive editor: *Vicki Malinee*
Developmental editor: *Lynda Huenefeld*
Editorial intern: *Aimee Mepham-Shirey*
Senior marketing manager: *Pamela S. Cooper*
Project manager: *Mary Lee Harms*
Production supervisor: *Enboge Chong*
Coordinator of freelance design: *David W. Hash*
Cover designer: *Rokusek Design*
Cover image: *©Corbis Stock Market*
Media technology producer: *Lance Gerhart*
Compositor: *Carlisle Communications, Ltd.*
Typeface: *10/12 Photina*
Printer: *R. R. Donnelley & Sons Company, Crawfordsville, IN*

The credits section for this book begins on page 252 and is considered an extension of the copyright page.

Library of Congress Cataloging-in-Publication Data

Carron, Albert V.
   The psychology of physical activity / Albert V. Carron, Heather A. Hausenblas,
Paul A. Estabrooks.—1st ed.
     p.   cm.
   Includes bibliographical references and indexes.
   ISBN 0–07–248901–4
   1. Exercise—Psychological aspects. I. Hausenblas, Heather A. II. Estabrooks, Paul A. III. Title.

RA781 .C325   2003
613.7'01'9—dc21

2002019088
CIP

This text was based on the most up-to-date research and suggestions made by individuals knowledgeable in the field of athletic training. The authors and publisher disclaim any responsibility for any adverse effects or consequences from the misapplication or injudicious use of information contained within this text. It is also accepted as judicious that the coach and/or athletic trainer performing his or her duties is, at all times, working under the guidance of a licensed physician.

www.mhhe.com

Contents

Preface

It Is Facts That Are Needed. Facts. Facts. Facts. When Facts Have Been Supplied, Each of Us Can Try to Reason from Them.

(James Bryce)

This book evolved from a course in the Psychology of Exercise and Physical Activity that we developed and taught as a team five years ago at The University of Western Ontario. At that time, we were faced with three important questions. The first and most fundamental question was, why introduce a new course into an already crowded curriculum? The answer to that one seemed relatively easy. Across the university in departments as diverse as psychology, health sciences, and medicine, no course in the psychology of exercise and physical activity was available. And if societal interest and concern are any criterion—then and now—there was a pressing need for such a course. Over the past 10 to 15 years, there has been an almost global endorsement of the value of physical activity.

The second important question we faced was, what should be included as content in any discussion of exercise and physical activity? It seemed to us that one natural, logical approach would be to parallel the major foci of research. That research can be categorized into one of three general areas. The first is research that has as its objective *description*. Typically, in the physical activity sciences, researchers have been interested in questions such as: Who is physically active? Who is not? What are the motives of those individuals who are physically active? What reasons are cited for inactivity? Any serious analysis of physical activity must begin with an understanding of research of a descriptive nature. So, in our

course, we naturally decided to discuss the individual and situational correlates of involvement in exercise and physical activity.

A second general research category has to do with *explanation*. It has been suggested by Kerlinger (1973) that "the basic aim of science is theory" (p. 8). Theory is an attempt to account for why events or behaviors occur. Thus, not surprisingly, scholars in the physical activity sciences have developed and tested a number of theories to explain why people are physically active (or not). So, as was the case with descriptive research, we felt that we should discuss the various theories and models advanced to account for physical activity behavior.

The final general research category involves research involved with the introduction and evaluation of *interventions* designed to change inactive behavior and/or sustain physically active behavior. Because physical activity is such an important health behavior, researchers have developed a variety of programs to encourage its adoption and then sustain it. Some of those programs have met with success and others have not. So, as was the case with descriptive and explanatory research, we made a decision to discuss what is known from research about successful intervention programs.

The third important question we faced was, what book would be useful as an addendum to the in-class experience? As it turned out, this question proved to be our most difficult. We examined all the books available at that time and none met our needs. Some were too specialized, focusing on only minimal aspects of the physical activity experience. Others, although more general, did not include all the content we felt is essential to understanding what research has to say about involvement in exercise and physical activity. As a consequence, we compiled a list of selected readings and provided that for our students. But our failure to find a suitable book led to the idea that what was sorely needed was a comprehensive overview of the psychological basis of physical activity behavior. Although we made a decision to undertake the project, nothing came of our plan until about a year ago. At that time, each of us was teaching a course in exercise psychology at our respective universities. Because, again, none of us was able to locate a book that met our needs, we acted on our earlier decision to write this book.

Today, with the completion of our project, we are reminded of a line by Alfred Lord Tennyson in his poem *Ulysses:* "I am a part of all that I have met." What insight! That quote has both general and specific application for each of us. From a general perspective, we owe a huge debt to researchers in the physical activity sciences. Any reader who peruses the pages and pages of references presented at the end of this book will readily understand what we mean. Without the substantial body of research evidence, our own efforts would not have been possible. We hope that we have adequately acknowledged our indebtedness through the citations in the text.

Also, from a specific perspective, each of us is a part of all those people who contributed directly or indirectly to our development. Therefore, we would like to specifically acknowledge our personal debts.

BERT

Historically, my general area of interest has been group dynamics in sport. However, over a period of approximately 15 years, I have developed an increasing interest in what is referred to as exercise psychology. Much of what I have learned in the area of exercise psychology is a product of the interactions and research collaborations I've had the good fortune to experience with bright innovative colleagues and graduate students. That group includes Larry Brawley, Neil Widmeyer, Kevin Spink, Harry Prapavessis, Heather Hausenblas, Diane Stevens, Paul Estabrooks, Michelle Colman, and Todd Loughead.

HEATHER

My interest in exercise psychology began early in my graduate school studies. I was, and still am, intrigued in general by human behavior and more specifically by why the majority of individuals select not to engage in a behavior that has so many physical and psychological benefits. I am indebted to the following colleagues and graduate students who have cultivated and fostered my interest in the field of exercise psychology: Bert Carron, Paul Estabrooks, Craig Hall, Bob Singer, Christopher Janelle, Pete Giacobbi, Claudio Nigg, Danielle Symons Downs, Brian Focht, Erin Dannecker, Becky Ellis Gardner, Beth Fallon, Aaron Duley, and Amy Hagan. Finally, thanks to my family and friends, especially my husband, Todd, and son, Tommy, for their unconditional support and encouragement.

PAUL

Being a part of this project has been an exciting experience for me. Like Bert, I feel that my input in this book was indelibly marked by the research and teaching relationships I have had with my colleagues and mentors. First and foremost I would like to thank my family, especially my wife, Jennie, for continual and unwavering support. For the comprehensive exposure I have had to the science of physical activity psychology, I would like to thank Kerry Courneya and Bert Carron. I also feel it necessary to acknowledge my close collaborators, David Dzewaltowski, Nancy Gyurcsik, Elaine Johannes, Krista Munroe, Rebecca Lee, Heather Hausenblas, and Claudio Nigg. Finally, I would like to dedicate my contributions in this book to Mike Hackett and Harry Huish—two great men who left us too soon.

Finally, from a collective perspective, we would like to point out that our book is intended for health professionals, researchers, professors, and students who are interested in learning more about the psychological basis of involvement in exercise and physical activity. It is our hope that this work will stimulate continued interest in an important aspect of human behavior—physical activity.

SECTION ONE

Introduction to the Psychology of Physical Activity and Exercise

The purpose of Section 1 is to introduce you to the field of the psychology of physical activity and exercise. In the first chapter, we discuss physical activity from the perspective of why it is important, the degree to which people are involved, and the generally accepted guidelines (i.e., minimum levels) for the general population. Also, a hallmark of effective communication is definitional clarity—it's important for you to understand some of the terms that are used throughout the book. So we provide in Chapter 1 definitions for exercise, physical activity, and so on. Finally, we outline the organization of the book.

The foundation of science is measurement. In the second chapter, we focus on measurement concerns. Specifically, we discuss terms used to describe physical activity (e.g., intensity, duration) and fundamental measurement concerns (e.g., reliability, validity). We also describe self-report and behavioral protocols commonly used to assess physical activity.

CHAPTER 1

The Psychology of Physical Activity

The Journey of a Thousand Miles Starts in Front of Your Feet.

(Lao-Tzu)

CHAPTER OBJECTIVES

After completing this chapter you will be able to

- Outline the importance of physical activity from a physiological perspective.

- Estimate the numbers of people who are physically active.

- Describe the currently accepted guidelines for a physically active lifestyle.

- Differentiate among the key terms used in the area known as the psychology of physical activity.

Key terms

active living	intervention
body image	physical activity
cognition	prediction
description	psychology of physical
environment	activity
exercise	psychophysiological
exercise addiction	reactivity
explanation	self-esteem
health	tomato effect

From the perspective of personal fitness, consider the quote used to introduce this chapter. The road to physical fitness and a healthy lifestyle starts in front of our feet. However, there is evidence that remarkably few of us are on that journey. In fact, it would seem that participation in physical activity and exercise shows signs of a **tomato effect**. An interesting term—you may ask, "What's a tomato effect?" Moreover, because it sounds mysterious and a bit dangerous, you may also be tempted to ask, "And how can this so-called tomato effect be eradicated?"

The *tomato effect* is a term James and Jean Goodwin (1984) used to describe a phenomenon whereby highly efficacious therapies are ignored or rejected. Generally, the reason for this rejection is that the therapies do not seem to make sense in light of popular beliefs or common understandings. A tomato effect can also occur if people simply ignore the evidence available.

The term tomato effect is derived from the history of the fruit in North America. The tomato was originally discovered in Peru and transported to

> **tomato effect** A phenomenon whereby highly efficacious therapies are ignored or rejected because the therapies do not seem to make sense in light of popular beliefs or common understandings, or because the available evidence is simply ignored.

Spain from which it made its way to Italy, France, and most of Europe. By 1560, the tomato played a significant role in the diet of most Europeans. In North America, however, tomatoes were avoided because they were considered poisonous. The basis for this belief was that tomatoes belong to the nightshade family of fruits and that several nightshade plants can cause death if eaten in sufficient quantities. Thus, for more than 200 years, tomatoes were not grown commercially in North America. In fact, a significant turning point did not occur until 1820. Apparently, in a dramatic gesture, Robert Gibbon Johnson ate a tomato on the courthouse steps in Salem, New Jersey—and survived! Subsequently, tomatoes began to be accepted as a nutritious food source. It wasn't until the 20th century, however, that commercial marketing of the tomato began in earnest. Today it represents one of the largest commercial crops in North America (Goodwin & Goodwin, 1984).

EFFICACY OF PHYSICAL ACTIVITY

According to Goodwin and Goodwin (1984), the use of aspirin for the alleviation of pain, swelling, and stiffness of rheumatoid arthritis was also characterized by a tomato effect—"high doses of aspirin became an accepted treatment some 70 years after the initial studies demonstrating its efficacy" (p. 2389). What about physical activity? Is a tomato effect toward physical activity prevalent in society?

One part of the answer to that question, of course, pertains to whether physical activity is an efficacious activity. Scientists have spent a large portion of the previous century conducting research on the physiological, physical, and biological benefits of chronic physical activity. What their research has shown is that every system of the body benefits when a person engages in frequent physical activity (Haskell, 1994). In terms of the skeletal system, for example, frequent physical activity leads to increased bone density in youth and an increased likelihood that bone mineral density will be retained in older adults. What about the muscle system? Fre-

quent physical activity brings hypertrophy, strength, and endurance as well as increased capillarization, maximal blood flow, and increased metabolic capacity. In the cardiovascular system, frequent physical activity contributes not only to increased cardiac mass but also to increased stroke volume and cardiac output at rest and during physical activity, and to lower heart rate and blood pressure at rest and during submaximal physical activity. The respiratory system experiences increased ventilatory-diffusion efficiency during physical activity as well as possible decreased work associated with breathing. What about the metabolic system? Being physically active is associated with decreased triglycerides, increased high-density cholesterol, increased insulin-mediated glucose uptake, and decreased adiposity (Haskell, 1994).

These substantial physiological benefits are no secret. Within the past 10 to 15 years, there has been an almost global endorsement of the value of physical activity. For example, Biddle (1995) noted that "physical activity is considered important in contemporary European society" (p. 3). As another example, Dr. Audrey Manley (1996), the former Surgeon General of the United States, in her preface to the report on the relationship of physical activity and health, pointed out:

> For more than a century, the Surgeon General of the Public Health Service has focused the nation's attention on important health issues . . . this new report . . . about the relationship between physical activity and health status, follows in this notable tradition. . . . We must get serious about improving

the health of the nation by affirming our commitment to healthy physical activity on all levels: personal, family, community, organizational, and national. Because physical activity is so directly related to preventing disease and premature death and to maintaining a high quality of life, we must accord it the same level of attention that we give other important public health practices that affect the entire nation. Physical activity thus joins the front ranks of essential health objectives, such as sound nutrition, the use of seat belts, the prevention of adverse health effects of tobacco. (p. 5)

There is absolutely no doubt that physical activity can be described as efficacious.

PREVALENCE OF PHYSICAL ACTIVITY

A second part of the question, is a tomato effect toward physical activity prevalent in society, pertains to whether the society in general tends to avoid physical activity. Are people eating the tomatoes? Or stated another way, is physical activity being embraced by a large portion of the world's population? Unfortunately, the answer seems to be a qualified no. Data collected in the United States shows that almost 30% of the population is physically inactive. An additional 40% to 50% of the population is characterized as not having participated in the recommended amount of physical activity necessary to gain health benefits [USDHSS] (United States Department of Health & Human Services, 2000). Further, these statistics have remained relatively consistent for the past decade (USDHSS, 2000).

Another perspective is provided by the comprehensive analysis undertaken by Caspersen, Merritt, and Stephens (1994). They attempted to summarize international physical activity patterns and trends in four countries: Australia, Canada, Finland, and the United States. Table 1-1 provides an overview from their work. These four countries were chosen because large, generally representative samples had been tested in each. Also, survey administration, sampling procedures, and measures of physical activity were consistent over the time periods studied.

It is apparent from Table 1-1 that substantial differences are present among the four countries. The number of sedentary individuals varies markedly, from a low of 16.1% in Finland to a high of 43% in Canada. Over the length of time between surveys, there was a slight decline in the number of sedentary individuals, from 2.3% in the United States to 15% in Canada. Also, the length of time between surveys did differ markedly across the four countries. Thus, a useful way to compare trends is to compute average annual increases. Using that method, the largest annual increases in physical activity from the lowest to the highest intensity of physical activity occurred in Australia and Canada.

The evidence in Table 1-1 provides the basis for suggesting that people are apparently becoming somewhat more active. However, the recent CDC (2001) findings contribute to the suggestion that the increases highlighted by Caspersen and his associates (1994) may have reached a plateau. The point is that few individuals are physically active on a regular basis, and this situation seems to generalize across a number of industrialized nations.

GUIDELINES FOR PHYSICAL ACTIVITY

A possible reason for the high rate of sedentariness may be a misperception that exercise-mediated health benefits can only be achieved by *strenuous, sustained* aerobic activity. Such perceptions were fostered by the original exercise guidelines established by the American College of Sports Medicine in 1978 (see Table 1-2 for the 1978 exercise guidelines). These guidelines were based on the improvement of cardiovascular fitness; however, these guidelines were often applied to general health (Haskell, 1994). Recently, recommendations by leading authorities have significantly influenced the traditional beliefs about the amount, intensity, and frequency of exercise that is necessary to elicit physical and psychological benefits.

How much physical activity do we need to achieve the health-related benefits? The new guidelines established by the American College of Sports Medicine and the Centers for Disease Control state

■ TABLE 1-1 Prevalence Estimates for Physical Activity in Selected Countries

	Physical Activity Level								
	Lowest			**Moderate**			**Highest**		
		Prevalence (%)			Prevalence (%)			Prevalence (%)	
COUNTRY	**DESCRIPTION OF ACTIVITY DEFINITION**	**MOST RECENT**	**TOTAL CHANGE**	**DESCRIPTION OF ACTIVITY DEFINITION**	**MOST RECENT**	**TOTAL CHANGE**	**DESCRIPTION OF ACTIVITY DEFINITION**	**MOST RECENT**	**TOTAL CHANGE**
Australia[a]	No aerobic activity reported over 2 weeks	26.5	−5	>0 to <1,600 kcal/wk over 2 weeks of aerobic activities	56%	+1.5	>1,600 kcal/wk over 2 weeks of aerobic activity	17.5	+3.5
Canada[b]	0 to 1.4 kcal/kg/day (<600 kcal/wk)	43	−15	1.5 to 2.9 kcal/kg/day of any intensity activity (>~600 to <~1,250 kcal/wk)	24	+7	3+ kcal/kg/day of any intense activity (>~1,250 kcal/wk)	33	+8
Finland[c]	A few times a year or less of physical activity to produce light sweating or cannot exercise	16.1	−6.6	1 time/wk or 2 to 3 times/month of physical activity to produce light sweating	33.3	−0.7	2+ times/wk and 30+ min/occasion of physical activity to produce light sweating	51.3	+7.3
United States[d]	No physical activity during the past month	30.5	−2.3	3+ times/wk & 20+ min/occasion of physical activity either not reaching 60% of age- and sex-specific max cardiorespiratory capacity or not involving rhythmic contractions of large muscles	31.9	+0.5	3+ times/wk & 20+ min/occasion of physical activity at 60%+ of age- and sex-specific max cardiorespiratory capacity involving rhythmic contractions of large muscles	9.1	+2.1

Note. From "International Physical Activity Patterns: A Methodological Perspective," by C. J. Caspersen, R. K. Merritt, and T. Stephens, 1994, in R. K. Dishman, Ed., *Advances in Exercise Adherence* (pp. 73–110), Champaign, IL: Human Kinetics. Used with permission.
[a]Dept. of Arts, Sport, Environment, Tourism, and Territories (1984–1987).
[b]Canada Fitness Survey (1981–1988).
[c]National Public Health Institute (1982–1991).
[d]Behavioral Risk Factor Surveillance System (26 states; 1986–1990).

■ **TABLE 1-2**   A Comparison of the Past and Present Guidelines for Physical Activity

ACTIVITY CHARACTERISTIC	FORMER ACSM GUIDELINES[a]	PRESENT CDC/ACSM GUIDELINES[b]
Frequency	3–5 times/week	4–7 ("most, preferably all") days of the week
Intensity	Vigorous (60%–80% of max)	Moderate
Duration	At least 20 min	Accumulation of ≥ 30 min of daily activity in bouts of at least 10 min
Type	Aerobic activity	Any activity that can be performed at an intensity similar to that of brisk walking

[a]ACSM, 1978.
[b]Pate et al., 1995.

that adults should accumulate a minimum of 30 minutes of moderate intensity physical activity on most, if not all, days of the week (Pate et al., 1995; see Table 1-2). Moderate intensity physical activity, for example, would include brisk walking at a pace of three to four miles per hour, climbing stairs, or doing heavy housework. The accumulation of physical activity indicates that people can engage in shorter bouts of activity spread out over the course of the day. For example, a person could go for a 10-minute brisk walk in the morning, afternoon, and evening to cumulate the daily goal of 30 minutes. The suggestion that physical activity can be accumulated over the course of the day, rather than performed continuously in a single session, was motivated by the difficulties reported by numerous individuals in trying to find a block of 30 minutes per day for physical activity (Sallis & Owen, 1998).

The current guidelines emphasize moderate intensity levels for a duration of 30 minutes. Does this guideline mean that people can achieve the health-related benefits of exercise without engaging in physical activity at vigorous intensity levels or for durations greater than 30 minutes? The answer to this question is an emphatic *no!* The benefits of physical activity are related to the effort that one devotes. Thus, additional health and fitness advantages are gained from physical activities that are undertaken for longer durations or at more strenuous intensity levels or both ([USDHHS], 1996).

What are the physical activity guidelines for youth? It is recommended that youth engage in a minimum of 30 minutes of moderate intensity physical activity per day (Biddle, Sallis, & Cavill, 1998). Maintaining the 30-minute minimal standard keeps the recommendation for youth consis-

The misperception that exercise-related health benefits can only be achieved by strenuous sustained aerobic activity is a possible reason for the high rate of sedentariness.
©PhotoDisk/Volume 67/Fitness and Well-Being

tent with the adult guidelines. The ultimate goal, however, is for youth to be active for at least one hour daily. Two specific research findings have led to the view that one hour per day of physical activity is preferred (Sallis & Owen, 1998). The first is that most young people are already active 30 minutes per day. The second is that despite 30 minutes of daily physical activity, the prevalence of obesity in developed nations is increasing (Biddle et al.). Thus, experts feel that the guideline of one hour might help deter the increase in childhood obesity (Sallis & Owen).

KNOWLEDGE OF BENEFITS OF PHYSICAL ACTIVITY

Scientists, health care professionals, and politicians are aware of the physical, biological, and physiological benefits of physical activity and exercise. A third part of the question pertaining to whether a tomato effect toward physical activity exists in society is whether the portion of the population who are not physically active (i.e., the non–tomato eaters) have a full understanding of the benefits of a physically active lifestyle. Godin, Cox, and Shephard (1983) queried physically active and inactive individuals on their knowledge and beliefs about physical activity. An overview is provided in Table 1-3. In most instances, inactive individuals held similar beliefs to active individuals about the benefits of physical activity. That is, in agreement with active people, inactive people see physical activity as a means to control body weight, be more healthy, relieve tension, improve physical appearance, feel better, and meet people. Yet they don't participate—in large numbers at least.

So the answer to the question, does participation in physical activity show evidence of a tomato effect? seems to be a qualified yes. An efficacious activity is not being wholeheartedly endorsed by a relatively large proportion of the population. The question then becomes, how do we overcome the tomato effect toward physical activity? One useful approach is through science—science that focuses on the psychology of physical activity and exercise.

■ **TABLE 1-3**   Differences in Beliefs About Exercise Held by Physically Active and Inactive Individuals

BELIEF	PHYSICALLY ACTIVE VS. INACTIVE INDIVIDUALS
Helps me control my body weight	Both active and inactive agree
Helps me be healthier	Both active and inactive agree
Is physically damaging	Both active and inactive disagree
Relieves my tension	Both active and inactive agree
Improves my physical appearance	Both active and inactive agree
Helps me feel better	Both active and inactive agree
Is time consuming	Both active and inactive agree
Helps me meet people	Both active and inactive agree
Improves my mental performance	Active agree more than inactive
Helps me be physically fit	Active agree more than inactive
Helps me fill my free time	Active agree more than inactive

Note. Adapted from "The Impact of Physical Fitness Evaluation on Behavioral Intentions Toward Regular Exercise," by G. Godin, M. H. Cox, and R. J. Shepherd, 1984, *Canadian Journal of Applied Sport Sciences, 8,* 240-245.

THE PSYCHOLOGY OF PHYSICAL ACTIVITY

If physical activity is efficacious, one important challenge facing scientists, health professionals, and governments is to help a large segment of the population become more physically active. This achievement is not likely to come through additional research in physiology of exercise, although that discipline will undoubtedly provide answers to important questions such as how much activity is necessary to obtain physiological benefits. As a science, physiology of exercise does not concern itself with general issues associated with understanding and modifying behavior, influencing public opinion, motivating people, and/or changing people's attitudes. Nor is it a concern of the biomechanics, history, or sociology of sport. Questions concerning human attitudes, cognitions, and behavior fall directly under the mandate of psychology.

Psychology is a science devoted to an understanding of human behavior. In turn, the area of science we refer to in this book as the **psychology of physical activity** is devoted to an understanding of (a) individual attitudes, cognitions, and behaviors in the context of physical activity and exercise and (b) the social factors that influence those attitudes, cognitions, and behaviors.

Historical Developments

Rejeski and Thompson (1993) noted that although interest has been directed toward the psychology of physical activity since 1897, the majority of research has appeared since the early 1970s. Several reasons were advanced by Rejeski and Thompson for the relatively slow development of the psychology of physical activity as a science. First, the popularity of sport preceded the popularity of general physical activity within the general population. Thus, scientists inevitably gravitated toward sport to ask and attempt to answer research questions. Second, the importance of physical activity for disease prevention and the maintenance of general health has long been suspected but not fully known until recently. Consequently, understanding the psychological dimensions of involvement in physical activity was not perceived to be a pressing priority. Finally, throughout history, the use of a biomedical model has been the traditional approach to understanding health and well-being; the dominant concern is with the treatment of disease as opposed to its prevention. Only recently has the importance of a biopsychological approach to disease prevention been acknowledged.

Topics of Interest

When research into the psychological aspects of involvement in physical activity increased in the 1970s, it tended to focus on an understanding of hu-

man attitudes, cognitions, and behaviors in the context of physical activity and exercise. Evidence of this focus is provided by the 10 most prevalent topics investigated to date (Rejeski and Thompson, 1993):

1. Mental health (examination of the influence of acute and chronic physical activity on mental health parameters such as anxiety and depression)
2. **Body image** and **self-esteem** (examination of the influence of acute and chronic physical activity on self-perceptions and self-esteem)
3. **Psychophysiological reactivity** (examination of the influence of acute and chronic physical activity on modulating psychological and physiological responses to social stressors)
4. Perceived exertion/fatigue/exercise symptoms (examining subjective perceptions of physical functioning during acute bouts of physical activity)
5. Adherence (identification of the determinants of involvement in chronic physical activity)
6. Performance and metabolic responses (identification of psychological correlates of physical performance and metabolic responses)
7. Sleep (examination of the impact of acute and chronic physical activity on quantity and quality of sleep)

psychology of physical activity   The area of science devoted to an understanding of individual attitudes, cognitions, and behaviors in the context of physical activity and exercise and of the social factors that influence those attitudes, cognitions, and behaviors.

body image   A subjective perception of one's external appearance.

self-esteem   A global and relatively stable evaluative construct reflecting the degree to which an individual feels positive about himself or herself.

psychophysiological reactivity   The influence of acute and chronic physical activity on modulating psychological and physiological responses to social stressors.

8. **Cognition** (examination of the influence of acute and chronic physical activity on mental acuity)

9. Corporate (examination of the influence of acute and chronic physical activity on outcomes in the workplace, e.g., absenteeism, stress)

10. **Exercise dependence** (examination of the nature and consequences of obsessive involvement in physical activity)

Because humans are by nature social creatures, later researchers have also focused on an understanding of the social factors that influence attitudes, cognitions, and behaviors associated with involvement in physical activity. The five main categories of social factors that have been examined in relation to involvement in physical activity are (Carron, Hausenblas, & Mack, 1996):

1. Family (examination of the role played by family members including siblings, spouses, children, and parents in sustaining involvement in physical activity programs)

2. Important others (examination of the role played by non–family members such as physicians and work colleagues in sustaining involvement in physical activity programs)

3. Other exercisers (comparison of being physically active alone or in the presence of others)

4. Cohesion (examination of an impact of a cohesive, unified group in sustaining involvement in physical activity programs)

5. Leadership (examination of the role played by the exercise leader in sustaining involvement in physical activity programs)

Related Terms

A variety of behaviors have been researched under the umbrella term *psychology of physical activity*. Researchers and practitioners, operating under the assumption that definitional clarity is essential for effective communication, have taken care to draw a distinction among these diverse behaviors (Gauvin, Wall, & Quinney, 1994). An overview of the various terms is presented in Table 1-4.

■ **TABLE 1-4**   Terms Used Within the Field of the Psychology of Physical Activity

TERM	DEFINITION
Physical activity[a]	Any body movement produced by skeletal muscles and resulting in a substantial increase over the resting energy expenditure
Exercise[a]	Form of physical activity undertaken with a specific objective such as the improvement of fitness, health, or physical performance
Health[a]	Human condition with physical, social, and psychological dimensions, each characterized by a continuum with positive and negative poles
Active living[b]	A way of life in which physical activity is valued and integrated into daily life

Note. Adapted from "Physical Activity, Fitness, and Health: Research and Practice," by L. Gauvin, A. E. T. Wall, and H. A. Quinney, 1994, in H. A. Quinney, L. Gauvin, and A. E. T. Wall, Eds., *Toward Active Living* (pp. 1-5), Champaign, IL: Human Kinetics.
[a]From Bouchard and Shephard (1991).
[b]From Fitness Canada (1991).

Physical activity is a term used to describe body movements produced by the skeletal muscles that require energy expenditures above what is typical at rest (Bouchard & Shephard, 1991, p. 3). Implicit within this definition is the fact that physical

cognition   Pertaining to the mental processes of comprehension, judgment, memory, and reasoning, as contrasted with emotional and volitional processes.

exercise dependence   Obsessive involvement in physical activity.

physical activity   Any body movement produced by skeletal muscles and resulting in a substantial increase over the resting energy expenditure.

activity includes exercise, sport, work, leisure time activity, and so on (Gauvin, Wall, & Quinney, 1994).

On the other hand, **exercise** is a specific form of physical activity in which the individual engages for the purpose of improving fitness, physical performance, or health (Bouchard & Shephard, 1991). According to Bouchard and Shephard, a characteristic that helps define exercise is that the individual must conform to a recommended frequency, intensity, and duration in order to achieve the specific purpose desired. If an individual does conform to recommended levels, the usual result is *fitness,* in other words, the ability to perform work satisfactorily.

Health may be viewed as a human condition with physical, social, and psychological dimensions, each characterized by a continuum varying from positive to negative poles (Bouchard & Shephard, 1991). Both physical activity and exercise, along with a number of other activities such as maintaining a proper diet and refraining from smoking, contribute to development and maintenance of health on the positive end of the continuum. Although every health behavior is important in its own right, our book concentrates on physical activity and exercise.

Finally, **active living** is a term introduced by Fitness Canada (1991) to represent a lifestyle in which physical activity plays a dominant role. Active living is intended to emphasize the importance of physical activity within the individual's total life experience.

Health Versus Physical Activity Versus Rehabilitation Psychology

Students interested in various activities associated with a healthy lifestyle are often uncertain about where various research issues might lie. For example, does the topic of how smoking cessation influences endurance performance fall within the domain of health psychology or the psychology of physical activity or rehabilitation psychology? Endurance performance seems relevant to the area of the psychology of physical activity, whereas cigarette smoking seems to relate to health psychology.

Rejeski and Brawley (1988) developed an organizational framework to answer questions pertaining to the classification of research findings. Essentially, they proposed that the dependent variable (i.e., outcome) should be used as the main classification factor. Thus, a research problem that deals with the influence of smoking cessation on endurance performance would fall within the domain of physical activity psychology because endurance performance is the outcome of interest. Conversely, a research problem that deals with the influence of endurance training on smoking cessation would fall within the domain of health psychology because smoking cessation is the outcome of interest. Also, according to Rejeski and Brawley, research in which physical activity is used as an intervention to offset disabled, impaired, or diseased states falls within the domain of rehabilitation psychology.

ORGANIZATION OF THE BOOK

This book is subdivided into five sections. Section 1 is devoted to introductory material and issues of definition (Chapter 1) as well as protocols used for the measurement of physical activity (Chapter 2).

The remaining sections of the book relate to the four general stages through which all areas of science proceed. The first stage is **description.** The descriptive stage is essential because it informs us about "what is." A large proportion of the research in exercise psychology has been descriptive in na-

exercise   A specific form of physical activity in which the individual engages for the specific purpose of improving fitness, physical performance, or health.

health   A human condition with physical, social, and psychological dimensions, each characterized by a continuum varying from positive to negative poles.

active living   A way of life in which physical activity is valued and integrated into daily life.

description   The first stage of science, which informs about "what is."

ture, and in Sections 2 and 3 of this book, we describe individual and situational correlates of physical activity. Section 2 is an overview of research that has centered on the individual. In Chapters 3, 4, 5, and 6, we discuss the cognitive, social, psychological, personality, and psychobiological benefits of a physically active lifestyle. In Chapter 7, we focus on the potential negative behaviors associated with physical activity—exercise dependence, steroid use, and eating disorders. In Chapter 8, we outline the individual correlates of physical activity.

An important characteristic that helps define the psychology of physical activity as a discipline is its focus on the social factors that influence individual behavior. Section 3 of the book is an overview of research that has centered on the individual participant's **environment.** In Chapter 9, we focus on the physical activity class. Social support from others has been linked to a number of positive outcomes including improved health and reduced morbidity, and in Chapter 10, we discuss the nature and consequences of social support. In Chapter 11, we outline the environmental correlates of physical activity.

The second and third stages of science, **explanation** and **prediction,** involve theory development and testing. In Section 4 of the book, we advance various theoretical models to explain and predict involvement in exercise and physical activity. In Chapter 12, we deal with one of the most extensively used theoretical models—self-efficacy theory. We introduce the health belief model and protection motivation theory—two somewhat similar theoretical approaches—in Chapter 13. The theories of rea-

soned action and planned behavior are outlined in Chapter 14. We present a currently popular approach to the study of involvement in physical activity, the transtheoretical model, in Chapter 15. In Chapter 16, the final chapter of Section 3, we discuss self-determination theory and personal investment theory.

The fourth stage of science is **intervention,** or control. The intervention stage involves the application of what has been learned from the other three stages. Because the benefits of physical activity are so important for the individual and for society in general, numerous attempts have been made to develop effective intervention strategies. Section 5 of the book is an overview of various interventions, including those that have focused on individual level strategies (Chapter 17), group level strategies (Chapter 18), and community level programs (Chapter 19). Finally, in Chapter 20, we focus on the efficacy and fidelity of intervention strategies.

environment   All of the many factors, physical and psychological, that influence or affect the life and survival of a person.

explanation   The second stage of science, which involves theory development.

prediction   The third stage of science, which involves theory testing.

intervention   The fourth stage of science (also called control), which involves application of what has been learned from the previous three stages.

Summary

Is there a tomato effect—a tendency for people to avoid physical activity? Many benefits are associated with involvement in physical activity and exercise. Further, large portions of the population consider physical activity to be healthy and beneficial. Nonetheless, throughout the world, the levels of inactivity are still unacceptably high. Behavior change and attitude change are necessary. Both

changes fall within the domain of psychology as a science. This book focuses on information from the area of science referred to as the psychology of physical activity.

We defined several terms related to the field of the psychology of physical activity. *Physical activity* is muscular movement that increases energy expenditure. *Exercise* refers to a specific type of physical activity that leads to improved fitness, physical performance, and/or health. *Health* is a combination of physical, social, and psychological dimensions that can vary from positive to negative. *Active living* represents a lifestyle that values physical activity and integrates it into daily life.

Topics in the area of the psychology of physical activity often seem to overlap with areas such as rehabilitation psychology or health psychology. In this book, we incorporate information from research in which physical activity was the dependent (outcome) variable.

CHAPTER 2

The Measurement of Physical Activity

It Is a Capital Mistake to Theorize Before One Has Data.

(Sherlock Holmes)

CHAPTER OBJECTIVES

After completing this chapter you will be able to

- Outline the importance of assessing physical activity.

- Describe the four parameters of physical activity.

- Differentiate among the terms *physical activity, energy expenditure,* and *metabolic equivalents.*

- Differentiate among the psychometric terms *validity, reliability,* and *objectivity.*

- Describe subjective, objective, and criterion measures of physical activity.

Key terms

accelerometer	partial time sampling
concurrent validity	participant reactivity
energy expenditure	pedometer
feasibility	physical activity
heart rate monitor	recency effect
metabolic equivalents	reliability
(METs)	test-retest reliability
momentary time sampling	validity
objectivity (interrater	
reliability)	

This chapter focuses on measuring physical activity—a fundamental consideration in the psychology of physical activity. This point was reinforced by Carron, Brawley, and Widmeyer (1989), who suggested "measurement lies at the heart of science" (p. 224). A primary reason for the Carron et al. claim is embedded in the quote, by Sir Arthur Conan Doyle's (1999) Sherlock Holmes, that introduces this chapter. Gaining an understanding of any phenomenon proceeds sequentially through various stages from description to explanation to prediction to control. It is impossible to develop explanations for physical activity behavior (i.e., what Sherlock Holmes referred to as theorizing) without the foundation provided by sound description (i.e., what Holmes referred to as data).

Why is it important to measure the amount of physical activity that people do? If researchers are to increase their understanding of the association between physical activity and health, accurate methods for assessing physical activity are needed (Montoye, Kemper, Saris, & Washburn, 1996). More specifically, accurately measuring physical activity will enable researchers and health-care professionals to

1. Specify which aspects of physical activity are important for a particular health outcome. For example, do people need to do aerobic, anaerobic, or a combination of both types of physical activities to reduce their risk of cardiovascular disease or depression?

2. Monitor changes in physical activity over time. For example, are people currently more or less active than people 20 years ago?

3. Monitor the effectiveness of an exercise intervention. For example, do people's physical activity levels increase from the beginning to the end of their exercise intervention (Wareham & Rennie, 1998)?

4. Determine the prevalence of people meeting the prescriptions for physical activity. For example, what percentage of the population is engaging in enough exercise to receive its health-related benefits (Sarkin, Nichols, Sallis, & Calfas, 1998)?

Physical activity, however, is difficult to measure because it is a complex behavior. To bring simplicity to this complex behavior, physical activity is described by four parameters: (a) type, (b) frequency, (c) intensity, and (d) duration. **Type** of activity refers to the main physiological systems that are activated during activity. Activities are often characterized as either aerobic (e.g., running, swimming) or anaerobic (e.g., lifting weights, stretching). **Frequency** represents the number of times a person engages in an activity over a predetermined period (e.g., walking three to four days per week). **Duration** refers to the temporal length of the activity and is often quantified in minutes (e.g., exercising for 30 minutes). Finally, **intensity** is the degree of overload an activity imposes on physiological systems compared to resting states. Terms commonly used to describe the intensity of physical activity include *mild, moderate,* and *strenuous/vigorous.* Several types of physical activity measures are available to assess some or all of the parameters of physical activity. For example, physical activity can be expressed in terms of energy expenditure, heart rate, units of movements (counts), or a numerical score derived from responses to questionnaires (Montoye et al., 1996). The ability of these different measures, however, to accurately assess physical activity varies greatly. In this chapter, *criterion* techniques (i.e., direct observation, doubly labeled water, and indirect calorimetry), *objective* techniques (i.e., heart rate monitors and motion sensors), and *subjective* techniques (i.e., self-report protocols and

■ **TABLE 2-1**   Techniques Used to Measure Physical Activity

LEVEL	TECHNIQUES
Criterion techniques	Direct observation, doubly labeled water, and indirect calorimetry
Objective techniques	Heart rate monitors, pedometers, and accelerometers
Subjective techniques	Self-report protocols: questionnaires and diaries

diaries) will be described (Sirard & Pate, 2001; see Table 2-1). However, before we discuss these measurement techniques, we address some important issues in measuring physical activity.

IMPORTANT ISSUES IN THE MEASUREMENT OF PHYSICAL ACTIVITY

One important consideration at the heart of measuring physical activity is the difference between physical activity and energy expenditure. **Physical activity** refers to body movement. Examples of physical activity include gardening, walking around the block, and running a marathon. In comparison, **energy**

---

type   Refers to the main physiological systems that are activated during activity.

frequency   The number of times a person engages in an activity over a predetermined period.

duration   The length of time that an activity lasts.

intensity   The degree of overload an activity imposes on physiological systems compared to resting states.

physical activity   Any body movement produced by skeletal muscles and resulting in a substantial increase over the resting energy expenditure.

energy expenditure   A consequence of body movement related to body size.

expenditure is a consequence of body movement and is related to body size (Montoye et al., 1996). For example, a lean child and an obese child may engage in the same physical activity, such as walking a mile. The obese child, however, because he or she weighs more, will expend more energy performing this physical activity than the lean child does.

All physical activities have an energy requirement, or metabolic cost. This cost is often expressed in **metabolic equivalents (METs).** METs are used to express the rate of oxygen use. Specifically, METs are multiples of the resting rate of oxygen consumption during physical activity. For example, one MET is the rate of oxygen use at rest (e.g., sitting quietly). An activity that uses oxygen at twice the resting rate is carried out at a 2 MET level (e.g., strolling very slowly on level ground); three times the resting rate of oxygen use equals a 3 MET level (e.g., walking downstairs); and so on (Ainsworth et al., 1993; Ainsworth et al., 2000). MET levels are unrelated to the duration of an activity; they stay the same as long as the intensity of the activity remains unchanged. Table 2-2 provides examples of common MET values developed by Ainsworth and her colleagues for various activities.

Another important consideration for measuring physical activity is the psychometric properties of the tests—their validity, reliability, objectivity,

and feasibility. **Validity** refers to the ability of a test to accurately assess what it is supposed to measure. For example, a very muscular person may weigh a great deal yet have very little body fat. Therefore, a person's weight is not a valid measure of body fat. As another example, a person's maximum oxygen consumption score ($\dot{V}O_2$ max) is a valid measure of aerobic capacity. In fact, it is considered to be the gold standard because it is the most valid measure of aerobic capacity available (ACSM, 2000). **Concurrent validity,** which is a common type of validity, involves the correlation of a measure with a criterion or gold standard measure. Usually, the higher the correlation, the more valid the measure is. For example, if a self-report measure of physical activity is highly correlated with $\dot{V}O_2$ max, then concurrent validity for the self-report measure is established.

---

metabolic equivalents (METs)   Multiples of the resting rate of oxygen consumption during physical activity.

validity   The ability of a test to accurately assess what it is supposed to measure.

concurrent validity   Type of validity involving the correlation of a measure with a criterion or gold standard measure.

■ **TABLE 2-2**   Metabolic Equivalent (MET) Scores for Common Physical Activities

ACTIVITY TYPE	LIGHT (<3.0 METs)	MODERATE (3.0 TO 6.0 METs)	STRENUOUS (>6.0 METs)
Walking/running	Slowly strolling at 1–2 mph	Walking briskly	Running or jogging
Golfing	Golfing with a power cart	Golfing while pulling a cart or carrying clubs	—
Tennis	—	Doubles tennis	Singles tennis
Bowling	All bowling		
Fishing	Fishing while sitting	Fishing while standing or casting	Fishing in a stream
Boating	Power boating	Canoeing leisurely	Canoeing rapidly
House cleaning	Carpet sweeping	General cleaning	Moving furniture
Lawn mowing	Riding mower	Power mower	Hand mower

Reliability is the ability of a test to yield consistent and stable scores. **Test-retest reliability** is a common measure of reliability; it assesses stability over time. For example, an individual might be asked on a Monday and then 2 days later, on a Wednesday, to recall her level of physical activity over the previous month. If highly similar or identical values are reported, the self-report would have adequate test-retest reliability. It is important to note that shorter times between test-retest assessment (e.g., 2 days) tend to be more accurate than longer times between assessments (e.g., 2 weeks).

Objectivity, also known as **interrater reliability,** refers to the ability of different testers or scorers to provide similar results for a given individual. For example, if five gymnastic judges all give very similar scores to a gymnast for her floor routine, then objectivity is achieved.

Finally, **feasibility** refers to how practical it is to administer a measure to a certain population. For example, it would not be feasible to conduct an epidemiological study of people's physical activity levels using $\dot{V}O_2$ max testing because this test is expensive, is time consuming, and requires trained experts for its administration. It is feasible, however, to conduct epidemiological studies using self-report questionnaires. In fact, self-report questionnaires are the most common method used to assess physical activity in epidemiological studies (Sarkin et al., 1998).

SUBJECTIVE TECHNIQUES TO ASSESS PHYSICAL ACTIVITY: SELF-REPORT PROTOCOLS

Self-report measures are the most frequently used protocol to determine the prevalence of physical activity in a population, the effectiveness of an intervention program, or the relationships between activity and various health outcomes (Sallis & Owen, 1998). Self-report protocols include self-report and interview questionnaires and activity diaries. A variety of questionnaires and diaries of differing complexity have been used to gauge the

physical activity level of individuals. For example, questionnaires and diaries vary in length from a few questions to a moderate number of questions to detailed inventories (Jacobs, Ainsworth, Hartman, & Leon, 1993). Also, questionnaires and diaries are used to assess physical activity involvement for the previous 24 hours, for a week or weeks, for a year, and even for a lifetime. As a final example, researchers have administered questionnaires through personal interviews, telephone interviews, paper and pencil tests, or the mail.

The four main advantages of self-report protocols that have led to their widespread use are (a) easy administration, (b) inexpensive administration, (c) easy scoring, and (d) ability to assess a large sample of individuals quickly. There are also four main limitations of self-report protocols. First, social desirability bias can result in peoples' overreporting of their physical activity level. Second, because recalling physical activity is a complex cognitive task, children and older adults are likely to have memory and recall limitations. Third, people can more accurately recall what physical activity they engaged in in the immediate past (e.g., last 7 days) compared to the distant past (e.g., last year). This phenomenon is known as the **recency effect.** Finally, phrases such as *physical activity, vigorous intensity, moderate intensity,* and *leisure time* are terms that lay people may

reliability   The ability of a test to yield consistent and stable scores.

test-retest reliability   Measure of reliability that assesses stability over time.

objectivity (interrater reliability)   The ability of different testers or scorers to provide similar results for a given individual.

feasibility   How practical it is to administer a measure to a certain population.

recency effect   The phenomenon by which people can more accurately recall what physical activity they engaged in in the immediate past (e.g., last 7 days).

Are lower levels of physical activity more enjoyable for the average person?

Yes. Increased intensity appears to be associated with reduced positive affect during and immediately following exercise. Thus, lower intensities, because they are more enjoyable, may be associated with increased adherence rates.

(Ekkekakis & Petruzzello, 1999)

not be familiar with (Sallis & Saelens, 2000). Thus, some self-report protocols provide examples, such as heavy breathing and sweating, and activities to describe the intensity level. In the following sections we describe several popular self-report and interview questionnaires and activity diaries that vary in complexity for adult, youth, and elderly populations.

Questionnaires

Questionnaires for Adults. A simple, self-administered measure of free-time physical activity is the *Leisure-Time Exercise Questionnaire*, which was developed by Godin and his colleagues (Godin, Jobin, & Bouillon, 1986; Godin & Shephard, 1985). This questionnaire assesses the number of times, on average, a person engages in strenuous (e.g., running, swimming), moderate (e.g., walking, doubles tennis), and mild (e.g., golf, gardening) activities in their free time for at least 15 minutes during a typical week. A METs score is obtained by multiplying the estimated rate of energy expenditure for each level of activity by the reported frequency of participation in each level of activity. For example, the frequency of strenuous exercise is multiplied by a value of 9, moderate by 5, and mild by 3. The total leisure-time activity is calculated as the sum of the three activity measures. Therefore, if an adult reports engaging in 4 bouts of mild activity, 3 bouts of moderate activity, and 2 bouts of strenuous activity in a typical week, his or her weekly total leisure activity would be 45 METs (i.e., 4 bouts of mild exercise times 3 equals 12, plus

3 bouts of moderate exercise times 5 equals 15, plus 2 bouts of strenuous activity times 9 equals 27, for a total of 45 METs). The Leisure-Time Exercise Questionnaire is considered to be a reliable and valid measure of exercise behavior in adults (Jacobs et al., 1993) and, to a lesser extent, in older children and adolescents (Sallis, Buono, Roby, Micale, & Nelson, 1993).

Two advantages of the Leisure-Time Exercise Questionnaire are its ease and speed of administration. Also, the fact that the questionnaire focuses on an individual's involvement in exercise during a *typical* week is an advantage. For example, a highly active exerciser might be sick or involved with exams in a particular week. Thus, a researcher is more likely to get a valid estimate of that individual's activity involvement if he or she is asked to recall activity during a typical week rather than during a specific week.

A disadvantage of the questionnaire is that the test-retest reliabilities for mild and moderate activity are not as high as they are for strenuous activity. The reason for this discrepancy is that people can more accurately recall the time that they have spent in strenuous activities (e.g., running) compared to moderate and mild activities (e.g., walking and gardening).

An example of a questionnaire that can be used in both an interview and self-report format is the *7-Day Physical Activity Recall Questionnaire* (Blair, Haskell, et al., 1985; Sallis et al., 1993; Sallis et al., 1985). To complete this questionnaire, participants indicate the number of hours spent in sleep and in moderate (e.g., brisk walking, volleyball), hard (e.g., scrubbing floors, doubles tennis), and very hard (e.g., running, singles tennis) activities during the previous week. The amount of time remaining each day is assumed to have been spent in light activities (e.g., bowling, office work, light housework). Because most adults in developed countries spend the greatest part of their day in light activity, it takes little time to recall the time spent in moderate, hard, or very hard activities. An estimate of energy expenditure is then obtained by multiplying moderate, hard, and very hard activity by the MET values of 4, 6, 10, respectively. Sleep has a MET value of 1. Once the time spent in sleep and in moderate, hard, and very hard activity has been determined, the amount of time spent in light activities is determined through subtraction. That is, all the time that is not spent sleeping or in moderate, hard, or very hard activity is presumed to be light and is scored as 1.5 METs. A limitation of this approach is that it does not consider the varying levels of occupational or home tasks that are performed during the day.

The strengths of the 7-Day Physical Activity Recall, similar to those of the Leisure-Time Exercise Questionnaire, include its focus on a relatively short recall period, its simplicity and ease to administer, and its application to a wide age spectrum. Another strength of the questionnaire is that it includes both occupational and leisure activity. A limitation of the 7-Day Physical Activity Recall is that it has the respondent recall physical activity undertaken during the past week only. Any given previous week may not accurately reflect habitual levels of physical activity.

The *Lifetime Total Physical Activity Questionnaire,* developed by Friedenreich, Courneya, and Bryant (1998), assesses lifetime patterns of activity. Specifically, within an interview format, respondents are asked to recall their lifetime involvement (i.e., frequency, intensity, and duration) in three areas of physical activity: occupation, household, and exercise or sport. To improve the accuracy of long-term recall, two procedures are used: (a) cognitive interviewing methods, and (b) recall calendars.

Cognitive interviewing methods incorporate several techniques to facilitate the participant's ability to understand the questions; retrieve the information asked; estimate the time, amount, and intensity of physical activity undertaken; and formulate a response. Examples of cognitive interviewing methods used to assess activity level are presented in Table 2-3. Also, two types of *recall calendars* are used to trigger memory. One calendar is for educational and occupational activities (e.g., college graduation, first job), and the other is for major life events (e.g., births, deaths in family). For example, the educational and occupational calendar asks participants to list their education and the jobs that they have held throughout their lives. For each job held, the level of physical activity that was required for that position is recorded.

■ **TABLE 2-3** Some Cognitive Interviewing Methods

METHOD	DESCRIPTION
Paraphrasing	The participant repeats the question in his or her own words. This method permits the interviewers to assess whether the participant understood the question.
Response latency	The length of time between the question and the participant's answer is measured to assess the difficulty of the question.
Confidence ratings	The interviewer asks respondents to relate the degree of confidence they have in the accuracy of their answers.

In the initial validation study, Friedenreich et al. (1998) examined the lifetime physical activity of 113 middle-aged women. Using the cognitive interview techniques, the authors found that the women spent approximately 56 hours a week in physical activity over their lifetime. The majority of their weekly activity was spent in household tasks (30 hours), less time was spent in occupational activity (23 hours), and relatively minimal amounts of time were allocated to sport and exercise activities (3.7 hours). In regard to intensity, the women spent, on average over their lifetime, 18.8 hours per week in light activity, 22.4 hours in moderate activity, and 5.8 hours in heavy activity. The remainder of time per week was assumed to have been spent in sedentary or resting activities.

A simple method frequently used to assess a person's subjective perceptions of his or her physical activity intensity (rather than the amount of activity) is the *Rating of Perceived Exertion Scale* (Borg, 1998; Noble & Noble, 1998). Perceived exertion is defined as the "act of detecting and interpreting sensations arising from the body during physical activity" (Noble & Noble, p. 351). Researchers often use perceived exertion ratings to monitor and prescribe exercise intensity. A typical scale to assess perceived exertion,

```
6 -
7 - Very, very light
8 -
9 - Very light
10 -
11 - Fairly light
12 -
13 - Somewhat hard
14 -
15 - Hard
16 -
17 -Very hard
18 -
19 - Very, very hard
20 -
```

Figure 2-1
Perceived exertion
scale.

developed by Borg (1971), is presented in Figure 2-1. The scale was designed so that it parallels the heart rate range of a normal, healthy male, that is, 60 to 200 beats per minute (bpm). According to the underlying theory, when scale ratings are multiplied by 10, heart rate can be estimated (Noble & Noble). Thus, if a person performed a light activity (e.g., slow walking) and indicated a rating of 9 on the perceived exertion scale, his heart rate would be estimated to be 90 bpm. In comparison, if another person performed very strenuous activity (e.g., running) and indicated a rating of 17 on the perceived exertion scale, her heart rate would be estimated to be 170 bpm. In general, rating of perceived exertion scales are considered to be valid and reliable tools for assessing physical exertion levels during continuous, aerobic exercise (Noble & Robertson, 1996).

Questionnaires for Children.   Self-report of children's physical activity includes both the child's responses of his or her activity level as well as proxy reports by parents and teachers. Most proxy reports of children's physical activity are not valid, probably because neither the parents nor the teachers are able to observe children all day (Sallis & Owen, 1998).

A critical question is, how old do children have to be before they can accurately recall their physical activity? This question was addressed in a study by

Sallis, Buono, and colleagues (1993). They evaluated the reliability and validity of the 7-Day Physical Activity Recall Questionnaire in three groups of children and adolescents in the 5th, 8th, and 11th grades. As predicted, test-retest reliability increased with age, with only the 11th graders' reliability values being in an acceptable range. Validity was assessed by comparing the children's reported time in high-intensity activities with minutes of high heart rates (i.e., greater than 140 bpm) on the same days. Once again validity increased by age, with acceptable values found for only the 11th graders. The authors concluded that 5th- and 8th-grade children are limited in their ability to recall their physical activity. Subsequently, Sallis and Owen (1998) recommended that physical activity recalls should *not* be used with children in less than the 4th grade. The researchers also stated that the reliability and validity of children's self-reports are limited until they reach high school.

Recalling physical activity is a difficult task for children, but it appears to be easier if they are asked to recall over a short time. In another study using the 7-Day Physical Activity Recall Questionnaire, children completed two recalls in less than a 7-day period (Sallis, Buono, et al., 1993). Across all ages, the reliability of recall was $r = .79$ when children had to remember only the previous 2 to 3 days. However, reliability was reduced to $r = .45$ when children had to remember the previous 4 to 6 days. Sallis and his colleagues concluded that to increase the accuracy of children's recall of physical activity, brief recall periods should be used.

A question that does arise is, how valid is a 1-day recall of physical activity for children? Sallis and his colleagues (1996) attempted to answer this question in a study with 5th-grade students. Researchers compared versions of the Physical Activity Recall Questionnaire that were either interviewer-administered to each child or self-administered to entire classrooms of children. Both versions used checklists of common physical activities to aid children's memories, and children reported the minutes they spent doing these physical activities the previous day. Selected sedentary behaviors, such as watching television and playing computer games, were also assessed. Before the questionnaires were administered, children received brief training in defining physical activities and in estimating time spent in the activities. Validity was assessed by correlations with heart rate and activity monitoring information gathered the day before the recall (these measures of physical activity are described in the section of this chapter titled "Objective Techniques to Assess Physical Activity). The researchers found that the self-administered and the interviewer-administered versions had similar levels of validity. The score from the self-administered recall correlated .59 with heart rate and .32 with activity monitoring information. Similarly, the interviewer-administered version correlated .54 with heart rate and .38 with activity monitoring data. Sallis and his colleagues concluded that the validity of both protocols for assessing 1-day physical activity recall was supported by correlations with two objective measures of physical activity. However, they suggested that the self-administered version be used because it can be administered to large numbers of children at a low cost.

Questionnaires for Older Adults.   An active lifestyle is associated with considerable benefits for older populations (i.e., post 65 years) just as it is with children, adolescents, and younger adults. However, limited information is available regarding the type, amount, duration, and frequency of physical activity necessary for maximum health benefits in older individuals. A primary reason for this limited information is a lack of physical activity assessment methods (Montoye et al., 1996). Typically, questionnaires designed specifically for younger populations are used with older populations (Washburn, Smith, Jetter, & Janney, 1993). However, this method is inappropriate for at least four reasons (Harada, Chiu, King, & Stewart, 2000; Washburn et al.). First, the time frame over which an activity is assessed can be too long (e.g., months, years) for older adults to recall accurately. Second, the types of activities engaged in by older adults are often not included or emphasized. For example, most elderly people are retired, so mild leisure-time activities are important, particularly household tasks, gardening, and walk-

ing (Montoye et al.). Also, only a small percentage of older people participate in moderate or strenuous physical activity (Dannenberg, Keller, Wilson, & Castelli, 1989). Third, open-ended response formats (e.g., asking how many minutes per week one engages in physical activity) can be difficult for older people to report accurately. Finally, older adults often perform activities on an irregular basis, which makes it more difficult for them to recall their physical activity patterns.

To overcome some of the limitations of using general adult physical activity measures, some researchers have developed surveys specifically for older adults. For example, Stewart and her colleagues (1998) designed and validated a questionnaire to assess physical activity for older adults called the *Community Healthy Activities Model Program for Seniors (CHAMPS)* survey. It addresses measurement issues for older adults by (a) asking about less vigorous activities (e.g., gardening, walking), (b) providing lists of specified activities to facilitate the recall of light-intensity activities, and (c) asking about the duration of activity performed over one week rather than per session to facilitate recording of irregular activity. Specifically, the CHAMPS survey provides respondents with a comprehensive list of light, moderate, and vigorous physical activities, and respondents report their frequency and duration of participation in a typical week over the last four weeks. The survey asks about the duration of participation for the total week rather than for each time the respondent performs an activity. The CHAMPS has been found to be a psychometrically sound measure and is sensitive to changes in light to moderate activities in older adults (Harada et al., 2001; King, Oka, Pruitt, Phillips, & Haskell, 1997; Stewart et al., 1997; Stewart et al., 2001).

Diary Methods

With the diary method, the individual periodically records his or her own physical activity involvement. Recordings are usually done once a day, often before the respondent goes to bed (Stetson et al., 1997). However, recordings can be done as often as every minute (Riumallo, Schoeller, Barrera, Gattas, & Vauy, 1989). The diary method has several advantages. Data collection involves little expense, does not require an observer, and can be undertaken by many individuals simultaneously. Also, detailed information regarding a person's physical activity can be obtained. Such detailed information includes the type, duration, intensity, and frequency of activity and also aspects of the social and physical environment. For example, a person could record that he engaged in 30 minutes of jogging with a friend on a wooded trail in the afternoon.

The diary technique also has its disadvantages. First, processing a large volume of data can be time consuming and expensive. Second, complete cooperation and conscientiousness by the participant is critical if accurate information is to be obtained. Even so, the individual may forget to log all entries or might make recording errors. Third, because logging activities is tedious, the longer the data collection period, the less accurate the results may be. Finally, the diary method is inappropriate with children under the age of 10 (Sallis & Owen, 1998).

Stetson and her colleagues (1997) used the diary method to examine the effects of stress on exercise in 82 community-residing women (M age = 34.8 years). The participants kept exercise diaries and reported their weekly stress for eight consecutive weeks. For the exercise diary, participants indicated each day whether they planned to exercise and whether they did exercise. An exercise omission was counted when participants reported that they planned to exercise on a specific day and did not. For days that the participants exercised, they reported the type of activity, duration of activity, rating of perceived exertion, and overall enjoyment of the exercise. At the end of each week, participants also rated their mood and their satisfaction with the week's exercise as well as self-efficacy for their ability to meet upcoming exercise goals. Results revealed that during the weeks with a high frequency of stressful events, participants exercised for less time and reported lower self-efficacy for meeting upcoming exercise goals. During the weeks of high perceived stress, participants exercised for significantly

fewer days, omitted more planned exercise sessions, were less satisfied with their exercise, and had lower self-efficacy for meeting exercise goals. The authors concluded that perceptions of stressful events and cognitive reactions to missed exercise may play a significant role in exercise relapse.

Overview

Sallis and Owen (1998) noted that commonly used measures of physical activity show evidence of validity. None of these subjective measures, however, are highly related with objective criteria. In short, even the best self-report questionnaire has considerable error. Nonetheless, these error-prone measures are able to show associations with health outcomes. So these measures can be relatively effective indicators of which people are more or less active. Still, questions of validity arise. For example, a physical activity intervention study was conducted by Wier, Jackson, and Pinkerton (1989). One subgroup of people in the intervention condition reported a 20% increase in physical activity. However, the $\dot{V}O_2$ max of that group—the laboratory gold standard for the assessment of cardiorespiratory fitness—was found to have decreased by 6%. Thus, if feasible, objective measures should be used in combination with self-report measures to obtain a more accurate estimate of physical activity or fitness level.

OBJECTIVE TECHNIQUES TO ASSESS PHYSICAL ACTIVITY

Technology has recently become available to monitor activity and objectively assess the minutes spent at different intensities of physical activity. Motion sensors and heart rate monitors are mechanical and electronic devices that pick up motion and acceleration of a limb or trunk, depending on where the monitor is attached to the body. There are several types of motion sensors that range in complexity and cost (Freedson & Miller, 2000). Activity monitors have the potential to provide substantial benefits over self-report measures because they avoid the biases and inaccuracies of recall, they provide quantitative data on both physical activity and energy expenditure, and they provide comparable data across ages and populations (Sallis & Owen, 1998). In the following sections, we discuss accelerometers, pedometers, and heart rate monitors, the most frequently used motion sensors.

Pedometers

Pedometers have been used since the 1920s to count steps while a person is walking or running (Montoye et al., 1996). Today, mechanical and electronic pedometers are available that can either count steps or compile the distance walked if stride length is estimated. Pedometers count steps by responding to vertical acceleration, which triggers a lever arm to move vertically and a ratchet to rotate (Freedman & Miller, 2000). Pedometers are inexpensive (approximately $20 to $25) movement device counters that estimate habitual physical activity over a long period without interfering with or modifying a participant's normal lifestyle. They tend to be nonobtrusive because they are lightweight and small, and they are usually clipped onto a belt or are worn around the ankle. The immediate feedback available from pedometers also makes them useful as behavior modification tools (Welk et al., 2000). Typically, for activities like walking or running, the pedometer is clipped onto a belt for the most accurate results. In an activity like bicycling, however, an ankle-mounted pedometer is more sensitive to leg movement (Montoye et al.).

Freedson and Miller (2000) noted that pedometers, despite their advantages of small size and low

cost, have some limitations. First, pedometers fail to provide temporal information about activity patterns because they do not store data over a specified time interval. Without a time-based indicator, it is impossible to determine the intensity or duration of the activity. Because a person can accumulate a large number of steps during normal activities of daily living, it is difficult to determine how many steps are needed to meet the current physical activity guidelines (Welk et al., 2000). Second, pedometers are not sensitive to (a) activities that do not involve locomotion, (b) isometric exercise, or (c) activities that involve the upper body. Third, pedometers are not as accurate at very slow or very fast walking speeds. Finally, there are limitations with the reliability and validity of mechanical and electronic pedometers. Early research with pedometers reported low validity and a great deal of interinstrument variability (Bassett et al., 1996; Welk et al.).

For example, a study comparing five electronic pedometers found some to be more valid than others. That is, based on the number of steps taken, the error rates among the five pedometers ranged from less than 1% to 15% (Bassett et al., 1996). The authors concluded that pedometers do not have equal sensitivity because some devices show high deviations from the actual step rate. They also noted that the Yamax Digi-Walker (Yamax Inc., Tokyo, Japan) exhibited exceptionally high reliability and validity. Because of the initial promising results of the Digi-Walker, investigators have recently examined its validity against more objective measures of physical activity.

Welk and his colleagues (2000), for example, examined the utility of Digi-Walker for quantifying physical activity levels with 31 adults. Participants wore a Digi-Walker and completed three 1-mile trials of walking (4 mph), jogging (6 mph), and running (7.5 mph) under both track and treadmill conditions. At the end of each mile, their time and number

Pedometers are used to count steps.

pedometer Instrument that can either count steps or estimate distance walked.

of steps were recorded. For the treadmill condition, participants' anthropometric measures (i.e., height, weight, percent body fat, leg and stride length) were obtained to determine if these measures influenced variability in step counts. The steps required to walk and jog a distance of 37.7 meters was recorded and used to verify steps recorded on the Digi-Walker.

Similar results were found for the track and treadmill conditions. Researchers also found that step counts decreased with increasing pace. That is, the average number of steps observed for the men was 1,875 for the walk pace, 1,605 for the jog pace, and 1,307 for the run pace. The corresponding values for the women were 1,996; 1,662; and 1,330 (see Figure 2-2). Also, step counts for all paces were negatively related to height, weight, leg length, and stride length and were positively related to body fatness.

Welk et al. (2000) concluded that walking or running a mile (1.61 km) requires approximately 1,300 to 2,000 steps (depending on pace and anthropometric characteristics). As expected, higher step counts were found for walking paces compared with jogging or running paces because average stride length is shorter. The step count data also provides useful benchmarks for quantifying activity lev-

els with the Digi-Walker. For example, using the step count data for the walking pace of 4 mph, which is equivalent to a 15-min mile, an average of 1,935 steps per mile for males and females is needed. Thus, about 3,870 steps is sufficient to meet the activity guidelines of 30 min of moderate intensity activity. This figure cannot be used, however, to categorize an active person if monitoring is conducted over the course of a whole day, because people accumulate a large number of steps going through their normal activities of daily living. Because much of this activity is of light intensity, it may not provide meaningful health benefits. Therefore, if the Digi-Walker is used to assess daily activity patterns, the target values for daily steps must be set higher. The authors concluded that although pedometers offer considerable promise for assessing daily physical activity patterns, additional work is needed to clarify daily step patterns across different ages, genders, and occupational classes.

Accelerometers

There are two types of **accelerometers:** unidimensional and triaxial. Unidimensional accelerometers assess vertical movement of the trunk, which is one characteristic of walking and running. How does an unidimensional accelerometer work? When the body moves vertically, a lever is displaced that generates an electrical current proportional to the energy of the acceleration. This current is used as a raw number to determine movement or is entered into a formula that takes into account age, sex, height, and weight to estimate energy expenditure. The unidimensional accelerometer commonly used in research is the *Caltrac* (Hemokinetics, Madison, WI). Several studies have shown that the Caltrac has adequate reliability for children and adults (Montoye et al., 1996). The benefits of the Caltrac are its small size, relatively low cost, and lack of interference with

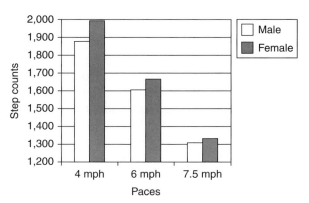

Figure 2-2 Step counts required to complete a mile at three different paces.
Note. From "The Utility of the Digi-Walker Step Counter to Assess Daily Physical Activity Patterns," by G. J. Welk et al., 2000, *Medicine and Science in Sports and Exercise, 32,* S481–S488.

accelerometer An instrument for measuring acceleration.

Triaxial
accelerometers detect
vertical, horizontal,
and lateral
movements.

ongoing activity (Sallis & Owen, 1998). Also, these devices have a large memory capacity that allows for monitoring and storage of temporal patterns of activity in small time intervals over days or weeks (Freedson & Miller, 2000). Additionally, unidimensional accelerometers measure both the amount and intensity of an activity. On the other hand, energy expenditure in activities such as bicycling, weight lifting, skating, and swimming cannot be assessed well with this device.

Some of the limitations of unidimensional accelerometers have been overcome with the newer triaxial accelerometers. Triaxial accelerometers detect vertical, horizontal, and lateral movements. Some triaxial accelerometers, such as the *Tritrac* (Hemokinetics, Madison, WI), can collect minute-by-minute data for up to 21 days. The Tritrac, however, is larger than the Caltrac and thus is cumbersome to use.

Research has shown that the reliability of the Caltrac and Tritrac accelerometers varies with different populations. That is, adequate reliability has been found with adult and youth population (Nichols, Patterson, & Early, 1992; Simons-Morton, Taylor, & Huang, 1994), but not with older adults (Fehling, Smith, Warner, & Dalsky, 1999). For example, Fehling and her colleagues compared the Tritrac and Caltrac accelerometers with two submaximal laboratory aerobic capacity tests using a group of 86 male and female older adults (*M* age = 71). The ac-

celerometers were worn while the participants performed both treadmill walking and bench stepping tests. Estimated energy expenditure from the two accelerometers was compared with energy expenditure from the submaximal tests.

The Caltrac overestimated energy expenditure for the treadmill test and underestimated energy expenditure for the step test. In comparison, the Tritrac underestimated energy expenditure for both the treadmill and step tests. Fehling et al. (1999) concluded that the magnitude of the differences between the accelerometer measures and estimated energy expenditure is affected by the mode and intensity of exercise.

Accelerometers are also used to examine the validity of self-report and diary methods of physical activity. For example, Coleman, Saelens, Wiedrich-Smith, Finn, and Epstein (1997) found that a triaxial accelerometer measure yielded a better estimate of activity in obese children than a diary self-report measure. In another example, Jakicic, Polley, and Wing (1998) compared self-reported exercise to measures obtained from a Tritrac accelerometer in 50 overweight females who were participating in a 20-week weight loss control program. The authors were interested in determining whether there was a difference in weight loss between individuals who under- and overreported their exercise involvement. The women were randomly assigned to either a long- or short-bout exercise condition, with both groups instructed to exercise 20 to 40 minutes a day for 5 days a week. Participants in the long-bout group exercised for one continuous 20- to 40-minute session per day. In comparison, participants in the short-bout group were instructed to divide their exercise into 10-minute sessions per day. All participants recorded their exercise in a daily log, and they also wore the accelerometer for one week to validate their self-reported exercise bouts.

It was found that approximately 45% of the women overreported the amount of exercise that they performed. Women who overreported their exercise had poorer weight loss across the 20-week program than did those who underreported their exercise. Figure 2-3 presents a graphic display of the

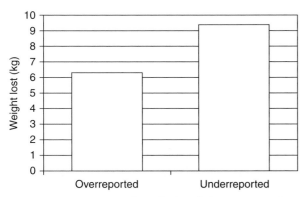

Figure 2-3   Amount of weight loss (kg) in women who underreported and overreported the amount of exercise they performed.

Note. From "Accuracy of Self-Reported Exercise and the Relationship With Weight Loss in Overweight Women," by J. M. Jakicic, B. A. Polley, and R. R. Wing, 1998, *Medicine and Science in Sports and Exercise, 30,* 634–638.

results. The researchers concluded that overweight women who overreport their exercise will have poorer weight loss while enrolled in a behavioral weight loss program compared to participants who more accurately report their activity level. Furthermore, the accelerometer may be useful in identifying individuals who inaccurately report their physical activity levels.

Heart Rate Monitors

A **heart rate monitor** is an effective device for measuring physical activity because of the linear relationship between heart rate and energy expenditure during steady-state exercise. This relationship means that heart rate can be used to estimate the intensity of an activity—with some qualifications. Two individuals working at the same heart rate may be engaged in activities of different intensity. For example, a sedentary

person may have a very high heart rate when walking for 10 minutes. In comparison, a physically fit person's heart rate when walking 10 minutes would be much less. Energy expenditure cannot be estimated from heart rate recordings alone unless the individual's heart rate is determined during a standardized fitness test (Sallis & Owen, 1998).

Small, affordable heart rate units have been used with a wide variety of populations. Polar Heart Rate Monitors (Polar Elector OY, Finland), which have been used in several studies, consist of a strap worn around the chest that contains electrodes and a transmitter. A receiving unit, worn like a wristwatch, has a memory that can store minute-by-minute data for up to 16 hours. The data are downloaded directly to a computer. Heart rate devices can be extremely valid, with a 2% error rate (Montoye et al., 1996).

There are some disadvantages in using heart rate monitors to assess physical activity. First, heart rate monitors cannot accurately distinguish between light and moderate intensity activities. Only high-intensity activity produces high heart rates, so using heart rate monitors is most appropriate for assessing vigorous physical activity. Second, elevated heart rates can be produced by mental stress in the absence of physical activity (e.g., your heart rate might increase before you give a presentation in class). Third, heart rate monitors can be inconvenient to use, especially in children, because the chest strap slips down when they sweat, stopping the recording. Fourth, individual variation in gender,

> **heart rate monitor**   An effective way to measure physical activity utilizing the linear relationship between heart rate and energy expenditure during steady-state exercise.

Heart rate monitor receiving unit.

age, body size, and training status can affect the relationship between heart rate and oxygen consumption (Strath et al., 2000; Trost, 2001). Fifth, heart rate tends to lag behind changes in activity movement and tends to remain elevated after the activity is stopped. Thus, heart rate monitoring may mask irregular physical activity patterns, such as when an individual changes from running to walking (Trost). Also, consecutive days of monitoring are difficult because the chest electrodes cause irritation and occasional rashes. Finally, various electronic devices, including televisions, microwaves, and other transmitters, interfere with the recording, which may result in lost data (Sallis & Owen, 1998).

Pate, Baranowski, Dowda, and Trost (1996) used heart rate monitors to track physical activity in 47 young children (*M* age = 3.45) for a three-year period. The children wore the heart rate monitors a minimum of two (and up to four) days from 7:00 a.m. to 7:00 p.m. during each of the three years of the study. Physical activity was quantified as the percentage of observed minutes between 3:00 p.m. and 6:00 p.m. during which heart rate was 50% or more above the individual's resting heart rate. The authors found that the children's physical activity level was relatively constant throughout the study. Thus, physical activity patterns tend to be maintained during early childhood, and less active children tend to remain less active over time. In short, physical activity has stability over time in young children.

In a validation study, Strath and his colleagues (2000) evaluated the utility of heart rate as a method for assessing moderate intensity physical activity. They measured heart rate and $\dot{V}O_2$ during a variety of field- and laboratory-based activities in 61 adults. Participants wore a Polar Heart Rate Monitor and a portable indirect calorimetry system (this method is described in greater detail in the subsequent section), which assessed $\dot{V}O_2$ while the participants performed a variety of activities. The activities were performed for 15 min at the participants' self-selected pace and included tasks such as vacuuming, mowing the lawn, doing laundry, raking, playing with children, playing doubles tennis, cooking, and walking. The researchers found that heart rate was strongly correlated with $\dot{V}O_2$ ($r = .68$) and heart rate accounted for 47% of the variability in $\dot{V}O_2$. After adjusting for age and fitness level, heart rate was an accurate predictor of energy expenditure. The researchers concluded that heart rate can be a moderate physiological indicator of $\dot{V}O_2$ during lifestyle physical activities.

CRITERION TECHNIQUES TO ASSESS PHYSICAL ACTIVITY

Behavioral Observation

One of the earliest methods employed to measure physical activity required an experimenter to watch a participant and record that person's physical activity involvement. For example, an observer could record the number of minutes during a 15-minute recess period that a 6-year-old spent walking, fidgeting, standing still, or running. The observer could also record who else was present, if the child was interacting with other students, the nature of the weather, and if the child was using any equipment (e.g., ball).

This example illustrates some of the advantages of using observational methods to assess physical activity. First, it is accurate. Accuracy is an advantage especially when considering that most other assessment methods, such as self-reports, are not suitable with younger populations. Second, observation is a valid method for obtaining physical activity data from a natural setting because it involves little interference with the participant's routine. That is, a participant should not be aware of the observer's presence and should continue on in his or her daily activities. Third, diverse dimensions related to physical activity can be quantified, such as the physical and social environment and the type, duration, intensity, and frequency of the activity. Fourth, because behavioral observation is a direct measure of activity requiring little inference or interpretation, it can be used as a criterion method for validating other measures of physical activity (e.g., self-report and motion sensors; Montoye et al., 1996).

There are also several disadvantages, however, that limit the widespread use of behavioral observations as a measure of physical activity (McKenzie, 1991). First, it is time-consuming, especially if one observer is required for each participant. Second, the necessity for an observer to be present to code data means that relative to other methods of measurement, observation is expensive. Third, observations are confined to relatively short periods and thus may not reflect habitual physical activity. Fourth, subjects, especially older children and adults, may alter their usual activity when they know they are being watched. This tendency is called **participant reactivity.** Thus, researchers must be trained to be sensitive to and reduce participant reactivity—which adds to the cost and time involved. Fourth, watching and recording is tedious, and accuracy decreases as the observation period lengthens. Various techniques and equipment have been used in an effort to improve reliability and provide permanent records of activity, such as the use of movie cameras and video recorders. Also, behavior can be coded and entered directly into portable computers, thereby reducing some of the logistical problems of collecting behavioral observations.

McKenzie (1991) noted that there are two common observation strategies that are used to record physical activity in children. First, with the **momentary time sampling method,** activity level is coded at the moment the observation interval ends. This method provides a snapshot, or sample, of activity levels. Second, with the **partial time sampling method,** observers code all activities that occur during a short interval, usually 5 to 20 seconds.

An example of the momentary time sampling method is provided in a study of play and leisure opportunities undertaken by McKenzie, Marshall, Sallis, and Conway (2000) at 24 middle schools in the Southern California region. The researchers used a behavioral checklist referred to as the *System of Observing Play and Leisure Activity in Youth* (SOPLAY) that was developed and validated for the purposes of their study. Observers recorded the children's activity as either sedentary (i.e., lying down, sitting, or standing), walking, or very active; and they also

recorded the time of the observation, the physical and social characteristics of each area (e.g., whether supervision, organized activities, and equipment were provided), and the type of activity (e.g., basketball, football). To obtain an overall activity measure, counts were tallied for those children engaged in sedentary, walking, and very active behavior. The counts were transformed into estimates of energy expenditure. Observers recorded children's physical activity levels before and after school as well as during lunch time in areas at the school that were designated as activity zones.

The results showed that very few students visited the activity areas during leisure time periods (i.e., the numbers varied from 2% to 4% for daily attendance before and after school to 20% during lunch time). Compared to girls, boys visited the physical activity areas more, were more physically active, and participated in activities that had more structure. McKenzie et al. (2000) noted that few students used opportunities to be physically active during

participant reactivity   The tendency for subjects to alter their usual activity when they know they are being watched.

momentary time sampling   Observation method in which activity level is coded at the moment the observation interval ends.

partial time sampling   Observation method in which observers code all activities that occur during a short interval, usually 5 to 20 seconds.

leisure time at school. Therefore, policies and environmental manipulations (e.g., supervision, equipment, structured programs) are needed to attract more adolescents, especially girls, to physical activity areas. The researchers also suggested that SOPLAY is a feasible measure of group physical activity in children.

Another example of a physical activity and dietary observation system, called *Behaviors of Eating and Activity for Child Health* (BEACHES), was developed for use with children by McKenzie and his colleagues (1991). To assess the instrument's reliability and validity, 42 children, ages 4 to 8 years, were observed for 8 consecutive weeks at home and at school. Five activity types—lying, sitting, standing, walking, and being very active—were recorded at the end of each 30-second observation interval. The first three types (i.e., lying, sitting, standing) are body positions that indicate a lack of activity. The very active category includes all activities that require more energy expenditure than walking. McKenzie et al. also simultaneously collected information on location of the activity type, whether eating occurred, whether other people were present, and various social interactions related to physical activity. The 30-second observation interval was followed by a 30-second recording interval, and the data were entered into a portable computer. The results showed that heart rates were highly related to activity types, ranging from a mean heart rate of 99 beats per minute for the lying category to 153 beats per minute for the very active category. Also, interobserver reliabilities during live and videotaped observations were high. The authors concluded that the BEACHES system is appropriate for studying physical activity correlates in children in a variety of settings.

Doubly Labeled Water

Some scientists consider the doubly labeled water technique to be the gold standard, or the most accurate and precise method, for the assessment of total energy expenditure in humans (Montoye et al., 1996; Schoeller & Racette, 1990). The accuracy of doubly labeled water for assessing total energy expenditure is 4% to 7%. Because this method measures all forms of energy expenditure, it is not a specific measure of physical activity. To assess doubly labeled water, participants must ingest known amounts of hydrogen and oxygen isotopes. These isotopes are not radioactive, so there is no health risk. The isotopes become distributed throughout the body's water in a matter of hours, and a baseline reading of their concentration is obtained from a urine sample. Labeled hydrogen leaves the body as water through urine, sweat, and moisture in respiration. Labeled oxygen leaves the body in the same way, plus as carbon dioxide from respiration. Because the amount of carbon dioxide lost through respiration is very closely related to oxygen consumption, energy expenditure can be calculated based on the difference between rates of loss of hydrogen and oxygen. Up to three weeks after the original urine sample was collected, participants provide another sample and energy expenditure can be calculated for the entire interval.

A major advantage of the doubly labeled water method is its high validity. That is why it is considered the gold standard. It is valid for children, adults, and elderly populations (Starling, Matthews, Ades, & Poehlman, 1999). Because measures are taken over a 1- to 3-week period, habitual physical activity is assessed. In short, doubly labeled water is safe, places little burden on the participant, and does not influence people's physical activity level.

What is the downside to doubly labeled water? The primary disadvantage is cost. Each dose of oxygen currently costs several hundred U.S. dollars and the analysis of samples requires a mass spectrometer, which costs about $250,000 U.S. dollars (Montoye et al., 1996). This technique's expense makes it impractical for use in large epidemiological studies or in educational programs. Second, the measure does not provide data on the type, frequency, intensity, or duration of physical activity. In short, doubly labeled water is valuable for small controlled studies and as a criterion to validate other physical activity measures (Montoye et al.; Starling et al., 1999).

In a validation study Ekelund et al. (2000) examined the validity of the Computer Science and Applications (CSA) unidimensional activity monitor (CSA Inc., Shalimar, FL) using doubly labeled water as a criterion measure in 26 9-year-old children. The children's physical activity was monitored for two weeks in their naturalistic environment. Physical activity was measured by the CSA activity monitor, and total energy expenditure was simultaneously assessed by the doubly labeled water method. The children wore the monitors during the daytime except when they were engaged in water activities such as swimming and bathing.

The researchers found that the CSA activity monitor was significantly associated with energy expenditure from the doubly labeled water method ($r = .39$). The researchers also calculated the relationship between physical activity level with the CSA activity monitor. Physical activity level was determined by expressing total energy expenditure as a multiple of basal metabolic rate using the following formula: physical activity level equals total energy expenditure divided by basal metabolic rate. The correlation between physical activity level and the CSA activity monitor was .58. The authors concluded that activity counts from the CSA monitor is a useful measure of the total amount of physical activity in 9-year-old children.

Another example of a validation study of self-report of physical activity and heart rate monitoring using doubly labeled water as the criterion was conducted by Racette and her colleagues (1995). They compared the 7-Day Physical Activity Recall Questionnaire and heart rate monitoring to doubly labeled water in 14 obese women in a weight loss program. Specifically, doubly labeled water was used to assess the accuracy of these two methods to determine physical activity and energy expenditure. Results revealed that both the heart rate monitor and self-report measure accurately assessed energy expenditure for the group. Individual variability, however, was high.

Indirect Calorimetry

Indirect calorimetry measures energy expenditure from oxygen consumption and carbon dioxide production by analyzing expired air. This method is considered an accurate and valid measure of short-term energy expenditure. What is the downside of this technique? Indirect calorimetry is difficult to use because it requires nonportable gas analysis equipment. That is, the person must wear a mask, a mouthpiece, and nose clip while expired air is gathered. Also, the person must carry a gas collection container or remain in the laboratory or near remote sensors (Dishman, Washburn, & Schoeller, 2001). Thus, this method is impractical for validating a questionnaire that measures weekly or habitual exercise behavior. So, when is this technique used? Indirect calorimetry is used mostly in laboratory settings to validate other physical activity measures (e.g., Eston, Rowlands, & Ingledew, 1998). Recently, manufacturers are introducing portable, lightweight metabolic systems that should improve the estimates of energy expenditure in field settings (Sirard & Pate, 2001).

Summary

For decades, assessment of physical activity has captured the interest of epidemiologists, exercise scientists, and clinicians. Driven by the increasing cost of health care and the strong negative relationship between physical activity and prevalence of chronic diseases, the search for accurate and reliable tests of physical activity is critical for clinicians and researchers interested in examining the health-related benefits of physical activity (Wood, 2000). This chapter examined several methods of assessing physical activity, including self-report questionnaires, pedometers, accelerometers, and doubly labeled water. These measures vary considerably in their feasibility, reliability, and validity.

Currently, there is no single field method to assess physical activity that is psychometrically sound and logistically feasible over a wide range of populations, settings, and uses. Wood (2000) stated that as "we move into the new millennium the accurate field assessment of physical activity will assume utmost importance as we further explore the relationship between physical activity and disease prevention" (p. vi). In short, until technological advances offer more valid, objective, and feasible field methods for assessing physical activity, multiple assessment devices must be used to obtain accurate activity profiles (Wood).

SECTION TWO

The Individual and Physical Activity

The general purpose of Section 2 is to discuss the antecedents and consequences of physical activity for the *individual* person. In the first three chapters in this section, we discuss the relationship of physical activity to cognitive functioning (Chapter 3), various manifestations of mood including anxiety and depression (Chapter 4), and personality including trait anxiety and self-esteem (Chapter 5). Researchers are interested in the role that physical activity plays in psychobiological outcomes such as sleep, tolerance for pain, and reactivity to stress, so these topics are discussed in Chapter 6. Although exercise is considered almost universally to be a positive behavior, it has become apparent that certain negative behaviors sometimes go hand in hand with physical activity. Chapter 7 outlines some of these behaviors, including exercise dependence, steroid abuse, and eating disorders. Finally, in the last chapter in this section, we discuss the individual correlates of (i.e., factors associated with) involvement in physical activity.

CHAPTER 3

Cognitive Functioning and Physical Activity

Mens sana in corpore sano.

(Homer)

CHAPTER OBJECTIVES

After completing this chapter you will be able to

- Understand a major protocol—meta-analysis—that is used to statistically summarize large bodies of research.

- Describe the relationship between involvement in physical activity and cognitive functioning.

Key terms

dose-response issue	moderate effect
effect size	moderator variables
large effect	small effect
meta-analysis	

In Chapter 1, we discussed the physiological, physical, and biological benefits of being active. You may recall that these benefits include increased bone density in youth; an increased likelihood that bone mineral density will be retained in older adults; increased muscle hypertrophy, strength, endurance, capillarization, maximal blood flow and metabolic capacity; increased cardiac mass, stroke volume, fibrinolysis, and cardiac output at rest and during exercise; reduced heart rate and blood pressure at rest and during submaximal exercise; increased ventillatory-diffusion efficiency during exercise; decreased triglycerides and adiposity, and increased high density cholesterol; and insulin-mediated glucose uptake (Haskell, 1994).

Given this impressive list, a case can be (and often is) made for increased physical activity on the basis of physically oriented benefits alone. Historically, however, there has also been a long-standing belief that being physically active has consequences far beyond the physical. One illustration of that long-standing belief is present in the quote used to introduce this chapter. In ancient Greece, Homer endorsed the link between the physical and the mental when he stated "a sound mind in a sound body" (i.e., *mens sana in corpore sano*). As another example, Hippocrates, who is acknowledged to be the father of medicine, strongly urged individuals suffering from mental illness to exercise (A. J. Ryan, 1984). Even in modern times, physicians see physical activity and exercise as having beneficial consequences beyond the physical. For example, A. J. Ryan (1983), reporting on a survey conducted with 1,156 primary care physicians, noted that many routinely prescribed exercise as a treatment for emotional disorders such as depression (85%) and anxiety (60%).

The implicit belief that a link exists between physical health and mental health led many social scientists to empirically test various relationships over the past 100 years. Not all of that research was scientifically sound. Further, not all of that research showed the same pattern of results. Thus, it was difficult to draw conclusions. This point was emphasized by North, McCullagh, and Tran (1990) when they attempted to summarize the literature on the impact of physical activity on depression. In their commentary, they pointed out that "given the discrepant findings . . . it is likely that a narrative review of literature would conclude that there is no consistent findings" (p. 383). North et al. offered a solution, however: **meta-analysis,** a method of reviewing a large body of research evidence that is both systematic and quantitative. Fortunately, much of the research on the impact of exercise on psychological variables has been summarized through the use of meta-analysis. Over the next four chapters, we present conclusions from those meta-analyses. Prior to discussing those conclusions, however, you might find it useful to understand what meta-analysis is and why it is used.

RESEARCH INTEGRATION THROUGH META-ANALYSIS

Consider the question, is physical fitness related to anxiety? Across different studies, the operational definition of anxiety could vary markedly. For example, it might be tested with a single statement such as "I feel very anxious." Responses then could be obtained on a 9-point scale containing anchor statements such as *strongly disagree* and *strongly agree.* Or anxiety might be tested with a psychometrically sound inventory containing 20 anxiety-relevant questions to which the individual responds "true" or "false." Or it might even be assessed using a physiological measure such as heart rate with responses indicated in beats per minute.

Across that same cross section of studies, the operational definition of fitness also could vary. For example, fitness might be assessed through amount of

---

meta-analysis   The statistical analysis of the summary findings of many empirical studies.

---

time spent running per week. Then responses could be obtained in minutes and/or hours. Or fitness might be defined through measures of muscular strength, and responses expressed in grams or kilograms (or ounces or pounds) lifted. Finally, fitness might even be assessed using a physiological measure such as maximal oxygen uptake, with responses stated in milliliters per kilogram of body weight.

Imagine carrying out a literature review focusing on the question of the relationship of fitness and anxiety. If 50 studies were located, they might vary in the operational definitions used for anxiety, operational definitions used for fitness, size of the samples tested, and the nature of the samples tested (i.e., age, gender, physical health status, mental health status). Also, the 50 studies might vary in their findings relative to the question. That is, 35 studies might show that fitness is associated with reduced anxiety; 10, that fitness is unrelated to anxiety; and 5, that fitness is associated with increased anxiety. Any scholar attempting to summarize this body of research with a narrative review would be forced to conclude that the results were "mixed" or "unclear."

Effect Sizes

In 1976, the protocol for meta-analysis was introduced by Glass as a means of quantifying the magnitude of treatment effects in individual studies and then averaging the results from several studies. As Glass, McGaw, and Smith (1981) stated, the essential characteristic of meta-analysis is that it "is the statistical analysis of the summary findings of many empirical studies" (p. 21).

In a meta-analysis, the result from an individual study is converted to a *standard score,* which is called an **effect size.** Because effect sizes are standard scores, the measures (and the units used to express the amount of those measures) in the various studies are not relevant. Moreover, standard scores can be added and then averaged so conclusions can be drawn about the overall impact of a particular treatment. Finally, and this point is also important, a meta-analysis can examine the possible influence of what are called **moderator variables.** Moderator variables directly influence the relationship of an independent variable to a dependent variable. So, in our fitness-anxiety relationship example, it would be possible to assess statistically through a meta-analysis whether age is a moderator variable in the fitness-anxiety relationship. If increased fitness is associated with reduced anxiety, does that relationship hold across the age spectrum from adolescents to older adulthood?

Meta-analysis is particularly useful in areas of research where a large number of studies are available, where not all the studies are of uniform quality, where there is wide variability in the operational definition of the variables, where differences in the nature of the subjects and differences in designs are present, and where the results have not been completely consistent. Meta-analysis offers the opportunity for researchers to statistically average the effects from various studies and come to some conclusion for the population as a whole. It is also possible, of course, to subdivide the pool of studies and examine conditions that might serve to moderate the basic relationship.

Interpretation of Effect Sizes

Most people can easily interpret quantities or amounts when commonly used measures such as inches, feet, seconds, and kilograms are used. People also have a common understanding of the meaning of some standard statistical scores such as a percentile (e.g., you scored in the 85th percentile on your SAT). However, interpretation of an effect size is not as intuitively obvious. Fortunately, Cohen (1969, 1992) has provided some guidelines that are useful for understanding the results from a meta-analysis. Thus, the descriptive term **small effect** can be used for any effect size within

---

FIT FACTS

Can you get into flow (i.e., the feeling state characterized by positive mood, a here-and-now focus, absorption, loss of self-consciousness, and spontaneous action) during physical activity?

Yes, but it is more likely to occur in more experienced exercisers and in individuals who are high in hypnotic susceptibility.

(Grove & Lewis, 1996)

---

the range of .10 to .30. Also, the descriptive term **moderate effect** can be used for effect sizes in the range of .40 to .70. Finally, the descriptive term **large effect** can be used for any effect size that is over .80.

There is another statistical way to interpret an effect size. Consider, for example, the improvement (i.e., reduction) in anxiety scores in an experimental group exposed to 16 weeks of exercise versus a control group that simply met and talked for the 16 weeks. An effect size of .33 for the improvement in anxiety scores in the experimental group over that in the control group would mean that the average experimental person improved in (showed a reduction for) anxiety one third of a standard deviation more than was the case for the average control person.

Most students find it easier to use the descriptive terms *small, medium,* and *large* for effect sizes of .20, .50, and .80 respectively. However, they sometimes

---

effect size   The result from an individual study converted to a standard score.

moderator variables   Variables that have a direct influence on the relationship between an independent variable and a dependent variable.

small effect   Any effect size within the range of .10 to .30.

moderate effect   Any effect size within the range of .40 to .70.

large effect   Any effect size that is over .80.

ask, "Well, what about effect sizes of .35 or .75? How are these effect sizes described? They are not included in the ranges." In response, we remind the students that the descriptive terms *small, medium,* and *large* are intended to be guidelines, not fixed criteria. So to a large extent, the verbal descriptors used for effect sizes that are outside the ranges we have presented here are a matter of personal choice. There is a parallel in academia. Universally, we might agree that someone in the 30th percentile is a poor student, someone in the 50th percentile is a good student, and someone in the 85th percentile is an excellent student. Where is the boundary between a poor and a good student, and a good and an excellent student? A wide variability would exist among the answers given by different groups.

PHYSICAL ACTIVITY AND COGNITIVE FUNCTIONING

An issue that has long intrigued researchers is contained in Homer's dictum *mens sana in corpore sano.* Etnier and her colleagues (1997) observed that almost 200 studies have been carried out to determine if acute and chronic bouts of physical activity influence cognitive functioning. The types of cognitive functioning tasks that have been tested in research are memory, mathematical ability, verbal ability, reasoning creativity, academic achievement, mental age, intelligence quotient, reaction time, and perception. Also, the research protocol has compared inactive individuals and physically active individuals on those cognitive tasks after exposure to either a single session (acute) or a long-term (chronic) program of physical activity.

Etnier and her colleagues (1997) carried out a meta-analysis on those 200 studies. As Table 3-1 shows, the results from all studies combined led the researchers to a conclusion that being physically active has a small beneficial effect on mental function (ES = .25).

Chronic Versus Acute Bouts of Physical Activity

An important issue pertains to the influence of a single exposure to physical activity (i.e., acute physical activity) versus a long-term sustained exposure

Cognitive functioning tasks used in research include logical and creative reasoning.

■ **TABLE 3-1**   The Relationship Between Physical Activity and Cognitive Functioning

COGNITIVE FUNCTIONING	AVERAGE EFFECT SIZE[1]
Overall effect	.25
Nature of physical activity involvement	
Chronic activity	.33
Acute activity	.16
Cross-sectional/correlational	.53
Age and chronic physical activity	
Elementary (6–13 yrs.)	.36
High school (14–17 yrs.)	.77
College (18–30 yrs.)	.64
Older adult (45–60 yrs.)	1.02
Oldest adult (60–90 yrs.)	.19

[1.] An effect size of .20 is small, one of .50 is medium, and one of .80 is large. The effect sizes are all positive, indicating improvements over control groups or baseline conditions.

(i.e., chronic physical activity). When Etnier and her colleagues (1997) examined the pool of studies that had tested cognitive functioning after acute bouts of physical activity, they found only a small effect of .16 (see Table 3-1). On the other hand, chronic physical activity was associated with an effect size more than twice as large (ES = .33). These findings led Etnier et al. to conclude that "exercise may not have a meaningful impact on cognition when it is administered in acute bouts, but exercise that is administered as a chronic treatment to produce fitness gains, or exercise that has been adopted by an individual for a sufficiently long period of time to produce fitness gains, may be a useful intervention for enhancing cognitive abilities" (p. 266).

Researchers use a variety of paradigms (approaches) to answer important questions. The paradigm used is often influenced by such considerations as availability of participants, of financial resources, and so on. Two of the simplest and easiest to use paradigms are cross-sectional and correlational. Typically, with a cross-sectional paradigm, the cognitive functioning of a sample of physically active individuals is compared with a sample of inactive or less active individuals. With a correlational paradigm, a single sample of individuals is tested and a correlation coefficient is computed to assess the degree of relationship between level of cognitive functioning and level of fitness. As Table 3-1 shows, in studies where either a cross-sectional or correlational paradigm was used, a moderate relationship between physical activity and cognitive functioning was observed (ES = .53).

A major limitation in cross-sectional and correlational designs is that they do not give any insight into the question, has the physical activity directly caused improved cognition ability? Clinical trials, which are used in behavioral and medical sciences, do permit inferences about cause and effect. With clinical trials, participants are randomly assigned to control and treatment groups and the treatment or intervention—physical activity in this case—is provided over an extended period of time. In the 17 clinical trial studies that Etnier et al. (1997) analyzed, physical activity had a small positive effect (i.e., ES = .18) on cognitive functioning.

Chronic Physical Activity and the Dose-Response Issue

Practitioners (and participants) are often interested in what is referred to as the **dose-response issue:** how much of the dose (physical activity in this case) is necessary to obtain the desired response (improved cognitive functioning). For people chronically engaged in physical activity, a "dose" can represent a number of different considerations. For example, it is possible to vary the duration of each training session, the days of training per week, and/or the total number of weeks of training.

Many researchers examining the relationship of physical activity to cognitive functioning varied the degree of involvement. When Etnier et al. (1997) summarized the results in their meta-analysis, they did not find any relationship between improved cognitive functioning and either the duration of individual training sessions, the number of days devoted to physical activity each week, or the total number of weeks of involvement. Thus, at this point, it is not possible to provide prescriptions for the specific doses of physical activity necessary to produce enhanced cognitive functioning.

Chronic Physical Activity and the Age of Participants

Researchers interested in the role that chronic physical activity plays in cognitive functioning have tested individuals of widely varying ages—from 6 to 90. Table 3-1 provides an overview of the results from the meta-analysis carried out by Etnier and her colleagues (1997). The largest improvements in cognitive functioning following long-term bouts of physical activity occur in older adults ages 45 to 60

---

dose-response issue   How much of the dose is necessary to obtain the desired response.

years (ES = 1.02), followed by high school students ages 14 to 17 years (ES = .77), college students ages 18 to 30 years (ES = .64), elementary school children ages 6 to 13 years (ES = .36), and oldest adults ages 60 to 90 years (ES = .19).

No discernible pattern is evident in the results summarized in Table 3-1. Nonetheless, physical activity is positively associated with enhanced cognitive functioning across the age spectrum.

Summary

Historically, a long-standing belief has held that being physically active has positive mental as well as physical consequences. Numerous studies have explored the degree to which involvement in physical activity is associated with enhanced cognitive functioning. In areas where a large number of studies exist, researchers often attempt to summarize the literature through the use of meta-analyses. A meta-analysis provides a statistical summary through the use of a standard score referred to as an effect size. Effect sizes are traditionally referred to as small, medium, and large if they are of the magnitude of .10 to .30, .40 to .70, and .80 or greater.

A meta-analysis concerned with the relationship of physical activity to cognitive functioning showed that there is, on average, a small relationship between involvement in physical activity and improvements in cognitive functioning. Also, the relationship is greater after chronic physical activity than after acute physical activity.

The dose-response issue is unclear at this point. No relationship has been shown between improved cognitive functioning and either the duration of individual training sessions, the number of days devoted to physical activity each week, or the total number of weeks of involvement.

Finally, the magnitude of the relationship between involvement in chronic physical activity and enhanced cognitive functioning varies across the age spectrum. Although there is no meaningful pattern in the results, the meta-analysis shows that physical activity is positively associated with enhanced cognitive functioning at every age.

CHAPTER **4**

Physical Activity and Mood

True Enjoyment Comes from Activity of the Mind and Exercise of the Body.
(Wilhelm von Humboldt)

CHAPTER OBJECTIVES

After completing this chapter you will be able to

- Differentiate among the various terms used to represent mood.

- Discuss the role that physical activity plays in the alleviation of anxiety.

- Discuss the role that physical activity plays in the alleviation of depression.

- Discuss the role that physical activity plays in other manifestations of mood.

- Understand the consequences of combining pharmacologic treatments with physical activity.

- Outline the explanations offered to account for the psychological benefits associated with being more physically active.

Key terms

clinical depression	positive affect
negative affect	state anxiety
nonclinical depression	trait anxiety
POMS	

onsiderable anecdotal testimony supports the popular belief that physical activity and exercise contribute to a "feel good" state in the individual. The quote by Wilhelm von Humboldt used to introduce this chapter is consistent with this popular belief. He suggested that exercise of the body contributes to feelings of true enjoyment. Science seldom relies on popular beliefs, however. As a consequence, researchers over a number of years have concentrated their efforts on examining the impact of physical activity and exercise on the mood states of the individual.

What does that research indicate? Interestingly, despite hundreds of studies, a number of meta-analyses (e.g., Calfas & Taylor, 1994; Craft & Landers, 1998; Kugler, Seelback, & Krüskemper, 1994; Landers & Petruzzello, 1994; Long & van Stavel, 1995; D. G. McDonald & Hodgdon, 1991; North et al., 1990; Petruzzello, Landers, Hatfield, Kubitz, & Salazar, 1991; Schlicht, 1994), narrative reviews (e.g., Ekkekakis & Petruzzello, 1999; Landers & Arent, 2001; Salmon, 2001), and even reviews of reviews (e.g., Scully, Kremer, Meade, Graham, & Dudgeon, 1998), there is still some debate.

One reason for the debate is that *mood* is a complex construct to operationally define and different authors have used the term in different ways. For example, Landers and Arent (2001) pointed out that a number of constructs fall under the category of mood-like states. Feelings of anxiety, depression, fatigue, anger, and confusion are considered to be manifestations of **negative affect** or mood. Conversely, feelings of vigor, pleasantness, and euphoria are considered to be manifestations of **positive affect** or mood. The researchers also noted, however, that theoreticians (Lazarus, 1991) make a distinction between mood versus affect, claiming that these constructs represent psychological states along an *emotional continuum*. Mood is considered to be more transient and less stable, whereas affect is considered to be more enduring. Consequently, for example, anxiety is a type of affect whereas vigor is a type of mood.

A second reason for the debate is that physical activity—particularly its intensity—is difficult to operationally define. Even "maximal intensity," for example, is difficult to identify. This point was illustrated by Salmon (2000), who noted that "maximal exertion is not a purely physiological limit; even when exercising 'to exhaustion,' the offer of financial reward further increases its intensity" (p. 34). It has been even more difficult to equate workloads described as being at less than maximal intensity (see Ekkekakis & Petruzzello, 1999, for a full discussion on this issue).

A third reason for the debate is that differences exist between people, that the same individual is not completely consistent in his or her response from one physical activity bout to another, and that considerable differences exist in the demands imposed by different activities. In short, all people do not respond to the same workload in the same way or even consistently from time to time. As Ekkekakis and Petruzzello (1999) pointed out, "affective responses to exercise have been shown to be affected by biological and psychological individual difference variables, the physical and social environment, and the objective and perceived attributes of the exercise stimulus, as well as several psychological states" (p. 339).

Finally, adding to the debate, some theoreticians (e.g., Morgan, 1997; Raglin, 1997) have even suggested that evidence showing a physical activity–improved mood relationship could easily reflect a behavioral artifact. Fundamentally, the argument they advance is that people who like to exercise and expect to feel good following physical activity will report that they do. Conversely, people who do not like exercise either avoid physical activity or do not report the positive mood benefits espoused by advocates. So the physical activity–mood relationship might reflect nothing more than the testimonials of advocates.

As is the case in any debate, it's necessary to finally draw conclusions based on the evidence available. The positions endorsed here (i.e., the conclusions we draw) are the ones most strongly supported by research evidence garnered to date and highlighted through empirical summaries (i.e., meta-analyses).

Because the research literature in the physical activity sciences has not progressed to the point where strong distinctions have been made in research between mood and affect, the two types of psychological states are combined in this chapter and referred to as mood. In the first part of this chapter, we discuss the two affective states most frequently examined in the physical activity sciences—anxiety and depression. In the final section of this chapter, we address the relationship of physical activity to a variety of other positive and negative moods—vigor, anger, and so on.

PHYSICAL ACTIVITY AND ANXIETY

Anxiety is considered to be a negative emotional state characterized by feelings of nervousness, worry, and apprehension and by activation or arousal of the body. It arises "in the face of demands that tax or exceed the resources of the system [emphasis removed] or . . . demands to which there are no readily available or automatic adaptive responses" (Lazarus & Cohen, 1977, p. 109). In modern society, anxiety represents a serious health problem. For example, a report from the National Institute of Mental Health (Regier et al., 1984) indicated that anxiety neurosis is the largest mental health problem in the United States, affecting 8% (13.1 million) individuals.

negative affect Feelings such as anxiety, depression, fatigue, anger, and confusion.

positive affect Feelings such as vigor, pleasantness, and euphoria.

Theorists consider it important to differentiate between **state anxiety** and **trait anxiety.** State anxiety is "an existing or current emotional state characterized by feelings of apprehension and tension and associated with activation of the organism" (Martens, Vealey, & Burton, 1990, p. 9). The critical phrase that serves to differentiate state from trait anxiety is *existing or current.* State anxiety refers to the level of anxiety that an individual experiences at any given point in time. Thus, for example, state anxiety is generally elevated for most individuals immediately prior to important events such as exams and piano recitals. The physical activity–state anxiety relationship is the focus of discussion in this chapter. The impact of physical activity on individual personality characteristics such as trait anxiety is discussed in Chapter 5.

General Effects

A number of meta-analyses have statistically summarized the research on physical activity and state anxiety (e.g., Calfas & Taylor, 1994; Kugler et al., 1994; Landers & Petruzzello, 1994; Long & van Stavel, 1995; D. G. McDonald & Hodgon, 1991; Petruzzello et al., 1991). The number (and types) of

> **state anxiety** The level of anxiety that an individual experiences at any given point in time.
>
> **trait anxiety** The predisposition to perceive certain environmental stimuli as threatening or nonthreatening and to respond to these stimuli with varying levels of state anxiety.

studies included in those different meta-analyses has varied widely. Nonetheless, the overriding conclusion reached was that physical activity is associated with a reduction in anxiety. The magnitude of the reduction reported has varied from small to moderate (i.e., ES = .15 to .56).

The beneficial effects that physical activity has on state anxiety seems to begin within 5 minutes of the cessation of acute exercise. Although there is some research that shows that this beneficial effect could last from 4 to 6 hours, it is generally accepted that the duration is substantially less—up to approximately 2 hours (Landers & Petruzzello, 1994).

Task Type. A question of interest for practitioners is whether the anxiety reduction found following physical activity is restricted to one particular type of task, such as those involving the aerobic system. In their meta-analysis, Petruzzello and his colleagues (1991) found that aerobic activities (e.g., walking, jogging, running, swimming, cycling) are all equally associated with a small reduction in state anxiety (ES = .26). Conversely, however, nonaerobic activities—activities such as weight training, for example—were not found to be associated with reductions in self-reported state anxiety (ES = −.05).

The Dose-Response Issue. A second question of interest for practitioners relates to the dose-response issue: what dosage of the treatment (physical activity in this case) is necessary to obtain the desired response (reduced state anxiety in this case). Ekkekakis and Petruzzello (1999) noted that two assumptions typically provide the foundation for any prescriptions pertaining to the amount of physical activity necessary to produce reductions in state anxiety. The first is that physical activity must reach some minimal threshold in terms of intensity and duration. They also noted that the threshold advocated varies slightly. For example, Dishman (1986) proposed that exercise should be carried out at an intensity of 70% of maximal oxygen uptake or 70% of maximal heart rate for at least 20 minutes. Similarly, Raglin and Morgan (1985) advocated an intensity of 60% of maximal oxygen uptake. The second assumption is that physical activity carried out at excessively high intensities (e.g., 80% to 90% of

Popular belief is that physical activity can have an affect on mood.

maximal heart rate) and/or duration (e.g., a marathon) will have a detrimental impact on state anxiety. In short, what is implicitly suggested here is a happy medium: Too little physical activity has no appreciable effect on anxiety and too much has a negative effect.

Ekkekakis and Petruzzello (1999) pointed out that research does not support either of these two assumptions. One way to consider the dose-response issue is from the perspective of the length of the physical activity session. In the meta-analysis carried out by Petruzzello and his colleagues (1991) the programs in the studies were categorized according to whether physical activity lasted 0 to 20 minutes, 21 to 30 minutes, 31 to 40 minutes, or greater than 40 minutes. The researchers found that anxiety reduction is present *following* physical activity regardless of the duration of the program.

Another way of looking at the dose-response issue is to consider the intensity of the physical activity stimulus rather than the time involved. Two possible measures of intensity are, of course, an individual's exercising heart rate and that person's exercising oxygen uptake as a percentage of his or her maximum. When Petruzzello and his colleagues (1991) carried out their analyses, they found that anxiety reduction is present *following* physical activity regardless of the intensity of the program.

A slightly different picture is present for anxiety responses *during* physical activity. Ekkekakis and Petruzzello (1999) noted that "affective responses during exercise appear to be sensitive to dose effects, with increasing intensity and progressing duration being generally associated with reduced affective positivity" (p. 366).

Physical Activity Versus Other Treatment Modalities. Individuals who are suffering from anxiety may choose any of a number of possible treatments to alleviate their symptoms. Some of the more popular treatments include quiet rest, progressive relaxation, meditation, biofeedback, and hypnosis. In some of the studies Petruzzello et al. (1991) reviewed, different types of treatments—including physical activity—were compared against a control condition. These studies offer insight into the comparative benefits of physical activity versus other treatment modalities.

When Petruzzello et al. (1991) examined the reductions in state anxiety across the various strategies used, no differences were found. In short, practitioners providing counsel to individuals suffering from anxiety can be confident that physical activity is as effective as treatments such as hypnosis, meditation, and so on.

PHYSICAL ACTIVITY AND DEPRESSION

In the health sciences, a distinction is made between **clinical depression** and **nonclinical depression.** The latter is viewed as a mental state characterized by feelings of gloom and listlessness. Generally, it arises as a result of a loss of some type, such as a death, a family breakup, or negative changes in job status. However, depression can also arise in periods immediately following completion of some

clinical depression A lowered mood or loss of interest/pleasure for a minimum of two weeks and accompanied by at least five of the following symptoms: loss of appetite, weight loss/gain, sleep disturbance, psychomotor agitation or retardation, energy decrease, sense of worthlessness, guilt, difficulty in concentrating, thoughts of suicide.

nonclinical depression A mental state characterized by feelings of gloom and listlessness.

long-anticipated pleasurable event, such as a birth, a holiday period, or a major assignment.

There is less consensus on what constitutes clinical depression. The American Psychiatric Association (1987) considers it to be a lowered mood or loss of interest/pleasure for a minimum of at least two weeks. Furthermore, at least five of the following symptoms must be present: loss of appetite, weight loss or gain, sleep disturbance, psychomotor agitation or retardation, decrease in energy, sense of worthlessness, guilt, difficulty in concentrating, and thoughts of suicide.

There has been a long-standing interest in the potential benefits of physical activity and exercise as an intervention strategy for the treatment of depression (e.g., Franz & Hamilton, 1905). Numerous studies have been undertaken, but some of those studies suffer from poor research design, and others, from small or nonrepresentative samples. Therefore, it is difficult for readers unfamiliar with the area to make sense out of the body of research. Fortunately, meta-analyses have been carried out over the past 10 years. One, by North et al. (1990), focused on all forms of depression. Another, by Craft and Landers (1998), focused on clinical depression only. The two reviews provide an opportunity for researchers to examine the role of physical activity on depression for both nonclinical and clinical individuals.

Nonclinical Depression

The purpose of the North et al. (1990) meta-analysis was to summarize the total population of studies dealing with depression and physical activity, and some of the studies they reviewed included samples of individuals undergoing treatment for depression. Nonetheless, in one of their analyses, North and his colleagues subdivided their studies according to the nature of the participants. As Table 4-1 shows, physically active high school students (ES = .60), health club members (ES = .49), community citizens (ES = .49), and college students and faculty (ES = .16) all exhibited reductions in depression as a result of their involvement in physical activity.

■ **TABLE 4-1** The Relationship Between Physical Activity and Nonclinical Depression

MEASURE	AVERAGE EFFECT SIZE[1]
Types of participants in the study	
High school students	.60
Health club members	.49
Community citizens	.49
College students/faculty	.16
Purpose underlying physical activity	
Academic experiment	.67
General health	.29

[1] An effect size of .20 is small, one of .50 is medium, and one of .80 is large. The effect sizes are all positive, indicating that reductions in depression are associated with involvement in physical activity.

In another set of analyses, North and his colleagues (1990) subdivided their studies on the basis of the stated purpose of the physical activity. They found that individuals involved in physical activity for general health (ES = .29) or as a result of an academic experiment (ES = .67) demonstrated reductions in depression. The results, taken as a whole, provide strong evidence that physical activity is beneficial for individuals experiencing nonclinical depression.

Clinical Depression

Eight years after the report by North and his colleagues (1990), Craft and Landers (1998) were able to include an additional 17 studies dealing with the influence of physical activity on individuals suffering from clinical depression or depression resulting from mental illness. The results from the North et al. and Craft and Landers meta-analyses were similar (see Table 4-2). North and his colleagues reported antidepressant effects from physical activity for indi-

■ **TABLE 4-2**   Physical Activity for Individuals Undergoing Treatment for Depression

MEASURE	AVERAGE EFFECT SIZE[1]
Individual's purpose for physical activity (North et al., 1990)	
Medical rehabilitation	.97
Psychological rehabilitation	.55
Individuals receiving treatment for depression (Craft & Landers, 1998)	.72

[1]An effect size of .20 is small, one of .50 is medium, and one of .80 is large. The effect sizes are all positive, indicating that reductions in depression are associated with involvement in physical activity.

viduals under medical treatment (i.e., for postmyocardial infarction, cardiovascular risk, pulmonary problems, or hemodialysis; ES = .97) as well as those undergoing psychological rehabilitation (ES = .55). Similarly, as Table 4-2 shows, Craft and Landers reported an overall moderate to large effect (ES = .72). Physical activity is therefore a useful treatment for individuals suffering from depression to such an extent that they must obtain professional help.

Factors Influencing the Impact of Physical Activity on Depression

The North et al. (1990) and Craft and Landers (1998) studies combined also provide some insight into how various conditions might moderate the impact of physical activity on depression. Keep in mind, however, that the North et al. search for moderators involved the total population of studies they analyzed (i.e., individuals of all levels of depression were included).

The Dose-Response Issue.   One conclusion that comes out consistently from both meta-analyses is that the duration of physical activity is important.

The longer the physical activity program goes on, the greater is the impact on depression. For example, Craft and Landers (1998) found that physical activity for 9 weeks or greater led to a large decrease in depression (ES = 1.18). Even physical activity periods of shorter duration are effective, however. Programs of 8 weeks or less were reported to produce a moderate change in depression (ES = .54). Although Craft and Landers found differences in effect sizes when they compared physical activity periods of different duration (i.e., minutes per session) as well as physical activity periods of different intensity, no statistically significant findings emerged.

Task Type.   All forms of exercise—weight training, aerobic activity, walking—are equally beneficial in terms of their impact on depression. Craft and Landers (1998) urged caution, however, in drawing conclusions about the role that type of physical activity might play in reducing depression in clinical populations. They noted that 83% of physical activity situations "alleging to be aerobic did not result in fitness gains over 5%. This makes a comparison between [aerobic and nonaerobic programs] difficult at best" (pp. 350–351).

Characteristics of the Individual.   Comparisons have been made of studies in which the characteristics of the individuals were different. No evidence has been found to suggest that the beneficial effects of physical activity are restricted to specific groups of individuals. Males and females, individuals across the age span, individuals varying markedly in health status, individuals undergoing psychological and medical treatment, and individuals initially depressed versus not depressed all showed reductions in depression as a result of involvement in physical activity. Craft and Landers (1998) did point out that the law of initial values is present in terms of physical activity and clinical depression in that individuals with moderate to severe depression benefited more than individuals with mild to moderate depression (i.e., ES = .88 versus ES = .34 respectively).

Physical Activity Versus Other Treatments. A word of caution is necessary before too much emphasis is placed on physical activity as a treatment for depression. Physical activity is effective. However, Craft and Landers (1998) found that it is no more effective than group or individual psychotherapy and behavioral interventions. North and his colleagues (1990) found that the combination of physical activity and psychotherapy produced the largest decrease in depression.

INTERACTION OF PHYSICAL ACTIVITY AND PSYCHOTHERAPEUTIC DRUGS

Psychotherapeutic medications such as the tricyclic antidepressants, neuroleptics, and benzodiazepines have been linked with numerous physical side effects. These side effects include dizziness, nausea, drowsiness, and dry mouth (Martinsen & Stanghelle, 1997). Although the physiological consequences of combining pharmacologic treatments with exercise has been thoroughly examined, knowledge of the synergistic effects of psychotropic medications and physical activity is limited. Because both exercise and psychotherapeutic drugs are routinely prescribed as part of the treatment strategy for psychological disturbance (Morgan & Goldston, 1987), knowledge of the effects that the interaction of these interventions may have on physical and psychological health is of great importance. To date, however, the relationship between exercise and psychotherapeutic medications has not been systematically investigated.

An obvious concern of combining exercise with drug therapy involves the potential health risks that may arise from the physical side effects of the medication and the physiological demands of exercise. Some studies indicate that tricyclic antidepressants may compromise cardiac output (Vohra, Burrows, & Sloma, 1975) and consequently impinge on a person's ability to exercise safely. In contrast to this assertion, other researchers have found that therapeutic doses of antidepressants have little impact on cardiac function and do not impair a person's ability to perform physical activity (Glassman & Bigger, 1981; Veith, Raskind, & Claswell, 1982). Thus, psy-

chotherapeutic drugs do not appear to make exercise an unsafe activity. Nevertheless, they are associated with numerous side effects that may make physical activity more difficult. For example, the use of psychotherapeutic drugs has been linked with drowsiness, decreased cardiac output, and reduced blood pressure responses both at rest and during exercise. It is possible that these physical changes may make exercise more difficult (Carlsson, Dencker, Grimby, & Heggendal, 1967) and subsequently decrease an individual's motivation to engage in regular physical activity. Nevertheless, due to the health benefits of physical activity, exercise is not contraindicated for individuals taking drugs (Martinsen & Stanghelle, 1997). Benzodiazapines may decrease psychomotor performance; however, findings do not indicate that they significantly impair exercise tolerance, duration, or cardiac function (Eimer, Cable, Gal, Rothenberg, & McCue, 1985; Stratton & Halter, 1985). Therefore, although psychotropic medications do impact physiological factors, exercising concomitantly with the use of psychotherapeutic drugs does not appear to increase the risk of adverse physical health complications.

Given that exercise has been consistently associated—with reductions in depression and anxiety (Morgan, 1994; Raglin, 1997), it is plausible that physical activity would enhance the beneficial effect of medications. However, only two studies have investigated this relationship, and the findings are mixed. In one study, Martinsen (1987) examined the influence of exercise therapy and a combination of exercise therapy with tricyclic antidepressants in a sample of 43 patients with major depressive disorder. Although both treatments had a beneficial effect on depression, the addition of exercise failed to increase the antidepressant effect of the medication. In the second study (Martinsen, Hoffart, & Solberg, 1989), results favored the combination of medication and exercise over exercise alone for the reduction of depression in a sample of 99 patients diagnosed with unipolar depressive disorder. Finally, in a related area, case studies of three male runners with bipolar disorder (Martinsen & Stanghelle, 1997) revealed that attempts to taper their lithium intake and replace it with running were unsuccessful. Specifically, all three men experienced a relapse and resumed their previous lithium treatment within a year. In short, although results that address the synergistic effects of exercise and medication remain equivocal, the efficacy of combining exercise with medication in the treatment of mental illness warrants additional inquiry.

In summary, findings indicate that people do not assume additional health risk when they combine exercise with psychotherapeutic drug therapy (Martinsen & Morgan, 1997). It appears that when each are prescribed under appropriate medical supervision, exercise can be safely combined with pharmacologic medications. It is unclear if the combination of psychotherapeutic medications and exercise is more effective than the use of either treatment alone. However, relatively little research addressing this possibility has been conducted at the present time, and the synergistic effects of exercise and psychotherapeutic medications requires further exploration.

PHYSICAL ACTIVITY AND OTHER MEASURES OF MOOD

A commonly used measure to assess mood has been the Profile of Mood States, or **POMS** as it is more commonly called (McNair, Lorr, & Droppleman, 1971). The POMS assesses six moods: the five negative moods of anger, tension, fatigue, depression, and confusion, and the one positive mood of vigor.

In 1991, D. G. McDonald and Hodgdon undertook a meta-analysis of studies available at that time that had examined the impact of physical activity on mood. An overview of the findings of their meta-analysis are presented in Table 4-3. All six of the mood states examined in the POMS are influenced by physical activity. The five negative mood states (i.e., anger, tension, fatigue, depression, confusion) all show significant reductions, varying from an effect

POMS   Profile of Mood States.

■ **TABLE 4-3**   The Relationship Between Physical Activity and Various Indices of Mood Assessed in the Profile of Mood States Test

MEASURE	AVERAGE EFFECT SIZE[1]
Tension	.32
Anger	.18
Vigor	.40
Fatigue	.27
Confusion	.40

[1]An effect size of .20 is small, one of .50 is medium, and one of .80 is large. A positive effect size indicates improvements over control groups or baseline conditions.

size of .18 for anger to an effect size of .40 for confusion. Similarly, the one positive mood state, vigor, shows a moderate increase in magnitude following a bout of physical activity (ES = .40).

More recently, Arent, Landers, and Etnier (in press) undertook a meta-analysis of 32 studies that had examined the influence of physical activity on the mood states of older (> 65 years) participants. Their results were consistent with those reported for younger participants: Physical activity was associated with significantly enhanced positive and significantly reduced negative mood states. Moreover, positive changes in mood states were more likely to occur in either aerobic activities or resistive training activities than in either motivational control groups, no treatment control groups, or groups involved in yoga.

POSSIBLE REASONS FOR THE BENEFITS OF PHYSICAL ACTIVITY

In Chapter 1, we pointed out that science proceeds from description to explanation to prediction to control/intervention. Investigations of the link between acute and chronic bouts of physical activity and psychological states and traits have produced a substantial body of descriptive research. That research shows that the link is positive—often small but nevertheless always positive. Acute and chronic physical activity are associated with positive psychological benefits, with the latter being more beneficial than the former. A question that now arises is, why is physical activity beneficial? What are the underlying reasons for these benefits? A number of explanations have been advanced.

Physiological Mechanisms

Some of the explanations offered for why exercise and physical activity have a beneficial impact on various psychological states have a biological basis. These include the thermogenic, monoamine, endorphin, opponent-process, and cerebral changes hypotheses.

Thermogenic Hypothesis. For thousands of years, humans have used techniques that raise body temperature (e.g., saunas, warm showers) as a form of therapy. The thermogenic hypothesis as an explanation for the psychological benefits of exercise was only advanced recently, however. DeVries, Beckman, Huber, and Dieckmeier (1968) found that the elevations that occur in core temperature during and after moderate to intense exercise are associated with concomitant decreases in muscle tension. This reduction in muscle tension, in turn, is associated with relaxation, enhanced mood states, and reduced anxiety.

The thermogenic hypothesis may help to account for the positive changes in state anxiety and stress reactivity following physical activity. However, there is no basis for suggesting that increased body temperature explains the positive changes in depression or cognitive functioning that are associated with acute or chronic physical activity.

Monoamine Hypothesis. The monoamine hypothesis has relevance for both the physical activity–depression and physical activity–cognitive functioning relationships. Fundamentally, it is based on a proposed facilitative effect from physical activity on neurotransmitters such as dopamine, norepinephrine, and serotonin. Specific neural pathways in the brain are associated with specific cognitive activities as well as specific mood states such as depression, pleasure, anxiety, and so on. The neuro-

transmitters serve as chemical messengers to help transmit neural impulses across the synapses between neurons. If the neurotransmitters are present in sufficient quantities to adhere to the receptor site, the neural impulse is transmitted; if not, neural impulses are not transmitted.

High levels of norepinephrine have been found to be associated with better memory (Zornetzer, 1985). Also, low levels have been associated with depression (J. M. Weiss, 1982). Furthermore, various medical treatments for depression, such as drugs and electroconvulsive therapy, have been found to produce an increase in dopamine, norepinephrine, and serotonin (e.g., Grahame-Smith, Green, & Costain, 1978).

Physical activity also has been identified as a stimulus that increases the quantity of neurotransmitters present in the brain—at least in laboratory rats (B. S. Brown, Payne, Kin, Moore, & Martin, 1979). However, the evidence from research on humans, while promising, is by necessity only indirect because monoamine levels can only be assessed in blood plasma, cerebrospinal fluid, and urine.

Endorphin Hypothesis. The endorphin hypothesis also has relevance to the relationship of physical activity to reduced depression. The beneficial psychological effects that accompany physical activity are attributed by many theorists to increased levels of endorphins—peptides similar in chemical structure to morphine. Endorphins (beta-endorphins, met-enkephalins, leu-enkephalins) act to reduce pain and can contribute to feelings of euphoria. The so-called runner's high is attributed to increased levels of endorphins. Also, endurance training is related to changes in levels of resting plasma beta-endorphins and reduced depression (e.g., Lobstein & Rasmussen, 1991). However, as Appenzeller, Standefer, Appenzeller, and Atkinson (1980) have cautioned, while endurance running may produce increases in beta-endorphins, "whether this increase persists after physical activity and is responsible for runner's high, the behavioral alterations of endurance trained individual's improved libido, heightened pain threshold, absence of depression, and other anecdotal effects of endurance training remains conjectural" (p. 419).

Research with animals has produced results that are promising to the endorphin hypothesis (e.g., Christie & Chesher, 1982). However, as with the monoamine hypothesis, research with humans, by necessity, has yielded indirect evidence only. Thus, in attempting to draw conclusions from that research, theorists have suggested that the interrelationships among increased physical activity, enhanced psychological states, and increased endorphin levels remains inconclusive (e.g., Morgan, 1985).

Opponent-Process Hypothesis. The opponent-process hypothesis, which was advanced by Solomon (1980), uses physiological mechanisms to account for psychological changes. According to Solomon, the brain is organized to oppose either pleasurable or aversive emotional processes—to bring the system back to homeostasis. Thus, the appearance of a stimulus (pleasurable or aversive) serves to activate the sympathetic nervous system. This activation is referred to as the *a process*. In an effort to return the body to homeostasis, a *b process* is also aroused—possibly through activation of the parasympathetic nervous system.

Moderate to high intensity physical activity can be considered the a process—a generally taxing, unpleasant stimulus. With acute or chronic bouts of physical activity, the strength of the a process remains constant (i.e., we continue to strive for a training effect by placing increasingly greater physical demands on our system). The opponent process activated by physical activity—or b process—could be enhanced psychological moods (or relaxation, or reduced state anxiety). Over time (i.e., with chronic physical activity), the a process remains constant while the b process increases in strength.

There is some support for the opponent-process hypothesis. Boutcher and Landers (1988) found that trained runners who had adapted to the demands of exercise showed reductions in anxiety; untrained runners did not. Also, Petruzzello and his colleagues (1991) proposed that Solomon's opponent-process hypothesis is "an attractive explanation for the exercise-induced anxiety reduction" (p. 160) they found in their meta-analysis.

Cerebral Changes Hypothesis. Two hypotheses pertaining to cerebral changes have been advanced to account for the relationship between chronic and acute physical activity and improved cognitive functioning (Etnier et al., 1997). One is related to the fact that exercise produces structural changes in the brain, including increased density of the vasculature of the cerebral cortex and shorter vascular diffusion distances (Issacs, Anderson, Alcantara, Black, & Greenough, 1992). A second is related to cerebral blood flow; moderate to high intensities of physical activity lead to large increases in cerebral blood flow (e.g., Heroltz et al., 1987). With this increased cerebral blood flow, there is an increase in essential nutrients such as glucose and oxygen available to the brain (Chodzko-Zajko, 1991). As a consequence, cognitive functioning is thought to be enhanced.

Etnier and her colleagues (1997) suggested that their meta-analysis on the relationship of physical activity to cognitive functioning (see Chapter 3) provided indirect evidence against both of the cerebral change hypotheses. They pointed out that none of the variables relating to the duration of the physical activity program—number of weeks of exercise, number of days of exercise per week—were related to the size of the effect for enhanced cognitive functioning. Furthermore, evidence of improved physical fitness was unrelated to enhanced cognitive functioning. Etnier et al. concluded that the mechanisms that might help to explain the improvements in cognitive functioning associated with physical activity "must be one of the following: (a) physiological mechanisms independent of aerobic fitness; (b) physiological mechanisms related to aerobic fitness, but occurring prior to changes in aerobic fitness; or, (c) psychological mechanisms independent of aerobic fitness and exercise" (p. 268).

Cognitive Mechanisms

Some of the explanations offered for why exercise and physical activity have a beneficial impact on various psychological states have a cognitive basis. These include the expectancy and distraction hypotheses.

Expectancy Hypothesis.   Is it possible that physical activity is one giant placebo effect? That is, individuals expect to feel better psychologically when they are more physically active, so, not surprisingly, they do. The proliferation of information in the popular media and other sources has convinced many people of the benefits of physical activity. Thus, when they begin to be active (or cease to maintain activity), they expect to and do experience psychological changes.

Desharnais, Jobin, Cote, Levesque, & Godin (1993) did find some evidence for a placebo effect. Patients who were informed that the program in which they were engaged was sufficient to enhance psychological well-being showed self-esteem improvements similar to physically active patients. However, other research that has manipulated expectancies (i.e., tested for a placebo effect) has shown that there are benefits from physical activity beyond those resulting from expectancy alone (e.g., McCann & Holmes, 1984).

Distraction Hypothesis.   The distraction or "time-out" hypothesis that was advanced by Bahrke and Morgan (1978) is based on the assumption that time away from the stress of day-to-day routines can serve as a distraction and contribute to the psychological benefits associated with physical activity. Thus, physical activity represents one activity from among a variety that can produce positive changes in mental health. Also, as Morgan (1988; Morgan & O'Connor, 1989) pointed out, the distraction hypothesis does not contradict other cognitive or physiological mechanisms. Distraction or time-out could simply be one reason for the positive psychological outcomes that come from being physically active.

The Bahrke and Morgan (1978) hypothesis has been tested in studies in which the effects of physical activity versus time-out (i.e., quiet rest periods) have been controlled. Physical activity was found to produce greater positive psychological changes than did time-out alone (Roth, 1989; Roth, Bachtler, & Fillingam, 1990). So, time-out may be useful and important, but the individual taking that time-out would be better advised to engage in physical activity.

Summary

Scientists have had a long-standing interest in the association between physical activity and improvements in both positive mood states such as vigor and pleasantness and negative mood states such as anxiety and depression. The results from that body of research are unequivocal. For males and females across the age spectrum, physical activity involvement is related to improvements in mood.

In some areas, because of the greater number of studies available, it has been possible to determine whether certain variables might serve to moderate the activity–mood change relationship. Insofar as anxiety is concerned, the type of activity is important. Aerobic activities such as jogging are associated with a reduction in state anxiety but nonaerobic activities such as weight training are not. The beneficial effects of physical activity are not dependent on either the duration of the activity or its intensity.

Within 5 minutes of the cessation of acute exercise, the individual begins to experience the reductions in state anxiety. Although some research shows that this beneficial effect could last from 4 to 6 hours, it is generally accepted that the duration is substantially less—up to approximately 2 hours. A variety of protocols have been used in an attempt to alleviate anxiety. Physical activity is as effective as other treatments such as hypnosis, meditation, relaxation, and so on.

Insofar as depression is concerned, both aerobic and nonaerobic activities are associated with reductions in depression. Also, the longer the physical activity program goes on, the greater impact it has on depression. All categories of individuals—males and females, individuals across the age span, individuals varying markedly in health status, individuals undergoing psychological and medical treatment, and individuals initially depressed versus not depressed—show reductions in depression as a result of involvement in physical activity. However, the law of initial values is present—individuals with moderate to severe depression benefit more than do individuals with mild to moderate depression.

Physical activity has proven to be effective as an intervention strategy to reduce depression. However, it is no more effective than group or individual psychotherapy and behavioral interventions. Finally, physical activity is associated with improvements in other positive and negative mood states such as vigor, confusion, anger, fatigue, and tension.

CHAPTER 5

Physical Activity and Personality

The Self Is Not Something Ready-Made, But Something in Continuous Formation Through Choice of Action.

(John Dewey)

CHAPTER OBJECTIVES

After completing this chapter you will be able to

- Better understand the meaning of the term *personality*.

- Discuss the role that physical activity plays in changing the personality trait of anxiety.

- Differentiate among terms used to describe the self, such as *self-esteem* and *self-concept*.

- Discuss the role that physical activity has in modifying self-esteem.

- Understand the relationship between physical activity and individual attitudes and beliefs about the body.

Key terms

affective measures	perceptual measures
behavioral measures	predisposition
body image	self-concept
cognitive measures	self-esteem
evaluation	self-presentation
per sonae	social physique anxiety

The origin of the term *personality* is unclear. However, the Latin phrase **per sonae,** which translates as "to speak through" (and denotes the masks worn by actors in ancient Rome), and the Greek word *personae*, which also denotes a theatrical mask, are the most frequently endorsed origins. Viewed from this perspective, personality might be considered as that facet, role, or aspect of the individual that is presented to the public. However, this view of personality is somewhat restrictive. Certainly, theorists consider personality to be much broader than a role presented publicly. For example, Allport (1924), one of the founders of the field of psychology, considered personality to be the dynamic amalgamation of the individual's psychological and physical characteristics that serve to influence behavior.

The complexity of personality—which is implicitly acknowledged in Allport's definition—is illustrated by the fact that it is considered to be relatively *stable and enduring* yet at the same time *dynamic and modifiable.* The stable and enduring aspects of the self provide for some degree of predictability in human behavior. The individual who possesses a high degree of global self-esteem, for example, is likely to exhibit behaviors generally consistent with that personality disposition across a wide variety of situations (social situations, work situations, and so on). Also, how-

per sonae   Latin for "to speak through."

ever, personality is dynamic and modifiable—it can be changed. The quote by John Dewey used to introduce this chapter is consistent with this perspective of personality. As Dewey noted, the self is in continuous formation through choice of behaviors. Thus, for example, the individual who is dissatisfied with his or her tendency to be loud and assertive can affect changes.

What about physical activity and personality? Over the years, scientists have questioned whether involvement in chronic physical activity can lead to changes in personality.

PHYSICAL ACTIVITY AND TRAIT ANXIETY

In Chapter 4, we pointed out that theorists consider it important to differentiate between state and trait anxiety. Trait anxiety refers to the "predisposition to perceive certain environmental stimuli as threatening or nonthreatening and to respond to these stimuli with varying levels of [state anxiety]" (Martens et al., 1990, p. 9). The critical word that serves to differentiate trait from state anxiety is **predisposition**. Some individuals have a predisposition to be more anxious than do other individuals.

The impact of physical activity on trait anxiety has typically been examined by comparing the responses on personality inventories of participants who have been involved in a long-term (chronic) physical activity program with the response of individuals who have not (i.e., a no-treatment control condition). In 1991, Petruzzello and his colleagues carried out a meta-analysis on 62 comparisons. They found that, on average, chronic physical activity is associated with a small to moderate reduction in trait anxiety (ES = .34; see Table 5-1). Neither the age of the participants nor their health status had an effect on the magnitude of the reduction in trait anxiety.

----

predisposition   A state of being particularly susceptible.

■ TABLE 5-1   Physical Activity and Personality

PSYCHOLOGICAL MEASURE	AVERAGE EFFECT SIZE[1]
Trait anxiety	.34
Self-esteem in children	.41
Self-esteem in children with handicaps	.57
Self-esteem in children without handicaps	.34
Self-esteem in young adults (<30 years)	.55
Self-esteem in middle-aged adults (>30 years)	.57
Self-esteem in older adults (>60 years)	.61
Duration of the program	
4 weeks or less	.45
5 to 8 weeks	.37
9 weeks or longer	.43

[1]An effect size of .20 is small, one of .50 is medium, and one of .80 is large. A positive effect size indicates improvements over control groups or baseline conditions.

The Dose-Response Issue

Length of the training program seems to be an important consideration (see Figure 5-1). Through their meta-analysis, Petruzzello and his colleagues (1991) found that at least 10 weeks are necessary for any meaningful reduction in trait anxiety to be evidenced. After only 4 to 6 weeks (ES = .14) or 7 to 9 weeks (ES = .17), the effect of physical activity is minimal. After 16 weeks, there is quite a large reduction in trait anxiety (ES = .90). As Petruzzello and his colleagues pointed out, "it may be that in order to change a relatively stable personality disposition like trait anxiety, exercise must be done over a longer time" (p. 153).

Petruzzello et al. (1991) also found that exercise bouts of less than 20 minutes per session are associated with *increases* in trait anxiety (ES = −.12). However, they felt that the presence of confounding variables in the studies they examined made it premature to draw conclusions about the dose-response issue from the perspective of the length of each training session.

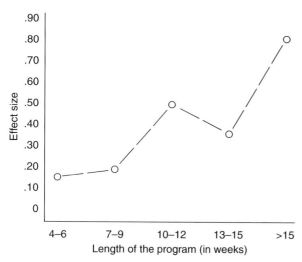

Figure 5-1   Impact of the length of the training program on reductions in trait anxiety.

Note. Adapted from "A Meta-Analysis on the Anxiety-Reducing Effects of Acute and Chronic Exercise," by S. J. Petruzzello et al., 1991, *Sports Medicine, 11.*

Task Type

Petruzzello and his colleagues (1991) also looked at the impact of aerobic activities and nonaerobic activities in terms of their relationship to reductions in trait anxiety. Although aerobic activities were found to be associated with a small to moderate reduction in trait anxiety (ES = .36) and nonaerobic activities were found to be associated with a slight increase in trait anxiety (ES = −.16), these differences were not statistically significant when subjected to further analysis. Nonetheless, in a subsequent discussion Landers and Petruzzello (1994), drawing on their own meta-analysis, concluded that reductions in trait anxiety are related to more aerobic-type physical activities that involve continuous, rhythmic exercises as opposed to activities that are less aerobic and that involve resistive intermittent exercises.

THE STRUCTURE OF THE SELF

Researchers have held considerable interest in the role that exercise and physical activity might play in self-perceptions. The reason for this interest is self-

evident. As K. R. Fox (1998) pointed out, how humans perceive themselves has important implications for their mental well-being. So, does involvement in exercise and physical activity influence how people perceive themselves? Unfortunately, it isn't possible to answer the question with a simple yes or no response because the self is "a complex system of constructs" (K. R. Fox, 2000, p. 229). A variety of terms have sprung up to describe the self because of this complexity: People hold perceptions of themselves as physical beings, academic beings, social beings, and so on. In addition, some of the self-perceptions people hold in each of those areas are simply descriptive in nature. Thus, renewed involvement in exercise and physical activity would undoubtedly influence a person's self-prescription from a descriptive perspective, for example, "I am a regular exerciser." Also, however, some self-perceptions are evaluative in nature. Thus, renewed involvement in exercise and physical activity might or might not influence self-perception from an evaluative perspective, for example, "I have/ have not become a more physically attractive person as a result of being more physically active." In order to ensure that communication is not misunderstood, theoreticians have attempted to clarify the terminology used pertaining to the self.

The term **self-esteem** is typically used to represent a "global and relatively stable evaluative construct reflecting the degree to which an individual feels positive about him- or herself" (K. R. Fox, 1998, p. 296). Self-esteem reflects people's **evaluation** of themselves—the degree to which they possess positive and/or negative self-perceptions. The term *self-worth* is considered to be a synonym for self-esteem. Thus, the statement "*I am a good person*" is evaluative in nature and would be a manifestation of the person's self-esteem.

self-esteem   A global, self-evaluative personality disposition that reflects the degree to which an individual feels positive about the self.

evaluation   The degree to which people possess positive and/or negative self-perceptions.

Involvement in physical exercise
may influence self-perception.

The term **self-concept** is typically used to refer to the "multitude of attributes and roles through which individuals evaluate themselves to establish self-esteem judgments (K. R. Fox, 1998, p. 296). It represents a *description* of the self and is synonymous with personal *identity*. Thus, the statement "I am a regular exerciser," because it is self-descriptive in nature, would reflect the individual's self-concept.

Historically, the conception and measurement of self-oriented constructs such as self-esteem, self-concept, and self-worth were unidimensional in nature. Thus, for example, self-esteem was considered (and measured) as one overall global index. The implicit assumption made with unidimensional approaches was that a single measure would provide insight into individual behavior in a wide cross-section of settings including, for example, academics, social situations, sport, exercise, and so on. More recently, however, the approach taken acknowledges that the self is multidimensional, that people are composed of a complex combination of many selves. Thus, for example, people's perceptions of their physical self may be dramatically different from their perceptions of their academic self.

> **self-concept**   A large variety of personal characteristics which are used in the process of self-evaluation to establish self-esteem.

Consistent with a multidimensional approach, theoreticians now suggest that perceptions of the self can be organized into a hierarchical structure (K. R. Fox, 1998; Shavelson, Hubner, & Stanton, 1976; Sonstroem, Harlow, & Josephs, 1994). The top of the hierarchy would be global self-esteem (see Figure 5-2). In turn, global self-esteem is thought to develop as a result of evaluative perceptions arising from a number of life areas—the physical self, the social self, the academic self, and so on. Figure 5-2 illustrates how physical self-esteem might contribute to global self-esteem. Similar schematics could be developed for social self-esteem, academic self-esteem, and so on.

As Figure 5-2 shows, physical self-esteem develops as a result of evaluative perceptions that arise from a number of dimensions including, for example, sport competence, physical strength, physical condition, body image, and so on. In turn, each of these dimensions develops from a hierarchy of self-perceptions. Thus, for example, a person's total weight may contribute to his or her feelings of being fat, which in turn may contribute to social physique anxiety and subsequently to a poor body image. That poor body image, in turn, would influence the individual's physical self-esteem, which in turn would influence the individual's overall self-esteem.

Although all dimensions (e.g., social self-esteem, academic self-esteem, etc.) contribute to global self-esteem, physical self-esteem seems to play a preeminent role. As K. R. Fox (2000) pointed out:

> The physical self has occupied a unique position in the self-system because the body, through its appearance, attributes and abilities provides substantive interface between the individual and the world. It provides the major vehicle for social communication and is therefore used to express status and sexuality, and therefore, takes on critical significance in overall self-rating. It is not surprising that the physical self has consistently demonstrated moderately strong correlations with global self-esteem across the lifespan. This is largely explained through ratings of physical appearance or body image but also specific physical competencies such as sport competence and perceived fitness and physical health. (p. 230)

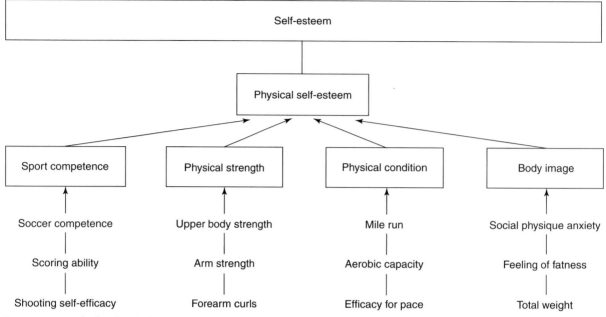

Figure 5-2 The levels of self-perceptions that influence self-esteem.
Note. Based on models suggested by K. R. Fox, 1998; Shavelson, Hubner, & Stanton, 1976; and, Sonstroem, Harlow, & Josephs, 1994.

Earlier we posed the question, does involvement in exercise and physical activity influence how people perceive themselves? We then pointed out that a yes/no response to that question wasn't possible because the self is a highly complex construct. Moreover, much of the research available has been criticized for limitations in the measurement of the various self-constructs as well as for shortcomings in experimental control. Thus, the following sections should be read within the constraints of these limitations.

PHYSICAL ACTIVITY AND SELF-ESTEEM

Historically, a considerable amount of research has been conducted with children to examine the role that various types of sports and physical activities play in the self-esteem of children. Typically, the research protocol involves a comparison of the self-esteem of individuals prior to and then after an intervention program—a sport program, an exercise program, and so on. In 1986, J. J. Gruber reported on the results from a meta-analysis that he conducted on studies from the previous 20-year period (see Table 5-1).

Gruber (1986) found that self-esteem is positively influenced by involvement in sport and physical activity, with an effect size in the moderate range (ES = .41). The total sample of studies analyzed by Gruber included research with children who were both handicapped and nonhandicapped. When the sample was subdivided, Gruber noted that physical activity has a greater effect on handicapped children (ES = .57) than on nonhandicapped children (ES = .34).

An analysis of the studies on the basis of type of activity showed that the largest beneficial effect is associated with fitness and aerobics activities (ES = .89). Because of the small number of studies available to him, Gruber was not able to provide information on the relationship of fitness and aerobics on the self-esteem of handicapped versus non-handicapped children.

D. G. McDonald and Hodgdon (1991) also conducted a meta-analysis that focused on subjects across the age span (see Table 5-1). The extent to which their sample of studies included handicapped and nonhandicapped individuals, however, is unclear. They did report that moderate relationships are present between physical activity and self-esteem in young adults (i.e., under 30 years; ES = .55), middle-aged adults (i.e., over 30 but under 60 years; ES = .57), and older adults (i.e., greater than 60 years; ES = .61).

Most recently, K. R. Fox (in press) carried out a comprehensive narrative review of 79 studies. Those studies had tested a wide variety of participants including children, college students, and special populations such as alcoholics, depressives, overweight people, and people with learning disabilities. In his summary, Fox concluded that exercise and physical activity:

- Can be used to enhance self-esteem and body image. However, in a considerable number of studies no effects were observed. In short, improvements in self-esteem do not automatically result from involvement in physical activity programs.
- Has a positive impact on males and females of all ages but the greatest effects are shown in children and middle-aged adults.
- Has the strongest positive effect on individuals with initially low self-esteem.

Fox also noted that a number of different types of tasks are useful for changing self-perceptions but aerobic activities and weight training are most beneficial. In fact, weight training has the quickest impact on self-perception.

In his meta-analysis, J. J. Gruber (1986) subdivided his studies into 3 categories on the basis of their duration: 4 weeks or less, 5 to 8 weeks, and 9 weeks or longer. Changes in self-esteem are evident even after a minimal amount of time (i.e., 4 weeks or less, ES = .45). Further, extending the program beyond that period to either 5 to 8 weeks (ES = .37) or 9 weeks or longer (ES = .43) did not have any additional positive effect on the magnitude of the effect produced.

PHYSICAL ACTIVITY AND BODY IMAGE

As Figure 5-2 shows, one integral component contributing to a person's physical self-esteem (which, in turn, has a major impact on global self-esteem) is **body image.** As the term suggests, body image refers to the self-perceptions and attitudes an individual holds with respect to his or her body and physical appearance. Increasingly, the lean and fit body for women and the lean and muscular body for men have been endorsed as an ideal. Males and females who deviate from these sometimes impossible ideals often experience body image problems.

Bane and McAuley (1998), in their recent summary of the relationship of body image and physical activity, cited reports published in *Psychology Today* that illustrate the increasing dissatisfaction felt for physical appearance (see Figure 5-3). Door-to-door

> **body image** A subjective perception of how one's body appears.

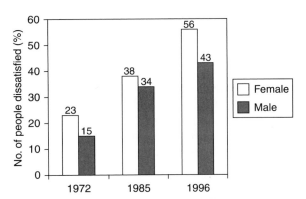

Figure 5-3 Prevalence of body dissatisfaction in females and males over time.

Note. Based on data from Berscheid et al., 1973; Cash et al., 1986; Garner et al., 1997.

surveys were carried out in successive decades beginning in the 1970s. In those surveys, respondents were queried about the satisfaction/dissatisfaction experienced in relation to their physical appearance.

In the first survey carried out in the early 1970s (Berscheid, Walster, & Bohrnstedt, 1973), 15% of the men and 23% of the women queried expressed dissatisfaction with various parts of their body. The areas particularly problematic for women were the abdomen, hips, thighs, and overall weight. For men, the most problematic areas were the abdomen and overall weight. When the survey was repeated in the mid-1980s (Cash, Winstedt, & Janda, 1986), the percentage of dissatisfied people had increased substantially, to 34% for men and 38% for women. Again, the same general body areas were identified as most problematic. A study carried out in the mid-1990s indicates that no change is in sight (Garner et al., 1997). The percentage of women and men between the ages of 18 and 70 who expressed dissatisfaction with their body increased to 56% and 43%. Again, the same general body areas were identified as most problematic.

The differences in levels of satisfaction/dissatisfaction shown by females and males in these studies is not atypical. A wide variety of studies with participants who varied in age show that women are found to express greater dissatisfaction with their physical appearance than are men (e.g., Whaaler Loland, 1998). Also, other research has shown that women are more likely than men to diet, see themselves as overweight despite objective evidence to the contrary, overestimate their body size, and exercise for weight-related reasons (Cash et al., 1986; Drewnowski & Yee, 1987; K. McDonald & Thomson, 1992; Thomson, 1986). Conversely, men are more likely to try to gain weight, and they see themselves as smaller than objective standards indicate (Cash & Brown, 1989; Gray, 1977).

A recent meta-analysis by Hausenblas and Symons Downs (2001b) provides support for the suggestion that sport is one setting in which females do not differ from males in body image. In their meta-analysis, Hausenblas and Symons Downs found that athletes generally have a better body image than do

people in the general population (ES = .26) and that female athletes (ES = .36) do not differ significantly from male athletes (ES = .31) in their body image.

In a discussion on the measurement of body image, Bane and McAuley (1998) suggested that to explore the exercise–body image relationship, it is useful to consider the various types of measures used to assess body image. **Perceptual measures** are employed to assess the *accuracy* of an individual's perceptions about his or her body size, whereas **cognitive measures** are used to assess the individual's general *attitude* about his or her body. **Affective measures** are used to assess an individual's level of *anxiety or discomfort* about his or her body. Research pertaining to these four approaches is discussed in the sections that follow. Finally, **behavioral measures** are used to determine the degree to which an individual engages in activities designed to avoid intimacy, hide his or her body, or avoid situations where his or her body might be the object of scrutiny by other people.

Physical Activity and the Accuracy of Self-Perceptions of the Body

Can you use your two hands or two beams of light on the wall and accurately estimate how wide your hips are or your waist is? If previous research is any indication, the chances are good that you will not be very accurate.

---

perceptual measures   Assessment of the accuracy of an individual's perceptions about his or her body size.

cognitive measures   Assessment of the individual's general attitude about his or her body.

affective measures   Assessment of an individual's level of anxiety or discomfort about his or her body.

behavioral measures   Determination of the degree to which an individual engages in activities designed to avoid intimacy, hide his or her body, or avoid situations where his or her body might be the object of scrutiny by other people.

Researchers have held considerable interest in the accuracy with which individuals estimate either their overall body size or the size of various parts of their body. Much of that research, however, has focused on individuals with eating disorders or other clinical disturbances. There is very little data on the role that exercise and physical activity might play in reducing any possible differences between perceptions and reality. One exception is a study by Fisher and Thompson (1994). They carried out an intervention study that compared both a cognitive behavioral therapy program and an exercise program with a control group with respect to the treatment of body image disturbances. Participants in the cognitive behavioral therapy intervention attended six sessions in which they received information on body dissatisfaction, relaxation training, training in imagery for desensitization of various body sites, body desensitization using a mirror, training oriented toward cognitive restructuring of thoughts about the body, and training in stress inoculation and relapse prevention. The participants in the exercise intervention also attended six sessions. In the first session, they received information on body dissatisfaction as well as instructions in aerobic and anaerobic training (weight lifting). The remaining five sessions were devoted to exercise, and the participants were encouraged to do "homework" by carrying out the exercise program at least twice a week. The objective width of specific sites (waist, hips) was determined with body calipers, and the participants estimated the size of those same sites by adjusting the width of horizontal beams of light projected on a wall.

Fisher and Thompson (1994) found that over the course of the study, all three groups—the control group, the cognitive behavioral therapy group, and the exercise therapy group—showed the same degree of improvement in their accuracy of perception of the size of their various body sites. Thus, the authors questioned the use of this type of measure for examining body image. That is, people may be short or tall, large or small, and be quite able to accurately appraise their physical dimensions—or get better at it. Where people may have difficulty, however, is in

FIT FACTS

Is feeling optimistic just whistling in the dark, or does it help?

Optimism, the dispositional tendency to generally expect that good things will happen, has been found to be positively related to physical recovery after coronary artery bypass surgery.

(Scheier et al., 1989)

being satisfied with that objective reality—no matter how attractive it might otherwise appear to be to other people.

Physical Activity and Attitudes Toward the Body

Another line of research has concentrated on the attitudes that individuals hold about their body. Whether involvement in physical activity is associated with better self-perceptions is not entirely clear. Certainly there is evidence to support the presence of a positive relationship. Both weight training programs and aerobics programs have been found to enhance self-perceptions (e.g., Ossip-Klein et al., 1989). Also, individuals who are active appear to possess better body image perceptions than do individuals who are inactive. A large representative study by Nina Waaler Loland (1998) is illustrative.

Waaler Loland (1998) administered a questionnaire to a random sample of 1,555 active and inactive Norwegian males and females between the ages of 18 and 67 years. Discrepancies between actual and desired weight and actual and desired height were also assessed. Waaler Loland found that low, moderately, and highly active women all evaluated their physical appearance and fitness better than inactive women did. Similarly, low, moderately, and highly active men all evaluated their physical appearance, fitness, and health status better than inactive men did.

Individuals who are more physically active also show less dissatisfaction with their weight and height. For example, 59% of active males in Waaler Loland's

(1998) sample expressed a preference for a weight that was different from what was reported—the majority (45%) wanted to lose weight whereas the remainder (14%) wanted to gain weight. In the case of inactive males, however, a larger percentage (66%) preferred a weight that was different from what they reported. The majority of those inactive males who preferred a different weight (55%) expressed a preference for a weight loss rather than a weight gain (11%). The discrepancy between reported weight and weight preference was even larger for females, with involvement in physical activity having only a minimal impact. That is, almost all the active (85%) and inactive (89%) females expressed preference for a weight that was different from what was reported. That dissatisfaction was associated with the perception of having too much weight—the overwhelming majority of both active (81%) and inactive (86%) females indicated a preference for a weight loss, not a weight gain.

Discrepancies between reported and preferred height were also found by Waaler Loland (1998). Twenty-seven percent of the active men and 51% of the inactive men expressed dissatisfaction with their height. The overwhelming majority indicated a preference for being taller (i.e., 93% of the dissatisfied active men and 98% of the dissatisfied inactive men). The pattern of findings for women was similar in that 28% of the active women and 21% of the inactive women showed dissatisfaction with their height, with only 25% of the former and all of the latter expressing a preference for being taller.

Can you assume that physical activity causes body image improvements? Although the evidence is encouraging, many researchers have urged caution. In fact, Waaler Loland (1998) noted that "participation in activities in which there is an emphasis on a trained and thin body (i.e., aerobics) can foster an increased focus on one's body, a critical view of one's appearance, and hence, an exaggerated concern with weight control" (p. 355).

Physical Activity and Anxiety About the Body

Anxiety can arise over concerns with **self-presentation** of the body. Self-presentation refers to the attempts by an individual to selectively present

aspects of the self and to omit self-relevant information to maximize the likelihood that a positive social impression will be generated and an undesired impression will be avoided (Leary, 1992a, 1992b; Leary & Kowalski, 1990). When the individual doubts that he or she will be able to generate a positive impression or forestall an undesirable impression, social anxiety results (Leary, 1992b). Because physical appearance is such an important component of both physical self-esteem and global self-esteem, social anxiety can arise as a result of concerns about the self-presentation of one's body. In fact, in 1989 Hart, Leary, and Rejeski proposed the presence of a trait—a stable personal disposition—that they called **social physique anxiety.**

Hart and her colleagues (1989) found that women who possess the trait of social physique anxiety to a greater degree have more stress and discomfort during physique evaluations and more negative thoughts about their body appearance. Also, Crawford and Eklund (1994) noted that women who are higher in the trait of social physique anxiety also reported a greater tendency to exercise for self-presentation reasons—weight control, body tone, and physical attractiveness. Conversely, women lower in the trait of social physique anxiety were more likely to exercise for motives generally unrelated to self-presentation—fitness, mood enhancement, health, and enjoyment. A similar result was found when Hausenblas and Martin (2000) tested 286 female aerobics instructors. Instructors who were involved in leading classes primarily for self-presentation reasons (e.g., weight loss, improved body tone) also possessed a larger degree of social physique anxiety. Conversely, instructors who were involved in leading classes for leadership opportuni-

---

self-presentation   The attempts by an individual to selectively present aspects of the self and to omit self-relevant information to maximize the likelihood that a positive social impression will be generated and an undesired impression will be avoided.

social physique anxiety   Social anxiety that arises as a result of concerns about the self-presentation of the body.

FIT FACTS

Does physical self-efficacy influence how anxious you feel about your body?

Yes. Initially sedentary middle-aged men and women who experience increases in self-efficacy for walking also have reductions in physique anxiety.

(McAuley, Bane, & Mihalko, 1995)

ties (e.g., educate, lead) or to affect enhancement (e.g., have fun, reduce stress) possessed a lower degree of social physique anxiety.

In a series of studies, McAuley, Bane, and their colleagues (Bane & McAuley, 1996; McAuley, Bane, & Mihalko, 1995; McAuley, Bane, Rudolph, & Lox, 1995) demonstrated that a program of physical activity will serve to lower social physique anxiety. In the various studies, the program of physical activity introduced by Bane, McAuley, and their colleagues also contributed to changes in fitness and body composition. However, the researchers pointed out that they had no way of validly concluding whether the physiological and anthropometric changes led to the changes in social physique anxiety.

In a series of studies, Carron and his colleagues (Carron & Prapavessis, 1977; Carron, Estabrooks, Horton, Prapavessis, & Hausenblas, 1999; Sardoni & Carron, 2000) showed that being a member of a group can help reduce social anxiety arising from self-presentation concerns. However, the composition of the group is important. Sardoni and Carron found that females experience less social anxiety when they enter into either an aerobics class or the weight training room in the company of a group of females versus alone. However, entering into either of those two exercise environments in the company of a group of males produces as much anxiety as entering alone.

Both Sardoni and Carron (2000) and Carron, Estabrooks et al. (1999) also explored the question of why the presence of other females might serve to reduce social anxiety in physical activity contexts. Four possibilities were examined: The presence of others serves as a distraction; the presence of others serves to diffuse evaluations; the presence of others

leads the individual to feel lost in the crowd; and the presence of others provides a sense of security. The possibility most strongly endorsed was that the presence of others serves to diffuse evaluations—spread evaluations among the individuals present.

Physical Activity and Behavior

It has been suggested that overweight people often choose not to exercise "because they feel self-conscious if others see them huffing and puffing (D. Blumenthal, 1984, p. 54). There is good empirical support for this suggestion. When Bain, Wilson, and Chaikind (1989) had overweight women list their reasons for not exercising in public or not attending exercise studios, the most important limiting reason was a concern for being observed and evaluated by others.

Social physique anxiety reflects people's tendency to experience social anxiety when they feel that other people are evaluating their physique. In order to avoid evaluative settings, individuals who experience higher degrees of social physique anxiety exercise in private rather than in public (Spink, 1992). Also, Crawford and Eklund (1994) found that individuals with high social physique anxiety have a preference for exercise outfits that are less revealing. The researchers presented college women exercisers with two videos of aerobics classes that were identical in every respect (i.e., music used, routines, angle of the camera, participants involved, etc.) except for the attire worn by the participants. In one video, the participants wore tights and thong leotards that served to emphasize their figure/physique. In the other video, the participants wore shorts and T-shirts over their tights and leotards, thereby serving to reduce the salience of their figure/physique. The viewers were then asked a series of questions designed to assess their perceptions of the favorability of participating in the two different situations. Crawford and Eklund found that women varying in social physique anxiety differed in their perceptions of the two situations. Higher social physique anxiety was positively associated with greater endorsements of the aerobics class in which emphasis on the physique was reduced and lower endorsement of the aerobics class in which emphasis on the physique was magnified.

Summary

The term *personality* is thought to come from the Latin or Greek words denoting theatrical masks. The complexity of personality is illustrated by the fact that it is considered to be both stable and enduring, and dynamic and modifiable. Research provides support for the suggestion that involvement in physical activity for at least 10 weeks is associated with changes in personality. The trait of anxiety is one stable disposition that is positively influenced. For anxiety reductions, however, aerobic activities appear to be superior to anaerobic activities. Self-esteem is another stable disposition that is positively influenced. Physical activity has a positive impact on males and females of all ages, but the greatest effects are shown in children, in middle-aged adults, and in individuals with initially low self-esteem. The positive effects of activity on self-esteem are evident quickly (i.e., as quickly as 4 weeks). Finally, it is clear that large proportions of the population have a negative or distorted body image. Females are more dissatisfied than males, and inactive people are more dissatisfied than active people. However, there is insufficient evidence to draw conclusions on the question of whether involvement in physical activity will produce more positive perceptions of the self.

CHAPTER 6

Psychobiological Benefits of Physical Activity

*I Have Never Taken Any Exercise Except Sleeping and Resting and
I Never Intend to Take Any.*

(Mark Twain)

CHAPTER OBJECTIVES

After completing this chapter you will be able to

- Understand the relationship between being physically active and sleeping longer or more deeply.

- Understand the relationship between being physically active and responding to life stressors.

- Differentiate between the various types of pain.

- Understand the relationship between pain and improvements in physiological function via involvement in physical activity.

Key terms

behavior
electroencephalography (EEG)
electromyography (EMG)
emotion
endogenous pain
nocioception
non-rapid eye movement sleep (NREM)
pain
perception of pain
rapid eye movement sleep (REM)
slow wave sleep (SWS)

Mark Twain is an American icon who has written with insight and humor. Not surprisingly, then, he has often been quoted for his perspectives on a variety of topics. As the quote used to introduce this chapter indicates, Mark Twain was not a strong proponent of being physically active. Ironically, if he were alive today and were to consult primary care physicians, exercise scientists, and/or the lay public, he would likely be advised to exercise more frequently in order to improve his sleep! As Youngstedt, O'Connor, and Dishman (1997) stated, "few behaviors are as closely linked with enhanced sleep as exercise" (p. 203).

In this chapter, we explore the suspected link between physical activity and sleep. We also discuss the research pertaining to another psychobiological benefit thought to be associated with involvement in physical activity and exercise—improved reactivity to stressors. Finally, physical activity is often advocated as a treatment for managing endogenous (naturally occurring) pain, and we examine the research pertaining to this issue.

PHYSICAL ACTIVITY AND SLEEP

For the majority of people, sleep is an inevitable, natural daily experience. However, insomnia affects 20% to 40% of the population around the world (cf. Janson et al., 1995; Mellinger, Balter, & Uhlenhuth, 1985). Further, the consequences of sleepiness can be severe. According to the National Commission on

61

FIT FACTS

Does level of fitness influence sleep?

Physical activity seems to improve sleep in both fit and unfit individuals. In order to obtain the sleep-associated benefits of physical activity, however, it is recommended that the activity session be longer rather than harder; sleep times seem to increase when activity sessions are an hour or longer.

(Youngstedt, 1997)

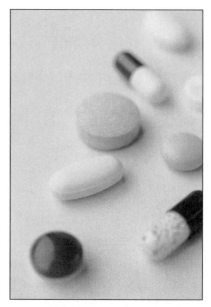

The regular use of sleeping pills is the mortality equivalent of smoking one to two packs of cigarettes daily.
©PhotoDisc/Volume 36/Nature Scenes

Sleep Disorders Research (1993), a lack of sleep can result in psychiatric disturbances, reduced productivity, and increased accidents. In fact, it has been suggested that major world catastrophes such as, for example, the Chernobyl nuclear plant accident can be traced to employee sleepiness (National Commission on Sleep Disorders Research).

As a consequence, there is an interest—particularly on the part of individuals suffering from insomnia—in determining how sleep can be facilitated. One common approach taken to improve the quality and quantity of sleep has been medication in the form of sleeping pills. However, sleeping pills do not seem to be the answer. In his recent review, Youngstedt (2000) noted that the individual becomes dependent on pills and tolerance develops to prescribed dosages. Also, sleeping pills are often associated with profound rebound insomnia. Even more importantly, however, the regular use of sleeping pills is the mortality equivalent of smoking one to two packages of cigarettes daily. So, sleeping pills don't work well over the long term, and their chronic usage represents a health risk.

Given that sleeping pills are problematic, what other approaches might work? One strategy used to answer this question has been to ask (using paper-and-pencil questionnaires) large samples of individuals what aids and/or disrupts their sleep. This strategy was employed in an epidemiological study undertaken in Tampere, Finland (Vuori, Urponen, Hasan, & Partinen, 1988). Eleven hundred and ninety males and females between the ages of 36 and 50 were asked to list in order of importance three practices, habits, or actions that promoted or improved their ability to fall asleep immediately or that enhanced the quality of their sleep. Interestingly, exercise was ranked number one.

At first glance, it might seem that insomniacs should become more active to alleviate their disorder. However, self-reports on sleep have been questioned from both a reliability and a validity perspective. For example, most people hold the common belief that physical activity promotes sleep. So if asked, most people would likely report that being physically active causes them to have longer and deeper sleep. Is this really true? Most people also hold the common belief that alcohol promotes sleep when, in fact, it disrupts sleep. Self-reports on physical activity and sleep could be as invalid as self-reports on alcohol and sleep. Thus, the greatest insights into the nature of sleep and the factors that might influence it come from laboratory research.

The Nature of Sleep

Physiological changes occur when a person sleeps. These changes have been demonstrated through **electroencephalographic (EEG)** recordings from the scalp (i.e., to assess electrical conductivity in the brain), **electromyographic (EMG)** recordings from around the eyes (i.e., to assess eye movements), **strain gauge recordings** from around the chest and abdomen (i.e., to assess breathing), and **EMG recordings** from the legs (i.e., to assess leg movements). Body movements diminish when we sleep so wrist movements have also been measured through **accelerometer recordings.** What do all these assessments indicate?

When the individual is awake, he or she exhibits EEG activity in the range of 13 Hz to 30 Hz with high levels of EMG activity. Dramatic reductions in activity occur during sleep. However, the nature of the data from EEG and EMG recordings show that sleep cannot be treated as a single physiological state; it consists of two distinct states that alternate cyclically throughout the night. One of those states, **nonrapid eye movement sleep (NREM),** is subdivided into four stages. Stage 1 of NREM is the period of transition between wakefulness and the onset of sleep; it occupies approximately 5% (or 1 to 7 minutes) of a night's sleep. During Stage 1 of NREM, there is a reduction in EMG activity, slow rolling eye movements, and EEG recordings of mixed frequency. Humans are in Stage 2 of NREM approximately 50% of their sleep time. It is characterized by EEG recordings in the range of 12 Hz to 14 Hz. Stages 3 and 4 of NREM, which occupy approximately 20% of sleep time, are typically combined and referred to as **slow wave sleep (SWS)** because EEG recordings are in the range of 2 Hz to 4 Hz.

Rapid eye movement sleep (REM), as the name suggests, is characterized by rapid eye movements, increased frequency and reduced amplitude of EEG recordings, and a reduction in EMG activity. Generally, REM represents 25% of an individual's sleep. NREM sleep and REM sleep alternate throughout the night in approximately 90-minute cycles. However, the duration of time spent in each state changes throughout the night, with SWS being most prevalent in the initial third of the night and REM sleep being the most prevalent in the last third.

There has been a tendency to characterize SWS as the *deepest form of sleep.* According to Kandel, Schwartz, and Jessell (2000), however, the terms *lighter* and *deeper* have little meaning in discussing the nature of sleep because

> by some criteria, REM sleep might be considered lighter than non-REM sleep; for example, humans are easier to awaken from REM sleep than from non-REM stages 3 and 4. By other criteria, non-REM sleep might be considered lighter than REM sleep; muscle tone, spinal reflexes, and the regulation of body temperature are maintained during non-REM sleep but are reduced during REM sleep. (p. 939)

Nonetheless, increased durations of SWS are considered most preferable for feelings of rejuvenation. Also, it is assumed that physical activity has its greatest (beneficial) impact on SWS.

The Impact of Acute Physical Activity on Sleep

There is contradictory evidence from research on the efficacy of physical activity for enhanced sleep. Some studies have reported that acute physical activity

---

electroencephalography (EEG)   The process of recording brain wave activity.

electromyography (EMG)   The process of electrically recording muscle action potentials.

nonrapid eye movement sleep (NREM)   A state of sleep characterized by four stages.

slow wave sleep (SWS)   Stages 3 and 4 of nonrapid eye movement sleep.

rapid eye movement sleep (REM)   A state of sleep characterized by rapid eye movements, increased frequency and reduced amplitude of EEG recordings, and a reduction in EMG activity.

enhances sleep, others have reported that it disrupts sleep, and others have shown that physical activity has no discernible influence on sleep. This conflicting pattern of research results has even led some scientists to question the popular assumption that there is a positive relationship between sleep and physical activity (Trinder, Montgomery, & Paxton, 1988).

In an attempt to empirically reconcile the research evidence, Youngstedt et al. (1997) conducted a meta-analysis on 38 studies that addressed this issue. As the results in Table 6-1 show, acute physical activity has no effect on the time it takes to fall asleep or the amount of wakefulness during the night. However, physical activity does have an effect—a significant moderate effect—on total duration of sleep. The total sleep time of individuals after bouts of physical activity is increased by 9.90 minutes over nonactive controls (ES = .42).

The nature of that sleep is different, however. Active individuals are asleep in Stage 2 of the NREM period 5.20 minutes more than are nonactive controls (ES = .18) and asleep in Stages 3 and 4 of the NREM period (i.e., slow wave sleep) 4.20 minutes more than are nonactive controls (ES = .19). Conversely, however, physically active individuals are in REM sleep 7.40 minutes less than are nonactive controls (ES = −.49).

■ **TABLE 6-1**   The Relationship Between Physical Activity and Sleep

MEASURE	AVERAGE EFFECT SIZE[1]	MEAN DIFFERENCE (MINUTES)
Sleep onset	−.05	−1.40
Wake after sleep onset	.07	2.10
Non-REM Stage 2 sleep	.18	5.20
Non-REM slow wave sleep (i.e., Stages 3 and 4)	.19	4.20
REM sleep	−.49	−7.40
REM latency	.52	13.10
Total sleep time	.42	9.90

[1]An effect size of .20 is small, one of .50 is medium, and one of .80 is large.

Elaborating on the practical meaning of the meta-analysis results, Youngstedt (2000) noted that the

> clinical relevance of these modest effects of exercise on sleep is quite dubious. [Also] the trivial effects of acute exercise on SWS contrasts with previous assumptions that exercise increases SWS. Not only is the assumption not true, but there is also several lines of evidence contradicting the notion that postexercise increases in SWS are particularly indicative of better sleep. (p. 247)

Youngstedt (2000) and Youngstedt, O'Connor, and Dishman (1997) did attach a strong qualifier to the findings from the meta-analysis, however. Research on the impact of acute exercise on sleep has been undertaken with individuals who are *good sleepers.* In short, a ceiling effect was in operation in the research. People who are sleeping well are unlikely to show large increases in the amount and/or type of sleep they experience. Consequently, "the fact that a consistent, albeit small, effect of exercise on sleep has been found may be important" (Youngstedt, p. 248).

The Dose-Response Issue. A number of moderators of the acute physical activity–sleep relationship were explored by Youngstedt, O'Connor, and Dishman (1997) in their meta-analysis. One of those moderators was the duration of the period of physical activity. The researchers found that the relationship between the duration of physical activity and total sleep time is linear in nature. That is, as the amount of time spent in physical activity increases, people sleep longer. Again, Youngstedt et al. interjected a note of caution. They pointed out that because reliable increases in sleep were obtained in their meta-analysis only for activity periods greater than one hour in duration, most of the population is unlikely to experience benefits. That is, large proportions of the population are not physically active generally, and especially not for periods greater than one hour.

Proximity to Bedtime. A common assumption is that engaging in vigorous bouts of physical activity just prior to bedtime will disrupt sleep. However, Youngstedt (2000) argued that research evidence does not support this assumption. Moreover, as he observed, the evening is a practical time for many people to exercise. Thus, an unsubstantiated assumption that sleep is negatively affected by activity might represent an unnecessary barrier to a physically active lifestyle.

PHYSICAL ACTIVITY AND REACTIVITY TO STRESS

Stress has been defined as "a substantial imbalance between psychological and/or physical demand and response capability, under conditions where failure to meet that demand has important consequences" (McGrath, 1970, p. 20). Feelings of stress are accompanied by a number of physiological changes including, for example, increases in heart rate, respiratory rate, blood pressure, and sweating. One general benefit espoused for physical activity is that it is assumed to reduce reactivity to stress—physical fitness helps individuals better cope with the onset of a stressor, and it dampens or reduces physiological changes.

Crews and Landers (1987) suggested that two general processes through which physical activity could serve to reduce stress are coping and inoculation. Physical activity could provide a more efficient *coping* system by reducing recovery time in the autonomic nervous system. Similarly, *inoculation* might occur if chronic physical activity enhances the individual's physical and psychological abilities to deal with stress. So, for example, when an individual is faced with a stressor, the autonomic nervous system responds with its flight or fight response. For those individuals who are physically active, the stress response might be of less magnitude, less time might be spent in a state of stress (and at perhaps a lower level), or there might be a faster recovery from the stress response.

Considerable research has been undertaken to examine the association between physical activity and reactivity to stressors. Typically in that research, participants were exposed to a stressor such as electric shock, a loud noise, or cognitive tasks to be per-

formed under time pressure. The question of interest was whether greater physical fitness or involvement in acute or chronic physical activity would help protect the individual from the effects of a stressor (i.e., by reducing his or her reactivity) and/or help the person recover more quickly than would an unfit or nonexercising individual (Landers & Petruzzello, 1994).

Crews and Landers (1987) undertook a meta-analysis in an attempt to empirically summarize the research pertaining to this issue. When the researchers combined the results from all studies, they found that aerobically fit individuals have a reduced reactivity to stress compared to unfit individuals (ES = .48).

Reduced reactivity and/or enhanced recovery from a stressor can be manifested through a variety of indices—heart rate, systolic blood pressure, diastolic blood pressure, skin response, hormonal changes, and EMG, for example. Because different researchers have used different indices, Crew and Landers (1987) also carried out sub-analyses using the different indices. The results for each of these physiological indices as well as participants' self-reports of their reactivity and recovery are presented in Table 6-2. The smallest differences between aerobically fit and unfit individuals in stress reactivity is for hormonal changes (ES = .15) while the largest is for muscle tension (ES = .87).

Landers and Petruzzello (1994) suggested that chronic physical activity could be analogous to

■ **TABLE 6-2**   The Relationship Between Physical Activity and Reactivity to and Recovery From Stressors

MEASURE	AVERAGE EFFECT SIZE[1]
Overall reactivity to recovery from stressors	.48
Heart rate	.39
Systolic blood pressure	.42
Diastolic blood pressure	.40
Skin response	.67
Hormonal changes	.15
Muscle tension	.87
Psychological self-report	.57

[1] An effect size of .20 is small, one of .50 is medium, and one of .80 is large. The effect sizes are all positive, indicating reduced reactivity and enhanced recovery over control groups.

repeated exposure to psychological stress in producing adaptations in the sympathetic nervous system. They also proposed that chronic exercise could lead to cognitions such as self-efficacy—the individual's fitness level leads him or her to believe that a stressor can be handled. Whatever the underlying mechanisms, it is clear that greater fitness is associated with better reactivity to and recovery from stress.

PHYSICAL ACTIVITY AND PAIN

Pain is frequently associated with physical activity, as evidenced by the common phrase "no pain, no gain." This no pain, no gain mentality may have deterred many people from engaging in physical activity. Luckily, researchers have illustrated that exercise does not need to be painful to be beneficial.

Pain is defined as "an unpleasant sensory and emotional experience associated with actual or po-

tential tissue damage, or described in terms of such damage" (Merskey & Bogduk, 1994, p. 210). Implied in this definition are three specific ideas. First, pain is always a subjective experience. Second, emotions are always an element of pain. Third, the perception of pain is not always related to the amount of tissue damage (O'Connor & Cook, 1999). Pain affects numerous people. For example, Von Korff, Dworkin, and Le Resche (1990) reported that 8% of new adult members to a health maintenance organization reported severe chronic pain. Similarly, Brewer and Karoly (1992) detected that 29% of college students described the occurrence of recurrent mild to moderate pain.

Not only is pain a common problem, it also causes functional and activity impairment in 3% to 13% of the population (Andersson, 1994). Functional impairments such as restricted mobility can significantly impact a person's daily activities. In addition, pain is associated with drug abuse and psychological disorders (Kouyanou, Pither, & Wessely, 1997) and is the most common reason for health care utilization (Knapp & Koch, 1984). Furthermore, poor pain management can lengthen hospital stays and increase morbidity and mortality (Rauck, 1996). In short, pain is common, disabling, and difficult to manage. The combination of these factors makes pain very costly to society. The estimated cost of health care and lost productivity due to pain was $100 billion in the United States in 1995 (National Institute of Dental and Craniofacial Research, 1995).

People's inability to effectively manage pain and the economic pressures to decrease the costs of health care have resulted in increased interest in nonsurgical and nonpharmacological treatments for pain. One adjunct to traditional pain treatment is physical activity (O'Connor & Cook, 1999). Clinical practice guidelines that recommend physical activity as a modality for pain are based on research that can be categorized into two general groups: (a) investigations into the effects of regular exercise on endogenous (i.e., naturally occurring) pain, and (b) research examining the effects of an acute bout of exercise on experimentally induced pain. Research in each of these areas as well as the components of pain are discussed in the following sections.

> **pain**   A negative sensory or emotional experience that is either accompanied by real or potential tissue damage or is described by such damage.

Components of Pain

Pain is a multidimensional construct with four different components: nocioception, perception of pain, emotion, and behavior (Loeser & Melzack, 1999). The first component, **nocioception,** is the detection of tissue damage by sensory receptors known as nociceptors. Two types of afferent nerve fibers act as nociceptors: A-delta fibers and C-fibers. A-delta fibers, which are small and myelinated, include nociceptors that quickly transmit sharp and localized pain (Wall, 1989). For example, when you burn your finger on a hot plate, nociceptive signals of tissue damage travel quickly to the central nervous system. C-fibers, which are nonmyelinated and predominantly nociceptors, slowly transmit dull and diffuse pain (Wall). For example, after you rake leaves for the first time in the fall, the soreness that you feel throughout your hands, arms, and shoulders is predominately due to these nonmyelinated nociceptors.

The second component is the **perception of pain;** it can be experienced with or without actual tissue damage. An example of the latter event is phantom limb pain, which is the perception of pain within an amputated limb. It is also possible for nocioception to occur without the perception of pain. For instance, myocardial ischemia without pain occurs in 4 million to 5 million people in the United States (Cohn, 1985).

The third component of pain is **emotion.** According to Price and Harkins (1992), there are two stages of pain-related emotion. The first stage is characterized by unpleasantness, distress, or annoyance. The level of the emotion in this stage corresponds to the intensity of the pain stimulus and amount of arousal. The second stage is characterized by an emotional reaction to the cognitive appraisal of how the pain influences one's life and activities of daily living. Cognitive appraisal is dependent on the context of pain, which includes such issues as the perceived origin of the pain and the perceived ability to control the pain.

Behavior, the fourth component, refers to activities that are performed or avoided as a result of the perception of pain. Health care seeking, medication consumption, moaning, crying, complaining, pain-related body postures, facial expressions, and activity avoidance are all pain behaviors. These behaviors communicate the perception of pain to others (Keefe & Williams, 1992).

Endogenous Pain

Endogenous pain is naturally occurring pain. Researchers examining endogenous pain typically access patients or population-based samples. This type of survey research assesses large numbers of individuals, including people who may not be under the supervision of a health care professional for their pain. However, such survey research is limited by researchers' inability to control the amount of nocioception. Anecdotes from athletes who continue strenuous exercise in the face of severe injuries, and later report that they felt no pain, have contributed to the notion that physical activity can alter pain perception (Koltyn, 2000).

Much of the research on regular physical activity and naturally occurring pain has concentrated on musculoskeletal pain. Research has revealed that aerobic and strengthening exercise may have beneficial effects on reducing the pain associated with osteoarthritis, rheumatoid arthritis (Minor & Brown, 1993), low back problems (Lahad, Malter, Berg, & Deyo, 1994), fibromyalgia (McCain, Bell, Mai, & Halliday, 1988), peripheral artery disease (Gardner & Poehlman, 1995), menstruation pain (Hightower, 1997), and labor pain (Artal, 1992). The mechanism for why exercise may be helpful in reducing endogenous pain is unknown (O'Connor & Cook, 1999).

---

nocioception   The detection of tissue damage by sensory receptors known as nociceptors; the first component of pain.

perception of pain   The second component of pain.

emotion   The third component of pain.

behavior   Activities that are performed or avoided as a result of the perception of pain; the fourth component of pain.

endogenous pain   Naturally occurring pain.

Experimentally Induced Pain

In contrast to endogenous pain, experimentally induced pain provides researchers with an opportunity to control the amount of nociception. Pain stimuli are used to induce nociception and can be applied to either healthy participants or pain patients. These stimuli can also be applied in either laboratory or clinical settings. For example, Fuller and Robinson (1995) had low back pain patients perform low back exercises of specific intensities at a physical therapy clinic. Their study illustrated how a painful stimulus may assist researchers in understanding the distinctions between patients with pain and healthy participants.

How is pain experimentally induced? Common experimental pain stimuli include: (a) pressure pain (e.g., a weighted edge applied to a finger or a football cleat applied against the tibia), (b) electrical pain (e.g., electrical current sent to electrodes attached to the skin or dental pulp), (c) thermal pain (e.g., cutaneous application of heat to the forearm), (d) ischemic pain (e.g., use of a blood pressure cuff to restrict blood flow to the hands), and (e) cold-pressor pain (e.g., immersion of a hand in a container of cold water). Typically, the noxious stimulus is applied before and after physical activity to see if relief occurs after physical activity (Koltyn, 2000). Recent reviews of the research on the effects of a single episode of exercise on pain have concluded that exercise can be an analgesic depending on the types of experimentally induced pain and the characteristics of the exercise bout (Janal, 1996; Koltyn; O'Connor & Cook, 1999).

For example, Koltyn, Garvin, Gardiner, and Nelson (1996) examined pain thresholds following exercise and quiet rest in 16 adults (M age = 29 years). The participants completed two randomly assigned conditions of exercise and no-exercise control. The exercise session was 30 minutes of cycle ergometer exercise at 75% of VO_2 max. The control condition consisted of resting quietly for 30 minutes. Pressure was applied to the participant's finger for 2 minutes before, immediately following, and 15 minutes following the exercise and control conditions. Pain

Not only is pain a common problem, it causes functional and activity impairment in 3% to 13% of the population.
©PhotoDisc/Volume 40/Health and Medicine 2

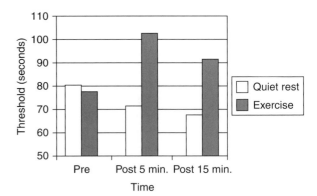

Figure 6-1   Mean scores for pain threshold responses in the exercise and quiet rest condition.
Note. From "Perception of Pain Following Aerobic Exercise," by K. F. Koltyn et al., 1996, *Medicine and Science in Sports and Exercise, 28,* 1418–1421.

threshold and pain ratings were assessed during the 2-minute pain exposure. Pain threshold was defined as the elapsed time from the initial application of the pain stimulus until the subject perceived the stimulus to be painful. Pain ratings were provided by the participants every 15 seconds during the 2-minute pain exposure.

It was found that pain threshold was significantly elevated both immediately and 15 minutes following exercise. In contrast, pain threshold did not change following the control condition (see Figure 6-1). Also, pain ratings were significantly lower after exercise than after the quiet rest condition. The authors concluded that an acute bout of exercise results in increased pain threshold and significantly lower pain ratings. The mechanisms responsible for exercise-induced analgesia, however, are not understood (Koltyn, 2000).

Summary

Physical activity is considered to have psychobiological benefits. One prevalent assumption is that physical activity contributes to enhanced sleep. In fact, in a large epidemiological survey, physical activity was listed as the most important practice, habit, or action for promoting or improving sleep (Vuori et al., 1988). Research evidence from well-controlled laboratory studies has not tended to support the suspected link between physical activity and enhanced sleep. Although acute physical activity increases the total amount of sleep by approximately 10 minutes, there is no evidence of increased quality of sleep. The clinical relevance of these modest effects of exercise on sleep is quite dubious (Youngstedt, 2000). An important qualifying note has been added, however. Generally, research on acute physical activity and sleep has been undertaken with healthy individuals who are not experiencing insomnia. Thus, a ceiling effect is present.

People experience feelings of stress when they perceive an imbalance between the demands of the situation and their ability to meet those demands. The body responds with a flight or fight response and with changes in the autonomic nervous system—increased heart rate, increased blood pressure, and so on. The good news, however, is that physical activity enhances the ability to deal with the stress. Repeated exposures to physical activity improves a person's overall reaction in terms of elevations in heart rate, blood pressure, and muscle tension as well as changes in various skin conductivity responses (i.e., sweating, temperature increases).

All people experience pain at some time in their life. Physical activity can help alleviate that pain. Research has shown that involvement in physical activity can have beneficial effects on the pain associated with osteoarthritis, rheumatoid arthritis, low back problems, peripheral artery disease, menstruation, and childbirth.

CHAPTER 7

Negative Behaviors and Physical Activity

Every Form of Addiction Is Bad.

(Carl Gustav Jung)

CHAPTER OBJECTIVES

After completing this chapter you will be able to

- Describe the criteria for exercise dependence, anorexia nervosa, bulimia nervosa, and muscle dysmorphia.

- Differentiate among overtraining and staleness.

- Describe the relationship between physical activity and eating disorders.

- Outline the psychological effects of steroid use and excessive exercise.

Since the fitness boom of the 1970s, much has been written about the benefits of exercise and physical activity. Now, it seems that everywhere you turn, you hear that you should be more physically active and with good reason, given the physiological benefits outlined in Chapter 1 and the psychological benefits discussed in Chapters 3 through 6. Does an activity associated with so many benefits have the potential to be harmful? The answer seems to be, it depends. Carl Gustav Jung held the belief that every form of addiction is bad. Thus, while he did not specifically address addiction to physical activity, presumably he would view it as negative.

Many people become physically active because it is fun or it makes them feel better. Also, psychological and physical benefits are derived. But exercise and physical activity can become addictive. Consider the following quote, for example:

> I am going to run until I'm 90. If the weather is bad on my last day, I'll collapse and die on an indoor track. Don't let anyone try to keep me alive, Fred. Just take a pushbroom and shove me off the running surface. Then, when you have finished your run, call the coroner. (Graham, 1981, p. 152)

Key terms

affective regulation explanation	personality trait explanation
anorexia analogue hypothesis	primary exercise dependence
β-endorphin explanation	reduction in other activities
β-endorphins	secondary exercise dependence
continuance	staleness
exercise dependence	subjective aversion
exercise deprivation sensations	sympathetic arousal explanation
intention	time
lack of control	tolerance
muscle dysmorphia	withdrawal
overtraining	

Although exercise may represent an addictive behavior for a small number of people who engage in it to an extreme and unhealthy level, habitual exercise is not inherently abusive (Davis, 2000; Dishman, 1986). This chapter focuses on the following potential negative effects of physical activity: (a) exercise dependence, (b) overtraining and staleness, (c) physical activity and eating disorders, and (d) physical activity and steroid use.

EXERCISE DEPENDENCE

For a very small number of people, physical activity goes into overdrive. Rather than exercise enhancing their lives, it ends up assuming a life of its own (Morrow & Harvey, 1990). These people continue to exercise despite injuries and mental and physical exhaustion. They may even watch their careers crumble and their family and friends drift away. This perspective is illustrated in the following quote:

> I have learned there is no need for haste, no need to worry, no need to agonize over the future . . . The world will wait. Job, family, friends will wait; in fact, they must wait on the outcome. And that outcome depends upon the lifetime that is in every day of running . . . Can anything have a higher priority than running? It defines me, adds to me, makes me whole. I have a job and a family and friends that can attest to that. (avid runner Dr. George Sheehan quoted in Waters, 1981, p. 51)

The term used to describe this compulsive behavior is **exercise dependence.** In this section exercise dependence is discussed with reference to how it is defined, what researchers have to say about it, and how it might be treated.

Exercise Dependence Defined

Descriptions of exercise dependence have focused on (a) behavioral correlates including physical activity duration, intensity, frequency, or history; (b) psychological correlates such as a pathological commitment to physical activity; or (c) a combination of both. However, just because someone runs 6 days a

Many people can be physically active every day of the week and not be classified as exercise dependent.

week for 45 minutes a session or has been regularly lifting weights for 3 years does not mean he or she is exercise dependent. In fact thousands of people who can be physically active 5, 6, or even 7 days a week *should not and could not* be classified as exercise dependent. Dependence is indicated not only by the behavior but by the psychological reasons underlying that behavior. Exercise dependence is defined as a craving for leisure time physical activity that results in uncontrollable excessive exercise behavior and that manifests in physiological symptoms (e.g., tolerance, withdrawal) and/or psychological symptoms (e.g., anxiety, depression). The exercise dependence literature, however, has been plagued by a myriad of terms, definitions, and measurements, which has made it difficult to draw conclusions regarding the existence of exercise dependence and its predisposing, precipitating, and perpetuating factors.

---

exercise dependence   A craving for leisure time physical activity that results in uncontrollable excessive exercise behavior and that manifests in physiological and/or psychological symptoms.

The operational definition that has received the most recognition was presented by Veale (1987, 1995). He advocated the adoption of a set of standards for the diagnosis of exercise dependence that are based on the *Diagnostic and Statistical Manual for Mental Disorders* (*DSM-IV*; American Psychiatric Association, 1994) criteria for substance dependence. The *DSM* provides a classification system for mental disorders.

Expanding on Veale's suggestion, Hausenblas and Symons Downs (2001b) stated that exercise dependence should be defined as a multidimensional maladaptive pattern of physical activity that leads to significant impairment or distress as manifested by *three or more* criteria from a list of seven (*DSM-IV*, 1994). The seven criteria are

1. **Tolerance**—Increased physical activity levels are needed to achieve the desired effect, or the same physical activity level produces markedly diminished effects.
2. **Withdrawal**—Cessation of physical activity produces negative symptoms (e.g., anxiety, fatigue), or physical activity is used to relieve or forestall the onset of these symptoms.
3. **Intensity** effects—Physical activity is undertaken with greater intensity, frequency, or duration than is intended.
4. **Lack of control**—Physical activity is maintained despite a persistent desire to cut down or control it.
5. **Time** effects—Considerable time is spent in activities essential to physical activity maintenance (e.g., vacations are related to physical activity).
6. **Reduction** in other activities—Social, occupational, or recreational pursuits are reduced or dropped because of physical activity.
7. **Continuance**—Despite any persistent physical or psychological problems, physical activity is maintained (e.g., an individual continues running despite shin splints).

Thus, for example, if a person reports feelings of anxiety and depression when unable to exercise, spends little to no time with family or friends because of physical activity involvement, and continues to run despite a doctor's advice to allow an overuse injury to heal, he or she could potentially be classified as exercise dependent.

Historical Contributions

Exercise dependence was first identified by "accident" by Frederick Baekeland in 1970. He was conducting a one-month longitudinal study on the effects of exercise deprivation (i.e., no physical activity) on sleep. Two key study findings led him to the conclusion that some individuals may become addicted to physical activity. First, he encountered great difficulty recruiting habitual male exercisers (i.e., individuals who exercised five to six days a week) who were willing to abstain from physical activity for one month. In fact, no amount of money was sufficient to persuade these habitual runners to participate in the study. He finally was able to recruit individuals who regularly exercised three to four days a week. Second, during the one month deprivation period, participants reported decreased psychological well-being.

tolerance   A criterion of exercise dependence in which increased physical activity levels are needed to achieve the desired effect, or in which the same physical activity level produces markedly diminished effects.

withdrawal   A criterion of exercise dependence in which the cessation of physical activity produces negative symptoms, or in which physical activity is used to relieve or forestall the onset of these symptoms.

intensity   A criterion of exercise dependence in which physical activity is undertaken with greater intensity, frequency, or duration than is intended.

lack of control   A criterion of exercise dependence in which physical activity is maintained despite a persistent desire to cut down or control it.

time   A criterion of exercise dependence in which considerable time is spent in activities essential to physical activity maintenance.

reduction in other activities   A criterion for exercise dependence that represents social, occupational, or recreational pursuits that are reduced or dropped because of physical activity.

continuance   A criterion of exercise dependence in which physical activity is maintained despite the awareness of a persistent physical problem.

Baekeland (1970) realized the importance of these complaints and designed a self-report questionnaire to assess the participant's distress sensations. It was found that the participants retrospectively reported that their exercise deprivation of one month evoked increased anxiety, nocturnal awakening and arousal, and decreased sexual drive. In short, he found that habitual runners refused to abstain from physical activity for a one-month period, while regular runners reported withdrawal symptoms during physical activity deprivation.

Subsequent early researchers debated the differences between positive versus negative addiction and whether excessive physical activity could be harmful (Glasser, 1976; Hailey & Bailey, 1982; Morgan, 1979; Sachs, 1981). In 1976, Glasser argued that excessive physical activity is a *positive addiction* because of its many beneficial effects on self-esteem, mood, and anxiety, for example. He also claimed that running is "the hardest but surest way to positive addiction" (p. 100).

On the other hand, in 1979, Morgan pointed to the increasing number of overuse injuries and the social and occupational problems present in individuals who ran "excessively." As a consequence, he concluded that, for some runners, the benefits of physical activity may be offset by a *negative addiction.*

Subsequently, the term *exercise addiction* has been replaced by a variety of terms such as *exercise dependence, compulsive exercise, and morbid exercise* (see Table 7-1 for a list of terms). It is not always apparent whether the various terms represent the same phenomenon because operational definitions are often not provided (Grange & Eisler, 1993). This hodgepodge of terminology has resulted in a body of literature with no consensus regarding the causes, consequences, and correlates of exercise dependence.

Exercise Dependence Research

Although research on exercise dependence had a slow and controversial beginning, in recent years an increased interest has been observed. For example, in a review of the literature, Hausenblas and Symons Downs (2001b) located more than 130 research, review, and popular press articles on exercise dependence. Based on their review, they concluded that the exercise dependence research is characterized by

■ **TABLE 7-1**   Terms Used to Describe Exercise Dependence

TERM	SOURCE
Exercise dependence	Adams & Kirkby (1997, 1998)
Exercise addiction	Anshel (1991); Chapman & DeCastro (1990)
Obligatory exercise	Brehm & Steffen (1998)
Excessive exercise	Davis & Fox (1993)
Compulsive runners	Diekhoff (1984)
Negative addiction	Furst & Germone (1993)
Chronic joggers	Kagan (1987)
Habitual runners	Powers, Schocken, & Boyd et al. (1998)
Obsessive exercise	Thornton & Scott (1995)
Fitness fanaticism	Little (1979)

three general approaches: (a) comparing exercisers to eating disorder patients (this literature is discussed in the subsequent section), (b) comparing "excessive" to "less excessive" exercisers, and (c) comparing exercisers to nonexercisers.

Despite considerable research and discussion, the question of whether an exercise dependent individual differs in significant ways from a sedentary individual or a less avid exerciser remains unclear. Unfortunately, in general, the research has suffered from a lack of experimental investigations, inconsistent or nonexistent control groups, failure to control for subject biases, discrepant classification criteria, and invalid or inappropriate measures for excessive dependence (Modin et al., 1996).

More recently, in an attempt to overcome some of the past research limitations, Hausenblas and Symons Downs (in press) examined exercise dependence symptoms in more than 2,300 exercisers who varied in their physical activity involvement. The researchers developed the Exercise Dependence Scale, which they used to assess the prevalence of exercise dependence in a physically active population. The scale operationalizes exercise dependence based on the *DSM-IV* criteria for substance dependence. The results showed that approximately 9% of the exercisers could be classified as at-risk for exercise dependence, 40% as nondependent-symptomatic (i.e., display some exercise dependence symptoms), and 41% as nondependent-asymptomatic (i.e., display no exercise dependence symptoms).

Hausenblas and Symons Downs (in press) also found a hierarchy of responses in the areas of degree of participation in strenuous exercise (as measured by the Leisure-Time Exercise Questionnaire, Godin & Shepard, 1985), self-efficacy for exercise, and the disposition of perfectionism. That is, the individuals classified as at-risk for exercise dependence scored higher on self-efficacy and perfectionism than did those classified as nondependent-symptomatic, and the latter scored higher than did individuals classified as nondependent-asymptomatic. The study was based exclusively on self-report measures and was correlational. Therefore, cause-effect conclusions were not possible. That is, the researchers were unable to state, for example, that being perfectionistic causes an individual to be exercise dependent.

Exercise Deprivation Research

Exercise deprivation sensations (also referred to as exercise withdrawal symptoms) are what Szabo (1995) refers to as the cardinal identifying components of exercise dependence. These sensations represent the psychological and physiological effects that occur during periods of no physical activity. The individual may either experience the withdrawal symptoms (e.g., anxiety, fatigue) because of a lack of physical activity or engage in physical activity to relieve or avoid the onset of the withdrawal symptoms (*DSM-IV*, 1994).

Research evidence is difficult to interpret; studies have used diverse methodologies, adopted different periods of deprivation (ranging from one day to one month), and examined participants in different age groups involved in a variety of physical activity modes (Hausenblas & Symons Downs, 2001b). It is assumed that exercise deprivation symptoms arise for the same reason that regular physical activity re-

---

exercise deprivation sensations   The psychological and physiological effects that occur during periods of no physical activity.

---

sults in positive psychological states (see Chapters 3 through 6 for a review of the psychological benefits of physical activity). That is, it is assumed that the onset of physical activity leads to the onset of positive psychological states, whereas the cessation of regular physical activity leads to the onset of negative psychological states. Research has generally supported this assumption. The most frequently reported feelings resulting from physical activity deprivation are guilt, depression, irritability, restlessness, tension, stress, anxiety, and sluggishness (Szabo, Frenkl, & Caputo, 1997). Table 7-2 displays a list of the withdrawal symptoms commonly reported during exercise deprivation studies. It is important to emphasize that exercise deprivation sensations could be experienced by both nondependent and dependent exercisers, but the former would experience less profound effects than the latter (Szabo, 1995).

One noteworthy study of exercise deprivation was undertaken by Mondin and his colleagues (1996) at the University of Wisconsin–Madison. The effects of three days of exercise deprivation on mood states and anxiety in 10 male and female habitual runners was examined. Participants had to run at least 6 to 7 days a week for a minimum duration of 45 minutes per session to be classified as a habitual runner.

The study design required that the runners complete their regular workout on a Monday, refrain from physical activity on Tuesday, Wednesday, and Thursday, and then resume their regular physical activity on Friday. Also, on the no-exercising days the participants were also asked to limit their lifestyle physical activity (e.g., take the bus instead of biking to work). Mood and state anxiety were assessed on the Monday and Friday following the workout as well as on the three days of physical activity deprivation. It was found that the participants displayed increases in mood disturbance and anxiety during the no-exercise days. When physical activity was resumed on Friday, participants showed improvements in mood and anxiety (see Figure 7-1 for a graphic display of the anxiety results). The authors concluded that a brief period of physical activity deprivation in habitual exercisers results in mood disturbance within 24 to 48 hours.

■ **TABLE 7-2**   Exercise Deprivation Symptoms

AFFECTIVE SYMPTOMS	COGNITIVE SYMPTOMS	PHYSIOLOGICAL SYMPTOMS	SOCIAL SYMPTOMS
Anxiety	Confusion	Muscle soreness	Increased need for
Depression	Impaired concentration	Disturbed sleep	social interaction
Irritability		Lethargy	
Hostility		Fatigue	
Anger		Increased galvanic skin response	
Tension		Gastrointestinal problems	
Guilt		Decreased vigor	
Frustration			
Sexual tension			
Decreased self-esteem			

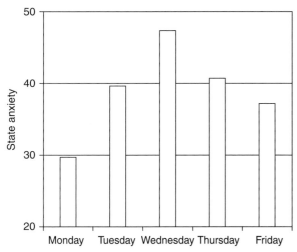

Figure 7-1   Examination of state anxiety during running days (Monday and Friday) and deprivation days (Tuesday to Thursday).
Note. From "Psychological Consequences of Exercise Deprivation in Habitual Exercisers," by G. W. Mondin et al., 1996, *Medicine and Science in Sports and Exercise, 28,* 1199–1203.

Explanations of Exercise Dependence

Potential explanations of exercise dependence can be classified into three domains: psychological (i.e., personality traits, anorexia analogue hypothesis, and affective regulation); physiological (i.e., β-endorphin and sympathetic arousal hypothesis); and psychobio-logical (i.e., general theory of addiction). Each of these explanations is described in the following sections.

Psychological Explanations.   The **personality trait explanation** is based on the belief that exercise dependent people have specific personality characteristics such as perfectionism, obsessive-compulsiveness, neuroticism, low self-esteem, and high trait anxiety. Researchers have usually found a positive relationship between exercise dependence symptoms and perfectionism (Coen & Ogles, 1993), obsessive-compulsiveness (Davis et al., 1995), trait anxiety (Coen & Ogles; Rudy & Estok, 1989), and extraversion (Davis & Fox, 1993). A negative relationship has been evidenced between exercise dependence symptoms and self-esteem (Rudy & Estok). The relationship, however, between narcissism and exercise dependence symptoms is inconclusive. That is, researchers have found either a positive relationship (Jibaja-Rusth, 1989), no relationship (Spano, 2001), or a negative relationship (Davis & Fox) between exercise dependence symptoms and neuroticism. Some of the inconsistent findings may be the result of the varied methods used by researchers to assess physical

personality trait explanation   An explanation of exercise dependence that states that exercise dependent individuals have specific personality characteristics such as perfectionism, obsessive-compulsiveness, neuroticism, low self-esteem, and high trait anxiety.

activity, personality, and exercise dependence. Also, the distinction between primary exercise dependence (independent disorder) versus secondary exercise dependence (secondary to an eating disorder) often is not made (Veale, 1995).

The **anorexia analogue hypothesis,** which is a type of personality explanation, was developed by Yates, Leehey, and Shisslak (1983). They argued that male obligatory runners resembled anorexia nervosa patients on personality characteristics such as introversion, inhibition of anger, high expectations, depression, and excessive use of denial. Although the authors reported no objective data, they claimed that running and anorexia nervosa were both dangerous attempts to establish an identity. Their article was heavily criticized as having no pertinent data, poor methodology, no relevance to the majority of runners, and an overreliance on extreme individuals, and as overstating the similarities between the groups. Researchers using empirical data have failed to find a common psychopathology between people with exercise dependence and those with eating disorders (e.g., Powers et al., 1998).

The basis for the **affective regulation explanation** is that physical activity leads to positive psychological states, whereas the cessation of exercise results in negative psychological states. For example, acute and chronic bouts of exercise are associated with reductions in depression and anxiety and increases in positive mood states in clinical and nonclinical populations (Landers & Arent, 2001). Exercise dependent individuals may use exercise for affective regulation, that is, they engage in physical activity to either avoid or reduce their anxiety levels. Research support for the affective regulation explanation is found in exercise deprivation studies. In general, researchers have found that exercise deprivation results in increased mood disturbance in habitual exercisers (Szabo, 1995).

Physiological Explanations. The **β-endorphin explanation** is based on the premise that β-endorphin levels in the blood rise with exercise due to an increased need for blood to be transported to the working muscles (Crossman, Jamieson, & Henderson, 1987). β-endorphins are endogenous compounds that decrease people's sensitivity to pain,

which results in euphoric effects and addictive behavioral tendencies. Thus, it has been suggested (Crossman et al.) that exercisers may become dependent on β-endorphins because they make the exercisers feel better and they mask pain.

Pierce, Eastman, Tripatni, Olson, and Dewey (1993) conducted the only located study examining the plausibility of the β-endorphin explanation for exercise dependence. They examined the relationship between β-endorphin levels after an acute bout of exercise in eight females who engaged in a minimum of three aerobics classes a week. Blood samples of the participants were taken before and following a 45-minute high-intensity aerobic session. Although their β-endorphin levels were elevated following the exercise session, no relationship was found between the β-endorphin levels and exercise dependence symptoms. It is important to note that the participants did not report high levels of exercise dependence. That is, their scores on the Negative Addiction Scale (Hailey & Bailey, 1982) ranged from 2 to 6 (M score $= 4$) out of a possible maximum score of 14, which indicates high dependence. Thus, future research needs to examine the β-endorphin explanation in individuals who report high levels of exercise dependence.

---

anorexia analogue hypothesis A type of personality trait explanation of exercise dependence that argues that male obligatory runners resemble anorexia nervosa patients on personality traits.

affective regulation explanation An explanation of exercise dependence that suggests that physical activity leads to positive psychological states, whereas the cessation of exercise results in negative psychological states.

β-endorphin explanation An explanation of exercise dependence that is based on the premise that β-endorphin levels in the blood rise with exercise because of an increased need for blood to be transported to the working muscles.

β-endorphins Endogenous compounds that decrease sensitivity to pain, which results in euphoric effects and addictive behavioral tendencies.

Thompson and Blanton (1987) suggested a **sympathetic arousal explanation** of exercise dependence. In this explanation, excessive exercise produces an increase in people's fitness level and in their efficiency of energy use. This increased efficiency is a result of lowered sympathetic output that is reflected in a decreased metabolic rate. Because of the lowered sympathetic output, the individual experiences lethargy, fatigue, and low arousal. Thus, regular exercisers must engage in higher intensities and durations of physical activity to produce the same level of physiological arousal during and following an exercise bout. No located studies have examined the plausibility of the sympathetic arousal hypothesis as an explanation of exercise dependence.

Psychobiological Explanations. This general theory of addictions suggests that physiological and psychology factors interact to produce a predisposition for people to exhibit dependent behaviors (Jacobs, 1986). Jacobs stated that the two major factors for developing a dependency are (a) **subjective aversion,** which is an excessively depressed or excited resting physiological state; and (b) a psychological state characterized by feelings of inadequacy and rejection based on experiences in childhood and early adolescence. Because both factors must be present for a person to develop a dependency, only a limited number of people will be predisposed to dependent behaviors. Furthermore, the dependency remains latent unless at-risk individuals come into contact with a situation that is associated with the alteration of the physiological state to a level that reduces the aversiveness of the existing state.

In the only located study examining the general theory of addiction to exercise behavior, Beh, Mathers, and Holden (1996) recorded EEG readings of three groups of university students who differed in their degree of dependency (i.e., high-dependent, low-dependent, and nondependent). EEGs measure the level of physiological activity, with low EEG frequencies being associated with depression and high frequencies being related to excitation. Thus, in this study depressed and excited states were defined by EEG parameters. The participants' EEG recordings were assessed before and after a 45-minute exercise session. It was found that the high-dependent group had higher EEG frequencies (i.e., excitation) than did the low-dependent group. The authors concluded that their results provided partial support for Jacob's (1986) general theory of addiction.

Treatment of Exercise Dependence

The scientific literature is relatively sparse regarding treatment for exercise dependent individuals. One of the few studies examining the treatment of exercise dependence was conducted by Adams and Kirkby (1997), who interviewed 24 physiotherapists with exercise-dependent clients. Treatment approaches listed by the physiotherapists included

- Providing education about the injury and likely outcomes
- Prescribing reduced or alternative activities
- Making referrals to other health professionals
- Using psychological strategies such as behavior modification, modeling, and counseling

The authors reported that 71% of the physiotherapists experienced problems communicating with their clients and ensuring that the clients complied with the rehabilitation programs; the injured clients refused to stop exercising.

OVERTRAINING AND STALENESS

Very few people (mostly athletes) may experience overtraining and staleness because of their excessive exercise behavior. **Overtraining** is a short period of training, usually lasting a few days to a few weeks, during which people increase their training loads to

---

sympathetic arousal explanation An explanation of exercise dependence that states that excessive exercise produces an increase in fitness level and in energy use efficiency.

subjective aversion An excessively depressed or excited resting physiological state.

overtraining A short period of training, usually lasting a few days to a few weeks, during which training increases to near or at maximal capacity.

near or at maximal capacity (O'Connor, 1997). O'Connor noted that overtraining has three distinct features. First, overtraining is a process that involves a series of acute exercise bouts. Second, overtraining consists of a significant increase in training compared with recent training history. Third, overtraining involves exercising at a high frequency (often more than one session per day) with an intensity-duration combination that is at or near maximal capacity.

In defining overtraining, attention must be given to (a) individual differences in performance capacity, and (b) exercise mode. First, for example, 10 days of running 5 km at 95% of VO_2 max is not overtraining for an elite athlete who is accustomed to running 10 km per day at 95% of VO_2 max. In contrast, this regimen would represent overtraining for a high school runner who is used to running 2 km at 95% of VO_2 max (O'Connor, 1997). Second, for example, 2 hours of daily running at 70% of VO_2 max is more likely to represent overtraining than is 2 hours of daily swimming at 70% of VO_2 max because long-duration exercise is tolerated better in non-weight-bearing activities (e.g., cycling, swimming) than in weight-bearing activities (e.g., running; O'Connor).

Although many coaches and athletes believe that overtraining is necessary for high-level performance, the process can also result in the negative outcome of staleness. **Staleness** is a psychological state of overtraining that manifests as deteriorated readiness (O'Connor, 1997). The principal behavioral sign of staleness is impairment of athletic performance. For example, the stale athlete has a significant reduction in performance, that is, 5% or greater, for an extended period (usually 2 weeks or greater) that occurs during or following overtraining and that fails to improve in response to short-term training reductions. The psychological symptoms of staleness are mood disturbance and increases in perceived effort during exercise. For example stale athletes perceive typical workouts as more effortful and finish them with extreme difficulty. The most common mood disturbance that is associated with staleness is depression. In fact, it has been reported that about 80% of stale athletes are clinically depressed (Morgan, Brown, Raglin, O'Connor, & Ellickson, 1987). The recommended treatment for staleness is rest. The amount of rest needed to recover from staleness, however, is unknown.

The dominant research design to identify early warning signs of staleness is to assess mood states in athletes prior to, during, and following a period of overtraining and then compare those athletes who develop performance difficulties with those who do not (O'Connor, 1997). The most consistent finding in the overtraining and staleness literature is that increases in training are associated with mood disturbance, whereas reductions in training load are associated with improved mood (O'Connor). For example O'Connor, Morgan, and Raglin (1991) examined mood states during 3 days of increased training in 40 college swimmers. The swimmers' training volume was increased from 6,800 to 11,200 m per day for the female swimmers and 8,800 to 12,950 m per day for the male swimmers. The swimmers completed the POMS for four consecutive days (baseline and days 1 to 3 of overtraining). Increased vigor, fatigue, and overall mood disturbance on the POMS were found during the overtraining period for the male and female

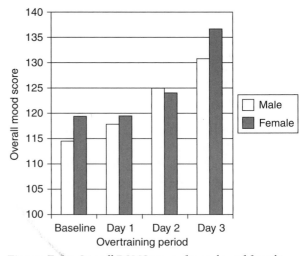

Figure 7-2 Overall POMS scores for male and female swimmers during a 3-day overtraining period.

Note. From "Psychobiologic Effects of 3 days of Increased Training in Female and Male Swimmers," by P. J. O'Connor, W. P. Morgan, and J. S. Raglin, 1991, *Medicine and Science in Sports and Exercise, 23,* 1055–1061.

---

staleness A psychological state of overtraining that manifests as deteriorated readiness.

swimmer (see Figure 7-2 for a graphic display of the results). The authors concluded that a short period of overtraining can have negative mood outcomes for college swimmers. Landers and Arent (2001) noted, however, that the vigor and fatigue subscales of the POMS may merely reflect a consequence of the actual and perceived exertion the athletes are experiencing. That is, during periods of overtraining athletes are likely to report increased fatigue and decreased vigor.

PHYSICAL ACTIVITY AND EATING DISORDERS

Although physical activity is often part of a safe and healthy program to control weight, individuals may have unrealistic expectations. People are bombarded with images of the ideal body: from advertisers thin and toned for females (i.e., low percent body fat and physically fit) and lean and muscular for males (i.e.,

low percent body fat and muscular, especially in the upper body; Brownell, 1991). To try to achieve these unreasonable body ideals, some individuals turn to dieting, which, taken to the extreme, can develop into the eating disorders of anorexia nervosa or bulimia nervosa. The cardinal feature of anorexia nervosa is an extreme pursuit of thinness. The primary criteria for bulimia nervosa involve eating binges followed by inappropriate compensatory methods to prevent weight gain (*DSM-IV*, 1994). Table 7-3 displays the diagnostic criteria for anorexia nervosa and bulimia nervosa. If progress seems slow, the individual may become frustrated with the results from diet alone and may add compulsive exercise to speed up weight loss. In fact, to lose or maintain weight, individuals with eating disorders often engage in excessive physical activity. For example, Davis (2000) noted that approximately 80% of female patients with eating disorders exercise excessively during the acute phase of their disorder.

■ **TABLE 7-3**   Diagnostic Criteria for Anorexia Nervosa and Bulimia Nervosa

BULIMIA NERVOSA

1. Recurrent episodes of binge eating. Binge eating is characterized by the following:
   a) eating in a discrete period of time (e.g., within a two-hour period), an amount of food that is larger than most people would eat during a similar period of time and under similar circumstances
   b) a sense of lack of control over eating during the episode (e.g., a feeling that one cannot stop eating or control what or how much one is eating)
2. Recurrent inappropriate compensatory behavior in order to prevent weight gain (e.g., self-induced vomiting; misuse of laxatives, diuretics, enemas, fasting or excessive exercise)
3. The binge eating and inappropriate compensatory behaviors both occur, on average, at least twice a week for three months
4. Self-evaluation is unduly influenced by body shape and weight
5. The disturbance does not occur exclusively during episodes of anorexia nervosa

ANOREXIA NERVOSA

1. Refusal to maintain body weight at or above a minimally normal weight for age and height
2. Intense fear of gaining weight or becoming fat, even though under weight
3. Disturbance in the way in which one's body weight or shape is experienced, unduly influence of body weight or shape on self-evaluation, or denial of the seriousness of the current low body weight
4. Amenorrhea

Note. From *Diagnostic and Statistical Manual for Mental Disorders* (4th ed.), by American Psychiatric Association, 1994, Washington, DC: Author. Copyright 1994 by the American Psychiatric Association. Reprinted with permission.

The relationship, however, between physical activity and eating disorders is far from clear. Some researchers state that there is no relationship between physical activity and eating disorders, whereas other experts feel strongly that physical activity and eating disorders are related (O'Connor & Smith, 1999). Three general lines of research have attempted to shed light on this issue. In one, comparisons are made between the profiles of individuals identified as having an eating disorder and those characterized as being an excessive exerciser. In the second, the physical activity behavior of individuals with an eating disorder, particularly anorexia nervosa, is examined. Finally, in the third, athletes are compared to nonathletes on eating disorder symptoms.

Eating Disorders Versus Excessive Physical Activity

Some researchers have argued that exercise dependence is merely a symptom of anorexia nervosa (Yates et al., 1983). Other researchers, however, state that a distinction must be made between **primary exercise dependence** and **secondary exercise dependence.** In primary exercise dependence, the physical activity is an end in itself. In contrast, for secondary exercise dependence, the excessive exercise is secondary to an eating disorder. Thus, for secondary dependence, the motivation for physical activity is the control and manipulation of body composition. Veale (1987, 1995) suggested that a diagnostic hierarchy must occur to validly identify exercise dependence. He argued that the diagnosis of an eating disorder (i.e., secondary dependence) must first be excluded before a diagnosis of primary exercise dependence can be made. That is, primary exercise dependence can be differentiated from an eating

---

primary exercise dependence   Exercise dependence in which the physical activity is an end in itself.

secondary exercise dependence   Exercise dependence in which the motivation for physical activity is the control and manipulation of body composition.

FIT FACTS

Does watching TV reduce muscular fitness in prepubescent children?

Apparently not. Children who are frequent viewers of television (3 hours or more a day) do no worse on strength tests than do moderate viewers (2 hours per day) or infrequent viewers (1 hour or less per day).

(Tucker & Hager, 1996)

---

disorder by clarifying the ultimate objective of the exerciser.

In the early 1980s researchers began to examine if excessive physical activity was merely one manifestation of anorexia nervosa. This area of research was stimulated by a controversial article by Yates and her colleagues (1983; see the section titled "Explanations of Exercise Dependence"), who argued that male obligatory runners resembled female anorexia nervosa patients on specific personality characteristics. Their article has been criticized for poor methodological design and inaccurate interpretation of the results.

Subsequent, more tightly controlled studies that have compared patients with eating disorders and those who exercise have yielded conflicting results. Generally, robust psychological similarities between individuals with eating disorders and individuals who exercise have not been identified (J. A. Blumenthal, O'Toole, & Chang, 1984; Coen & Ogles, 1993; Krelstein, 1983; Larsen, 1983; Powers et al., 1998; Wells, 1983). For example, Powers and her colleagues examined psychological and physiological characteristics of 40 male and female obligatory runners and 17 female anorexia nervosa patients. The runners had the following characteristics: (a) they ran over 25 miles/week; (b) they ran despite injury or illness; (c) they considered running to be an important part of their life; and (d) they felt guilty, irritable, or depressed when unable to run. Measures of depression, personality, obsessions, and body image were obtained. Also, physical examinations were carried out, skin-fold assessments to estimate percent body fat were obtained, and exercise treadmill tests were undertaken to determine the participants' aerobic fitness. The researchers found that the patients with anorexia nervosa displayed significant psychopathology, whereas the runners were in the normal range. Percent body fat was in the normal range for the runners and in the low range for the anorexia nervosa group. Also, runners had excellent fitness levels compared to the anorexia nervosa patients. In short, despite hypothesized similarities, individuals suffering from anorexia nervosa and individuals characterized as habitual runners were found to have few similar psychological or physiological features.

Physical Activity Behavior of Individuals With Eating Disorders

Despite a lack of compelling empirical evidence, a misconception is that excessive exercise leads to the development of anorexia nervosa (O'Connor & Smith, 1999). In a review of the literature O'Connor and Smith stated that "logic and empirical evidence dictate that excessive exercise cannot be a sole cause of anorexia nervosa" (p. 1010). To illustrate their point, O'Connor and Smith pointed out that approximately 12% of the adult population participates in regular vigorous physical activity but that the overwhelming majority of these individuals never develop anorexia nervosa. Also, increased physical activity with anorexia is paradoxical because starvation results in reduced physical activity and fatigue. Furthermore, the majority of studies that examine exercise patterns of patients with eating disorders have been cross-sectional and retrospective and have failed to use valid physical activity assessments, thus rendering conclusions regarding a causal relationship as premature.

For example, Davis, Kennedy, Ravelski, and Dionne (1994) at the University of Toronto collected historical and current physical activity data on 45 hospitalized patients with eating disorders and an age-matched control group. The patients with eating disorders also completed a checklist of eating disorder symptoms and a semistructured interview regarding eating behaviors and physical activity. The researchers found that involvement in a competitive sport or a regular physical activity program predated the onset of dieting among a large portion of patients with anorexia nervosa. Also, relative to individuals in the control group, individuals with eating disorders were more physically active from adolescence onward as well as just prior to the onset of their eating disorder. Specifically, 78% of the patients reported engaging in excessive physical activity, 60% were competitive athletes prior to the onset of their disorder, and 75% claimed that their physical activity levels steadily increased during the period in which food intake and weight loss decreased the most. These results, however, should be viewed with caution because validity data for the physical activity instrument was unknown and because interview and symptom checklist data were not obtained from the controls (O'Connor & Smith, 1999).

Bouten, Van Marken Lichtenbelt, and Westerderp (1996) conducted the only study that examined daily physical activity in nonhospitalized anorexic individuals (O'Connor & Smith, 1999). Bouten et al. determined the daily physical activity and metabolic rate of 11 females with anorexia nervosa and 13 normal-weight controls. Physical activity was assessed by a movement counter, and metabolic rate was measured via the doubly labeled water method (see Chapter 2 for a description of these measures). On average, daily physical activity did not differ between the anorexic group and the control group. However, the anorexic women with a very low body mass index, less than 17, tended to be less active than the controls. In comparison, anorexic participants with a body mass index higher than 17 tended to be more or equally active compared with the controls. This finding illustrates that starvation leads to reduced physical activity and fatigue.

Comparison of Athletes to Nonathletes

Over the past 20 years, considerable scientific attention has been directed toward the potential role that sport involvement plays in athletes' development of attitudes and behaviors about disordered eating. The bases for the expectation that athletes as a population

FIT FACTS

Does a placebo work as well as anabolic steroids?

Apparently. National-level weight lifters, led to believe that the saccharin tablets they were taking were a powerful anabolic steroid, showed improvements in performance that would have garnered them international status.

(Maganaris, Collins, & Sharp, 2000)

might be at risk for eating disorders are threefold. First, societal norms in western cultures—historically for females, but also increasingly for males—favor a lean, physically fit physique, and these societal norms are salient for athletes (Brownell, 1991). Second, it has been suggested that high activity levels and strenuous exercise associated with sport participation can reduce the value of food reinforcement, which results in weight loss (Epling & Pierce, 1988). Third, the psychological characteristics consistent with high-level athletic achievement, such as perfectionism and motivation, are also evident in individuals with eating disorders (M. D. Johnson, 1994). Research is needed to examine the plausibility of these explanations.

Although it is not possible on the basis of current research to answer questions pertaining to why, it does appear that athletes as a population self-report more eating disorder symptoms than do nonathletes. Hausenblas and Carron (1999) undertook a meta-analysis of 92 studies that examined eating disorder symptoms in male and female athletes. They found a small but significant effect for female athletes to self-report more bulimic and anorexic symptomatology compared to females from the general population. Similarly, a small but significant effect was found for male athletes to self-report more of the symptomatology for bulimia, anorexia, and the drive for thinness (i.e., the cardinal feature of an eating disorder) compared to males from the general population.

There has also been an implicit expectation that certain types of athletes could be at risk for developing eating and dieting pathologies because of the specific task demands of their sport (Sundgot-Borgen, 1994). Sports in which competition is determined by weight-based classification systems (e.g., wrestling, rowing) have been one focus of concern. Another focus has been sports that have a strong aesthetic component (e.g., figure skating, gymnastics, diving). Results of the Hausenblas and Carron (1999) meta-analysis revealed that male athletes in aesthetic and weight-dependent sports self-reported more bulimic and drive for thinness symptomatology than did male comparison groups. Relative to females in the general population, females in aesthetic sports self-reported more anorexic and drive for thinness indices. For example, the mean effect size for the anorexic indices was significantly higher for the female aesthetic sport athletes compared to female athletes engaged in ball game sports (e.g., basketball, soccer) and endurance sports (e.g., long distance running).

STEROID ABUSE AND PHYSICAL ACTIVITY

Within the last two decades scientific and public interest in the effects of anabolic-androgenic steroid use have been evidenced. These drugs are synthetic versions of the primary male sex hormone, testosterone. In contrast to popular beliefs, athletes are not the only population using steroids. Steroid use has been documented, for example, in firefighters, police officers, military personnel, personal trainers, regular exercisers, models, and movie stars (Yesalis & Cowart, 1998). Many of these individuals are trying to improve their body image, not enhance sport performance. For example, one bodybuilder, when confronted with the serious health risks of steroids, said "life's too short to die small!" (quoted in Klein, 1995, p. 113).

Just how prevalent is steroid use? "Arnold Schwartzenegger, the prototype of the action hero, readily admits using steroids to achieve the look during his bodybuilding days, explaining that 'everyone did it' back then" (Yesalis & Cowart, 1998, p. 6). Until the late 1980s, very little data were available on the prevalence of steroid use. A 1988 study by Buckley and his colleagues was the first U.S. nationwide survey of steroid use among teenage boys. The survey revealed that approximately 7% of high school seniors reported that they had used steroids. Users were more likely to participate in athletics, especially wrestling and football. A revealing point of interest, however, was that 35% of the steroid users did not participate in sports. As Figure 7-3 illustrates, the main reason that high school students reported taking steroids was to improve athletic performance (47%), followed by improve physical appearance (27%), prevent or treat injury (11%), and fit in socially (7%). The results of the Buckley et al. study subsequently have been confirmed by more than 40 national, regional, and local studies (Yesalis & Cowart, 1998).

Steroids produce not only the well-documented physical effects (e.g., increased muscle mass) but also psychological effects. For example, Pope and Katz (1994) examined the psychological effects of steroid use in 156 men who had lifted weights for at least 2 years. The weight lifters were interviewed about their steroid use and medical history, were administered a questionnaire for mental disorders, and re-

ceived a physical examination. Urine samples were obtained to assess actual steroid use. Of the total sample, 88 had used steroids (37 current users and 51 past users), while 68 had not. Among the steroid users, 23% reported experiencing major mood disturbances such as mania, anxiety, depression, or major depression. The authors concluded that major mood disturbances associated with steroids may represent an important public health problem.

Some weight lifters, no matter how large they become, see themselves as small. What seems to other people to be nothing more than an exaggerated physical vanity may be a manifestation of a distorted body image associated with steroid abuse. Pope, Gruber, Choi, Olivardia, and Phillips (1997), in their discussion of the problem, provided the following example:

> All of his waking hours are consumed with preoccupations of getting bigger. He tries to resist these thoughts, but reports success only half of the time. He weighs himself 2–3 times daily and checks mirrors 10–12 times a day to monitor his physique. He wears baggy sweatshirts and long pants even in the heat of summer to disguise his perceived smallness. (p. 554)

A large variety of terms have been used to describe **muscle dysmorphia,** a form of body image distortion in which the individual perceives himself or herself as unacceptably small. These terms include, for example,

- *bodybuilding anorexia* (Siff, 1992)
- *inverse anorexia* (i.e., virtually everything in the bodybuilder is the inverse, or opposite of, what characterizes anorexia, except the psychologically distorted preoccupation with body mass; Siff, 1992)
- *reverse anorexia* (Pope, Katz, & Hudson, 1993)
- *megorexia nervosa* (Kessler, 1997)

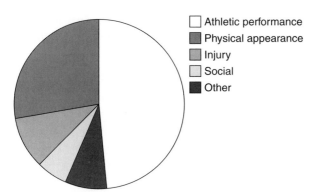

Figure 7-3 Reasons for taking steroids in a male high school sample.
Note. From "Estimated Prevalence of Anabolic Steroid Use Among Male High School Seniors," by W. A. Buckley et al., 1988, *JAMA, 260,* 3341–3445.

Legend:
- ☐ Athletic performance
- ■ Physical appearance
- ▨ Injury
- ☐ Social
- ■ Other

muscle dysmorphia A form of body image distortion in which the individual perceives himself or herself as unacceptably small.

- *bigameraria* (W. N. Taylor, 1985)
- *body image disorder of the '90s* (Pope et al., 1997)

Pope and his colleagues (1993, 1997, 1998) were the first researchers to examine muscle dysmorphia. Based on their research, they proposed that persons with muscle dysmorphia are (a) pathologically preoccupied with the appearance of the whole body; (b) concerned that they are not sufficiently large or muscular; and (c) are consumed by weight lifting, dieting, and steroid abuse. As a consequence, these individuals experience profound distress about having their bodies seen in public, they exhibit impaired social and occupational functioning, and they abuse anabolic steroids and other drugs.

A. J. Gruber and Pope (1998) conducted interviews and medical examinations with 36 females who incorporated weight lifting into their fitness program and were taking ephedrine (a central nervous system stimulant). These women were recruited by advertisements in gymnasiums seeking females who had competed in a bodybuilding contest or had worked out at least five times per week for two years or more. It was found that 97% ($n = 35$) of the female bodybuilders displayed muscle dysmorphia, and that 44% ($n = 16$) reported a history of an eating disorder (i.e., anorexia nervosa, bulimia nervosa, binge eating disorder). The generalizability of these results, however, are limited because of the selected sample.

Finally, Olivardia, Pope, and Hudson (2000) conducted interviews with 24 young men with muscle dysmorphia and 30 normal comparison weight lifters. The researchers found that the men with muscle dysmorphia, in comparison to the normal weight lifters, scored higher in the areas of body dissatisfaction, disordered eating, anabolic steroid abuse, and lifetime prevalence of mood and anxiety disorders. The authors also found that the men with muscle dysmorphia frequently reported shame, embarrassment, and impairment of social and occupational functioning in association with their condition. In contrast, the normal weight lifters reported little pathology.

Summary

This chapter examined some potential negative effects of exercise and physical activity including exercise dependence, staleness, eating disorders, and steroid use. For some people, exercise may represent a negative behavior when it becomes excessive, and it is associated with pathological behaviors such as binging, purging, and taking steroids. We want to emphasize, however, that exercise is largely a positive behavior—a behavior that few adults engage in on a regular basis.

CHAPTER 8

Individual Correlates of Physical Activity

If a Man Would Move the World, He Must First Move Himself.

(Socrates)

CHAPTER OBJECTIVES

After completing this chapter you will be able to

- Differentiate between the keys terms of *correlates* and *determinants* of physical activity.

- Outline the demographic, biological, psychological, behavioral, and physical activity correlates of physical activity.

Key terms

determinants	tracking
social physique anxiety	

Socrates might be correct in his belief that people must first move themselves, but researchers, health care professionals, and government agencies are concerned about the number of people who have yet to move themselves into a physically active lifestyle. For example, the statistics generally considered applicable in North America are that 40% of the adult population is sedentary (USDHHS, 1996, 1999, 2000) and that approximately 50% of sedentary adults who begin an exercise program drop out within 6 months (Dishman, 1994).

To better promote the adoption and maintenance of regular physical activity, those same researchers, health care professionals, and government agencies have tried to gain insight into the characteristics of individuals who are active or inactive, who sustain or terminate their exercise involvement.* To date, a large number of the individual characteristics that influence exercise behavior have been identified. These characteristics are referred to as **determinants** of adherence to exercise and physical activity (Sallis & Owen, 1999). Given that the research examining physical activity determinants has largely been generated in cross-sectional or retrospective studies (Dishman, 1994), the implicit suggestion of causation is not appropriate. In fact, a more accurate term would be the *correlates* of adherence in exercise and physical activity.

It is well documented that as people get older they tend to be less active. It is not true, however, that aging causes people to be less active. Many older people are very active. No single variable explains all

---

determinants Individual characteristics that influence exercise behavior.

---

*Exercise scientists also have tried to gain insight into the characteristics of the situations and environments that are associated with cessation or maintenance of physical activity. That work is discussed in Chapters 9 and 11.

physical activity behavior (Sallis, Hovell, Hofstetter, & Barrington, 1992). Different variables exert different degrees of influence on different people. For example, spousal support may be important in helping some people exercise, but not others. In addition, the strength of spousal influence for each person may vary during different stages of life (Sallis & Owen, 1999). Spousal support for physical activity may be relatively unimportant in early adulthood but important in older adulthood. More than 300 studies have examined the correlates of physical activity (Sallis & Owen, 1999). In this chapter, we outline the main demographic, biological, psychological, behavioral, and physical activity correlates of involvement in exercise and physical activity.

DEMOGRAPHIC AND BIOLOGICAL CORRELATES OF PHYSICAL ACTIVITY

Demographic and biological characteristics include age, ethnicity, socioeconomic status, and gender. These types of characteristics cannot be altered. So, even if differences in demography and biology are associated with differences in involvement in physical activity, why is it important to study them? One reason is that knowledge of the demographic and biologic correlates of physical activity allows researchers and health care professionals to identify groups more at risk for inactivity (Dishman, 1994). This information provides insight for health care professionals to target different intervention strategies for different populations.

Age

Physical activity declines with age, resulting in an almost 50% decrease between ages 6 and 16 (Rowland, 1990). Figure 8-1 graphically displays the decline in vigorous physical activity by grade for male and female high school students (USDHHS, 2000). Further declines in activity occur throughout adulthood (Leslie, Fotheringham, Owen, & Bauman, 2001; Stephens, Jacobs, & White, 1985). Although

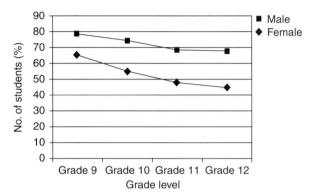

Figure 8-1   The percentage of high school male and females who engage in vigorous physical activity 3 or more days per week for 20 minutes or more per session. *Note.* From USDHHS, 2000.

data are limited for older adults, what is available supports the conclusion that this decline continues after age 50, with progressively larger proportions of men and women reporting that they get no leisure time physical activity through age 80 (King et al., 1994; Ruuskanen & Puoppila, 1995).

One frequently cited study was carried out by Ruuskanen and Puoppila (1995). They conducted interviews with 1,244 Finnish participants aged 65 to 84 years and found that physical activity decreased markedly with age. Their results are not atypical. Figure 8-2 graphically displays the decline in vigorous physical activity by age for adults (USDHHS, 2000).

The relationship of advancing age and declining involvement in vigorous physical activity is not easily explained. Because advancing age is also associated with reductions in cardiovascular fitness, impaired health (e.g., arthritis), retirement, and isolation from others due to poor health, it may not be surprising that elderly individuals engage in more mild and moderate physical activity compared to vigorous activity (Caspersen et al., 1994). Another reason for the negative relationship between age and physical activity may be the cohort effect. That is, people born earlier (e.g., 1930s) have not grown up with the same norms and beliefs around physical activity as people born later (e.g., 1980s).

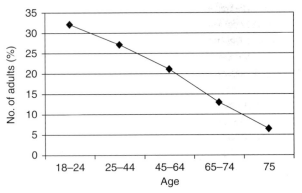

Figure 8-2   The percentage of adults by age grouping who engage in vigorous physical activity 3 or more days per week for 20 minutes or more per session.
Note. From USDHHS, 2000.

Gender

Gender differences in the physical activity patterns of infants are minimal (Eaton & Enns, 1986). Studies, however, of preschoolers (Kucera, 1985), preadolescents (J. G. Ross & Pate, 1987; Trost et al., 1996; Trost et al., 1997), adolescents (Fuchs et al., 1988), adults (Leslie et al., 2001), and older individuals (Ruuskanen & Puoppila, 1995) continually find that males engage in more vigorous and moderate physical activity than females do (see Figure 8-1). The fact that males are more active than females may be due, in part, to different family and sociocultural influences pertaining to participation in physical activity.

Ethnicity

Surveys and epidemiological studies have found that ethnic differences exist for sedentariness. For example, research conducted by the Centers for Disease Control and Prevention (USDHHS, 2000) show that 36% of White Americans are sedentary, followed by 42% of Asians or Pacific Islanders, 46% of American Indians, 52% of Black or African Americans, and 54% of Hispanic Americans (see Figure 8-3). These discrepancies are apparent even at the high school level, with 67% of White students engaging in vigorous physical activity compared to only 60% of Hispanics and 54% of Blacks (USDHHS, 2000).

Occupation

Research has revealed that blue-collar workers are more likely to drop out of rehabilitative exercise programs following myocardial infarction than are white-collar workers. Blue-collar workers are also less likely to use worksite exercise facilities (Andrew, Oldridge, Parker, Cunningham, Rechnitzer, Jones, Buck, Kavanagh,

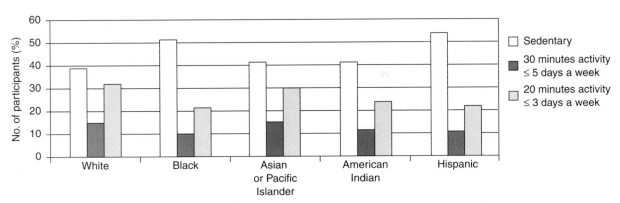

Figure 8-3   Percentage of Hispanic, American Indian, Asian and Pacific Islander, Black, and White adults who engage in various levels of physical activity.
Note. From USDHHS, 2000.

Blue-collar workers are less likely to be active when total leisure activity is considered.
©PhotoDisc/Volume 88/Shipping and Handling

Shepard, & Sutton, 1981). The generalizability of these findings to other supervised settings is less clear. In general, however, blue-collar workers are less likely to be active when total leisure activity is considered (Dishman & Buckworth, 1997). There may be an explanation for this finding. As Dishman (1993) noted, "many blue-collar occupations may carry with them the perception of on-job activity adequate for health and fitness despite low actual exertion" (p. 782).

Education

Level of education is positively associated with leisure time physical activity (King et al., 1994; Kuh & Cooper, 1992; C. E. Ross, 2000). For example, only 6% of adults (aged 25 years or older) with less than a 9th grade education engage in vigorous physical activity compared to 32% who have a college degree or greater (USDHHS, 2000). A higher level of parental education is also positively related to children's physical activity level. For example, the Centers for Disease Control and Prevention found that 68% of high school students who reported engaging in vigorous physical activity had parents with at least some college education. For students whose parents were high school graduates only, 54% reported engaging in vigorous physical activity. Finally, the figure fell to 50% for individuals whose parents had less than a high school education (USDHHS, 2000).

What about the education level of other people in the community? When C. E. Ross (2000)

posed this question, she found that people are more likely to walk in their neighborhoods if they have many neighbors who hold college degrees. Interestingly, she found that the influence of neighbors' education level was more important than personal education level for predicting physical activity. Ross concluded that her results provided evidence for a contagion effect in which people adopt the behaviors of people seen on the streets in their neighborhood.

Biomedical Status

Not surprisingly, researchers have consistently found that healthy people are more active than persons with medical and psychological conditions (King et al., 1994; Tsuang, Perkins, & Simpson, 1983). The Centers for Disease Control and Prevention reported that 13% of adults with disabilities engaged in vigorous physical activity compared to 25% without disabilities (USDHHS, 2000). It also appears that individuals from special populations have high dropout rates from exercise programs. For example, McArthur, Levine, and Berk (1993) found a 75% dropout rate during a 24-week exercise program with HIV patients. This dropout rate is significantly higher than the 50% typically reported at 6 months in healthy adult populations (Dishman, 1994).

Body composition is also a factor. Overweight and obese men and women are less likely to participate in physical activity than are normal-weight individuals (Brownell, Stunkard, & Albaum, 1980). Despite the common belief that obese children and adolescents are less active than lean youth, data from numerous studies are inconclusive at this point (Vara & Agras, 1989). There is some evidence, however, that parental obesity is negatively related to children's physical activity (Klesges, Eck, Hanson, Haddock, & Klesges, 1990).

Injury

Injury rates are estimated to be as high as 50% per year for individuals who regularly engage in high-intensity physical activities such as running (Pollock

& Wilmore, 1990). Sallis, Hovell, Hofstetter, Elder, Faucher et al. (1990) asked adults to recall how many times they had stopped exercising for three months or more during adulthood. They found that approximately 20% of both exercisers and nonexercisers reported three or more relapses. The most common reason for the most recent relapse was injury, reported by 40% of current exercisers and 22% of current nonexercisers. The authors concluded that because exercisers are more likely to report injuries, it appears that injuries do not cause many people to drop out of exercise completely.

PSYCHOLOGICAL CORRELATES OF PHYSICAL ACTIVITY

In an extensive literature review, Sallis and Owen (1999) identified several psychological factors associated with involvement in physical activity. The psychological factors that are positively associated with physical activity include enjoyment of the activity, expectation of positive benefits, intention to exercise, perceived fitness or health, self-efficacy, self-motivation, self-schemata for exercise, and extra-version. The psychological factors reported to be negatively associated with physical activity include perceived barriers to exercise and mood disturbances. The psychological factors reported to be unrelated to involvement in physical activity include knowledge of health and exercise, and perceived susceptibility to illness. In the following sections, we expand upon some of these areas.

Barriers

Researchers have continually reported a negative relationship between an individual's perception that there are barriers (impediments) to participation and that individual's actual involvement in physical activity (Sallis et al., 1992). The major barriers that people report when they are trying to increase their physical activity are (a) lack of time, (b) lack of access to convenient facilities, and (c) lack of safe environments in which to be active (USDHHS, 2000). Researchers suggested that lack of time is an *excuse*

rather than a barrier. That is, people find the time during the day to do the things that they really want to do, and if they wanted to exercise they would find the time to do so. For example, studies in the United States and Canada have found that adolescents watch more than 20 hours of television per week (Pate, Long, & Heath, 1994), and that younger children watch even more (USDHHS, 2000).

Self-Efficacy

Self-efficacy is the confidence to execute a course of action (see Chapter 12 for a comprehensive discussion of self-efficacy and its relationship to involvement in physical activity). Albert Bandura (1997) stated that self-efficacy is the most powerful determinant of behavior. Bandura's statement is strongly supported because the majority of studies that have examined self-efficacy have found it to be the strongest determinant of physical activity (Sallis et al., 1992; Sallis & Owen, 1999). For example, Trost et al. (1997) found a strong positive relationship between self-efficacy in overcoming barriers in fifth grade children and their actual physical activity behavior one year later. Interestingly, the authors found gender differences in self-efficacy. For girls, self-efficacy to exercise despite tiredness and homework obligations was the most important predictor of physical activity. For boys, on the other hand, self-efficacy to exercise despite bad weather conditions was most strongly related to physical activity.

Attitudes and Intention

Researchers have continually found that intention is the primary determinant of exercise when it is under personal control (Hausenblas, Carron, & Mack, 1997; see Chapter 14 for a comprehensive discussion of intention and its relationship to involvement in physical activity). That is, if a person has a strong intent to engage in physical activity, he or she is likely to be active. Also, people's intentions to exercise are positively influenced by their attitudes. That is, those individuals who have a positive attitude toward exercise are more likely to have a strong intention to exercise and, thus, are more likely to engage in the behavior. For example, Courneya, Friedenreich, Arthur, and Bobick (1999) found that intention to exercise before becoming ill in postsurgical colorectal cancer patients was a positive determinant of postsurgical exercise. The researchers also found that attitude was a positive determinant of the cancer patients' intention to exercise.

Enjoyment

People tend to do things that they enjoy. Not surprising, then, is the finding that people who enjoy physical activity are more likely to be active. When Sallis, Prochaska, Taylor, Hill, and Geraci (1999) examined 22 potential determinants of physical activity in 1,504 children in grades 4 to 12, they found that enjoyment of physical education was one of the strongest.

Body Image

Body image is an umbrella term that represents self-attitudes toward one's body with an emphasis on physical appearance (Cash & Pruzinsky, 1990). In their review of the literature, Sallis and Owen (1999) found a small negative relationship between body image disturbance and exercise adherence. That is, people with poor body image were less likely to adhere to an exercise program. A recent meta-analysis by Hausenblas and Fallon (2001) confirms that body image disturbance is associated with less physical activity.

In their research, Treasure, Lox, and Lawton (1998) examined whether social physique anxiety, an affective form of body image, could predict adherence to a 12-week walking program in 31 obese females. **Social physique anxiety** represents a fear of negative evaluation of the physique in social situations (Hart et al., 1989). Treasure and his colleagues found that younger participants with high social physique anxiety were more likely to drop out of the walking program than were older participants with high social physique anxiety. The researchers suggested that social physique anxiety's negative effects on adherence might be lessened if young obese females were encouraged to exercise initially in a private setting or in classes designed specifically for obese individuals.

Stages of Change

It is assumed that individuals vary along a continuum in terms of their stage of behavior change (Prochaska & DiClemente, 1984; Reed, Velicer, Prochaska, Rossi, & Marcus, 1997). This assumption forms the basis for the transtheoretical model of behavior change (see Chapter 15 for a detailed discussion of the transtheoretical model and its relation to physical activity involvement). The continuum for stages of change is precontemplation (not intending to make changes), contemplation (intending to make changes), preparation (making small changes), action (actively engaging in the new behavior), and maintenance (sustaining change over time). Researchers have hypothesized that as individuals change from an unhealthy to a healthy behavior they will move through these stages at varying rates and in a cyclical fashion with periods of progression and relapse (Prochaska & DiClemente; Reed et al.).

Researchers have usually found that physical activity behavior increases across the stages of change (e.g., Hausenblas, Dannecker, Connaughton, &

---

social physique anxiety   Social anxiety that arises as a result of concerns about the self-presentation of the body.

Lovins, 1999). That is, precontemplators and contemplators report the least amount of activity, and maintainers report the most activity. For example, Cardinal (1997) classified 235 adults by their stage of change and then had the participants complete a bicycle submaximal aerobic fitness test and a self-report measure of exercise behavior. He also determined the participants' body mass index. Cardinal found a linear improvement in body mass index, submaximal aerobic fitness, and self-reported involvement in exercise across the various stages. That is, participants in the precontemplation stage were the least aerobically fit, had the highest body mass index scores, and were the least involved in exercise, whereas participants in the maintenance stage were the most aerobically fit, had the lowest body mass index scores, and were the most involved in exercise.

Knowledge of Physical Activity

Several studies have shown that knowledge of the health effects of physical activity is not correlated with activity level, even though the health belief model would predict such a relationship (Janz & Becker, 1984; see Chapter 13 for a detailed description of the health belief model and its relation to involvement in physical activity). That is, most people know that exercise is good for their health, but many people are not regularly active. The lack of a relationship between knowledge and involvement indicates that other factors are more important in the control of physical activity habits and that interventions intended solely to increase knowledge would not be effective (Sallis & Owen, 1999).

Personality Traits

There are five major dimensions, or traits, of personality: neuroticism, extraversion, openness, conscientiousness, and agreeableness (Costa & McCrae, 1992). The tendency to experience negative affects such as fear, sadness, anger, and guilt are the core features of a neurotic person (Costa & McCrae). Extraverts are, of course, sociable, assertive, and talkative. The elements of openness include imagination, aesthetic sensitivity, and intellectual curiosity. The

agreeable person is altruistic, sympathetic to others, and eager to help. Finally, the conscientious individual is purposeful, strong-willed, and determined. Researchers have found that neuroticism is negatively related, whereas extraversion and conscientiousness are positively related, to exercise behavior and adherence (Courneya & Hellsten, 1998; Young & Hemsley, 1997). These findings are consistent with the fact that individuals seek situations that are congruent with their personalities. The excitement and sensory stimulation sought by extraverts leads them to activities such as sport and exercise, whereas neurotics will tend to avoid such situations. Highly conscientious individuals are determined, persistent, and systematic in carrying out tasks, qualities that are important in exercise and physical activity.

CHARACTERISTICS OF THE PHYSICAL ACTIVITY

Physical activity can vary in its intensity and duration. Researchers have been interested in the question of whether these two characteristics will influence adherence behavior.

Intensity and Perceived Effort

Intensity of exercise and perceived effort are negatively related to physical activity (Sallis & Owen, 1999). That is, the higher the perceived effort and intensity of the physical activity, the less likely people are to adhere. For example, Sallis and his colleagues (1986) found that not only are adults more likely to *adopt* moderate-level activities compared to high-intensity activities, but they are also more likely to *maintain* their involvement in moderate-level activities. Sallis et al. found that the dropout rate for participating in moderate activities was approximately 30%—considerably less than the 50% rate generally cited for vigorous physical activity dropouts (Dishman, 1994).

Duration

Does exercising in multiple (shorter) bouts of exercise result in increased adherence compared to exercising in one longer bout? Jakicic, Wing, Butler, and Robertson (1995) examined this question in 56 overweight sedentary female adults who were randomly assigned to either a short- or a long-bout exercise program. Duration of the exercise was set at 20 minutes per day for weeks 1 to 4, 30 minutes per day for weeks 5 to 8, and 40 minutes per day for weeks 9 to 20. The long-bout group performed the specified duration of exercise in one continuous bout (e.g., 1 session for 30 minutes per day), whereas the short-bout group performed the specified duration of exercise in multiples of 10 minutes. Jakicic et al. found that adherence was influenced by activity duration—participants in the short-bout group exercised for more days and for a longer duration compared to participants in the long-bout group. This finding also coincides with the current American College of Sports Medicine (ACSM)/Centers for Disease Control (CDC) guidelines that physical activity can be accumulated in 10-minute increments during the day to reach the daily goal of 30 minutes of moderate to strenuous physical activity.

BEHAVIORAL CORRELATES OF PHYSICAL ACTIVITY

Descriptive research has shown that a number of behaviors are related to involvement in physical activity. These behaviors include smoking, diet, and previous history of being active.

Smoking and Diet

Contrary to popular opinion, the negative relationship between cigarette smoking and physical activity level appears to be relatively modest. Some studies show no association, whereas others show a weak relationship (King et al., 1994). Although cigarette smoking has been associated with higher dropout rates from vigorous leisure time physical activity programs (Blair, Jacobs, & Powell, 1985), smoking status may not be associated with overall physical activity level (Dishman, Sallis, & Orenstein, 1985). Researchers have also found that good dietary habits are positively correlated with physical activity levels (Sallis & Owens, 1999).

Physical Activity History

An important issue in assessing influences on physical activity is to establish whether physically active children become physically active adults. The phenomenon of children maintaining their relative ranking on a variable over time is called **tracking** (Taylor, Baranowski, & Sallis, 1994). Tracking requires longitudinal observation with assessments taken for at least two different points in time (e.g., assessing physical activity at age 6 and then again at age 12). Most studies that track physical activity are based on correlations (Malina, 2001). In general, researchers have found moderate tracking of physical activity from childhood to adolescence, lower levels of tracking from adolescence to young adulthood, and relatively weak tracking from childhood and adolescence to older adulthood (Janz, Dawson, & Mahoney, 2000; Malina, 2001; Taylor, Blair, Cummings, Wun, & Malina, 1999).

For example, in a prospective study, Pate and his colleagues (1996) used heart rate monitors to track physical activity in 47 young children (average age, 3.5 years) over a three-year period. The authors found that the level of physical activity was relatively constant throughout the study. Thus, physical activity behavior tends to track during early childhood, and less active children tend to remain less active than the majority of their peers.

In a retrospective study, Dennison, Straus, Mellits, and Charney (1988) compared self-reported

---

tracking The phenomenon of children maintaining their relative ranking on a variable over time.

physical activity levels of 453 young men (23 to 25 years of age) with their physical fitness scores as children. The researchers found that the group of physically active adults had significantly better childhood fitness test scores than did the group of inactive adults. Also, parental encouragement for exercise, level of education, participation in organized sports after high school, and spousal encouragement of physical activity were all positive predictors of adult physical activity. The authors concluded that physical fitness testing in boys facilitates the identification of those at increased risk of becoming sedentary adults.

Summary

Unfortunately most adults are not physically active on a regular basis. Furthermore, only a small percentage of those individuals who are active do so at an intensity sufficient to receive the health-related benefits associated with physical activity. The low adherence rate to physical activity has prompted researchers to study the factors associated with sticking with this behavior. Individual factors associated with physical activity can be categorized into demographic, biological, psychological, behavioral, and physical activity correlates. The biological and demographic correlates of physical activity—such as age, gender, ethnicity—are not modifiable. That is, people cannot change their age, gender, or ethnicity. These correlates, however, can identify groups at risk for being inactive. In comparison, modifiable correlates of physical activity include self-efficacy, perceived barriers, and enjoyment. Researchers can use these individual correlates of physical activity to design interventions based on a theoretical framework in an attempt to increase people's levels of exercise (see Chapters 12 through 17 for theoretical frameworks that have been applied to physical activity behavior).

SECTION THREE

The Environment and Physical Activity

A long-standing dictum in psychology is that behavior is a product of the individual and the situation (environment). Thus, it follows directly from this dictum that researchers need to gain an understanding of the physical environment if they hope to understand individual involvement in physical activity. In the three chapters of Section 3, we explore various aspects of the physical activity environment. Often, physical activity is carried out in class settings. Therefore, in Chapter 9, we present some of the main factors influencing individual involvement in groups—the cohesiveness of the class, its leadership, and its size. In Chapter 10, we discuss the role that support from others has in both motivating people to be more physically active and helping them sustain that activity. Finally, in the last chapter in this section, we discuss the environmental correlates of (i.e., factors associated with) involvement in physical activity.

CHAPTER 9

Physical Activity Groups

Those Who Are Enjoying Something, or Suffering Something, Together, Are Companions.

(C. S. Lewis)

CHAPTER OBJECTIVES

After completing this chapter you will be able to

- Outline the importance of group dynamics to physical activity promotion.

- Differentiate among the four dimensions of group cohesion.

- Describe the relationships between group cohesion, class attendance, and individual level cognition.

- Describe the relationships between class leadership, class attendance, and individual level cognition.

- Describe the relationships between class size, class attendance, and individual level cognition.

Key terms

Group Environment
  Questionnaire (GEQ)
group cohesion
instructor efficacy

Physical Activity Group
  Environment
  Questionnaire (PAGEQ)

The dynamics of group behavior has long been of interest to the scholar and layperson alike. *Group dynamics,* a term coined by Lewin (1948), can be defined as the positive and negative forces within a group of people (Dion, 2000). More specifically, it refers to both the study of groups *and* the energy, vitality, and activity characteristic of all groups (Carron & Hausenblas, 1998).

The importance of group dynamics to physical activity promotion resides in its ability to identify (a) the forces that bind members to their groups, (b) the critical parameters of leadership, and (c) the impact of group structure (Forsyth, 2000). By applying this information to physical activity programs, it is hypothesized that effective and sustained physical activity participation can be attained. Within the domain of physical activity, a number of group dynamics variables have been related to sustained behavior (Carron, Hausenblas, & Estabrooks, 1999). In this chapter, three of those topics are examined: class cohesion, exercise class leadership, and exercise class size.

CLASS COHESION: FORCES THAT BIND MEMBERS TO THEIR GROUPS

When examining the forces that bind individuals together, a logical starting point is the cohesive nature of the physical activity group. Physical activity groups, like other action-based groups (e.g., sport, work, or military groups), become bound together based on the task and social components of the environment (Widmeyer, Carron, & Brawley, 1993). This bond is referred to as **group cohesion** and is defined as "a dynamic process that is reflected in the tendency for a group to stick together and remain united in pursuit of its instrumental objectives and/or for the satisfaction of member affective needs" (Carron et al., 1998).

A Conceptual Perspective of Group Cohesion

A number of studies have attempted to determine if perceptions of group cohesiveness are related to adherence in physical activity programs. The majority of that research has been based on a conceptual model (and inventory) for group cohesion developed by Carron, Widmeyer, and Brawley (1985). In the multidimensional model, which is illustrated in Figure 9-1, cohesion is assumed to be composed of four distinct dimensions distinguished on two levels. The first level is the individual basis versus group basis for cohesion. For example, an individual has personal attractions to the group as well as perceptions regarding the collectivity of the group. Simply said, the individual basis for cohesion is exemplified by "I" and

> **group cohesion** A dynamic property of groups that is manifested by the tendency for members to stick together and remain united as they work toward collectives goals and/or for social purposes.

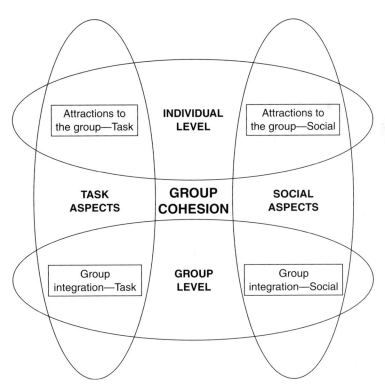

Figure 9-1 A conceptual model for class cohesion.
Note. Adapted from "The Development of an Instrument to Assess Cohesion in Sports Teams: The Group Environment Questionnaire," by A. V. Carron, W. N. Widmeyer, and L. R. Brawley, 1985, *Journal of Sport Psychology, 7,* 244–266.

"me" statements (e.g., "I like the exercises I do in this class"), whereas the group basis for cohesion is exemplified by "we" and "us" statements (e.g., "We all like the exercises we do in this class").

The second level of group cohesion is based on a distinction between the task aspects and social aspects of group involvement. That is, both individuals and groups have social outcomes (activities related to the development and maintenance of social relations) and task outcomes (activities related to accomplishing a task, to productivity, and to performance). A typical social outcome of physical activity classes could be the development of friendships. A typical task outcome could be the increased attraction to the exercises done in class.

Based on these two levels of distinction (i.e., individual versus group and social versus task), four dimensions of group cohesion were conceptualized: Individual Attractions to the Group—Task, Individual Attractions to the Group—Social, Group Integration—Task, and Group Integration—Social (Carron et al., 1985). It is hypothesized that individuals can feel personally attracted to the specific physical activity offered in the class (Individual Attractions to the Group—Task) and to the people who attend the class (Individual Attractions to the Group—Social). Individuals may also perceive that the physical activity

group as a whole interacts with one another to get the best work out (Group Integration—Task) or to socialize (Group Integration—Social).

The Measurement of Cohesion in Physical Activity Classes

Perceptions of cohesion are generally assessed using the **Group Environment Questionnaire (GEQ).** Carron et al. (1985) originally developed the inventory for use with sport teams; however, minor changes were made in the wording of the various items in the GEQ and the inventory was then used to assess cohesiveness in exercise classes (Carron, Widmeyer, & Brawley, 1988). Some sample items from the four scales are presented in Table 9-1. The GEQ was validated and tested on a number of young adult samples and has been shown to be reliable. The measure has also shown good content and concurrent and predictive validity (Carron et al., 1998).

The earliest research on the relationship of cohesion to involvement in physical activity programs was undertaken with university-aged samples of partici-

> **Group Environment Questionnaire (GEQ)**   Inventory used to assess cohesiveness.

■ **TABLE 9-1**   Sample Items from the Group Environment Questionnaire (GEQ) and the Physical Activity Group Environment Questionnaire (PAGEQ)

SCALE	SAMPLE ITEM FROM THE GEQ	SAMPLE ITEM FROM THE PAGEQ
Individual Attractions to the Group—Task	I am unhappy with the group's level of commitment to exercise.	I like the amount of physical activity I get in this program.
Individual Attractions to the Group—Social	Some of my best friends are in this exercise group.	I enjoy my social interactions within this physical activity group.
Group Integration—Task	We all take responsibility if one of our exercise classes goes poorly.	Members of our group are satisfied with the intensity of physical activity in this program.
Group Integration—Social	Members of our exercise class rarely socialize together.	We spend time socializing with each other before or after our activity sessions.

Note. From Carron et al., 1985; and from Estabrooks and Carron (2000). The Physical Activity Group Environment Questionnaire: An instrument for the assessment of cohesion in exercise classes. *Group Dynamics: Theory, Research, Practice, 4,* 230–243.

pants. More recently, however, Estabrooks and Carron (e.g., 1999a, 1999b) undertook a series of studies with older adults (i.e., more than 65 years of age). In that research, Estabrooks and Carron encountered three persistent problems that drew into question the utility of the GEQ for use in an older population. First, there were problems with the psychometric properties of the test. In some samples, for example, the internal consistency values for specific scales were marginal (i.e., under .70); (Estabrooks & Carron, 1999a). For other samples (Estabrooks & Carron), the entire data set was unusable because the internal consistency values on all scales were less than .60. A second and possibly related point is that many older participants expressed dissatisfaction, confusion, and/or uncertainty when they completed the negatively worded items on the GEQ (see Table 9-1 for some examples). Some participants found the negative items difficult to evaluate; others expressed uneasiness about considering their group in a negative light. Finally, some participants questioned the applicability (face validity) of the items that required them to evaluate the degree to which the group was united around its collective goals (e.g., see the Group Integration—Task item from the GEQ presented in Table 9-1).

As a result of these three considerations, the **Physical Activity Group Environment Questionnaire (PAGEQ)** was developed specifically for use in older adult samples (Estabrooks & Carron, 2000). Sample items are also illustrated in Table 9-1. Early research utilizing the PAGEQ has found the measure to be internally consistent and to have sound predictive, concurrent, content, and factorial validity (Estabrooks & Carron).

Cohesion and Adherence Behavior

Carron et al. (1988) were the first to examine the effect of cohesion on adherence and withdrawal from exercise groups. Participants were fitness class adher-

> **Physical Activity Group Environment Questionnaire (PAGEQ)** Inventory developed specifically for use in older adult samples to measure cohesiveness in physical activity classes.

ers and nonadherers. Adherers were individuals who were still involved in a physical activity program, whereas nonadherers were people who had voluntarily stopped attending physical activity classes. The GEQ modified for exercise classes was administered to determine a perception of the cohesion constructs (Carron et al., 1998). In comparison to the exercise nonadherers, the exercise adherers had stronger perceptions of Individual Attractions to the Group—Task and Individual Attractions to the Group—Social.

Spink and Carron (1992) then examined the relationship between group cohesion and nonadherence (operationally defined as absenteeism and lateness) in females participating in exercise classes. Four weeks of attendance and punctuality data were collected during Weeks 8 to 12 of a 13-week program. The GEQ was administered in Week 13. Two cohesion dimensions, Individual Attractions to the Group—Task and Individual Attractions to the Group—Social, were negatively associated with absenteeism. The researchers also found that Individual Attractions to the Group—Task accounted for the greatest difference between those participants who were never late and those who were late four or more times.

Although these results were considered promising, each of the studies was retrospective in nature, leaving the reader unsure as to the direction of the relationship between group cohesion and exercise adherence. For this reason, Spink and Carron (1994) conducted two prospective studies to examine the predictive ability of group cohesion on exercise adherence. The purpose of Study 1 was to determine if perceptions of group cohesion assessed relatively early in an exercise program would predict subsequent participant adherence or nonadherence. The female participants attended exercise classes that were offered 1 hour per day for 3 days each week at a major university. Cohesion was assessed in Week 3 of a 13-week program. Adherence was operationalized as attendance during the final 4 weeks of the program. The results showed that dropouts from the 13-week program had possessed lower perceptions of cohesion (manifested as Individual Attractions to the Group—Task) in Week 3 than the adherers had.

Spink and Carron (1994) then replicated Study 1 within a private fitness facility rather than in a university setting. The participants again completed the GEQ during the 3rd week of a 13-week program and attendance again was monitored for the final 4 weeks of the program. The results showed that dropouts from the 13-week program had possessed lower perceptions of cohesion (manifested as Individual Attractions to the Group—Social and Group Integration—Social) in Week 3 than the adherers had.

Blanchard, Poon, Rodgers, and Pinel (2000) recently examined whether a modified GEQ would be related to adherence. The participants were volunteers involved in exercise classes offered by the recreation department at a local university. There were 35 female and 8 male participants with a mean age of 36.58 years. Attendance was self-reported by the participants over the last 6 weeks of classes. The GEQ was administered at the end of the 3rd week and the beginning of the 7th week. In this study none of the four subscales of cohesion were related to exercise attendance. There was also no change in the participants' perceptions of cohesion from Week 3 to Week 7. The authors suggest that these results were obtained because the participants in the study were generally adherent.

In the research that we have discussed so far, the exercise participants were exclusively in the age range of university-age students to young adults (i.e., < 35 years). More recently, researchers have examined the role that cohesiveness might play in the exercise involvement of older adults (Estabrooks & Carron, 1999a; Estabrooks & Carron, 1999a, 1999b; Estabrooks & Carron, 2000). Several good reasons exist for determining the cohesion–exercise involvement relationship in older adults.

First, aging has a deleterious effect on body composition, the cardiovascular system, the respiratory system, visceral functions, and the nervous system (Shephard, 1997). However, regular physical activity is positively associated with physical and psychological maintenance and improvements for older adults (e.g., Dustman, Emmerson, & Shearer, 1994; Green & Crouse, 1995; Mihalko & McAuley, 1996). Despite the benefits of exercise, participation

Regular physical activity is positively associated with physical and psychological maintenance and improvements for older adults.
©PhotoDisc/Volume 58/Mature Lifestyles 2

in a physically active lifestyle declines with age (Fitness and Lifestyle Research Institute, 1996).

A second, related constellation of reasons pertains to the fact that researchers need to gain an understanding of the role that other factors, including the existence of a cohesive group, might play in the exercise programs of older adults. A finding that older adult exercisers benefit from high group cohesion offers important implications for program planning.

Estabrooks and Carron (1999a) conducted two studies to examine the relationship between class cohesion and exercise adherence in older adult exercisers. In Study 1, older adults in 14 exercise classes completed the GEQ during the first month of a new exercise term. Attendance at the program was then documented for 1, 6, and 12 months of the program. The results showed that three measures of cohesion, Individual Attractions to the Group—Social, Group Integration—Social, and Group Integration—Task, were all significantly related to exercise class attendance following a 1-month interval. Group Integration—Task was significantly related to class attendance following a 6- and 12-month interval. Estabrooks and Carron concluded that previous cohesion research in exercise classes could be extended to classes for older adults. They also concluded that the dimensions of group cohesion seem to have differential impacts on adherence based on short- and long-term attendance.

In Study 2, Estabrooks and Carron (1999a) examined the effectiveness of a team-building intervention designed to enhance class cohesion (and, ultimately, exercise adherence and return rates following a summer vacation period). Participants were assigned to a team-building, placebo, or control condition. Study 2 showed that participants in the team-building condition attended more classes than did the control and placebo conditions, and they had a higher return rate following a 10-week hiatus than did the control condition.

Given the consistent findings of these studies and others, the positive relationship between group cohesion and exercise adherence exists (Estabrooks, 2000). It is true that this relationship between cohesion and attendance has not been universally observed (e.g., Blanchard et al., 2000). However, the Blanchard et al. study excluded dropouts from the analysis. Previous studies have shown that the dimensions of cohesion have been successful in discriminating adherers from dropouts (Spink & Carron, 1994). By excluding dropouts from their study, Blanchard and his associates probably reduced their chances of finding a relationship.

Cohesion and Cognitions About Physical Activity

In several domains, groups have been shown to have an impact on the members' cognition and self-conceptions (Hogg & Williams, 2000). In Chapters 12 through 17, we highlight a number of salient cognitions. These cognitions include variables like attitude, self-efficacy, and intentions to be physically active. Within the domain of physical activity, research has also demonstrated that the presence of perceptions of cohesiveness is also positively associated with a number of important cognitions. For example, Brawley, Carron, and Widmeyer (1988) found that perceptions of Group Integration—Task significantly discriminated between participants with high and those with low perceptions of the class' ability to withstand the negative impact of disruptive events.

There is also research that provides initial evidence of the interrelatedness of group cohesion and perceptions about the types of interactions that occur among exercise class members. Hill and Estabrooks (2000) studied the relationship between the cohesive nature of the physical activity groups of older adults and the degree to which feelings of cooperation, communication, and competition were present. Their findings revealed that competition (defined as "wanting to be the healthiest person in the class") had a strong positive relationship with the measures of Individual Attractions to the Group—Task and Group Integration—Task, whereas communication had the strongest positive relationship with the measure of Individual Attractions to the Group—Social, and finally, all three group-interaction variables were positively related to the measure of Group Integration—Social. Hill and Estabrooks concluded that when program planners are developing intervention strategies for older adult exercise classes, special care should be taken to foster an atmosphere that provides opportunity for friendly competition and open lines of communication.

The relationship of cohesion within a broader framework of individual determinants of adherence behavior has also been studied. For example, Estabrooks and Carron (1999b) examined the relationship between individual perceptions of control and the dimensions of Individual Attractions to the Group—Task and Social. In this study, cohesion and perceptions of control, in the form of perceived behavioral control (see Chapter 14), were assessed during the first week of a physical activity program for older adults. The results of the study showed that only the measure Individual Attractions to the Group—Task was positively related to perceived control.

Estabrooks and Carron (2000) followed with a second study on cohesion and perceptions of control to answer two questions. First, can group cohesion predict perceptions of control in a prospective manner? Second, could the dimension Group Integration—Task add to the prediction of control beliefs? To answer these questions, Estabrooks and Carron assessed both task components of group cohesion during the first week of physical activity classes after a holiday break. Subsequently, at the midpoint of the program, perceptions of control were assessed (in the form of self-efficacy to schedule physical activity classes into one's regular routine; see Chapter 12). The results showed that both measures, Individual Attractions to the Group—Task and Group Integration—Task, were positive predictive of perceptions of control.

Two primary conclusions can be made from these studies. First, task cohesion does have a consistent relationship with individual control. Second, by fostering both individual attractions and integration to the group's task, program developers could provide opportunities for improved perceptions of control for program participants.

Cohesion and Affect About Physical Activity

An important implication of varying perceptions of cohesion is that "changes in one's belongingness status will produce emotional responses, with positive affect linked to increases in belongingness and negative affect linked to decreases in it" (Baumeister & Leary, 1995, p. 505). However, by 1995, researchers had yet to examine the hypothesized influence of exercise class cohesion on affect. As a result Courneya (1995a) conducted a study to examine the relationship between cohesion in structured exercise classes and affect during exercise. Courneya hypothesized that higher perceptions of cohesion would be positively related to affect during exercise classes. Volunteers from aerobic exercise classes completed an assessment of cohesion within the first 3 weeks of each program. The feeling scale, a measure to determine general affect (on a scale that ranges from "very bad" to "very good") was then used to assess the affect of participants over the final 8 weeks of the program. The results supported Courneya's hypothesis with the exception of the measure of Group Integration—Social, which was not related to affect. Courneya concluded that members of more cohesive exercise classes report more positive affect during exercise.

Two studies have provided additional support to Baumeister and Leary's (1995) conclusion that belongingness or cohesion is related to affective variables. First, Courneya and McAuley (1995a) examined the relationship of group cohesion to individual attitudes toward physical activity participation. Cohesion and attitude were assessed 4 weeks into a physical activity program offered through a university fitness facility. The researchers found that each dimension was positively related to attitude; however, the largest relationship was associated with the measure of Individual Attractions to the Group—Task. In a similar study, Estabrooks and Carron (1999b) examined the relationship between the measures of Individual Attractions to the Group—Task and Social and attitude toward physical activity class participation using a sample of older adults. Results showed that both Individual Attractions to the Group components were positively related to attitude, except in this case the measure Individual Attractions to the Group—Social had the strongest relationship. Although cohesion has a consistent positive relationship with affect and attitude, different dimensions of cohesion may be salient within different samples of participants.

LEADERSHIP

Researchers and program planners also have been interested in the role that exercise leaders play in participants' attitudes toward and adherence in physical activity programs. The conclusions from early research seem unequivocal. For example, Oldridge (1977) concluded that the exercise leader is "the pivot on which the success or failure of a program will depend" (p. 86). When Franklin (1988) compiled a list of more than 30 variables that influence dropout behavior from physical activity programs, he identified the exercise leader as "the single most important variable affecting exercise compliance" (p. 238). In contrast, however, a recent meta-analysis by Carron et al. (1996) on social influences in exercise adherence showed only a small positive effect for the influence that exercise leaders have on adherence behavior.

Qualities of Physical Activity Leaders

Considerable anecdotal testimony exists about the qualities that good exercise class leaders should possess. Peterson (1993), for example, identified

24 qualities that can be reduced to three general categories—behavioral, communicative, and motivational. Peterson suggested that program class leaders should have the ability to instruct with the proper technical execution, stay focused, and be energetic (behavioral); class leaders should possess the ability to express themselves clearly and listen to class members (communicative); and class leaders should have the ability to motivate both the participants and themselves, be decisive, and use group processes (motivational). Note, however, that these qualities are simply suggestions; no empirical evidence was provided to validate their respective relationships with adherence.

McAuley and Jacobson (1991) examined the relationship between member adherence and instructor influence with formerly sedentary females. Following an 8-week exercise program, participants were asked how they felt the instructor had influenced their adherence to the program. McAuley and Jacobson concluded that participant perceptions of leader influence did have a small positive association with in-class adherence. In a similar study, Gyurcsik, Culos, Bray, and DuCharme (1998) examined the relationship between elements of leadership and the adherence of regular exercisers. After assessing participants' confidence in their activity leader's abilities (a measure referred to as **instructor efficacy**), the researchers monitored attendance for 12 weeks. A small but significant positive relationship was found between instructor efficacy and attendance.

Physical Activity Leaders and Adherence

Recently, L. D. Fox, Rejeski, and Gauvin (2000) investigated the impact of leadership style and group dynamics on intention to return to a structured fitness class. Each participant completed a single program session under four conditions in which both leadership style (i.e., an enriched versus a bland leadership style) and group environment (i.e., an en-

---

> **instructor efficacy**   A measure of participants' confidence in their activity leader's abilities.

riched versus a bland class environment) were systematically varied. Table 9-2 provides an overview of the approach taken in each instance. The enriched group environment was manipulated with the use of trained confederates. At the end of the session, the participants completed assessments of intention to return to a similar class and enjoyment of the previous session. Interestingly, a positive effect was found for the interaction between the leader style and group environment for enjoyment of the aerobics session. That is, the participants enjoyed the class more when the environment offered both enriched leadership and group dynamics. It was also found that a positive relationship existed between the group environment and intention. So, those participants in the enriched group environments intended to return to a similar exercise session regardless of the style of the leader.

At the beginning of this section on leadership, we quoted Oldridge (1977) and Franklin (1988), who both stated that the physical activity class leader may be the most important adherence-related variable. However, research has not supported this hypothesis. A number of possible explanations exist for the seemingly contradictory perspectives. First, the comments by Oldridge and Franklin were broad statements of impact with little empirical data behind them. Second, most physical activity leadership research compares the standard care (i.e., a regular instructor) to a special treatment. Consequently, it may be that the small effect of exercise leaders on adherence is not the product of a comparison of good versus poor leadership but rather of good versus superior leadership. Unfortunately, this second explanation is not adequate; that is, other group interventions have compared standard (or good) care to superior group environments and have shown large effects (e.g., Estabrooks & Carron, 1999a). Third, it is possible that the research evidence obtained to date is 100% valid—that the relationship between a leader and the adherence of group members is small.

Do these findings mean that leadership is not an important correlate of physical activity adherence? Not necessarily. It is possible that different or inadequate criteria (measurement, manipulations) were

■ **TABLE 9-2**   Bland Versus Enriched Leadership Style and Group Environment

Leadership Style		Group Environment	
SOCIALLY ENRICHED	**BLAND**	**SOCIALLY ENRICHED**	**BLAND**
Use participants' names	Do not use participants' names	Introduce themselves to others as soon as they arrive in class	Do not introduce themselves to others at any time in class
Engage participants in general conversation before, during, and after class	Do not engage in general conversation before, during, or after class	Initiate casual interactions with other members early in each session	Do not initiate or promote casual interactions with other members at any time in the class
Provide specific reinforcement for positive behaviors	No reinforcement or praise for positive behaviors	Be compliant with the instructor's wishes	Be compliant but not enthusiastic
Give encouragement before and after a skill or mistake	Fail to follow up with praise after a skill or mistake	Provide encouragement to the group as a whole	No encouragement to others or the instructor
Focus on positive comments during instruction	Focus on negative comments during instruction	Respond to all questions the leader directs to the group	Do not respond to questions the leader directs to the group
Specific instructions	Vague instructions		
Verbal reward of effort and ability immediately after the exercise; ignore mistakes	Verbally note mistakes; do not reward effort and ability after the exercise	Make positive and encouraging remarks to the instructor about the class in general	No remarks to the instructor even if she or he directed instructions or corrections toward an individual

Note. From "Effects of Leadership Style and Group Dynamics on Enjoyment of Physical Activity," by L. D. Fox, W. J. Rejeski, and L. Gauvin, 2000, *American Journal of Health Promotion, 14,* 277–283.

used to represent leadership in the physical activity domain. Within general leadership theory, research has "been regarded as a fractured and confusing set of contradictory findings and assertions without coherence or interpretability" (Chemers, 2000). The literature to date in the exercise domain is clearly (or unclearly) in the same state. For example, the focus of literature on leadership within the physical activity domain has examined how one should lead (Oldridge, 1977; Gillett et al., 1993), the influence of the leader (McAuley & Jacobson, 1991), the impact of different leadership styles (L. D. Fox et al., 2000), and participants' confidence in their leaders (Gyurcsik et al., 1998).

Physical Activity Leaders and Member Cognitions and Affect

Just as group cohesion is related to other cognitive and affective factors in addition to adherence in the physical activity domain, so too is class leadership. Turner, Rejeski, and Brawley (1997) examined the influence of leadership behavior on participants' self-efficacy and the exercise-induced feeling states of revitalization, positive engagement, tranquility, and physical exhaustion. College women were assigned to classes structured to be either socially enriched or socially bland in terms of interactions from the program leader. The participants in the socially enriched

The socially enriched leadership style has a greater impact on self-efficacy beliefs.
©PhotoDisc/Volume 67/Fitness and Well-Being

classes reported more enhanced mood states from involvement in the exercise than did those in the bland classes. Further, the socially enriched leadership style had a greater impact on participants self-efficacy beliefs than the socially bland leadership style.

PHYSICAL ACTIVITY CLASS SIZE

Issues associated with group size have long intrigued group dynamics researchers. Across a wide variety of settings—the military, business, education—group size has a substantial impact on psychological and social variables (Carron, 1990). Researchers also have been interested in the impact of class size on involvement in physical activity.

Class Size and Adherence

The seminal physical activity setting–class size research was conducted a decade ago by Carron, Brawley, and Widmeyer (1990). In a study focusing on adherence behavior, the researchers examined archival data from 47 university physical activity classes ranging in size from 5 to 46 members. A quartile split was used to separate the classes into four categories: small classes (from 5 to 17 members), medium classes (from 18 to 26 members), moderately large classes (from 27 to 31 members), and large classes (from 32 to 46 members). Carron and his associates found that the small and large classes had the highest retention rates (i.e., fewest dropouts) and superior attendance (i.e., percentage of classes attended by adherers).

Based on the findings of Carron et al. (1990), Remers, Widmeyer, Williams, and Myers (1995) undertook a study to further explore the nature of the relationship between group size and adherence behavior. In particular, the purpose of the Remers et al. study was to determine if the Carron et al. findings could be replicated and what variables might moderate or mediate the group size–adherence relationship. In the Remers et al. study, adherence was operationalized in two ways—as attendance and perceived exertion. Further, only medium classes (18 to 26 members) and large classes (70 to 90 members) were examined. The results, consistent with Carron et al., showed that participants in large classes attended more classes than did those in medium-sized classes. Remers et al. also found that participants in large classes reported higher rates of perceived exertion. Although it was not clear why participants in larger classes perceived themselves to be exercising harder than those in smaller classes, it may be that large or full classes are generally the most popular and are taught by a facility's best instructor.

Class Size and Cognitions

Research outside the physical activity sciences shows that increasing group size generally has negative effects on group member perceptions (Carron

& Hausenblas, 1998). Certainly, increasing group size does mean that more resources are available to carry out group-related responsibilities. Also, increasing group size does increase a participant's chances of meeting other attractive and interesting people. Beyond these two potentially positive outcomes, however, members generally see little positive benefit to increased group size. What about physical activity classes? Is the issue of group size relevant to participant perceptions?

Carron and his associates (1990) examined intact physical activity classes (with four size categories) and assessed the relationship between group size and member perceptions of their leader, crowding, opportunities for interaction, density, and satisfaction with the group. The researchers found, first, that as physical activity classes became larger, participant perceptions of the instructor decreased in a linear fashion. Second, the data indicated that participants in small and moderate-sized classes perceived more opportunity for social interaction than did those in large classes. Third, participant satisfaction decreased in a linear fashion from small to large classes.

The relationships between class size and perceptions of cohesion have also been examined (Carron & Spink, 1995). In a series of studies, group cohesion was assessed at different times during ongoing small and large physical activity classes. The researchers determined that the group integration components of cohesion could effectively distinguish members of small and large groups in that participants in large groups held lower perceptions. Interestingly, this relationship was only present when group cohesion was assessed late in the program (the 8th week of a 13-week program). However, when cohesion was assessed earlier in the program, only individual attractions to the group could discriminate members. In sum, the studies showed that members of small exercise groups held stronger perceptions of cohesion than did members of large groups.

Finally, Remers and her associates (1995) presented a number of interesting findings based on the perceptions of participants in medium- and large-sized classes. The researchers found that participants in the larger classes felt that the classes were associated with more positive perceptions of the exercise environment. These perceptions included feelings of crowding, noise, leader motivation, leader availability, and attractiveness of classmates. Larger classes were also more satisfied with the exercise music and held higher perceptions in the measure of Group Integration—Social.

Summary

The importance of group dynamics to physical activity promotion resides in its ability to identify the forces that bind members to their groups, the critical parameters of leadership, and the impact of group structure (Forsyth, 2000). As such, this chapter reviewed the topics of exercise class cohesion, leadership, and size.

Class cohesion can be described as multidimensional in terms of individual attractions and group integration. A distinction is also made between task and social activities of a group. Research support has been provided for the positive impact of the various dimensions of group cohesion on adherence to physical activity programs for both young and older adults. Further, higher perceptions of cohesion have been shown to relate to more positive perceptions of personal attitudes, affective states, and confidence. Finally, group interactions such as cooperation, friendly competition, and communication have been identified as important for the development of class cohesion.

Like class cohesion, exercise class leadership is also multifaceted. The focus on leadership in research within the physical activity domain has been on how one should lead (Oldridge, 1977; Gillett et al., 1993); the influence of the leader (McAuley et al., 1991); the impact of different leadership styles (L. D. Fox et al., 2000); and participants' confidence in their leaders (Gyurcsik et al., 1998). However, the research examining the impact of leadership on adherence has been equivocal. It is clear that enriched leadership styles are related to participant enjoyment and positive affect.

Finally, research examining exercise class size has consistently shown that large and small classes have better retention and adherence rates than do medium-sized classes. However, the mechanisms of the adherence-size relationship are not well understood. The research by Carron and his associates (1990) showed that as physical activity classes became larger, participant perceptions of the instructor, opportunity for social interaction, group cohesion, and satisfaction decreased. In contrast, Remers and her associates (1995) found that participants in the larger classes felt that the classes were associated with more positive perceptions of the exercise environment.

CHAPTER 10

Social Support and Physical Activity

Cherish Your Human Connections, Your Relationships with Friends and Family.
(Barbara Bush)

CHAPTER OBJECTIVES

After completing this chapter you will be able to

- Differentiate among the various manifestations of social support.

- Understand how social support has traditionally been assessed.

- Explain how the presence of social support influences thoughts about physical activity.

- Explain how the presence of social support influences involvement in physical activity.

Key terms

attachment
enacted support
guidance
nurturance
perceived support
reassurance of worth
received support
reliable alliance

social integration
social support
subjective norm
support appraisal
support behavior
support networks
supportive climates

Supporting others appears to be "wired in." Argyle (1992) has pointed out that the complex social relationships that develop among humans—in families, among friends, and in professional (work) situations—have a biological basis. Among animals, helping and cooperation are associated with the degree of genetic resemblance present. However, even among animals of the same species that do not share the same genetic pool, evidence exists for what is referred to as reciprocal altruism. Along this same vein, Baumeister and Leary (1995) also observed that the need to belong—the desire for interpersonal attachments in humans—is fundamental. Social relationships influence people's thoughts, emotions, and behavior. Moreover, the absence of supportive social relationships can have a detrimental impact on physical and psychological health. Barbara Bush was correct in her advice to cherish human connections; people need the social support that results.

Interestingly, the term *social support* is relatively new in the social sciences. In fact, Veiel and Baumann (1992) observed that "two decades ago, social support was rarely used in a research context. The seminal paper by Nuckolls, Cassel, and Kaplan (1972), for example, did not use the term at all" (p. 2). In short, the study of the nature, antecedents, and consequences of social support represents an emerging field of study. In this new field of social support, like in any emerging field of study, researchers and theoreticians have advanced a variety of perspectives. The result is almost universal consensus that social support is important for health and well-being, but there is also considerable discrepancy in the understanding of what social support actually is and how it should be defined and measured. In this chapter, we discuss the nature of social support, and we outline findings from research that have examined the impact of social support on physical activity.

THE NATURE OF SOCIAL SUPPORT

Social support is a complex phenomenon. One measure of that complexity is the number of perspectives adopted in attempts to define it. In one general perspective, the role of *information* is emphasized. Cobb (1976), for example, defined social support as information that leads the individual to feel cared for; feel loved, esteemed and valued; and feel a sense of belonging to a reciprocal network. Another, similar perspective emphasizes the role of *emotion*. Thus, for example, Cassel (1976) proposed that social support reflects the gratification of an individual's basic needs. In yet another perspective, social support is viewed as a *process*. As an example of this perspective, Vaux (1992) suggested that social support is a dynamic process that involves transactions between individuals within a specific social context. Finally, yet another perspective draws on the idea of *networks* of support. From this perspective the individual is seen as the focus of networks (collections) of people—networks that can vary in structure (e.g., size, number of links), nature of the linkages (e.g., frequency, intensity of interactions), and function or functions provided (e.g., instrumental, emotional support; Isreal, 1982). Perhaps the complexity of social support was best summed up by Vaux (1988), who stated that social support represents a wide cross section of concepts including "belonging, bonding, and binding; attributes of groups, relationships, and persons; and processes that are social, behavioral, and affective in nature" (p. 33).

Taxonomies for Social Support and Social Networks

A second manifestation of the complexity of social support is the variety of terms used interchangeably. In an attempt to distinguish among social support–related concepts, Laireiter and Baumann (1992) proposed a taxonomy. One of the components, **social integration** (also known as social embedment), represents the degree to which the individual participates and is involved in family life, the social life of the community, churches, and so on and has access to resources and support systems. Social integration is similar to social networks. To what extent does the individual have regular contact with friends? neighbors? family?

A second component, **support networks** (also known as network resources), represents the individual's social network from a functional perspective. Who does the individual turn to for assistance? for emotional support? Who are the individual's potential supporters? Who are the individual's actual supporters? The people that an individual routinely turns to for support represent his or her network resources. As the term implies, support networks represent the pool of support resources available to the individual.

Supportive climates (or supportive environments, as the concept is also called) represent the

---

social support   An umbrella term used to represent a wide variety of (a) concepts such as belonging, bonding, and binding; (b) attributes that characterize groups, relationships, and/or people, and, (c) interpersonal processes that are social, behavioral, and/or affective in nature.

social integration   The degree to which the individual participates in family life, the social life of the community, church, and so on and has access to resources and support systems; also known as social embedment; network support.

support networks   The individual's social network from a functional perspective; also known as network resources.

supportive climates   The quality of social relationships and systems; also known as supportive environments.

quality of social relationships and systems. Is the family unit cohesive? To what extent is there frequent conflict in the family? As might be expected, cohesive families, work groups, and friendship groups are perceived by the individual to be more supportive.

Two aspects of the social support exchange, **received support** and **enacted support,** make up the fourth component of the taxonomy. When social support is viewed as a process, there are two individuals involved. One, the provider of social support, represents enacted support; the other individual in the exchange, the recipient, represents received support.

Another component, **perceived support,** represents the individual's cognitive appraisal. Support received is not synonymous with support perceived. An individual might receive advice, encouragement, financial assistance, and so on from a large network of people that includes family, close friends, fellow workers, and even health and business professionals. Yet that same individual could perceive that he or she is socially isolated or has been abandoned insofar as access to support is concerned. Thus, social support cannot simply be determined by counting the amount of contacts between a focal person and his or her social network.

According to Laireiter and Baumann (1992), the complex phenomena in their taxonomy are related to one another in a hierarchical manner. As Figure 10-1 shows, social integration represents the broadest, most fundamental category. Without social integration, there could be no support networks, supportive climates, enacted and received support, and/or perceived support. In turn, support networks are a necessary precondition of supportive climate, or received and enacted support, or perceived sup-

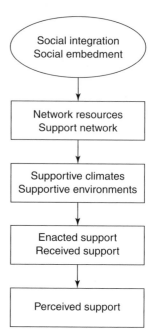

Figure 10-1   The nature of social support.

port. The hierarchy continues until, finally, received and enacted support serve as preconditions for perceived support.

Negative Aspects of Social Support

A third reflection of the complexity of social support is the fact that, recently, various authors (e.g., Chogahara, O'Brien Cousins, & Wankel, 1998; Rook, 1992; Vaux, 1992) have cautioned against the implicit assumption that social support is always positive. For example, Chogahara and his colleagues noted that there have been numerous negative social influences identified through research in other fields, such as health psychology. The labels attached to those negative social influences include, for example, social hindrance, social rejection, social inhibition, unsupportive behaviors, unhelpful behaviors, negative social ties, social strain, negative social interactions, perceived barriers, environmental barriers, leisure constraints, social disproval, and stereo-

---

received support   Support received by the recipient in a social support exchange.

enacted support   Support offered by the provider in a social support exchange.

perceived support   The individual's cognitive appraisal of his or her social network.

types. None of these influences constitute positive social support; all can have an impact on behavior.

According to Chogahara et al. (1998), negative social support occurs less frequently than positive social support does but likely will have a greater influence on health outcomes. Negative social support also has a stronger immediate impact, and it retains its influence over a longer duration. Thus, a supportive statement to parents and grandparents, such as "you can do it," could positively influence physical activity involvement. However, the negative impact of statements such as "act your age" and "you're too old to ride a bike" would likely carry more weight initially and persist as an influence on activity behavior over a longer period of time.

Social Support As a Personality Trait

A final reflection of complexity lies in the fact that although social support is by its very definition a *social* construct, there is also evidence that it is also an *individual* construct. In their research, the Sarasons and their colleagues (B. R. Sarason, Pierce, & Sarason, 1990; B. R. Sarason et al., 1991; I. G. Sarason, Levine, Basham, & Sarason, 1983; I. G. Sarason, Sarason, & Pierce, 1992) observed that perceptions of the availability of social support represent a stable personality trait. People possess an enduring disposition to see themselves as being supported by others. Some people, of course, may see themselves as the chronic recipients of considerable support from others (even in the presence of evidence to the contrary). Conversely, some people may have the tendency to see themselves as receiving minimal or no support from others (again, even in the presence of evidence to the contrary). The Sarasons and their associates have reported that the tendency to perceive oneself as being supported is positively related to both self-concept and self-esteem (I. G. Sarason et al.).

THE MEASUREMENT OF SOCIAL SUPPORT

Given the complex nature of social support, it is hardly surprising that a number of approaches have been taken in its measurement. Generally, these different approaches have reflected differences in the specific research question asked. Who gives the person social support? What type or types of social support does an individual receive? What is the quantity and quality of that social support?

The measurement of social support has taken three general approaches (see Table 10-1). One approach is concerned with determining an individual's *social network resources* (e.g., Vaux, 1992). Throughout the school year, for example, a student might have the need for financial assistance, practical assistance (e.g., for a ride to school or work), emotional support (e.g., for love, affection), advice or guidance (e.g., in course selection), and positive social interactions (e.g., someone to go to coffee with). Measures of social network resources determine who that student would or could go to for support. There could be more than one person in any one or all of the categories, of course. When social support is assessed through measures of social network resources, the focus is on size and density. The index or measure could be in the form of global estimates (e.g., how many people in total are available to provide support) or domain-specific estimates (e.g., how many people are available to provide financial assistance).

A second approach to measurement of social support is concerned with determining an individual's **support appraisal** (e.g., Russell & Cutrona, 1984). In this approach, the focus is on satisfaction, sufficiency, or helpfulness of the support. The student in our previous example might have a number

■ **TABLE 10-1** Typical Approaches in the Measurement of Social Support

APPROACH	CONCEPT	EXAMPLES OF POSSIBLE MEASURES
Social network resources	Significant others available to provide support	Size of the network Density of the network
Support appraisal	Satisfaction, sufficiency, or helpfulness of support in important domains	Attachment (emotional support) Social integration (network support) Opportunity for nurturance (self-worth from assisting others) Reassurance of worth (esteem support) Reliable alliance (tangible aid) Guidance (information support)
Support behavior	Frequency of occurrence or likelihood of behavior	Financial assistance Practical assistance Emotional support Advice or guidance Positive social interactions

Note. Adapted from "Assessment of Social Support," by A. Vaux, 1992, in H. O. F. Veiel and U. Baumann, Eds., *The Meaning and Measurement of Social Support* (pp. 193–216), New York: Hemisphere Publishing.

of individuals available for positive social interactions (e.g., to go for coffee). However, the student's support appraisal, that is, the student's satisfaction with his or her positive social interactions, could be moderate or low. The student could say, "I have support but it's just not very good."

Support appraisal has been examined frequently insofar as its relationship to issues such as self-efficacy for physical activity in older participants (e.g., Duncan, Duncan, & McAuley 1993). Generally, the appraisal of social support has centered on six important social needs identified by R. S. Weiss (1974): **attachment,** which reflects emotional support; **social integration,** which reflects network support; **opportunity for nurturance,** which reflects increased self-worth from assisting others; **reassurance of worth,** which reflects esteem support; sense of **reliable alliance,** which reflects tangible aid; and **obtaining of guidance,** which reflects information support. The relationship of these various forms of social support to physical activity is discussed throughout the rest of this chapter.

A third, somewhat related approach is concerned with determining **support behavior** (e.g.,

Barrera, Sandler, & Ramsay, 1981). In this approach, the focus is on frequency of occurrence or the likelihood that others will provide the behavior. Although the student in our example might have a large number of individuals to go for coffee with, he

support appraisal The satisfaction expressed with positive social interactions.

attachment Emotional support.

social integration The degree to which the individual participates in family life, the social life of the community, church, and so on and has access to resources and support systems; also known as social embedment; network support.

nurturance Increased self-worth from assisting others.

reassurance of worth Esteem support.

reliable alliance Tangible aid.

guidance Information support.

support behavior Frequency of occurrence or the likelihood that others will provide the behavior.

or she might rate the frequency of social interactions to be minimal over a 1-month period.

The three approaches are similar in that they are designed to assess some manifestation of social support. However, they have subtle differences as well. Thus, the specific approach taken would depend on the question being asked. Is the health professional or researcher interested in whether the person has a large number of people available for social support? If so, social network resources would be assessed. Is the health professional or researcher interested in whether the person's social support is frequent or infrequent? If so, support behavior would be assessed. Finally, is the interest in whether the social support available to the person is more or less satisfying? If so, support appraisal would be assessed.

SOCIAL SUPPORT AND COGNITIONS RELATING TO PHYSICAL ACTIVITY

The degree to which people sense that they receive the support of others will influence the development of cognitions associated with involvement in exercise and physical activity.

Intention to Be Physically Active

A considerable number of research studies using the theories of reasoned action and planned behavior (see Chapter 14) as a framework have examined the relationship between intention to be physically active and the behavior itself. When Hausenblas et al. (1997) carried out a meta-analysis on the results of that research, they found a large effect size, 1.09, between intention and behavior. (See Chapter 3 for a full discussion on the meaning and interpretation of effect sizes.) In short, when people express an intention to be physically active, that intention is usually translated into behavior.

Carron, Hausenblas, and Mack (1996) also statistically summarized through the use of meta-analysis available research on the relationship between social support and intention to be physically

■ **TABLE 10-2**   Meta-Analysis Results of the Influence of Social Support on Cognitions About Physical Activity

NATURE OF THE SOCIAL SUPPORT	COGNITIVE VARIABLE INFLUENCED	EFFECT SIZE
Support from family	Intention to be physically active	.49
Support from important others	Intention to be physically active	.44
Support from family	Efficacy for physical activity	.40
Support from family	Affect associated with physical activity	.59
Support from important others	Affect associated with physical activity	.63

Note. Effect sizes of .20, .50, and .80 are considered to be small, medium, and large, respectively. Adapted from "Social Influence and Exercise: A Meta-Analysis," by A. V. Carron, H. A. Hausenblas, and D. A. Mack, 1996, *Journal of Sport and Exercise Psychology, 18,* 1–16.

active. Table 10-2 provides a summary of their results. Social support from family members has a moderate effect (ES = .49) on an individual's intention to engage in physical activity. In addition, important others—physicians and work colleagues, for example—also have a moderate effect on intention (ES = .44), although their influence is slightly lower than that of the family. So, social support has an important role to play in terms of its impact on a person's intentions to be physically active.

Perceptions of Exercise Class Cohesiveness

Courneya and McAuley (1995b) observed that the overwhelming majority of theoretical models advanced to account for physical activity behavior "hypothesize various social constructs to be important determinants of behavior (e.g., interpersonal behavior, personal investment, planned behavior)" (p. 325). Thus, one question Courneya and McAuley addressed in their research pertained to the degree of relationship between two of those social constructs—social support and cohesion. Social support was measured using the Weiss (1974) conceptual model in which five important support needs are taken in consideration: attachment, nurturance, reassurance of worth, guidance, and social integration.

Group cohesion, an integral component of group dynamics theory (see Chapter 9), is "a dynamic process that is reflected in the tendency for a group to stick together and remain united in the pursuit of its instrumental objectives and/or for the satisfaction of member affective needs" (Carron et al., 1998, p. 213). From a conceptual and a measurement perspective, group cohesion is considered to be a multidimensional construct composed of perceptions about how the group meets individual needs, and it is integrated from both a task and a social perspective.

Exercisers in classes through a university recreation department that met for minimum of 12 weeks were tested at three time points in their program. Courneya and McAuley (1995a) found that the various measures of cohesion were related to the various measures of social support, with average correlations being .20, .27, and .30 at Times 1, 2, and 3, respectively. Courneya and McAuley emphasized that while cohesion and social support are related, they are sufficiently distinct to warrant consideration as independent forms of social influence.

In their research with older adults (i.e., < 65 years), Estabrooks and Carron (1997) also found that cohesion was related to social support. However, task cohesion (i.e., Individual Attractions to the Group—Task; see Chapter 9 for a definition and discussion) was found to be related to reliable alliance and guidance—the task manifestations of social support. On the other hand, social cohesion (i.e., Individual Attractions to the Group—Social) was found to be related to reassurance of worth and attachment—the affective manifestations of social support.

Subjective Norm

A second question explored by Courneya and McAuley (1995a) in their research pertained to the degree of relationship between social support and subjective norm. The two constructs are sometimes approached as if they were synonymous, but as the definitions for each one shows, they are different. **Subjective norm,** an integral component of the theories of reasoned action and planned behavior (see Chapter 14), is "the perceived social pressure to perform or not to perform the behavior" (Ajzen, 1991, p. 188). Social support is the existence of information that leads individuals to possess a feeling of being cared for; the belief that they are loved, esteemed, and valued; and a sense of belonging to a reciprocal network (Cobb, 1976).

Courneya and McAuley (1995a) found average correlations of .06, .20, and .30 over the three time periods that they tested. These correlations are similar, albeit somewhat lower, than the ones they found between social support and cohesion. Again, Courneya and McAuley concluded that although a relationship is present, social support and subjective norm should be considered distinct constructs.

Self-Efficacy

Does social support increase an individual's self-efficacy for physical activity? Available research evidence points to the fact that it does. That research also shows, however, that not all of the six fundamental social provisions identified by R. S. Weiss (1974) are equally important in every context.

Duncan, McAuley, Stoolmiller, and Duncan (1993) asked male and female exercisers 45 years to 64 years to indicate their efficacy to overcome barriers to exercise as well as the social support they received from instructors and other participants in the class. Barriers efficacy was related only to reassurance of worth (e.g., I have relationships in the class

subjective norm   The social pressures people feel to carry out a specific behavior.

where my competence and skill are recognized). No relationships were found between efficacy to overcome barriers and guidance (e.g., there is someone in the class that I could talk to about important decisions), reliable alliance (e.g., there are people in the class that I can depend on to help me if I need it), nurturance (e.g., there are people in the class who depend on me to help them), social integration (e.g., within my class I feel a part of a group of people who share my attitudes and beliefs), and attachment (e.g., I have relationships in the class that provide me with a sense of emotional security and well-being).

Attitude

Another issue that has interested researchers is the relationship of social support to attitudes and feelings about physical activity. Through the use of meta-analysis, Carron et al. (1996) summarized the research that was available. Because of the relatively small number of studies focusing on attitudes and feelings, Carron and his associates combined the research on attitudes and feelings into a single category, which they called affect. As Table 10-2 shows, social support from family members has a moderate effect on affect associated with physical activity.

Interestingly, as Table 10-2 also shows, social support from important others (e.g., work colleagues) has an even more important role to play than does family in terms of the positive affect participants develop around physical activity. The reason for this finding is uncertain. Possibly it is related to the informational and motivational aspects of social reinforcement. Social reinforcement from people who are not intimates can be more motivating because it is generally less frequent and more selective, and therefore it provides more information to the recipient.

SOCIAL SUPPORT AND PHYSICAL ACTIVITY BEHAVIOR

Table 10-3 provides an overview of the results of the meta-analysis by Carron et al. (1996) that examined the relationship between social support from a vari-

■ TABLE 10-3 Meta-Analysis Results of the Influence of Social Support and Subjective Norm on Physical Activity Behavior

NATURE OF THE SOCIAL SUPPORT	NATURE OF THE BEHAVIOR	EFFECT SIZE
Support from family[a]	Adherence behavior	.36
Support from family[b]	Compliance behavior	.69
Support from important others[a]	Adherence behavior	.44
Subjective norm[b]	Adherence behavior	.18

Note. Effect sizes of .20, .50, and .80 are considered to be small, medium, and large, respectively.
[a]From Carron et al. (1996).
[b]From Hausenblas et al. (1997).

ety of sources and adherence to physical activity regimes. The effect of social support on adherence is in the small to moderate range. Nonetheless, social support is important.

As Table 10-3 also shows, adherence behavior is more strongly influenced by social support from important others than from family members. Again, the reason for this finding is unknown. Possibly social support from important others is more motivating because it provides more information.

The difference between adherence and compliance is the difference between maintaining involvement in a self-selected program (i.e., adherence) versus maintaining involvement in a prescribed program (i.e., compliance). Physical activity is often prescribed by physicians and health care professionals for a variety of reasons, such as to treat obesity, to facilitate recovery after surgery for coronary heart disease, and so on. Social support from family plays an important role in compliance behavior (see Table 10-3).

As was pointed out above, subjective norm is sometimes confused with social support. The essential difference between the two concepts is one of encouragement (social support) versus pressure (subjective norm). As Table 10-3 shows, the encouragement afforded through social support has more effect on adherence behavior than does the pressure applied through subjective norms.

Research reported by Duncan and his colleagues (Duncan & McAuley, 1993; Duncan & Stoolmiller, 1993) offers insight into how social support might play a role in involvement in physical activity. These researchers found that both barriers efficacy and exercise efficacy served as mediators between social support and physical activity. That is, social support contributes directly to efficacy, which in turn contributes directly to physical activity behavior.

TWO FINAL CONSIDERATIONS: SICKNESS AND DEATH

In the beginning of this chapter, we pointed out that the absence of supportive social relationships could have a detrimental impact on physical and psychological health. In fact, there is some evidence to support the conclusion that social support is linked to sickness and even death. Although issues surrounding social support and general health are not directly pertinent to the focus of this book, it is useful to examine how social support might be related to health in general. In a series of meta-analyses over a 3-year period, Schwartzer and Leppin (Leppin & Schwartzer, 1990; Schwartzer & Leppin, 1989, 1992) attempted to summarize research bearing on this issue.

Mortality

One avenue pursued by Schwartzer and Leppin (1989) was to examine the relationship between social integration (or social embedment; see Figure 10-1) and mortality. Social integration represents the degree to which an individual is involved in family life and/or the social life of the community and has access to resources and support systems. Research has taken one of two approaches: large-scale epidemiological studies where the role of social integration is examined (e.g., do married people live longer than single or divorced people?); and life event studies where the impact of a breakdown in social

FIT FACTS

Can family physicians help their sedentary patients become active?

Yes. Verbal advice on exercise from a family physician followed by a pamphlet on exercise mailed to the patient's home within 2 days of his or her doctor visit can help reduce inactivity.

(Bull & Jamrozik, 1998)

networks is examined (e.g., does the death of a spouse contribute to premature death?).

In their meta-analysis, Schwartzer and Leppin (1989) found a correlation of $r = -.07$ between marital status and mortality. They pointed out that although

> this might seem a negligible correlation . . . if there were 100 persons with weak social embeddedness, 53.5% . . . [would] die [whereas] in another group of 100 persons with strong social embeddedness, only 46.5% would die during the same time range. This example may show that small correlations may well be of importance where matters of life and death exist. (p. 78)

Because social integration (e.g., marital status) is important for longevity, it might be expected that when a spouse dies, the loss will have a devastating effect on the health status of the survivor. But how devastating? Could premature death result? Schwartzer and Leppin (1989) provided evidence that it could. Individuals who lose a spouse have an increased risk of passing away, particularly within the first six months after the loss. Moreover, widowers are at greater risk than widows are.

Schwartzer and Leppin (1989) suggested two reasons for the gender differences. One is that men, on average, have smaller social networks than women do. The second is that widowhood occurs at an older age for men. Men are typically the older person in the relationship, and they die earlier. Thus, when their spouse dies, women are typically younger and possess a larger social network, whereas men are older and possess a smaller social network.

Morbidity

A second avenue pursued by Schwartzer and Leppin (1989) was to examine the relationship between social integration and morbidity. Again, the researchers found an overall relationship of r = −.07.

Individuals who are single or divorced are more likely to suffer health problems than are married people. Satisfaction with support also seems to be important. Schwartzer and Leppin reported a correlation of −.31 between satisfaction and morbidity.

Summary

The definition and measurement of social support is an ongoing source of discussion and debate in the health sciences. What seems to be generally accepted, however, is the belief that social support is essential for human well-being. It influences people's emotions, cognitions, and behavior. Thus, not surprisingly, it influences involvement in exercise and physical activity. Among the cognitions and emotions found to be positively associated with social support are intention to be physically active, perceptions of the degree of cohesiveness present in the exercise class, perceptions of normative pressures to be active (i.e., the subjective norm), self-efficacy, and attitudes toward physical activity. Moreover, social support is also positively associated with both adherence and compliance to activity programs. Finally, the probability of illness or premature death is increased in the absence of social support.

CHAPTER 11

Environmental Correlates of Physical Activity

The Physical Jerks Would Begin in Three Minutes . . . "Smith!" Screamed the Shrewish Voice from the Telescreen. "6079 Smith W! Yes You! Bend Lower, Please!"

(George Orwell)

CHAPTER OBJECTIVES

After completing this chapter you will be able to

- Outline the importance of the physical environment on physical activity participation.

- Describe the influence of the environment on travel patterns.

- Describe environmental prompts that increase physical activity.

- Differentiate between perceived and actual access to physical activity resources.

Key Terms

delayed gratification	perceived access
environment	actual access
environmental prompts	

George Orwell's (1949) classic novel *1984* describes a dark picture of a futuristic society in fear of the ever-present, watchful eye of Big Brother. Members of the party in *1984* were awakened with a whistle every morning at the same time. Three minutes after the sound of the whistle, a fitness instructor would appear on the telescreen. Party members did not think about having time for exercise; they did not consider if they had the confidence to complete the exercise; nor did they have intentions regarding the frequency, duration, intensity, or type of physical activity. They simply did it. Why? Because their **environment** was structured so that each day they would do The Physical Jerks. No questions, no options. And if they did attempt to miss the physical activity, they would be quickly chastised and brought back into behavioral conformity. In Big Brother's world, there were no adherence problems—100% prevalence, 100% maintenance.

Did Orwell find the answer to promoting the initiation and maintenance of physical activity? Maybe. Is it a plausible model for current society? Definitely not. However, some components of Big Brother's world are appealing (i.e., there are no motivational problems associated with being physically active). What is clear is that a person's environment can be related to behavioral outcomes. In the preceding chapters, we have focused on some social en-

---

environment An organism's surrounding conditions, influences, or forces.

vironmental variables that are related to behavior. In this chapter we focus on factors within the physical environment that may be related to improved or diminished levels of physical activity.

ENVIRONMENTAL INFLUENCES ON DELAYED GRATIFICATION

A functional starting point is with research by Mischel, Shoda, and Rodriguez (1989) regarding **delayed gratification** in children. In these studies, which used primarily laboratory research techniques, a researcher showed children toys, marshmallows, or candies, and the children were told that they could either have (play with) the treat immediately or have additional toys, candies, or more preferred alternatives if they would simply wait until the researcher returned to the room. The researcher would then leave the room and return 20 minutes later. As expected, the children, on average, were not very successful in delaying their gratification. That is, most would quickly play with the toys or eat the candies. Some children, however, could wait until the researcher returned.

Mischel et al. (1989) offered a number of potential explanations for why some children could wait and others couldn't. They hypothesized that some children simply have the skills necessary to wait for gratification. Potentially, these skills could be taught to other children, or the temptation of early consumption could be removed from children's environments. In subsequent studies, Mischel and his associates (1989) examined different strategies that could help children become more successful. First, the researchers suggested to some of the children that they think about fun thoughts while waiting for the researcher to return. The children were then assigned to one of two possible environments. In Condition 1, the children were asked to wait while the candy was in plain view on the table. In Condition 2, the children were asked to wait while the candy was on the table but under a cover. For Condition 1, children who had been taught to cope by thinking about fun thoughts were more successful than those who were not taught the coping strategy. However, for Condition 2, both groups of children were more successful in waiting for their reward.

How do these findings relate to physical activity participation? Dzewaltowski, Johnston, Estabrooks, and Johannes (2000) made the following comparisons. First, the benefits of physical activity participation are like waiting for a second candy; they are sometimes more distal than the acute benefits of sedentary behaviors. Second, like the wait for candy, physical activity often requires coping skills to complete. Take, for example, a young man who plans to exercise after work. Before he goes to the gym, he decides to stop at home. While at home, he turns on the television and finds an entertaining program, and in the end he does not exercise. If the television option were removed from the environment, then the young man would not have been tempted and would have followed through on his plans to exercise. So, when an environment is risky (i.e., there is a candy to be eaten or a television show to be watched), individuals need to have appropriate coping skills. But when the environment is supportive (i.e., no candy, accessible physical activity options), even those people without appropriate coping skills can be successful (Dzewaltowski et al). In short, it was the physical environment that changed the children's behavior regardless of the skills they possessed.

THE WESTERN ENVIRONMENT

Do the studies on delayed gratification in children generalize to physical activity? That is, if people have a physical environment that makes it easy to be active, will people be more active? The answers to these questions are a current hot topic in the psychology of physical activity. Research in the area of environments that promote physical activity is in a very exploratory stage. Rode and Shepard (1994, 1995a, 1995b) have published a number of manuscripts on the effect of changing environments on Inuit people

---

delayed gratification   Consciously avoiding or performing an action to receive a reward, enjoyment, or satisfaction at a later time.

living in Canada's Northwest Territories. The people in the sample were examined with surveys and tests that were administered every ten years from 1970 until 1990. During this time, the Inuit people were faced with a period of rapid acculturation to a sedentary lifestyle. Their hunter-gatherer lifestyle was quickly shifting to a more mechanized, western lifestyle. One measure that was used in the study was a skin-fold measure, which assesses the amount of subcutaneous body fat, a primary indicator of less physical activity. A higher number on the assessment is related to increased adiposity. Forty-year-old to 49-year-old Inuit people assessed in 1970 had a relatively low sum of skin folds (16mm for males, 21mm for females). Individuals in the same age category in 1990 had scores that quadrupled their predecessors (46mm for males, 82mm for females)! The researchers concluded that the Inuits' change in environment was responsible for their reduction of lifestyle physical activity.

ENVIRONMENTAL INFLUENCES ON TRAVEL PATTERNS

The relationship between physical activity and environment can be seen in the travel patterns of people from different industrialized countries. In the Netherlands, walking and bicycling account for a large proportion of the transportation patterns of its population. When the distance to be traveled is 1 kilometer or less, 32% and 60% of the trips are traveled by bicycle and walking, respectively. When the distance to be traveled is between 1 and 2.5 kilometers, 46% and 21% of the trips are traveled by bicycle and walking, respectively. Perhaps the most impressive statistic is that transportation by car accounted for only 44% of all trips within urban areas. In contrast, North American countries have very low bicycle and walking patterns within urban areas. Canadians use a bicycle for only 1%, walk for 10%, and travel by car for 74% of all trips (travel by public transportation accounts for the remainder). Similarly, Americans travel by car for 84% of all urban trips, bicycle for 1%, and walk for 9% (Pucher & Lefevre, 1996).

One factor that may account for the differences between these three populations is the physical environment of the roadways (Pucher & Lefevre, 1996). In the Netherlands, urban roads and paths are constructed to facilitate cycling and walking. Right of way and separate lanes are provided for cyclists. In North America, many urban communities are developed without sidewalks and clearly with car travel in mind (Pucher & Lefevre). Many North American homes have an attached garage so people don't even have to walk from the front doorway to the side of the road. Some researchers could argue that cultural norms are the primary influence on the travel patterns of populations in the Netherlands, United States, and Canada. Although cultural norms undoubtedly have some impact on travel patterns, studies in both the United States and Canada have shown that 46% and 70% of respondents, respectively, would cycle to work more often if safe bicycle lanes were provided (Pucher & Lefevre).

Once again, a supportive environment encourages physical activity. The environment in the Netherlands is free of connected garages and has easily accessible and well-developed mass transit roadways. The population there does not see the attractive, "speedy" option of physically inactive modes of travel. They do not need any coping skills to avoid using their cars for short trips.

ENVIRONMENTAL INFLUENCES ON PHYSICAL ACTIVITY

Changing travel patterns may be one approach to increasing the physical activity of a population. However, most research to date has focused on the relationship between a variety of other environmental influences and leisure-time physical activity. In 1985, Dishman and his associates provided a review of literature on the general determinants of physical activity. They categorized the determinants into personal characteristics and environmental influences. The weather, distance from facilities, and time pressures were all considered to be influences in the environment. Also in 1985, Iverson, Fielding, Crow, and Christenson reviewed research examining physical activity promotion in medical, work site, community, and school settings. They suggested that less active individuals would become more active if facilities were more accessible, of better quality, and cheaper. Further, community environmental changes—such as the building of bicycle paths, walking trails, basketball courts, and swimming pools—were proposed as a medium to increase physical activity participation.

A pattern of research emerges from a review of the literature examining the impact of environmental factors on physical activity participation. First, investigations have focused on *climate variations* and physical activity. Second, studies have examined **environmental prompts** to physical activity participation. Third, a number of studies have examined **perceived access** to physical activity resources. Fourth, studies have explored the **actual access** that a person has to resources for physical activity.

Climate Variations and Physical Activity

The climate is potentially one of the most influential environmental variables on physical activity participation. Very hot and humid weather or very cold weather may be related to reductions in physical activity participation. Research that has examined barriers to physical activity participation in both the young and the old has highlighted the inhibiting role of inclement weather (e.g., Pageot, 1987; Tappe, Duda, & Ehrnwald, 1989). Further, rain and snow can also reduce visibility and limit mobility, thus reducing physical activity (Patla & Shumway-Cook, 1999).

> **environmental prompts**   Surrounding conditions, influences, or forces, that influence and modify an organism's behavior, growth, and development.
>
> **perceived access**   An individual's belief in his or her right to make use of opportunities within the environment.
>
> **actual access**   The right to make use of opportunities within the environment.

When researchers design studies that focus on physical activity, they typically take great care to assess physical activity at a consistent time of the year across study groups or over time. For example, if an intervention study targeting increased physical activity completed the baseline measure in the middle of a cold winter and then completed the postassessment in the temperate weather of the spring, chances are good that the group would show increased physical activity. This practice highlights the recognition in the scientific community that physical activity varies based on climatic changes.

The climate is potentially one of the most influential environmental variables on physical activity participation.
©PhotoDisc/Volume 15/Family and Lifestyles

Interestingly, little research has examined physical activity across an entire year (Stephens & Caspersen, 1994). The research that has been completed points toward a relationship between weather and physical activity that is associated with seasonal changes in temperature. For example, in the temperate climate of Australia, only swimming varies with the seasons, and every other form of physical activity remains unchanged (Stephens & Caspersen, 1994). In contrast, data collected from Canada and Scotland show wide variations in physical activity across the seasons. For example, walking and cycling are highest in the months of June, July, and August and lowest during November, December, January, and February (Stephens & Caspersen, 1994).

Environmental Prompts to Physical Activity

Brownell et al. (1980) provided the seminal study on the potential impact of a person's environment on the promotion of physical activity. Their paper outlined the impact of a simple environmental manipulation intended to increase stair use at a shopping mall, a train station, and a bus terminal. In each setting, the stairs and escalator were side by side. Prior to the intervention, the research team documented the naturally occurring activity patterns of individuals confronted with the option of using a set of stairs or an escalator. To ensure that the recorded usage rates were reliable, each site was visited on two occasions and stair use was monitored at peak times (i.e., 11:00 a.m. to 1:00 p.m. at the mall, 7:30 a.m. to 9:30 a.m. at the train station, and, 3:30 p.m. to 5:30 p.m. at the bus terminal). In the initial observations, an average of only 5% to 6% of the people used the stairs.

The environmental manipulation consisted simply of the provision of a sign at the stairs/escalator choice point. The sign—which was 3 ft by 3.5 ft in size—depicted a lethargic heavy heart riding up the escalator and a healthy slim heart climbing the stairs (Figure 11-1). More than 21,000 observations were made during the baseline and intervention phases of the study. Following the intervention, the percentage

of people using the stairs increased to 13% to 16% (Brownell et al., 1980).

Interestingly, Brownell and his colleagues (1980) found that the impact of the intervention was significantly different for Caucasians and African Americans. Although there were no baseline differences between the groups, African Americans were less likely than Caucasians to use the stairs following the intervention. Further, although males and females differed in stair use at baseline (7% and 5% respectively), both increased at the same rate following the intervention (15% and 13% respectively). Perhaps the most important finding of the study was that the percentage of obese individuals who used the stairs (1.5%) quadrupled (6.7%) during the intervention phase.

In a second study, Brownell and his associates (1980) examined the lasting impact of their environmental intervention on stair use. To do so, they collected baseline data for a week to determine the typical frequency of stair use at a commuter train station. This time the sign was placed by the set of stairs and escalator for 2 weeks. Average stair use increased from 11% to more than 18% during the 2-week intervention period. The sign was then removed and follow-up assessments were conducted to examine how long the change would last. After 1 month without the sign, stair use had decreased to about 15%; 3 months later, stair usage had returned to baseline levels.

More recently, a study conducted in a subway in Glasgow, Scotland, used a similar design. The researchers placed a sign that read "Stay healthy, save time, use the stairs" in close proximity to a set of stairs that was adjacent to an escalator (Blamey, Mutrie, & Aitchison, 1995). Just as in the Brownell et al. (1980) studies, the stair use in this study nearly doubled for men (12% to 22%) and nearly tripled for women (5% to 14%).

In an attempt to determine if the Brownell et al. (1980) findings would generalize to a more traditional physical activity environment, Estabrooks, Courneya, and Nigg (1996) also used a simple prompt for attendance at a university fitness facility. Members of the facility were randomly assigned to a control, placebo, or experimental condition. Those in the experimental condition were provided with a complimentary key chain that was intended to prompt the participants to attend the facility. The key chain was plastic, 1 in. by 2 in., had a white background, and contained large red lettering that read "EXERCISE!" This prompt for exercise had no influence on participation rates. Through the use of various manipulation checks, the authors found that the participants did use the key chain, they did see it regularly, and it did make them think about exercising at the facility. Unfortunately, however, the prompt was not a strong

enough cue to initiate participation. The researchers concluded that a simple cue that was effective for changing lifestyle physical activity (a large sign by the stairs) was ineffective for changing complex behaviors associated with exercising at a specific facility.

Perceived Access to Physical Activity Resources

One category of environmental determinants repeatedly cited in discussions on the initiation and maintenance of physical activity is access to facilities. Access

Figure 11-1   The 3 ft by 3.5 ft sign used by Kelly Brownell and his associates to encourage stair use.
Note. Adapted from "Evaluation and Modification of Exercise Patterns in the Natural Environment," by K. D. Brownell, A. J. Stunkard, and J. M. Albaum, 1980, *American Journal of Psychiatry, 137,* 1540–1545.

can be examined in a number of different ways. Sallis, Johnson, Calfas, Caparosa, and Nichols (1997) suggested that access to physical activity resources could be examined by identifying various behavioral settings—homes, recreation centers, fitness clubs, parks, bicycle paths, and school grounds—and comparing the extent to which each of those settings is perceived to facilitate or hinder physical activity. In their research, participants' perceptions of their home and neighborhood physical activity settings were assessed.

A sample of undergraduate students rated their home and neighborhood environments. The participants rated their home environment by indicating the supplies or pieces of exercise equipment they had available. The neighborhood environment was rated on three distinct levels: first, the features of the neighborhood, such as sidewalks, hills, and enjoyable scenery; second, the perceived safety of the neighborhood; third, whether the neighborhood was residential, mixed residential and commercial, or mainly commercial. The participants also reported the convenience of 18 physical activity facilities and the proximity of those facilities to a frequently traveled route (i.e., on your way to or from university or work). Finally, physical activity was measured in terms of strength training, vigorous exercise, and the frequency and duration of walking.

The results indicated that the neighborhood environment was not related to any measure of physical activity, whereas convenience of facilities was mildly related to increased vigorous exercise. Interestingly, the home environment was positively associated with both vigorous exercise and strength training. Unfortunately, the presence of home equipment is also related to socioeconomic status. Hence, those participants in a lower socioeconomic climate are much less likely to have the means to acquire home equipment (Sallis et al., 1997).

More recently, Leslie and her associates (1999) in Australia have also examined the relationships be-

perceived access   An individual's belief in his or her right to make use of opportunities within the environment.

tween access to resources and physical activity behavior. In Australia, leisure-time physical inactivity rates for individuals between 20 years and 29 years of age are double the rates of individuals less than 20 years of age. Leslie and her colleagues suspected that this increase in physical inactivity might be due to the fact that older adults no longer have access to a school environment with the associated sports programs. To test this possibility, access to physical activity facilities was operationalized as the college undergraduate students' awareness of any on-campus facilities and possession of a gymnasium membership.

Of the 2,000 students who participated in the study, 40% were not sufficiently active as indicated by guidelines from either the American College of Sports Medicine or the Centers for Disease Control and Prevention. Leslie et al. (1999) replicated the findings that fewer participants over 20 years of age were sufficiently active (about 50%) than were those under 20 years of age (about 70%). Participants who were insufficiently active, irrespective of age, were also much less aware of potential resources and, not surprisingly, were much less likely to have a gymnasium membership. However, when other variables, such as enjoyment and social support, were included, awareness of resources was not significantly related to level of activity. The researchers concluded that students who choose to be physically active might also choose to do that activity in locations that are not necessarily related to the campus setting.

As is often the case in research, many of the initial studies examining access to physical activity resources have focused on undergraduate students or young adults. Potentially, older adults who possess greater needs for physical activity resources should be more dependent on the accessibility of those resources. In a recent study, Booth, Owen, Bauman, Clavisi, and Leslie (2000) examined the relationship between perceptions of the environment and physical activity in Australians aged 60 years and older. Personal interviews were conducted with 449 participants, and access to physical activity resources were determined by asking the older adults about the equipment they had within their home, the safety of walking in the neighborhood during the day, and access to the local exercise hall, recreation center, bicycle paths, swimming pool, and so on. Physical activity participation was assessed by a 2-week recall of vigorous and moderate leisure time activity.

A number of differences were found between the older adults who were sufficiently active and those who were not. Contrary to the study undertaken with undergraduate students (Sallis et al., 1997), access to home equipment did not differ between the two groups. Also, participants who were more active perceived that they had greater access to a local hall, recreation center, bicycle track, gymnasium, and parks. Further, more active individuals perceived footpaths to be safer. Booth and his associates (2000) found that access to a local park and footpath safety were the only environmental variables that predicted physical activity.

The relationship between perceived environments and physical activity participation is far from clear. Some research has shown that it is positively related, whereas other research has shown no relationship. The research does suggest that the relationship may be influenced by factors such as age. For younger adults, home access seems to be salient for participation, whereas for older adults, access to safe community parks and pathways may be more important.

Actual Access to Physical Activity Resources

Perceptions of one's environment and one's actual environment can be quite different. You may perceive a walking path to be quite safe; your friends may not. In many cases, personal perceptions are a stronger determinant of behavior than the actual environment is. However, a number of objective environmental criteria could potentially influence behavior. Cost is one. For minority women, for example, cost has been identified as one of the top

environmental barriers to physical activity (Eyler et al., 1998).

Estabrooks and Gyurcsik (2000) undertook a cost-related analysis to determine the availability of physical activity resources in relation to socioeconomic status within a small midwestern American city (population 123,000). First, the Internet, the telephone directory, and the city map were used to identify city resources for physical activity participation (e.g., schools, parks, fitness centers, dance studios, running paths). Second, a number of agencies (e.g., county and city parks and recreation, the metropolitan planning department, the city police department) were contacted to obtain global information system (GIS) data on physical activity resources and community characteristics. GIS is a system that provides accurate city demographic information on factors such as socioeconomic status, crime rates, and ethnicity.

Estabrooks and Gyurcsik (2000) identified high ($n = 4$ tracts; population 20,000) and low ($n = 6$ tracts; population 16,000) socioeconomic tract areas using a combination of poverty rate and average income. On average, the high socioeconomic tracts had seven resources for physical activity and the low socioeconomic tracts had five. Interestingly, in the high socioeconomic tracts, 25% of the resources were pay-for-use facilities. In contrast, 40% of the resources in the low socioeconomic tracts were pay-for-use facilities. Estabrooks and Gyurcsik concluded that the well-documented disparity in physical activity participation between low and high socioeconomic individuals might be related to access to free recreation facilities within close proximity.

Sallis, Hovell, Hofstetter, Elder, Hackley et al. (1990) also examined cost (i.e., free versus pay-for-use facilities) and density of facilities (i.e., the number of facilities in a given space) as two key barometers of access. The researchers contacted a random sample of 2,053 residents in San Diego, California, and the participants agreed to provide their addresses, which were matched with the addresses of local facilities. With this information, researchers were able to calculate the density of facilities around each participant.

actual access The right to make use of opportunities within the environment.

The results showed that the density of facilities around a participant's home was significantly related to physical activity habits. Sallis, Hovell, Hofstetter, Elder, Hackley et al. (1990) provided five factors related to their study that should increase the confidence in the validity of their results. First, regardless of the distance between home and facility, the density of facilities was consistently related to participation. Second, the density was assessed through an objective protocol that was independent of the assessment of physical activity. Therefore, participant biases had no impact on the rating of density. Third, age, education, and income level, all potential determinants of physical activity, were controlled for in the statistical analyses. Fourth, the results were consistent for people who exercised at facilities and for those who exercised elsewhere (i.e., at home, jogged on public streets). Fifth, the limitations of the study should hypothetically have biased the investigation against finding a relationship. For example, facilities like walking trails and bicycle paths were not measured. So there seems to be little doubt that access does influence participation.

Summary

In his book *1984* George Orwell (1949) described the fictional world of Big Brother, where behavior was simply a reaction to environmental cues and stimulants. More scientifically, Mischel and his associates (1989) showed that a person's environment has the potential to be related to behavioral outcomes. They concluded that when an environment is supportive, both individuals with and individuals without appropriate coping skills could be successful.

To examine the generalizability of Mischel et al.'s (1989) findings, Pucher and Lefevre (1996) contrasted the Netherlands, a nation with an environment that does not promote physically inactive travel modes (i.e., automobile travel) for urban trips, against Canada and the United States, nations with environments that do promote physically inactive travel modes. Clearly, the population within the Netherlands used physically active travel options with a much higher prevalence than did their North American counterparts.

As common sense may predict, climate changes are related to increased or decreased physical activity. Also, Brownell and associates' (1980) seminal study on the impact of a simple sign to promote the use of stairs rather than escalators provided good support for "point of choice" (i.e., stairs or escalator) environmental influences on physical activity. However, the translation of those findings to more distal physical activity participation within a fitness facility was not supported. Finally, individual perceptions of access and actual access to physical activity resources have an impact on physical activity. Because of the relative infancy of the field, a clear consensus on how best to change environments to promote activity is not available. Some research suggests that the relationship may be influenced by factors such as age. For example, home access may be salient for participation of younger adults, whereas it may be more important for older adults to have access to safe community parks and pathways.

SECTION FOUR

Models for Involvement in Physical Activity

A story is told about a group of blind people who set out to describe an elephant. Each person is directed to a different area of the body, and after spending some time palpating the elephant, each writes up a description. Each description is completely accurate in its own right but none is entirely complete. This story serves as a metaphor for the various explanations that have been advanced to account for why people do or do not embrace a physically active lifestyle. Each of the theories is accurate in its own right but none fully account for involvement in physical activity. The chapters in this section present those theories. Self-efficacy theory is discussed in Chapter 12, the health belief model and protection motivation theory in Chapter 13, the theories of reasoned action and planned behavior in Chapter 14, the transtheoretical model in Chapter 15, and two theories of motivation—self-determination theory and personal investment theory—in Chapter 16.

CHAPTER 12

Self-Efficacy for Physical Activity

Confidence Is a Plant of Slow Growth.

(William Pitt)

CHAPTER OBJECTIVES

After completing this chapter you will be able to

- Describe the main factors that serve to influence self-efficacy.

- Explain how self-efficacy can be measured.

- Outline the relationship between self-efficacy and physical activity behavior.

- Outline the relationship between self-efficacy and individual thoughts and emotions concerning physical activity.

Key terms

barriers efficacy	perceived behavioral
disease-specific efficacy	control
exercise efficacy	scheduling efficacy
generality of self-efficacy	self-efficacy
health behavior	strength of self-efficacy
efficacy	triadic reciprocal
imagery experience	causation
level of self-efficacy	verbal persuasion
mastery experience	vicarious experience
outcome expectation	vicarious learning

Self-efficacy "refers to beliefs in one's capabilities to organize and execute the courses of action required to produce given attainments" [emphasis removed] (Bandura, 1997, p. 3). As William Pitt noted, self-efficacy develops slowly. It is, however, the foundation for human behavior. Bandura (1997) noted that "unless people believe they can produce desired effects by their actions, they have little incentive to act. Efficacy belief, therefore, is a major basis for action" (pp. 2–3).

The claim is far from extravagant. Self-efficacy influences the course of action an individual chooses. Will you jog or cycle with friends or attend a box aerobics class? Or avoid all these activities? A belief that you have the capability to successfully carry out any or all of these activities will influence your decision. Also, the amount of effort you expend in these activities will be influenced by your efficacy belief. If you have a weak belief in your personal capability to keep up or perform successfully, you will more likely be tentative. Self-efficacy will influence the degree of perseverance you demonstrate when obstacles and adversities arise. It will also impact on whether your thought patterns hinder or facilitate your performance. Expectations of failure generally

self-efficacy The belief that one has the personal capability to carry out the actions required to produce a given outcome.

serve as a self-fulfilling prophecy. Similarly, individuals with low self-efficacy are more likely to feel anxious, stressed, or depressed if environmental demands become high. Finally, if your self-efficacy is low as a result of all these factors, your level of accomplishment will be detrimentally affected.

Given the important role that self-efficacy plays in human behavior generally, it's hardly surprising that numerous researchers have studied its specific role in physical activity. Researchers have examined whether self-efficacy is related to (a) the intention to become active, (b) the initiation of a more physically active lifestyle, (c) the maintenance of a more physically active lifestyle, (d) effort expended on physical activity, and (e) thought patterns about physical activity. We discuss the results from that research in this chapter after we introduce the nature, structure, and sources of self-efficacy.

SELF-EFFICACY IN SOCIAL COGNITIVE THEORY

Self-efficacy is an integral component of social cognitive theory, a conceptual approach useful for understanding human behavior. Social cognitive theory combines aspects of operant conditioning, social learning theory, and cognitive psychology. Figure 12-1 provides a schematic illustration of the main tenets of the theory as proposed by Bandura (1997).

Behavior, internal personal factors, and external environmental factors are three classes of determinants assumed to coexist in what is referred to as **triadic reciprocal causation.** That is, behavior (its type, frequency, duration, and so on) is influenced by and influences internal personal factors (e.g., individual cognitions such as self-efficacy, attitudes, emotions, and so on). An individual's attitude and self-efficacy beliefs, for example, would influence dieting behavior. In turn, the effectiveness (or ineffectiveness) of dieting behavior would serve to shape the individual's attitudes and beliefs. Behavior also influences and is influenced by environmental factors. Thus, for example, a new employee of a corporation who is also an avid exerciser could exert a positive influence on his/her sedentary confederates. Similarly, a work environment with exercise facilities could go a long way toward changing the physical activity attitudes and behavior of employees. As another example, an athlete's teammates (i.e., environment) might influence his or her attitudes and beliefs about dieting behavior. Again, in turn, the athlete's own attitudes and beliefs would have a reciprocal influence on teammates.

What are some of the implications of accepting a triadic reciprocal causation perspective? One

> **triadic reciprocal causation**   The theory that behavior is influenced by internal personal factors and external environmental factors.

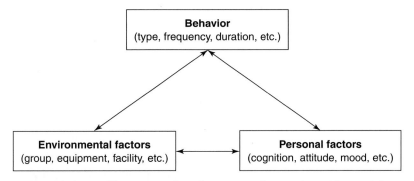

Figure 12-1   An illustration of triadic reciprocal causation within social cognitive theory.
Note. From *Self-Efficacy: The Exercise of Control,* by A. Bandura, 1997, New York: W. H. Freeman.

implication is relatively straightforward: Cognitions such as self-efficacy are assumed to play a role in behavior. A cardiac rehabilitation patient may be physically capable of moderate physical activity. However, if the patient does not possess the belief that he or she has that capability, physical activity behavior is unlikely.

Second, a patient also could learn through the consequences of his or her own actions. A cardiac rehabilitation patient who engages safely in physical activity would gain self-efficacy from the experience.

A third implication is that an individual's beliefs can be influenced by external environmental factors. A person does not have to engage directly in a behavior to develop the belief about personal capabilities. In short, self-efficacy can be influenced through social persuasion as well as the success of (similar) others. That same cardiac rehabilitation patient may gain efficacy by coming to a class and observing other patients with similar health problems engaging in physical activities.

SOURCES OF SELF-EFFICACY BELIEFS

As Figure 12-2 shows, self-efficacy can arise from a number of sources (see Bandura, 1997). The most important and potent source of self-efficacy is **mastery experience.** A person who successfully carries out a task will believe that he or she has the capabilities necessary. In this regard, success is obviously important for self-efficacy to develop. However, Bandura has pointed out that an efficacy belief is more resilient if the individual has also had to overcome obstacles and adversity—and has done so successfully. Similarly, of course, self-efficacy can be fragile; initial failures can serve to undermine efficacy beliefs.

Another source of efficacy is **vicarious experience,** or observational learning. The behavior (and successes or failures) of other people can be used as a comparative standard for the individual. Observing the success of other people in similar circumstances increases self-efficacy whereas observing them fail diminishes it. The individual is persuaded that if a similar other has the capability, he or she does as well.

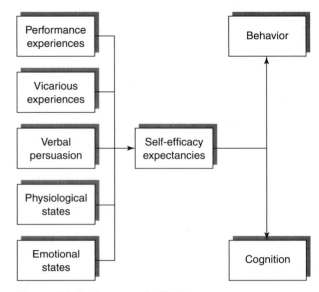

Figure 12-2   Sources of self-efficacy.
Note. Based on discussions from *Self-Efficacy: The Exercise of Control,* by A. Bandura, 1997, New York: W. H. Freeman.

Bandura (1997) has pointed out that although vicarious experiences are generally a less powerful source of self-efficacy beliefs than mastery experiences are, there are conditions under which vicarious experiences could be more powerful. For example, a woman may experience failure in her initial attempts to use a stair climber and, as a result, lose self-efficacy. She may, however, observe a friend who is perceived to be similar (or less fit) exercising successfully, which could serve as a catalyst to enhance her self-efficacy.

A specialized form of vicarious experiences is cognitive self-modeling—**imagery experiences.**

mastery experience   The experience of carrying out a task successfully.

vicarious experience   Behavior of others that serves as a reference for our own personal capabilities, enjoyment and/or understanding.

imagery experience   The use of visualization to repeatedly and successfully confront and master challenging situations.

Here, the individual uses visualization to repeatedly and successfully confront and master challenging situations.

A third source of information that has an impact on self-efficacy is **verbal persuasion.** Its influence is generally weak. However, as Bandura (1997) has pointed out, although "verbal persuasion alone may be limited in its power to create enduring increases in perceived efficacy . . . it can bolster self-change if the positive appraisal is within realistic bounds" (p. 101). Generally, verbal persuasion has its greatest self-efficacy impact on those individuals who have some reason to believe that they could be successful if they persist.

The fourth source of information for self-efficacy beliefs is the individual's *physiological state.* Bodily sensations such as increased heart rate, increased sweating, and increased respiratory rate can provide a signal to the individual about his or her current level of efficacy. Bandura (1997) emphasized that the individual's physiological state—like performance experiences, vicarious experiences, and verbal persuasion—is not, by itself, an indicator of self-efficacy. The individual's appraisal of the information is crucial. If, for example, an elevated heart rate is interpreted as confirmation of suspected poor physical condition, it could serve to reduce self-efficacy. On the other hand, if an elevated heart rate is interpreted as evidence of being adequately warmed up, it could serve to enhance self-efficacy.

The final factor, *mood states,* can influence self-efficacy through either affective priming or cognitive priming. Affective priming occurs because previous successes and failures are stored in memory (and recalled) with associated mood states. Thus, when individuals are successful, they store that experience in memory along with the feelings of joy, elation, vigor, and so on that initially accompanied the experience. Similarly, when individuals fail, they store that experience in memory with the feelings of frustration, sorrow, depression, and so on that initially accompanied the experience. Therefore, the presence of a negative mood state prior to an effect primes memories of failures and thereby serves to reduce self-efficacy.

The cognitive priming perspective is similar but with a subtle distinction. Memory of a failure might be stored with the negative mood state but it is also stored with an accompanying cognition—an attribution, for example. Consider the athlete who has just had a poor performance in a 10km race. The memory of that performance, the emotion associated with it (e.g., feeling depressed), and any accompanying attribution (e.g., "my failure to arrive one hour prior to the start was one reason for my poor performance") would be stored in memory together. Given similar or related experiences in a subsequent race, the cognition of the earlier causal event (arriving too close to the start time) would prime both the emotion (feeling depressed) and memory of the failure. The result would be diminished self-efficacy.

NATURE AND MEASUREMENT OF SELF-EFFICACY

Self-efficacy is the belief that one has the personal capability to carry out the actions required to produce a given outcome (Bandura, 1977, 1986, 1997). A related construct that is often confused with self-efficacy is **outcome expectation,** the belief about the effects of a behavior (Maddux, 1995; McAuley & Mihalko, 1998). There is some debate about the relatedness of these two constructs, with many theoreticians arguing that the two are quite distinct. Thus, for example, a person may have total confidence in his or her ability to maintain a diet (i.e., have self-efficacy for the task of dieting). However, that same person also may have minimal or no confidence that maintaining the diet will produce a loss in weight (i.e., have a low outcome expectation).

Also, theoreticians have stated that self-efficacy is a complex construct that can vary along three

---

verbal persuasion   The act of providing participants with considerable information about the why, what, and where of physical activity.

outcome expectation   The belief about the effects of a behavior.

dimensions. One dimension, **level of self-efficacy,** reflects a belief in personal ability to accomplish a particular task or component of a task. This dimension is the one most people consider to be self-efficacy. However, an individual's self-efficacy can also vary in **strength**—degree of conviction that a particular task or component of a task can be carried out successfully. Thus, for example, an individual might hold the belief that he or she can complete a 30-minute aerobics class (i.e., the level of self-efficacy). However, he or she might also be only 75% (not 100%) confident about this belief (i.e., the strength of self-efficacy). The third dimension, **generality,** reflects the degree to which efficacy beliefs transfer to related tasks. An individual who has high self-efficacy for an aerobics class may also have similarly high efficacy in all activities requiring aerobic fitness.

Because self-efficacy is a situation-specific construct, different manifestations (operational definitions of self-efficacy) have been assessed, depending on the context and interest of the researcher. After carrying out a comprehensive review of the research, McAuley and Mihalko (1998) identified four main categories. The first, most common category is **exercise efficacy.** It represents the individual's beliefs about the capability of successfully engaging in incremental bouts of physical activity. Thus, for example, respondents could be asked about their efficacy for engaging in physical activity at varying intensities and/or for different durations.

Another commonly examined form of self-efficacy is **barriers efficacy.** It represents an individual's beliefs about possessing the capability to overcome obstacles to physical activity. Those obstacles or barriers could be social, such as spousal lack of encouragement, or personal, such as reduced motivation, or environmental, such as bad weather that might interfere with physical activity. Respondents indicate, for example, their confidence that they can attend exercise classes 3 times a week in spite of inclement weather. A special form of barriers efficacy is **scheduling efficacy.** It reflects the individual's confidence that physical activity can be scheduled into a daily or weekly routine.

McAuley and Mihalko (1998) also noted that many studies assessed **disease-specific efficacy** or **health behavior efficacy.** Disease-specific efficacy is similar to exercise efficacy except that it is directly aimed at the assessment of efficacy beliefs in specific populations engaged in the secondary prevention of disease through exercise rehabilitation (e.g., arthritis programs). Similarly, health behavior efficacy pertains to individuals' beliefs about their capability to engage in health-promoting behaviors.

A fourth protocol used to assess efficacy beliefs involves the assessment of **perceived behavioral control,** a construct included in the theory of planned behavior (see Chapter 14). It is somewhat similar to barriers efficacy in that it assesses the individual's beliefs about the degree of personal control in the decision to engage in physical activity.

---

level of self-efficacy   Belief in personal ability to accomplish a particular task or component of a task.

strength of self-efficacy   Degree of conviction that a particular task or component of a task can be carried out successfully.

generality of self-efficacy   Degree to which efficacy beliefs transfer to related tasks.

exercise efficacy   Beliefs about the capability of successfully engaging in incremental bouts of physical activity.

barriers efficacy   Beliefs about possessing the capability to overcome obstacles to physical activity.

scheduling efficacy   Confidence that physical activity can be scheduled into a daily or weekly routine.

disease-specific efficacy   Beliefs about the assessment of self-efficacy in specific populations engaged in the secondary prevention of disease through exercise rehabilitation.

health behavior efficacy   Beliefs about the capability of engaging in health-promoting behaviors.

perceived behavioral control   Beliefs about the degree of personal control in the decision to engage in physical activity.

A student examining research on self-efficacy and physical activity behavior for the first time might wonder if all the ways of measuring efficacy are necessary, why one reliable and valid measure of self-efficacy can't be adopted and used. McAuley and Mihalko (1998) addressed this issue. They noted that the specificity of self-efficacy makes it unwise to adopt one general omnibus measure of self-efficacy. Self-efficacy has been shown to be a reliable predictor of physical activity behavior. A primary reason that it is a reliable predictor is that assessments of efficacy beliefs have directly focused on the targeted behavior. People are not confident about all the areas in which they are involved. Thus, an individual might have extremely high self-efficacy for overcoming the barriers to distance running but minimal or low efficacy for completing a 20km run. By assessing both task efficacy and barriers efficacy (or if the research question dictates it, assessing one or the other), researchers obtain a better understanding of physical activity behavior.

SELF-EFFICACY AND PHYSICAL ACTIVITY BEHAVIOR

As Figure 12-2 has shown, various factors contribute to self-efficacy. In turn, when self-efficacy is present, it positively influences behavior. In the physical activity domain, efficacy beliefs have been found to be associated with a wide cross section of behaviors.

Initiation and Maintenance of Physical Activity

Changes in behavior unfold slowly. One reason is that people see the presence of a number of (real or perceived) barriers and they are not confident about their ability to overcome those barriers. Not surprisingly, barriers efficacy plays a role in situations in which people initiate a lifestyle that involves being physically active. People who intend to become more active in the immediate future (but have not actually done so) have greater barriers efficacy than do people who have no intention of adopting a physically active lifestyle (Armstrong, Sallis, Hovell, & Hofstetter, 1993).

Self-efficacy also plays a role in situations in which people want to maintain a physically active lifestyle. In fact, a number of researchers, including Marcus and her colleagues (Marcus & Owen, 1992; Marcus, Pinto, Simkin, Audrain, & Taylor, 1994; Marcus, Selby, Niaura, & Rossi, 1992), have found that the degree of barrier efficacy present was different for individuals in *each* of the categories of involvement in physical activity listed in Table 15-1 in Chapter 15. That is, individuals more advanced along the continuum from the precontemplation stage to the termination stage were more confident about their capability to overcome barriers to physical activity.

Exercise efficacy also plays a role in situations in which people want to maintain a physically active lifestyle. In a series of studies, McAuley and his colleagues (Courneya & McAuley, 1994; McAuley, 1993; McAuley & Rowney, 1990; Rudolph & McAuley, 1995) observed that an individual's beliefs about personal capability of successfully engaging in incremental bouts of physical activity (i.e., exercise self-efficacy) are related to frequency of participation as well as adherence to exercise programs and/or a more physically active lifestyle.

Effort Expended in Physical Activity

One expected consequence of self-efficacy pertains to the amount of effort expended. That is, efficacious individuals could be expected to try harder. Research has supported this expected relationship in regard to physical activity. A variety of indices of physical effort or exertion such as perceived exertion, self-reports of activity intensity, peak heart rate, vital capacity, expiratory volume, and time to reach 70% of maximal heart rate have been found to be related to exercise efficacy as well as disease/health-related efficacy (see McAuley & Mihalko, 1998, for an overview of this research).

Physical Activity and Self-Efficacy

The strongest, most viable source of efficacy beliefs are mastery experiences. Thus, not surprisingly, the relationship between self-efficacy and involvement in physical activity is reciprocal. Efficacy beliefs are associated with the initiation and maintenance of physical activity. In turn, both acute and long-term involvement in a program of physical activity lead to significant gains in self-efficacy (e.g., McAuley, Bane, & Mihalko, 1995).

The positive effects of physical activity on self-efficacy are not restricted to general populations only. Individuals involved in cardiac rehabilitation programs (Gulanick, 1991), patients with chronic obstructive pulmonary disease (Oldridge & Rogowski, 1990), and psychiatric patients (S. W. Brown, Welsh, Labbe, Vitulli, & Kulkarnie, 1992) also have demonstrated increased efficacy beliefs following a program of physical activity.

SELF-EFFICACY AND MENTAL STATES

Figure 12-2 is intended to illustrate schematically that when self-efficacy beliefs are stronger, cognitions about physical activity are greater, stronger, and more positive. Research on the role that efficacy beliefs play in physical activity has demonstrated this relationship.

Intention to Be Physically Active

The individual could bring up a number of questions that might influence his or her *intention* to become physically active: Am I capable of doing the activity? What obstacles or barriers might arise that could prevent me from being physically active, and can I overcome those obstacles? Will it be possible to schedule regular bouts of physical activity into my already crowded schedule? Perceptions of personal capability in regard to these three questions are not unimportant. Considerable research evidence has been accumulated that shows intention is a reliable predictor of physical activity behavior* (Hausenblas et al., 1997).

In turn, research also shows that efficacy beliefs are related to intention. For example, the first question

---

*The role that intention plays in exercise behavior is discussed in detail in Chapter 14.

posed in the previous paragraph pertains to capability to carry out the activity. The degree to which the individual is confident that he or she is capable of doing the activity is, of course, referred to as *exercise efficacy.* Both Biddle, Goudas, and Page (1994) and Fruin, Pratt, and Owen (1991) have shown that exercise efficacy is positively related to intention to exercise. When people have a stronger belief that they can sustain activity at a given frequency or duration, they form a stronger intention to engage in the activity.

The second and third questions that the individual might pose pertain to *barriers efficacy* and *scheduling efficacy.* Again, research has shown that both barriers efficacy and scheduling efficacy are related to intention to become physically active (e.g., Ducharme & Brawley, 1995; Poag-Ducharme & Brawley, 1993). When individuals develop a stronger cognition that they can fit physical activity into their schedule and that they can overcome barriers—personal, social, or environmental—their intention to be more active is also stronger.

Other Mental States

Bandura (1986, 1992) demonstrated that individuals who possess greater self-efficacy also have lower levels of depression and anxiety. Similarly, efficacy beliefs are interrelated with *emotional responses* following acute sessions of physical activity. For example, individuals possessing greater exercise efficacy report more positive and less negative affect (e.g., McAuley, Shaffer, & Rudolph, 1995) following an acute bout of activity. Similarly, they also report enjoying the experience more (e.g., McAuley et al., 1991).

Efficacy beliefs also are associated with a number of positive intrapersonal characteristics. For example, Kavussanu and McAuley (1995) noted that individuals with greater self-efficacy tend to be more *optimistic*. As another example, exercise efficacy has been positively associated with *self-esteem* (Sonstroem et al., 1994).

ENHANCING SELF-EFFICACY

Efficacy beliefs play an important role in involvement in physical activity—from initiation to maintenance, from effort to frequency and duration, from attitudes to cognitions. How can efficacy be enhanced in individuals uncertain about their capability to organize and execute the actions associated with a physically active lifestyle? McAuley, an authority on the correlates of self-efficacy in physical activity, addressed this question in 1994. As he noted,

> It is vitally important for practitioners and programs to provide experiences that maximize individuals' beliefs in their sense of personal capabilities with respect to exercise and physical activity. If practitioners fail to organize, present, and develop their programs in such a way as to cultivate efficacy beliefs, participants are likely to perceive the activity negatively, become disenchanted and discouraged, and discontinue. On the other hand, adequately organizing exercise and physical activity sessions in a manner such that a strong sense of personal efficacy is promoted will result in individuals displaying more positive affect, evaluating their physical self-worth more positively, embracing more challenging activities, putting forth more effort, and persisting longer. (p. 87)

McAuley then went on to propose a series of strategies within each of the main categories of antecedents for self-efficacy identified in Figure 12-2: mastery experiences, vicarious learning, verbal persuasion, and physiological states. A summary of that list of strategies is provided in Table 12-1.

The principle strategy for mastery experiences is gradual progression. Opportunities for initial success should be maximized. One way to ensure success is to gradually increase the physical challenge on equipment such as treadmills, stair climbers, bi-

cycles, and weights. Also, as Table 12-1 shows, gradual increases in activity should be promoted in daily endeavors, for example, walking instead of riding. Finally, participants should be encouraged to chart their progress both in terms of physical accomplishments and physiological parameters such as heart rate.

The principle strategy for **vicarious learning** is to ensure that participants see other people successfully engaged in the target activity. Vicarious learning might be achieved through videotapes or demonstrations or by having the participants themselves model the activity. An example of participant modeling is to have a prospective exerciser mount and stand without moving on a stair climber, begin stepping but against large resistance, and finally, begin stepping against appropriate resistance but for a limited duration.

The principle strategy for **verbal persuasion** is to provide participants with considerable information about the why, what, and where of physical activity. This information might be disseminated through orientation sessions, pamphlets, articles, newsletters, and so on, or through media presentations (e.g., videotapes, television, newspapers).

Finally, the principle strategy for *physiological states* is to ensure that participants understand the body's response to activity. Physical activity produces increases in heart rate and sweating, for example. The meaning that the individual attaches to those physiological changes is important. Individuals who are frequently active expect and understand the body's response to a physical load. Participants new to physical activity may not. Therefore, they must be helped to interpret what those physiological changes mean and how those physiological responses change with training.

---

vicarious learning   The act of learning through watching other people successfully engaged in the target activity.

verbal persuasion   The act of providing participants with considerable information about the why, what, and where of physical activity.

■ **TABLE 12-1**   Strategies for Strengthening Self-Efficacy Expectations

SOURCE	POTENTIAL STRATEGY FOR ENHANCING SELF-EFFICACY
Mastery experiences	Exercises: Gradually increasing the (a) speed, grade or duration of treadmills, (b) resistance or duration of stationary bicycles, and (c) load, repetitions, or sets in weight lifting
	Daily activities: Walking to work, school, or errands instead of using motor transportation; Using stairs instead of elevators or escalators; Walking around golf courses instead of riding
Vicarious learning	Showing videotapes of successful models similar in age, physical characteristics, and capabilities
	Providing frequent leader or expert demonstrations
	Encouraging attendance at orientation sessions at health and exercise facilities to observe others
	Employing participant modeling in which gradually diminished aid is provided to participants for more difficult activities
	Using cooperative activities in groups or with partners
Verbal persuasion	Providing information and orientation seminars for participants
	Providing videotape and multimedia health promotion information
	Providing articles, magazines, or information pamphlets and booklets
	Developing social support networks through the implementation of "buddy systems" and group social activities
	Providing a telephone hot line or telephone reminders for frequent absentees
	Providing a physical activity and health bulletin board and newsletter
Physiological states	Instructing participants how to accurately and positively interpret: heart rate, perspiration, muscle soreness, weight changes, and general fatigue

Note. From "Enhancing Psychological Health Through Physical Activity," by E. McAuley, 1994, in H. A. Quinney, L. Gauvin, and A. E. T. Wall, Eds., *Toward Active Living: Proceedings of the International Conference on Physical Activity, Fitness, and Health* (pp. 83–90), Champaign, IL: Human Kinetics. Copyright 1999 by Human Kinetics. Used with permission.

Summary

Bandura (1997) has defined self-efficacy as the belief that one is capable of organizing and executing the action required to produce an outcome. Self-efficacy is influenced by a variety of factors including mastery experiences, vicarious experiences (i.e., observational learning), imagery experiences, verbal persuasion, physiological states, and mood. In the context of exercise and physical activity, self-efficacy has been assessed with a variety of operational definitions including exercise efficacy (capability of successfully engaging in incremental bouts of physical activity), barriers efficacy (capability of overcoming obstacles to physical activity), scheduling efficacy (capability of scheduling physical activity into routine), disease-specific efficacy and health behavior efficacy (capabil-

ity of successfully engaging in incremental bouts of physical activity for a specific disease), and perceived behavioral control (degree of personal control in the decision to engage in physical activity).

Efficacy plays an important role in exercise and physical activity. For example, it has been shown to be positively associated with the intention to be physically active as well as the initiation of a program of physical activity, maintenance of involvement, and expenditure of effort during participation. Also, more efficacious individuals are also likely to report more positive and less negative affect following acute bouts of activity and more enjoyment. Finally, efficacy is positively related to the personal qualities of optimism and self-esteem.

CHAPTER 13

Health Belief Model, Protection Motivation Theory, and Physical Activity

Those Who Are Enamored of Practice Without Science Are Like a Pilot Who Gets Into a Ship Without a Rudder or Compass and Never Has Any Certainty of Where [He or She] Is Going.

(Leonardo da Vinci)

CHAPTER OBJECTIVES

After completing this chapter you will be able to

- Describe the constructs of the health belief model and protection motivation theory.

- Describe research that has applied the health belief model and protection motivation theory to physical activity.

- Discuss the advantages and limitations of the health belief model and protection motivation theory.

Key terms

coping appraisal
cues to action
perceived barriers
perceived benefits
perceived severity
perceived susceptibility
perceived vulnerability
precaution strategy
response efficacy
self-efficacy
threat appraisal

Fred Kerlinger (1973), in a discussion on the scientific process, noted that, "the basic aim of science is theory . . . perhaps less cryptic, the basic aim of science is to explain natural phenomena" (p. 8). Leonardo da Vinci made a similar observation hundreds of years ago. Science generally, and the theories of science specifically, provide the rudder or compass to guide practice.

Throughout this book, we have emphasized that scientists and public health practitioners are trying to explain the natural phenomenon of why more people are not physically active. Physically inactive people are at risk for several chronic disorders such as heart disease, stroke, obesity, and diabetes (USD-HHS, 1996, 1999). Moreover, even though these individuals are at risk, they may not experience any symptoms associated with these diseases. Thus, they may not consider it necessary to discuss their inactive lifestyle with a physician or to increase their physical activity level. Two scientific theories—the *health belief model* (N. Janz & Becker, 1984) and *protection motivation theory* (Rogers, 1975, 1983)—may be useful in explaining the phenomenon of sedentary living.

Hundreds of years ago, Leonardo da Vinci observed that science generally, and the theories of science specifically, provide the rudder or compass to guide practice.

HEALTH BELIEF MODEL

The health belief model was one of the first models that adapted theory from the behavioral sciences to health problems, and it remains one of the most widely recognized conceptual frameworks for health behavior. It was introduced in the 1950s by social psychologists Godfrey Hochbaum, Stephen Kegels, and Irwin Rosenstock, who all worked for the U.S. Public Health Service. During the early 1950s the Public Health Service was oriented toward prevention of disease rather than treatment of disease. Thus, the originators of the health belief model were concerned with the widespread failure of individuals to engage in preventive health measures, such as getting a flu vaccine. They postulated that individuals will comply with preventive regimens if they possess minimal levels of relevant health motivation and knowledge, perceive themselves as potentially vulnerable, view the disease as severe, are convinced that the preventive regimen is effective, and see few difficulties or barriers in undertaking the regiment. In addition, internal or external cues that individuals associate with taking health-related actions are considered to be an essential catalyst.

The first research based on the health belief model was initiated by Hochbaum (1952). He attempted to identify factors underlying people's decision to obtain the then-available preventive service of a chest X ray for the early detection of tuberculosis. Subsequently, the model has been applied to screening utilization rates for high blood pressure, cervical cancer, dental disease, polio, and influenza. More recently, it has been applied to predict patient responses to symptoms (Kirscht, 1974) and to compliance with prescribed medical and health regimens (Becker, 1974) such as hypertension medication, diet, and physical activity (Aho, 1977; Frewen, Schomer, & Dunne, 1994; Hayslip, Weigand, Weinberg, Richardson, & Jackson, 1996; Tirrell & Hart, 1980). In short, the health belief model has become a major framework for explaining and predicting the reasons people engage in a variety of preventive health behaviors.

Health Belief Model Constructs

"The basic components of the Health Belief Model are derived from a well-established body of psychological and behavioral theory whose various models hypothesize that behavior depends mainly upon two variables: (a) the value placed by an individual on a particular goal, and (b) the individual's estimate of the likelihood that a given action will achieve that goal" (N. Janz & Becker, 1984, p. 2). When these two variables were conceptualized in the context of health-related behavior, the focus was on either (a) the desire to avoid illness or, if ill, to get well; or (b) the belief that a specific health action will prevent or improve illness.

The model was originally composed of the following four constructs: perceived susceptibility, perceived severity, perceived benefits, and perceived barriers. These concepts accounted for people's "readiness to act." An added concept, cues to action, would activate that readiness and stimulate the actual behavior. A recent addition to the model is self-efficacy, or confidence in the ability to successfully perform a behavior (see Chapter 12 for a detailed description of self-efficacy and physical activity). Self-efficacy was included in the model by Rosenstock, Stretcher, and Becker (1988) to accommodate the challenges of changing unhealthy behaviors, such as being sedentary, smoking, or overeating, to healthy behaviors. In addition to these constructs, the following three other variables are considered important for predicting health behavior: (a) demographic factors such as age, sex, and race; (b) psychosocial factors such as personality and peer pressure; and (c) structural factors such as knowledge (Rosenstock et al., 1988). Figure 13-1 provides a schematic illustration of the health belief model. Each of the model's constructs is discussed in detail in the following sections. (Also see Table 13-1 for definitions and applications of the health belief model constructs.)

Perceived Susceptibility.   To engage in a behavior and thereby avoid an illness, an individual must first believe that he or she is personally susceptible to that illness. Individuals vary in their **perceived susceptibility** to a disease or condition. Those people at the low end of the extreme deny the possibility of contracting an adverse condition. Individuals in a moderate category admit to a possibility of disease susceptibility. Finally, those individuals at the high extreme of susceptibility feel there is danger that they will experience an adverse condition or contract a disease. An individual's perceptions of

> **perceived susceptibility**   Person's opinion of his or her chances of getting a disease.

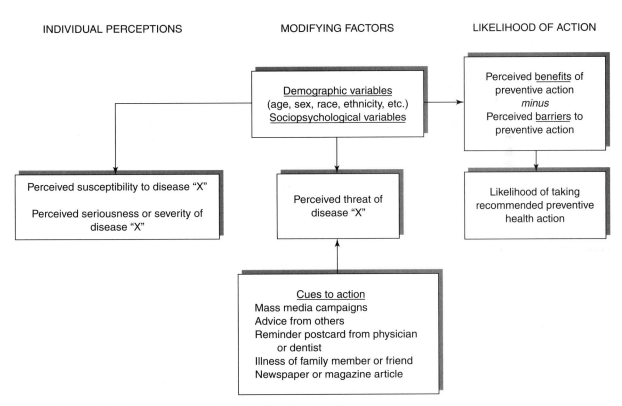

Figure 13-1   Graphic representation of the health belief model.
Note. From "The Health Belief Model: A Decade Later," by N. Janz and M. Becker, 1984, *Health Education Quarterly, 11,* 1–47.

■ **TABLE 13-1** Definitions, Applications, and Examples of the Health Belief Model Constructs

CONSTRUCT	DEFINITION	APPLICATION	EXAMPLE
Perceived susceptibility	Person's opinion of the chances of getting a disease	Define populations at risk. Personalize risk based on a person's features or behavior. Heighten perceived susceptibility if too low.	My chances of getting cardiovascular disease are high because I am sedentary and overweight.
Perceived severity	Person's opinion of the seriousness of a condition and its consequences	Specify consequences of the risk and condition.	Cardiovascular disease is a serious illness that may cost me my life.
Perceived benefits	Person's opinion of the efficacy of the advised action to reduce risk or seriousness of impact	Define when, where, and how to take action. Clarify the positive effects to be expected.	I will walk for a half hour 6 days a week. Becoming physically active will make me healthier and reduce my chances of a heart attack.
Perceived barriers	Person's opinion of the physical and psychological costs of the advised action	Identify and reduce barriers through reassurance, incentives, and assistance.	Becoming physically active will take time away from other things I enjoy doing.
Cues to action	Strategies to activate readiness	Provide how-to information, promote awareness, give reminders.	I will buy physical activity videos and magazines and post reminder notes on the fridge.
Self-efficacy	Confidence in one's ability to take action	Provide training and guidance in performing action.	I will start slow and gradually increase my frequency, intensity, and duration of walking.

personal susceptibility are related to a variety of health behaviors including immunization (Cummings, Jette, Brock, & Haefner, 1979), dental visits (Becker, Kaback, Rosenstock, & Ruth, 1975), and screening for tuberculosis (Haefner & Kirscht, 1970). In regard to physical activity, if a person believes she is at risk for cardiovascular disease, she may begin an exercise regimen to reduce her perceived susceptibility to the disease.

Perceived Seriousness or Severity. **Perceived severity** refers to an individual's feelings concerning the seriousness of a health condition if it is contracted or treatment is not obtained or both. Feelings concerning the seriousness of contracting an illness (or leaving it untreated) also vary from person to person. These feelings can be considered from the point of view of the difficulties that an illness (or potential illness) would create. For example, an individual may evaluate the severity of cancer in terms of the (a) medical consequences such as pain, discomfort, death, and disability; (b) social consequences such as difficulties for family, friends, and significant others; and (c) occupational consequences such as loss of work time and financial burdens (Rosenstock, 1990).

perceived severity Person's opinion of the seriousness of a condition and its consequences.

Perceived Benefits of Taking Action.   **Perceived benefits** is the efficacy of the advised action to reduce risk or seriousness of impact. The direction of action that a person chooses will be influenced by his or her beliefs regarding the action. For example, a sedentary individual at high risk for cardiovascular disease would not be expected to increase his or her physical activity level unless it was perceived as feasible and efficacious. The concept of perceived benefits is identical to the concept of outcome expectation discussed in Chapter 12.

Self-efficacy.   **Self-efficacy** is a judgment regarding a person's ability to perform a behavior required to achieve a certain outcome, and it is an important component of behavior change (Bandura, 1997). Because of its recent inclusion in the health belief model, self-efficacy has not been evaluated as extensively as the other constructs. Researchers who have examined self-efficacy with the health belief model have found overwhelming support for it. For example, a recent study by Chen, Neufeld, Feely, and Skinner (1998) found that self-efficacy was the only health belief model construct to predict exercise compliance among patients with upper-extremity impairment.

Perceived Barriers to Take Action.   Action may not take place even though the individual believes that the benefits to taking action are effective, and he or she possesses self-efficacy about performing that behavior. This inactivity may be due to **perceived barriers.** Common barriers to undertaking physical activity include low motivation, inconvenience of facilities, expense, lack of time, and discomfort (e.g., muscle soreness). These barriers may cause a person to not engage in the health behavior. For example, an individual may acknowledge the severity of his diabetes and that he is at risk for the disease. He may also believe that physical activity will reduce his chance of developing diabetes. However, he may not become active because of the perceived barrier of lack of time to engage in physical activity.

Cues to Action.   An individual's perception of the degree of both susceptibility and severity provides desire to take action, and the perceptions of benefits provide the preferred path of action. However, an event or cue is necessary to trigger the decision-making process and motivate an individual's readiness to take action. These **cues to action** might be internal, external, or both. Internal cues could include perceptions of bodily states such as dizziness, elevated heart rate, and shortness of breath. External cues could include mass media communications (e.g., watching a physical activity video or television commercial) or receiving a postcard from a physician that outlines the health benefits of exercise. Such factors as use of mass media, postcard reminders, and the presence of symptoms have been found to influence people to take a recommended health action (Rosenstock, 1974).

The following example illustrates how the components of the health belief model are hypothesized to predict behavior. A sedentary person believes that he or she could have a heart attack (*is susceptible*), that inactivity can lead to heart attack (*the severity is great*), and that becoming physically active will reduce the risk (*benefits*) without negative side effects or excessive difficulty (*barriers*). Print materials and letters of reminder sent to the person might promote physical activity adherence (*cues to action*). And if the individual has had a hard time being active in the past, a strategy involving the use of behavioral contracts could be used to establish achievable short-term goals so that the person's confidence (*self-efficacy*) to engage in physical activity increases.

Application of the Health Belief Model to Physical Activity

Different research paradigms have been used to examine the utility of the health belief model. Thus, it is useful to categorize the discussion accordingly.

---

perceived benefits   Person's opinion of the efficacy of the advised action to reduce risk or seriousness of impact.

self-efficacy   Confidence in one's ability to take action.

perceived barriers   Person's opinion of the physical and psychological costs of the advised action.

cues to action   Strategies to activate readiness.

Cross-Sectional Studies. Slenker, Price, Roberts, and Jurs (1984) examined the utility of some of the health belief model constructs (i.e., perceived susceptibility, perceived severity, barriers, benefits, and cues to action) for predicting jogging and nonexercising behaviors. Participants were 124 joggers and 96 nonexercisers. A jogger was defined as an individual who jogged at least 3 times a week for 20 minutes, while a nonexerciser was defined as a person who had not exercised regularly for the past 6 months.

The researchers found that the four health belief model constructs—perceptions of severity to health problems, barriers to jogging, benefits of jogging, and cues to jogging—differed between the joggers and nonexercisers. As the model would suggest, in comparison to the nonexercisers, joggers reported a greater perception of severity to health problems if unable to jog, more benefits of and cues to jogging, and less barriers to jog. Contrary to predictions from the model, however, perceived susceptibility did not predict jogging behavior.

It is important to note that perceived barriers to action was by far the most important factor differentiating the joggers from the nonexercisers. The nonexercisers accounted for their sedentary status by listing constraints such as lack of time, family or job responsibilities, unsuitable weather, and lack of desire or interest. The authors concluded that physical and health educators might more effectively change the behavior of sedentary individuals by utilizing strategies that address perceived barriers to jogging.

Other researchers examining health beliefs have also found that perceived barriers are strong determinants of physical activity behavior (e.g., Sommers, Andres, & Price, 1995; Taggart & Connor, 1995). For example, Sommers and her colleagues utilized the health belief model constructs in their examination of motivation for mall walking. Possibly because of its numerous benefits, walking in the mall is a physical activity that is growing in popularity, especially among older adults. Benefits of mall walking include consistent temperature, personal safety, convenience, safe walking surface, and opportunities for so-

cialization (Schacht & Unnithan, 1991). The participants in the Sommers et al. study were 123 older male and female mall walkers (M age = 66 years).

Sommers and her colleagues (1995) found that the males perceived significantly more barriers to walking in the mall than did the females. Also, participants with higher education demonstrated a greater level of knowledge of the benefits of exercise and the perceived severity of not exercising. The health problems that the participants perceived themselves to be the most susceptible to if they did not walk in the mall were stiff joints and legs, followed by a lack of energy and an increase in cholesterol level. The authors noted that their most significant finding was that participants who were told to exercise by their physician perceived greater susceptibility and severity of health problems if they did not exercise compared to those who were not told to exercise by their physician. The researchers concluded that health educators should work with physicians and other health professionals to educate older populations in the benefits of exercise for improving health, increasing longevity, and providing the skills necessary to engage in appropriate and effective physical activity.

Researchers have also found that health beliefs differ across health behaviors. This finding was illustrated in a study by O'Connell, Price, Roberts, Jurs, and McKinely (1985). They tested 69 obese and 100 nonobese adolescents to determine if both dieting and exercise behavior could be predicted using the health belief model constructs. The health beliefs that were examined were knowledge of the (a) etiology, pathology, and demographic variables associated with obesity; (b) proper means of losing weight by dieting and exercising; (c) perceived severity of obesity; (d) perceived susceptibility to the causes of obesity; (e) cues to losing weight by dieting and exercising; (f) benefits of losing weight by dieting and exercising; (g) barriers to losing weight by dieting and exercising; and (h) social support for dieting and exercise. To determine salient beliefs within the health belief model, an elicitation study was undertaken with 58 obese and nonobese adolescents. The most prevalent responses were then used to construct the health belief model questionnaire.

The researchers found that benefits of dieting was the most powerful predictor of dieting for the obese adolescents, whereas susceptibility to the causes of obesity best explained the current dieting practices of the nonobese adolescents. Exercising behavior of obese teenagers was best explained by cues to exercising. The salient cues for exercising included the external cue of peer pressure and the internal cues of poor health and poor muscle tone. None of the health belief model constructs were significant predictors of exercise behavior of nonobese adolescents. The authors concluded that weight control programs for obese adolescents should emphasize cues to encourage participation in aerobic exercise. The cues should be provided in the form of both internal and external stimuli for maximal results. The authors also concluded, however, that the utility of the health belief model was limited for explaining exercise behavior.

Prospective Studies. Bond, Aiken and Somerville (1992) examined the predictive utility of the health belief model for adherence with a medical regimen in 56 adolescents with insulin-dependent diabetes mellitus (M age = 14 years). The medical regimen consisted of testing glucose levels twice a day, exercising regularly, controlling diet, and administering insulin injections. At baseline, the adolescents completed a series of questionnaires designed to assess the health belief model constructs of perceived susceptibility/severity, benefits/costs, and cues in relation to their medical regiment. Five to 8

weeks after completing the questionnaires the adolescents had blood drawn to assess their actual blood glucose level.

The researchers found that the adolescents were motivated to comply with the medical regimen; perceived low susceptibility but high severity of the disease; perceived greater benefits than costs to compliance; and had a sensitivity to and willingness to act on the cues of cold sweats, shortness of breath, vomiting, and inability to concentrate. Compliance to the medical regimen was positively associated with cues to action and with perceived benefits and costs of the diabetic regiment. The greatest compliance was achieved with low perceived threat and high perceived benefits and costs. The researchers also found that, consistent with the pattern that exists in the general population, as age increased, exercise behavior decreased.

In another prospective study, Oldridge and Streiner (1990) examined the ability of the health belief model to predict exercise compliance and dropout rate in a cardiac rehabilitation population. They also examined whether the model added predictive utility to routinely assessed patient demographics and health behaviors such as age, weight, occupation type, and smoking status. The researchers assessed the following health beliefs of 120 male patients with coronary artery disease: severity of the disease, perceptions of susceptibility to the disease, perceptions of effectiveness of exercise, barriers to exercise, and cues to action. The patients were given a 6-month exercise program consisting of twice-weekly supervised exercise sessions lasting approximately 90 minutes. Home-based exercise also was recommended for at least 3 days a week. At the end of the program, the patients were divided into either compliers or dropouts. Dropouts were defined as those participants who missed either more than 50% of all the sessions or more than 8 consecutive sessions. Dropouts were then further classified as either unavoidable or avoidable. Reasons for unavoidable dropout included cardiac complications, death, and moving away. Reasons for avoidable dropouts included loss of motivation/interest, inconvenience, and fatigue.

It was found that 62 patients (52%) dropped out of the program. Of those who dropped out, 34 were categorized as avoidable and 28 were classified as unavoidable. Compliers were more likely to be non-smokers, have a white-collar occupation, have active leisure habits, and be younger than the dropouts. In regard to the health belief model constructs, the only significant difference between the compliers and dropouts was in perceptions of the severity of the disease but this finding was in the opposite direction to what was hypothesized. That is, the compliers perceived less susceptibility than the dropouts did. The predictive ability of the health belief model was found to be very small. The authors concluded that the results of the study provided limited evidence for the usefulness of the health belief model in accounting for compliance behavior.

PROTECTION MOTIVATION THEORY

Television advertisements often attempt to instill fear in observers in order to change their attitudes and behavior. For example, a dramatic car crash is followed by the observation that drinking and driving do not mix. But appeals based on fear do not consistently result in attitude and behavior changes. The protection motivation theory was originally developed to explain inconsistencies in research on fear appeals and attitude change (Rogers, 1975, 1983), but since that time it has been employed primarily as a model to explain health decision making and action. Protection motivation theory is concerned with the decision to protect oneself from harmful or

stressful life events, although it can also be viewed as a theory of coping with such events. In the protection motivation theory, decisions to engage (or not engage) in health-related behaviors are thought to be influenced by two primary cognitive processes: (a) **threat appraisal,** which is an evaluation of the factors that influence the likelihood of engaging in an unhealthy behavior (e.g., smoking, sedentary lifestyle); and (b) **coping appraisal,** which is an evaluation of the factors that influence the likelihood of engaging in a recommended preventive response (e.g., physical activity). The most common index of protection motivation is a measure of *intentions* to perform the recommended preventive behavior (intention is a fundamental construct in the theories of reasoned action and planned behavior, which are discussed in Chapter 14). Figure 13-2 provides an illustration of the constructs of protection motivation theory.

Threat Appraisal

The threat appraisal component depends on (a) **perceived vulnerability,** which is a person's estimate of the degree of personal risk for a specific health hazard if a current unhealthy behavior is continued (e.g., risk for developing lung cancer if one continues smoking); and (b) *perceived severity,* which is a person's estimate of the threat of the disease (e.g., perceived severity of lung cancer). It is assumed that as perceptions of vulnerability and severity increase, the likelihood of engaging in the unhealthy behavior

threat appraisal   An evaluation of the factors that influence the likelihood of engaging in an unhealthy behavior

coping appraisal   An evaluation of the factors that influence the likelihood of engaging in a recommended preventive response.

perceived vulnerability   Person's estimate of the degree of personal risk for a specific health hazard if a current unhealthy behavior is continued.

Protection Motivation Theory

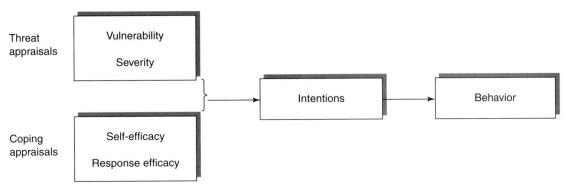

Figure 13-2   Graphic representation of the protection motivation theory.
Note. From "Cognitive and Physiological Processes in Fear Appeals and Attitude Change: A Revised Theory of Protection Motivation," by R. W. Rogers, 1983, in J. R. Cacioppo and R. E. Petty, Eds., *Social Psychology: A Source Book* (pp. 153–176), New York: Guilford Press.

decreases. However, the likelihood of continuing to engage in the unhealthy behavior is increased by the perceived intrinsic rewards (e.g., pleasure) and extrinsic rewards (e.g., approval) associated with that behavior.

Coping Appraisal

Coping appraisal consists of (a) **response efficacy,** the person's expectancy that complying with recommendations will remove the threat (e.g., quitting smoking will reduce one's risk for lung cancer); and (b) *self-efficacy,* the person's belief in his or her ability to implement the recommended coping behavior or strategy (e.g., belief that one can quit smoking). As response efficacy and self-efficacy increase, so does the likelihood of engaging in the recommended preventive behavior. In addition, however, the likelihood of carrying out the preventive coping response is decreased by the perceived response costs (e.g., loss of pleasure, loss of social support).

> **response efficacy**   Person's expectancy that complying with recommendations will remove the threat.

Protection motivation theory assumes that the motivation to protect oneself from danger is a positive linear function of four cognitive beliefs. That is, motivation to implement the coping response is at its maximum when the individual perceives that (a) the threat is severe, (b) he or she is personally vulnerable to the threat, (c) the coping response is effective to avert the threat, and (d) he or she has the ability to perform the coping response. Thus, the emotional state of fear is thought to influence attitudes and change behavior indirectly through the appraisal of the severity.

Application of the Protection Motivation Theory to Physical Activity

This section focuses on research that has examined the protection motivation theory. Discussion has been divided into review studies, prospective studies, and cross-sectional studies.

   Review Studies.   Two recent meta-analytic reviews on protection motivation theory representing more than 20 health issues, including exercise and physical activity, have found support for the utility of the theory (Floyd, Prentice-Dunn, & Rogers,

2000; Milne, Sheeran, & Orbell, 2000). The meta-analysis carried out by Floyd and her colleagues on 65 studies (with 29,650 participants) found that, in accordance with the theory, increases in threat severity, threat vulnerability, response efficacy, and self-efficacy facilitated adaptive intentions and behaviors. The magnitude of the effect sizes obtained was in the moderate range.

In the meta-analysis undertaken by Milne and her colleagues (2000), a more stringent criteria for including studies was used. As a result, only 29 studies with approximately 7,700 participants were analyzed. Nonetheless, Milne et al. obtained results that were similar to those of Floyd et al. (2000), with effect sizes in the small to moderate range. Specifically, Milne et al. found that the threat and coping appraisal components of the protection motivation theory were useful in predicting ongoing behavior. They found, however, that the model had less utility for predicting future behavior. It is important to note that these two meta-analyses examined a variety of health behaviors (e.g., quitting smoking, wearing sunscreen, healthy eating, physical activity). Thus, in the next two sections, we describe in more detail studies that examined the protection motivation theory solely for exercise and physical activity behavior.

Prospective Studies. Plotnikoff and Higginbotham (1998) examined the relative contributions of the protection motivation theory to predict intentions to engage in both a low-fat diet and exercise for the prevention of further cardiovascular heart disease in 151 patients who had recently suffered a heart attack. The participants completed baseline measures of threat appraisal (i.e., vulnerability and susceptibility) during their hospital stay following a heart attack. Six months later the participants completed measures of threat appraisal and coping appraisal (i.e., self-efficacy and response efficacy) via mail. It was found that self-efficacy was the strongest predictor of exercise and diet intentions and behaviors. The authors concluded that health education for this population should promote activities that enhance self-efficacy for such behaviors.

Cross-Sectional Studies. Wurtele and Maddux (1987) examined the relative effectiveness of threat appraisals (i.e., severity and vulnerability) and coping appraisals (i.e., self-efficacy and response efficacy) for increasing exercise behavior in 160 nonexercising undergraduate females. Nonexercisers were defined as engaging in less than two bouts of exercise per week. Each participant received a written persuasive message containing none, one, two, three, or four of the protection motivation theory components (see Table 13-2 for examples of the persuasive messages). After reading the message, all participants completed a postexperimental questionnaire. Participants were then given a list of suggested means of achieving aerobic fitness. Two weeks later the participants reported on any changes in their exercise behavior since the initiation of the study.

It was found that perceptions of both vulnerability and self-efficacy enhanced exercise intentions and behaviors. Furthermore, intentions predicted changes in exercise behavior. The researchers also found that the participants adopted a **precaution strategy.** That is, they intended to adopt exercise even though they held weak beliefs about its effectiveness and were not convinced of their at-risk status.

RESEARCH EXAMINING BOTH THEORIES

An important construct in both the health belief model (Rosenstock, 1990) and protection motivation theory (Rogers, 1975) is perceived severity—an individual's feelings about the seriousness of a health condition if it is contracted or not treated. Courneya (1995) noted that previous research has been unable to consistently find that perceived severity is an important construct for motivation to engage in physi-

precaution strategy Person's intention is to adopt exercise even though he or she holds weak beliefs about its effectiveness and is not convinced of his or her at-risk status.

■ **TABLE 13-2**   Persuasive Messages Read by the Participants

APPRAISAL CONSTRUCT	MESSAGE FOCUS	EXAMPLE
Severity	The seriousness of remaining sedentary by describing the immediate and long-term effects of having a heart attack or stroke	"Suddenly, the victim is overwhelmed with a crushing pain in the chest as if the ribs were being squeezed in a vise. . . . Nauseated, the victim vomits; pink foam comes out of the mouth. The face turns an ashen gray, sweat rolls down the face, and the victim, very weak, staggers to the floor."
Vulnerability	The susceptibility to developing heart disease and circulatory problems	"Because you do not exercise regularly, your cardiovascular system has already begun deteriorating, which puts the health of your body in jeopardy."
Response efficacy	The importance and efficacy of exercise in preventing health problems by presenting evidence that the physiological changes in the body resulting from a regular exercise program serve vital protection functions	"Since exercise leads to higher levels of high-density lipoprotein, which in turn lowers the level of cholesterol, exercising thus prevents heart attacks."
Self-efficacy	Reasons why participants would be able to begin and continue with a regular exercise program	"We all have a built-in urge for physical activity and this basic human physical need will serve as an energizer. . . . At your age you now have the cognitive abilities to commit yourself to a long-term exercise program."

Note. From "Relative Contributions of Protection Motivation Theory Components in Predicting Exercise Intentions and Behavior," by S. K. Wurtele and J. E. Maddux, 1987, *Health Psychology, 6,* 453–466.

cal activity. People may agree that being physically inactive can contribute to severe coronary problems, but there is no link between perceptions of the severity of the problem and the tendency to adopt a physically active lifestyle. Courneya suggested that the absence of a relationship between perceptions of severity and motivation to change could be due in part to the tendency for researchers to adopt a two-stage model of exercise behavior change. In a two-stage model, the population is considered to be either inactive or active. He also noted that perceived severity is similar to the process of change strategy of

dramatic relief in the transtheoretical model (see Chapter 15 for a detailed description of the transtheoretical model and physical activity). Dramatic relief refers to experiencing and expressing feelings about the consequences of being inactive. Researchers have shown that dramatic relief motivates a person to seriously consider a behavior change (i.e., to move from precontemplation to contemplation), but not necessarily to move onward to and through the active stages (Prochaska & Marcus, 1994).

Consequently, Courneya (1995) compared perceptions of the severity of a sedentary lifestyle among 270 senior citizens who were classified within one of the five stages of change of the trans-theoretical model (i.e., precontemplation, contemplation, preparation, action, and maintenance). He hypothesized that perceived severity would discriminate individuals in the precontemplation stage from individuals in the four subsequent stages. He also hypothesized that there would not be differences in perceived severity among individuals in those four subsequent stages. Consistent with his hypothesis, Courneya found that individuals in the precontemplation stage reported the least perceived severity of the consequences of an inactive lifestyle compared to those in the contemplation, preparation, action, and maintenance stages. Courneya concluded that the main function of perceived severity of physical inactivity is to motivate people to seriously consider becoming physically active. This perception of severity is then maintained through the active stages of preparation, action, and maintenance. Figure 13-3 displays the perception of severity of the participants across the stages of change.

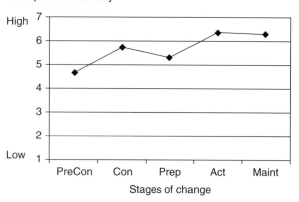

Perceptions of severity

Figure 13-3 Perceived severity of physical activity across the stages of change.
Note. PreCon = precontemplation; Con = contemplation; Prep = preparation; Act = action; Maint = maintenance. 7 = high perceived severity of inactivity; 1 = low perceived severity of inactivity.

An unexpected finding in Courneya's (1995) study, however, was that perceived severity of the consequences of an inactive lifestyle was lower for individuals in the preparation stage compared to individuals in the action and maintenance stages. He suggested that individuals who are in the preparation stage, who are physically active at a low level, will be motivated to increase their level of physical activity if they believe that the effects of being sedentary are very severe.

LIMITATIONS OF THE HEALTH BELIEF MODEL AND PROTECTION MOTIVATION THEORY

One of the problems that has plagued the health belief model is that different questions are used in different studies to determine the same beliefs. Consequently, it is difficult both to design appropriate tests of the health belief model and to compare results across studies. Furthermore, research does not always support the health belief model. One possible reason for this lack of support is that factors other than health beliefs also heavily influence health behavior practices. These factors may include cultural factors, socioeconomic status, and past physical activity behavior.

Although many researchers view the health belief model and protection motivation theory as limited because of their focus on cognitive factors, some of the potential determinants of physical activity that the models emphasize, particularly perceived barriers, are strong correlates of physical activity. It is important to note that perceived barriers are amenable to change. It also should be noted that the models were originally designed for risk-avoiding, not health-promoting, behaviors. Thus, their utility may be reduced in terms of understanding the behavior of individuals who view physical activity as a health-promoting behavior.

Summary

This chapter examined the health belief model and protection motivation theory and the research utilizing these models to explain and predict physical activity behavior. The components of the health belief model are perceived susceptibility, perceived seriousness or severity, perceived benefits of taking action, self-efficacy, perceived barriers to take action, and cues to action. In comparison, the premise for protection motivation theory is that decisions to engage in exercise are thought to be influenced by threat appraisals and coping appraisals. Despite limitations of both theories, they provide unique insight into physical activity behaviors—in particular, perceived severity (i.e., an individual's feelings about the seriousness of a health condition if it is contracted or not treated). In short, the health belief model and protection motivation theory have provided a compass to guide research to explain exercise behavior.

CHAPTER **14**

The Theories of Reasoned Action, Planned Behavior, and Physical Activity

Man Can Alter His Life by Altering His Thinking.

William James

CHAPTER OBJECTIVES

After completing this chapter you will be able to

- Describe the constructs of the theories of reasoned action and planned behavior.

- Discuss the research that has applied the theories of reasoned action and planned behavior to physical activity.

- Discuss the advantages and limitations of the theories of reasoned action and planned behavior.

Key terms

attitude
behavioral beliefs
control beliefs
intention

normative beliefs
perceived behavioral
  control
subjective norm

This chapter examines two social cognitive theories that have guided a large majority of theory-based research on physical activity—the theories of *reasoned action* (Ajzen & Fishbein, 1980; Fishbein & Ajzen, 1975) and *planned behavior* (Ajzen, 1985, 1988). These theories specify that some or all of the following psychological variables influence behavior: (a) behavioral intention; (b) attitude toward the behavior; (c) subjective norm; (d) perceived behavioral control; and (e) behavioral, normative, and control beliefs. The combination of an individual's expectations about performing a particular behavior and the value attached to that behavior form the conceptual basis of both theoretical models. This expectation by value approach provides a framework for understanding the relationship between people's attitudes and their underlying beliefs. Both theories concern attitude-behavior relationships and assume that individuals are capable of forethought and make rational decisions about their behavior and its consequences. Where they differ is in the importance attached to perceptions of behavioral control in the theory of planned behavior (Ajzen, 1988).

THE THEORY OF REASONED ACTION

The theory of reasoned action, developed by Fishbein and Ajzen (Ajzen & Fishbein, 1980; Fishbein & Ajzen, 1975), was designed to explain volitional (i.e., freely chosen) behavior. The theory is based on the assumption that people behave in a sensible and rational manner by taking into account available information and considering the potential implications of their behavior. The theory of reasoned action is composed of three principal constructs considered to influence behavior: intention, attitude, and subjective norm.

Intention

Intention to perform a behavior is the central determinant of whether an individual engages in that behavior. Intention is reflected in a person's willingness and how much effort he or she is planning to exert to perform the behavior. It is believed that the stronger a person's intention to perform a behavior, the more likely he or she will be to engage in that behavior. Thus, if you have a strong intent to go for a walk this afternoon, you are likely to go for that walk.

As might be expected, a person's intention can weaken over time. The longer the time between intention and behavior, the greater the likelihood that unforeseen events will produce changes in people's intention. For example, a young adult may intend to be a regular lifetime runner. However, after running for a few years, she may become bored with the activity and start to swim instead. She did not expect boredom to affect her intention to run. A person's behavioral intentions are influenced by both his or her *attitudes* about the behavior and the perceived social pressures to perform the behavior (i.e., *subjective norm*).

Attitude

Within the theory of reasoned action, **attitude** represents an individual's positive or negative evaluation of performing a behavior. Attitude is a function of **be-**

Intention to perform a behavior is the central determinant of whether an individual engages in that behavior.
©PhotoDisc/Volume 27/International Sports

havioral beliefs, which refer to the perceived consequences of carrying out a specific action and a personal evaluation of each of these consequences. For example, an individual's beliefs about physical activity could be represented by both positive expectations (e.g., it will improve my personal health) and negative expectations (e.g., it will reduce my time with friends and family). In shaping behavior, the person evaluates the consequences attached to each of these beliefs. Researchers have shown that the most common

---

intention   Person's willingness and how much effort he or she is planning to exertperform the behavior.

attitude   Positive or negative evaluation of performing the behavior.

behavioral beliefs   Perceived consequences of carrying out a specification and a personal evaluation of each of these consequences.

---

behavioral beliefs for physical activity in healthy populations are that it improves fitness/health, improves physical appearance, is fun/enjoyable, increases social interactions, and improves psychological health (Willis & Campbell, 1992).

Subjective Norm

Subjective norm reflects the perceived social pressure that individuals feel to perform or not perform a particular behavior. Subjective norm is believed to be a function of **normative beliefs,** which are determined by the perceived expectations of important significant others (e.g., family, friends, physician, priest) or groups (e.g., classmates, teammates, church members) and by the individual's motivation to comply with the expectations of these important significant others. For example, an individual may feel that his wife thinks he should exercise three times a week. The husband, however, may not be inclined to act according to these perceived beliefs.

A Caveat for the Theory of Reasoned Action

Within the theory of reasoned action, it is assumed that people will intend to perform a behavior once they evaluate it positively and believe that important others think they should perform it. This intention is assumed to lead to behavior (Ajzen, 1988). Thus, for example, a person is likely to go swimming at the beach if she has a strong intent to go swimming later that day, believes swimming is fun, and is motivated by the encouragement of friends. This example illustrates volitional behavior—behavior the individual

---

subjective norm   Perceived social pressure that individuals feel to perform or not perform a behavior.

normative beliefs   Perceived expectations of important significant others or groups and the motivation to comply with the expectations of these significant others.

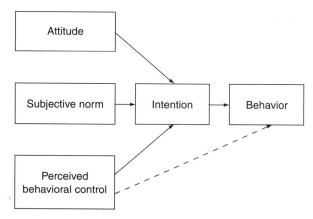

Figure 14-1 Schematic representation of the theories of reasoned action and planned behavior.
Note. From "Intentions to Actions: A Theory of Planned Behavior," by I. Ajzen, 1985, in J. Kuhl and J. Beckman, Eds., *Action Control: From Cognition to Behavior* (pp. 11–39), Heidelberg: Springer.

can undertake if he or she desires. What would happen, however, if a severe storm watch was announced and the beaches were closed from public access? Despite having a strong intention, positive attitude, and perceived social support, the individual would not be able to go swimming.

As the theory of reasoned action began to take hold in the social sciences, Ajzen and other researchers realized that it had limitations (Godin & Kok, 1996). One of the greatest limitations, as seen in the swimming example, was in predicting or explaining behavior in situations where people had little (or, more importantly perhaps, perceived that they had little) power over events around them. If a behavior is not under volition control, even a person who is highly motivated by his or her own attitudes and subjective norm may not perform the behavior. To more fully understand behavior in these types of situations, Ajzen added a third construct to the original theory. This construct, the concept of *perceived behavioral control,* reflects the fundamental difference between the theory of reasoned action and the theory of planned behavior (see Figure 14-1).

THE THEORY OF PLANNED BEHAVIOR

Perceived behavioral control represents the perceived ease or difficulty of performing a behavior. With the inclusion of this new construct, the theory of planned behavior assumes that perceived behavioral control influences behavior either directly or indirectly through intention (see Figure 14-1). People may hold positive attitudes toward a behavior and believe that important others would approve of their behavior. However, they are not likely to form a strong intention to perform that behavior if they believe they do not have the resources or opportunities to do so (Ajzen, 1991).

Ajzen (1985) stated that when perceptions of control are high, the theory of planned behavior operates like the theory of reasoned action. In short, perceived behavioral control is not an important factor, and behavior can be predicted from intention, attitude, and subjective norm. Perceived behavioral control is similar to Bandura's concept of self-efficacy (see Chapter 12 for a discussion of self-efficacy). In fact, in some studies using the theory of planned behavior, researchers have assessed self-efficacy rather than perceived behavioral control.

Perceived behavioral control is a function of **control beliefs.** Control beliefs represent the perceived presence or absence of required resources and opportunities (e.g., there is a road race this weekend), the anticipated obstacles or impediments to behavior (e.g., the probability of rain on the weekend is 90%), and the perceived power of a particular control factor to facilitate or inhibit performance of the

behavior (e.g., even if it rains this weekend, I can still participate in the road race; Ajzen & Driver, 1992). Researchers have shown that the most common control beliefs for physical activity in healthy populations are lack of time, lack of energy, and lack of motivation (Canadian Fitness and Lifestyle Research Institute, 1996a).

ELICITATION STUDIES

A strength of the theories of reasoned action and planned behavior is that an elicitation study forms the basis for the development of questions to assess the various constructs. Elicitation studies are conducted to determine the pertinent beliefs concerning a behavior. Protocol suggested by Ajzen and Fishbein (1980) for conducting elicitation studies include: (a) using open-ended questions to determine the important behavioral, normative, and control beliefs in the targeted population; (b) carrying out a content analysis (i.e., a simple frequency count) to determine which beliefs are most salient; and (c) developing structured items from the content analysis. Ajzen and Fishbein also proposed that structured items emanating from the elicitation study should be specific to the target at which the behavior is directed, the action or specificity of the behavior under study, and the context and time in which the behavior is being performed.

A recent study provides an illustration of an elicitation study. Courneya and Friedenreich (1999) were interested in determining the salient beliefs of 24 breast cancer survivors. The women answered open-ended questions about exercising during their cancer treatment. For *behavioral beliefs,* participants were asked to list the main advantages and disadvantages of exercising during their cancer treatment. For *control beliefs,* participants were asked to list the main factors that prevented or helped them exercise during their cancer treatment. Finally, for *normative beliefs,* participants were asked to list the individuals or groups who were most important to them when they thought about exercising during their cancer treatment.

---

perceived behavioral control   The perceived ease or difficulty of performing a behavior.

control beliefs   The perceived presence or absence of required resources and opportunities, the anticipated obstacles or impediments to behavior, and the perceived power of a particular control factor to facilitate or inhibit performance of the behavior.

Courneya and Friedenreich (1999) found that the most salient behavioral beliefs among the breast cancer patients were: (a) it gets my mind off cancer and treatment, (b) it makes me feel better and improves my well-being, (c) it helps me maintain a normal lifestyle, (d) it helps me cope with my life and the stress over cancer, (e) it helps in my recovery from surgery and treatment, and (f) it helps me control my weight. The five salient sources for normative beliefs were: (a) spouse, (b) other family members, (c) friends, (d) physicians, and (e) other persons with cancer. The seven control beliefs that emerged for the breast cancer survivors were: (a) nausea experienced, (b) fatigue/tiredness experienced, (c) lack of time to exercise, (d) lack of support for exercise, (e) pain and soreness experienced, (f) lack of counseling for exercise, and (g) work at regular job. The elicitation study revealed that the salient beliefs of breast cancer patients concerning exercise were different from those of healthy populations.

RESEARCH EXAMINING THE THEORIES

A meta-analysis of studies using the theories of reasoned action and planned behavior was carried out by Hausenblas, Carron, and Mack (see Hausenblas et al., 1997; Spence, 1999). A meta-analysis is considered to provide an adequate summary of research on a topic. Prior to providing the results from the Hausenblas et al. meta-analysis, however, we discuss some studies published after 1997. These later studies serve to illustrate how the theories of reasoned action and planned behavior have been used as a framework to guide research in the study of physical activity.

Research Using a Retrospective Design

With a retrospective design, participants are asked to recall events that have occurred previously. Courneya and Friedenreich (1997) used a retrospective design with the theory of planned behavior construct to gain insight into the role that physical ac-

FIT FACTS

Is body appearance or body function more important to older adults?

Attitudes about body image begin to change when adults pass the age of 50. Body function becomes more important to older adults than body appearance.

(Reboussin et al., 2000)

tivity plays in colorectal cancer treatment. First, they carried out an elicitation study to determine the salient beliefs about physical activity during cancer treatment. The salient beliefs found for colorectal cancer survivors were identical to those found in the Courneya and Friedenreich (1999) study with breast cancer patients. These beliefs formed the basis for scale development.

The authors then surveyed 110 survivors of colorectal cancer who had recently undergone treatment. The participants were asked to recall their beliefs, attitudes, subjective norms, perceptions of control, intentions, and exercise behavior during their treatment. Courneya and Friedenreich (1997) found that exercise during treatment was determined by intention and perceived behavioral control. Furthermore, intention was determined solely by attitude. Thus, patients with positive attitudes, a strong intention, and a high perception of control were more likely to exercise during treatment. These results led Courneya and Friedenreich to conclude that the theory of planned behavior could be a viable framework on which to base interventions to promote exercise in patients with colorectal cancer.

A limitation of retrospective studies, however, is that participants may provide a current perception based on what they now know versus what they felt previously. For example, a person's attitude toward physical activity as well as the support of others can change over time (Courneya & Friedenreich, 1997, 1999). Thus, questions about beliefs held 6 months ago may elicit responses more closely allied with current beliefs.

Research Using Prospective Designs

With a prospective design, an attempt is made to predict into the future based on current factors such as intention, perceptions of control, attitude, and subjective norm. Courneya and his colleagues (1999) used a prospective design to examine the ability of the theory of planned behavior to predict exercise behavior in postsurgical colorectal cancer patients over a 4-month period. Initially, the participants completed a questionnaire designed to assess the constructs of the theory of planned behavior as well as physical activity involvement. Then, on a monthly basis over the next 4 months, the participants were contacted by phone to determine their physical activity over the previous month.

The study showed that cancer treatment leads to a reduction in an individual's physical activity level. Following surgery for their colorectal cancer, the participants reported less strenuous exercise over the 4 months than was typical for them prior to diagnosis. The best predictors of postsurgical physical activity were presurgical levels of physical activity, intention, and perceived behavioral control. Also, attitude was the only significant determinant of intention.

Another example of a prospective study was reported by Brenes, Strube, and Storandt (1998). They examined the ability of the theory of planned behavior to predict exercise behavior in 105 older adults (average age, 68 years) enrolled in YMCA exercise classes. Within the first two weeks of beginning an exercise class, participants completed measures that assessed the theory of planned behavior constructs as well as their exercise habit. The habit measure was used to assess participation in regular exercise in each decade of their life beginning with childhood. The participants were contacted by telephone 1, 3, and 9 months later and were asked to make ratings of their exercise behavior. The researchers found that only perceived behavioral control predicted exercise behavior at 1 month. Also, perceived behavioral control was the only significant predictor of intention to exercise. Brenes and her colleagues felt that that one reason why the theory of planned behavior proved to be such

a poor predictor of exercise behavior might have been a lack of variability among the participants in both their intention and exercise behavior. That is, 100% of the participants stated that they intended to exercise at the beginning of the study, and nearly all (89%) were still exercising 9 months later.

Summary of Research Using Meta-Analysis

Several narrative reviews (Blue, 1995; Godin, 1993, 1994; Godin & Kok, 1996) and statistical reviews (Hausenblas et al., 1997) have examined research that has applied the theories of planned behavior and reasoned action to physical activity. In short, these reviews offer support for the theories as useful frameworks for examining physical activity behaviors. However, although both theories have been applied successfully within the physical activity domain, the theory of planned behavior has been applied with more success (Blue; Godin, 1993; Hausenblas et al.). Research examining the theory of planned behavior has, thus, been conducted at an increasing rate in recent years (Culos-Reed, Gyuresik, & Brawley, 2001).

In the meta-analysis undertaken by Hausenblas and her colleagues (1997) to statistically review the theories of reasoned action and planned behavior, 31 studies yielded 162 effect sizes based on more than 10,000 participants. As the results in Table 14-1 show, large effect sizes were evidenced between intention and attitude, intention and perceived behavioral control, behavior and intention, behavior and perceived behavioral control, and behavior and attitudes. Moderate effect sizes were found between intention and subjective norm. And finally, no effect was found between behavior and subjective norm. Hausenblas and her colleagues concluded that the theory of planned behavior constructs has considerable utility in predicting and explaining exercise behavior and that a knowledge of the theory of planned behavior could help exercise practitioners understand the key elements associated with initiating and maintaining physical activity behavior.

■ **TABLE 14-1** Effect Sizes for the Relationships Among the Theories of Reasoned Action and Planned Behavior Constructs

RELATIONSHIPS	EFFECT SIZES
Intention and	
Attitude	1.22
Subjective norm	.56
Perceived behavioral control	.97
Behavior and	
Intention	1.09
Perceived behavioral control	1.01
Attitude	.84
Subjective norm	.18

Note. From "The Theories of Reasoned Action and Planned Behavior: A Meta-Analysis," by H. A. Hausenblas, A. V. Carron, and D. A. Mack, 1997, *Journal of Sport & Exercise Psychology, 19,* 47–62.

THEORY LIMITATIONS

Although the theory of reasoned action, and to a greater extent the theory of planned behavior, has been successful in explaining and predicting physical activity behavior, limitations of the theory and research examining the theory exist. First, factors such as personality (e.g., anxiousness, perfectionism), demographic variables (e.g., age, gender, socioeconomic status), and past exercise behavior (Bozionelos & Bennett, 1999) are not directly taken into consideration within the theories. This neglect is a limitation because researchers examining the determinants of physical activity have consistently found, for example, that the percentage of the population reporting no physical activity is higher among females than males, among older adults than younger adults, and among the less affluent than the more affluent (USDHHS, 2000).

Second, there is ambiguity regarding how to define perceived behavioral control, and this ambiguity creates measurement problems (see Ajzen, in press). In fact, Estabrooks and Carron (1998) noted that

Ajzen (1985, 1987, 1991) has been inconsistent in the manner in which he has defined perceived behavioral control, representing it both as self-efficacy and as the perceived ease or difficulty of performing the specific behavior. Because there is no agreed-on protocol for the assessment of perceived behavioral control, Estabrooks and Carron (1998) compared the relative merits of three different measures in a study using the theory of planned behavior to examine the physical activity of older adults (average age, 68 years). In one approach, the participants indicated their confidence in their ability to schedule exercise into their daily routine (*scheduling self-efficacy*). In another approach, the participants indicated their confidence in their ability to overcome barriers that might arise to inhibit attendance (*barrier self-efficacy*). For the third approach, the participants rated the ease or difficulty of attending exercise classes (*perceived behavioral control*). Estabrooks and Carron found that scheduling self-efficacy was the best predictor of exercise behavior.

Recently, Ajzen (in press) stated that the term *perceived behavioral control* may be misleading, and to avoid misunderstanding, he suggested that *perceived behavioral control* should be read as a "perceived control over performance of a behavior." Ajzen further noted that perceived behavioral control is composed of two components: self-efficacy (i.e., ease or difficulty of performing the behavior) and controllability (i.e., beliefs about the extent to which performing the behavior is up to the actor). Thus, measures of perceived behavioral control should contain items that assess both self-efficacy and controllability. Terry and O'Leary (1995), in a prospective study examining the ability of the theory of planned behavior constructs to predict regular exercise over a 2-week period, found support for the two components of perceived behavioral control. They also reported that self-efficacy predicted intention but not behavior, whereas perceived controllability predicted behavior but not intention. Further research is needed to examine the utility of the two proposed components of perceived behavioral control in the physical activity domain.

A third limitation of the theory of reasoned action is that the longer the time interval between behavioral intention and behavior, the less likely it is that the behavior will occur. Fishbein and Ajzen (1975; Ajzen & Fishbein, 1980) have argued that the predictive power of intention will vary inversely with the time between the measurement of intention and performance of the behavior. They have suggested that the longer the time interval is between intention and behavior, the more likely it is that intention will change with new available information. This new information would result in a diminished relationship between intention and behavior.

Courneya and McAuley (1993) found support for this contention. They examined 42 undergraduate students' short-term (2 days) and long-term (4 weeks) intention to engage in physical activity. Short-range intention was assessed by asking the students to respond to the question "Do you intend to be physically active between this class and next class?" Two days later the students reported their physical activity behavior. Long-range intention was assessed by having the students respond to the statement, "During the next 4 weeks I intend to be physically active ____ times." Four weeks later the students listed their physical activity for the past month. The correlations between short- and long-range intention and physical activity were .59 and .39 respectively, confirming the expectation that short-range intention is a better predictor of physical activity than is long-range intention.

A fourth potential limitation pertains to the construct of subjective norm. The theory of planned behavior variables of attitude and perceived behavioral control have been significant and consistent predictors of behavioral intention throughout the physical activity literature. Subjective norm, however, is generally a weak predictor (Courneya & McAuley, 1995; Culos-Reed et al., 2001; Hausenblas et al., 1997). One reason that has been offered by Culos-Reed and her colleagues for the inconsistent usefulness of subjective norm is that the role of significant others may not be important in encouraging participation of physically active individuals. The researchers found support for this view from the fact that subjective

FIT FACTS

Do perceptions of stress influence one's intention to be active and to adhere to a program of physical activity?

When life stressors are high, planned sessions of physical activity are reduced in number, are less satisfactory, and are enjoyed less.

(Stetson et al., 1997)

norm is a stronger predictor of behavioral intention for health behaviors such as contraceptive use in which the role of significant others is deemed to be more important for the decisions made and, thus, cannot be ignored.

Culos-Reed et al. (2001) proposed that a second reason for the weak contribution of subjective norm to the prediction of physical activity might lie in its operationalization. Some authors have suggested that a better operational definition for subjective norm might be one that more closely approximates the concept of social support (e.g., Courneya, Plotnikoff, Hotz, & Birkett, 2000; see Chapter 10). Is your motivation (or intention) to be involved in physical activity more the result of your belief that important others wish you to do so (i.e., subjective norm), or is it more the result of the support and praise you receive from others who are significant in your life (i.e., social support)? Physical activity scientists increasingly favor the latter alternative.

USING THEORY FOR PRACTICE

The theories of reasoned action and planned behavior are useful in identifying psychosocial determinants of physical activity. Therefore, they could be useful for developing community and individual exercise programs. Based on the results of the studies reviewed in this chapter, physical activity programs would be more efficient if they included components that would encourage positive beliefs and the evaluation of those beliefs for the individual. Blue (1995) stated that "changing beliefs about exercise can improve attitude, which in turn affects intention. According to the results of the studies reviewed, people intend to exercise when they hold a positive evaluation of exercise. Exercise programs that offer a positive experience would enhance intention to exercise, which in turn influences exercise behavior" (p. 119). Positive behavioral beliefs and their evaluation may be enhanced if people are given experiences with easy, enjoyable types of physical activities and then gradually encouraged to increase the intensity, duration, and frequency of those activities. Perceived behavioral control is an important factor in a person's intention to be physically active (Blue). When individuals perceive physical activity as difficult to do, intention is low. Assisting people to overcome barriers such as time involvement, other obligations, or feelings of inability should enhance their perceptions of control about carrying out exercise. The next step in research using the theories is to determine whether belief-based programs will lead to increased levels of exercise and to determine whether beliefs about exercise behavior change as a person initiates and continues an exercise program (Blue).

Summary

Changing people's behaviors is very difficult to do, especially when dealing with a complex health behavior such as physical activity. Thus, to increase the success of predicting, understanding, explaining, and changing physical activity behavior, researchers and practitioners should use a theoretical framework as a guide. This chapter explored the constructs in the theories of reasoned action and planned behavior as guides for examining physical activity. Researchers have found support for the utility of attitude, perceived behavioral control, and to a lesser extent, subjective norm in explaining people's intention to become physically active. Research has found a strong relationship between a person's intention to be active and whether that person actually engages in the behavior. Furthermore, a person's perception of the control he or she has over engaging in physical activity can also directly predict behavior.

In general, the theory of reasoned action is a good theory for predicting exercise behavior. Its extension, the theory of planned behavior, is even more successful. Because the theory of planned behavior can explain and predict exercise behavior, it offers a useful framework to guide physical activity interventions.

CHAPTER 15

The Transtheoretical Model and Physical Activity

One Size Does Not *Fit All.*

CHAPTER OBJECTIVES

After completing this chapter you will be able to

- Describe the constructs of the transtheoretical model.

- Discuss the research that has applied the transtheoretical model.

- Discuss the advantages and limitations of the transtheoretical model.

Key terms

action	preparation
contemplation	processes of change
decisional balance	self-efficacy
maintenance	stages of change
precontemplation	temptation
precontemplation believers	termination
precontemplation nonbelievers	

For most people, changing unhealthy behaviors to healthy behaviors is often challenging. Change usually does not occur all at once; it is a lengthy process that involves progressing through several stages. At each stage, the cognitions and behaviors of the individual are different, so one approach to facilitating behavioral change is not appropriate. The concept of stages—or a "one size does not fit all" philosophy (Marcus et al., 2000)—forms the basis for the transtheoretical model of behavior change (also referred to as the stages of change model) developed by Prochaska and his colleagues at the University of Rhode Island. This model emerged from a comparative analysis of leading theories of psychotherapy and behavior change. In developing the model, the goal was to provide a systematic integration of a field that had fragmented into more than 300 theories of psychotherapy (Prochaska & Velicer, 1997). The transtheoretical model includes five constructs—stages of change, decisional balance, processes of change, self-efficacy, and temptation—that are important for an understanding of the process of volitional change. After applying it to their work on smoking cessation, the researchers extended the model in an attempt to better understand a broad range of health and mental health behaviors such as nutrition, weight control, alcohol abuse, eating disorders, unplanned pregnancy protection, mammography screening, sun exposure, substance abuse, and physical activity (Prochaska & Velicer). The latter, of course, represents the focus in this chapter.

CONSTRUCTS OF THE TRANSTHEORETICAL MODEL

Five main constructs make up the transtheoretical model: stages of change, decisional balance, processes of change, self-efficacy, and temptation. Each of these constructs is outlined in detail in the following sections.

Stages of Change

One of the major contributions of the transtheoretical model to the health field is the recognition that behavior change unfolds slowly over time through a series of stages. Benjamin Franklin recognized this fact more than 300 years ago when he noted:

> To get the bad customs of a country changed and new ones, thought better, introduced, it is necessary first to remove the prejudices of the people, enlighten their ignorance, and convince them that their interests will be promoted by the proposed changes; and this is not the work of a day. (cited in USDHHS, 1999, p. 73)

There are three main aspects to the stages of change construct. First, stages fall somewhere between traits and states. Traits are stable and not open to immediate change. States, on the other hand, are readily changeable and typically lack stability. Thus, for example, an individual who is chronically anxious would be known to have high trait anxiety. Conversely, an individual who has severe butterflies before a race would be known to possess high state anxiety.

Second, stages are both stable and dynamic. That is, although stages may last for a considerable period, they are susceptible to change. Prochaska and DiClemente (1986) have hypothesized that as individuals change from an unhealthy to a healthy behavior, they move through a number of stages at varying rates and in a cyclical fashion with periods of progression and relapse. For example, a sedentary man initially may begin to think about physical activity's benefits (e.g., have more energy) and costs (e.g., time away from watching television). Then, a few months later, he may buy a pair of walking shoes. Six months

later he may go walking three times a week. After a year of walking regularly, however, he may become overwhelmed with the stress of work and stop walking. The cessation of physical activity would represent a regression to an earlier stage. In short, individuals going through the process of behavioral change typically cycle (or progress and relapse) through a series of stages as they recognize the need to change, contemplate making a change, make the change, and finally, sustain the new behavior (Culos-Reed et al., 2001). Figure 15-1 provides a graphic illustration of the stages of change.

Third, there are six stages through which people pass in attempting any health behavior change: **precontemplation** (not intending to make changes), **contemplation** (intending to make changes within the foreseeable future, which is defined as the next

precontemplation The stage at which a person does not intend to make changes.

contemplation The stage at which a person intends to make changes within the foreseeable future, which is defined as the next 6 months.

preparation The stage at which a person intends to change in the immediate future, which is defined as within 1 month.

action The stage at which a person actively engages in a new behavior.

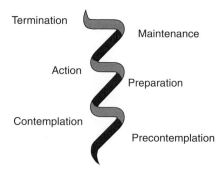

Figure 15-1 Stages of change. The spiral pattern represents the dynamic forward and backward movement through the stages.

6 months), **preparation** (intending to change in the immediate future, which is defined as within 1 month), **action** (actively engaging in the new behavior), **maintenance** (sustaining change over time), and **termination** (eliminating the probability of relapse; Cardinal, 1999; Cardinal, 2000; Reed et al., 1997). Operational definitions for the various stages are outlined in Table 15-1. Also, a more comprehensive description of each stage is provided in the following sections.

Precontemplation ("I won't or I can't"). People in the precontemplation stage are not considering or do not want to change their behavior. The so-called couch potato is an example of someone in the precontemplation stage. Precontemplators typically deny having a problem and have no intention of making a behavior change in the foreseeable future. As Table 15-1 shows, the foreseeable future is typically defined as within the next 6 months—the period of time most people might use if they are considering a behavior change (Prochaska & Marcus, 1994).

The hallmark of precontemplation is a lack of intention to take action regardless of the reason or excuse (Reed, 1999). An individual may be in precontemplation because he or she does not think

■ **TABLE 15-1**   Operational Definitions of the Stages of Exercise Change

STAGE	OPERATIONAL DEFINITION
Precontemplation	I do not intend to begin exercising in the next 6 months.
Contemplation	I intend to begin exercising in the next 6 months.
Preparation	I intend to begin exercising regularly in the next 30 days.
Action	I have been exercising, but for less than 6 months.
Maintenance	I have been exercising for more than 6 months.

Note. Adapted from "What Makes a Good Algorithm: Examples from Regular Exercise," by G. R. Reed, W. F. Velicer, J. O. Prochaska, J. S. Rossi, and B. H. Marcus, 1997, *American Journal of Health Promotion, 12,* 57–66.

physical activity is valuable or thinks it's valuable but may be overwhelmed by barriers such as lack of time. Precontemplators are the most difficult people to stimulate into behavioral change. They often think that change is not even a possibility. Educating them about the problem behavior is critical in helping them to start thinking about becoming more healthy.

Reed and her colleagues (1999) reported the existence of two types of precontemplators, each of whom have different reasons for not planning to engage in physical activity. **Precontemplation nonbelievers** either do not believe in regular physical activity or do not see the value of engaging in it. **Precontemplation believers** do believe that physical activity is a worthwhile behavior but they cannot seem to start participating in it. The precontemplation nonbelievers need to become aware of and learn to appreciate the pros, or benefits, of physical activity, such as improving mood states and energy levels. In contrast, the precontemplation believers need help overcoming the cons of exercising, such as taking time away from other activities (Reed, 1999).

Contemplation ("I might").   Individuals in the contemplation stage acknowledge that they have a problem and are thinking about changing their behavior sometime within the next 6 months. They see a need for change because they are aware of the costs and benefits of changing their behavior. For example, they may realize that physical activity reduces their chance of having heart disease (a pro, or

maintenance   The stage at which a person sustains change over time.

termination   The stage in which a person has 0% temptation to engage in old behavior and 100% self-efficacy in all previously tempting situations.

precontemplation nonbeliever   A person who either does not believe in regular physical activity or does not see the value of engaging in it.

precontemplation believer   A person who believes that physical activity is a worthwhile behavior but cannot seem to start participating in it.

benefit, of exercise). However, they also acknowledge that physical activity will take time away from doing other things such as working and spending time with family and friends (a con, or cost, of exercise). Contemplators are generally open to new information and interested in knowing more about the benefits of change. At this stage, however, people are not committed to the change because they are only contemplating or thinking about it. Therefore, they may become a chronic contemplator, never moving beyond the information-gathering phase (Prochaska & Marcus, 1994; Reed, 1999).

Preparation ("I will"). In the preparation stage, people are seriously considering or planning to change their activity level in the near future, usually within the next month. The preparation stage has both a behavioral and an intentional component. For example, preparers may have bought a pair of running shoes, joined a running club, and even gone for a half-hour walk once a week. They may also intend to increase the frequency of their walk from once to three times a week within the next month. These individuals often have strong incentives to change based on optimistic views about the beneficial outcomes. Preparation is a relatively unstable stage because people in this stage are more likely than precontemplators or contemplators to progress over the next six months (Prochaska & Marcus, 1994).

Action ("I am"). Individuals who have recently changed their behavior (i.e., within the last 6 months) are considered to be in the action stage. This stage requires the greatest commitment of time and energy. To be classified within the action stage insofar as physical activity is concerned, the individual must meet the minimal physical activity recommendations developed by the American College of Sports Medicine and Centers for Disease Control and Prevention (USDHHS, 1996). The recommendations state that adults should accumulate 30 minutes or more of moderate intensity physical activity (e.g., brisk walking) on most, preferably all, days of the week (Pate et al., 1995). Because the person in the action stage has only recently established the new habit, attentiveness is necessary because relapse is common (Reed, 1999).

Maintenance ("I have"). Once the individual has been regularly active for 6 consecutive months, he or she is deemed to have progressed into the maintenance stage. Although the new behavior has become better established, boredom and a loss of focus can become a real danger. The constant vigilance initially required to establish a new habit is exhausting and difficult to sustain. It is at this time that a person works to reinforce the gains made through the various stages of change and strives to prevent lapses and relapses (Reed, 1999).

Termination. Once a behavior has been maintained for more than 5 years, the individual is considered to have exited from the cycle of change, and a fear of relapse is eliminated. This stage is the ultimate goal for all people searching for a healthier lifestyle. Termination is the stage in which the person has 0% temptation to engage in the old behavior and 100% self-efficacy in all previously tempting situations. Research on the termination stage for physical activity is limited. For example, Cardinal (1999) examined whether a termination stage exists for physical activity. The criteria he used were the same as those just outlined—5 or more years of continuous involvement in physical activity and 100% self-efficacy in an ability to remain physically active for life. Of the 551 adults surveyed, 16.6% were classified within the termination stage. Cardinal concluded that individuals in the termination stage are resistant to relapse irrespective of common barriers given for not being physically active (e.g., lack of time, bad weather, no energy). The existence of a termination stage for exercise has also been found in research conducted by Fallon and Hausenblas (2001).

Decisional Balance

Decision making was first conceptualized by Janis and Mann (1977) as a decisional "balance sheet" that assesses the importance that an individual places on the potential advantages, or *pros*, and disadvantages, or *cons*, of a behavior. The **decisional balance** between

> **decisional balance** The balance between the potential advantages and disadvantages of a behavior.

the pros and cons varies depending on which stage of change the individual is in. When the cons of exercise (e.g., takes time away from other activities) are of greater importance than the pros of exercise (e.g., improves psychological well-being), motivation to change behavior (i.e., move from being sedentary to engaging in physical activity) is low. Thus, for example, in the precontemplation and contemplation stages, the cons are assumed to outweigh the pros. In the preparation stage, the pros and cons are believed to be relatively equal. In the action, maintenance, and termination stages, the pros are thought to outweigh the cons. DiClemente and his colleagues (1991) noted that an assessment of the pros and cons is relevant for researchers to understand and predict transitions among the first three stages of change (i.e., precontemplation, contemplation, and preparation). During the action and maintenance stages, however, these decisional balance measures are much less important predictors of progress.

Processes of Change

Ten **processes of change** represent the behaviors, cognitions, and emotions that people engage in during the course of changing a behavior. These processes are (a) *gathering information* (i.e., determining the pros and cons of the positive behavior); (b) *making substitutions* (substituting a positive behavior for a negative one); (c) *being moved emotionally* (experiencing and expressing feelings about the consequences of the positive behavior); (d) *being a role model* (considering how the negative behavior impacts on significant others); (e) *getting social support* (using significant others to effect change); (f) *developing a healthy self-image* (instilling the positive behaviors as an integral component of self-image); (g) *taking advantage of social mores* (taking advantage of social situations that encourage the positive behavior); (h) *being rewarded* (being rewarded by oneself or others for engaging in the positive behavior); (i) *using cues* (using cues as a catalyst for the positive behavior); and (j) *making a commitment* (becoming committed to the positive behavior). The 10 processes of change can be divided into 5 experiential or cogni-

tive processes (i.e., gathering information, being moved emotionally, being a role model, developing a healthy self-image, and taking advantage of social mores), and 5 behavioral or environmental processes (i.e., making substitutions, getting social support, making a commitment, being rewarded, and using cues).

Table 15-2 outlines the various processes of change and provides a description for each. The processes of change provide information on *how* shifts in behavior occur. As Culos-Reed and her colleagues (2001) noted, there is limited evidence about the processes that individuals experience as they move from being sedentary to engaging in regular physical activity.

Self-Efficacy

Self-efficacy is a judgment regarding a person's ability to perform a behavior required to achieve a certain outcome. Not surprisingly, self-efficacy is believed to be critical to behavior change (Bandura, 1997; see Chapter 12 for a detailed discussion of self-efficacy). Self-efficacy is proposed to change with each stage, presumably increasing as the individual gains confidence through, for example, successful attempts to increase physical activity. Conversely, self-efficacy may decrease if an individual falters and spirals back to an earlier stage.

Support for the role that self-efficacy plays in the transtheoretical model was provided by Gorely and Gordon (1995) in a study of Australian adults 50 to 65 years of age. The researchers found that self-efficacy to overcome barriers to exercise increased systematically from precontemplation to contemplation to preparation to action to maintenance. Further support for the effectiveness of self-efficacy was found by Sullum, Clark, and King

processes of change The behaviors, cognitions, and emotions that people engage in during behavior change.

self-efficacy Judgment regarding a person's ability to perform behavior.

■ **TABLE 15-2**   The Processes of Change

CLASSIC TERM	REVISED TERM	DESCRIPTION
Consciousness raising	Gathering information	Gathering information about regular physical activity (learning the pros and cons of exercising)
Counter-conditioning	Making substitutions	Substituting sedentary behavior with activity
Dramatic relief	Being moved emotionally	Experiencing and expressing feelings about the consequences of being active
Environmental reevaluation	Being a role model	Considering and assessing how inactivity affects friends, family, and citizens
Helping relationships	Getting social support	Getting support for one's intention to exercise
Self-reevaluation	Developing a healthy self-image	Appraising one's self-image as a healthy regular exerciser
Social-liberation	Taking advantage of social mores	Taking advantage of social policy, customs, and mores that enhance physical activity (e.g., New Year's resolutions)
Reinforcement management	Being rewarded	Rewarding oneself or being rewarded by others for making changes
Stimulus control	Using cues	Using cues to remember to engage in physical activity
Self-liberation	Making a commitment	Committing oneself to becoming or staying a regular exerciser

Note. Adopted from "Adherence to Exercise and the Transtheoretical Model of Behavior Change," by G. R. Reed, 1999, in S. Bull, Ed., *Adherence Issues in Sport and Exercise* (pp. 19–46), New York: Wiley.

(2000) in a study of 52 physically active college students. The researchers assessed the students' levels of self-efficacy at baseline and then tracked their physical activity behavior for approximately 8 weeks. They found that students who became inactive (i.e., relapsed) over the 8 weeks had lower self-efficacy at baseline than did those who maintained their exercise level.

Temptation

Temptation represents the intensity of the urges to engage in a specific behavior (or habit) when in the

temptation   Urge to engage in a behavior during difficult situations.

midst of difficult situations (Grimley, Prochaska, Velicer, Blais, & DiClemente, 1994). Temptation and self-efficacy function inversely across the stages of change, with temptation being a better predictor of relapses (Redding & Rossi, 1999). For example, in the maintenance stage, in which a smoker has successfully eliminated smoking behavior for at least six months, temptation is one of the best predictors of a relapse and the subsequent recycling to earlier stages of change (Redding & Rossi). Research examining the temptation construct for physical activity behavior is limited. In a recent study, Hausenblas and her colleagues (2001) found a negative relationship between temptations to *not* exercise and self-efficacy. That is, maintainers reported the lowest temptation to not exercise and the highest confidence in engaging in exercise behavior compared to individuals in the other stages.

There are many ways to avoid temptations.

ADVANTAGES AND LIMITATIONS OF THE TRANSTHEORETICAL MODEL

Advantages

Reed (1999) noted at least three advantages to dividing a population into the stages of change. The first is that using a stages perspective provides researchers with the opportunity to match interventions to the different needs of individuals in each of the stages. As a consequence, researchers and health care professionals are able to target specific interventions for the total population (i.e., those who have not yet made a behavior change and are at risk as well as those who have changed but may be at risk of relapse). For example, limited success has been observed for traditional interventions in terms of promoting the adoption and maintenance of a physically active lifestyle. This lack of success may be attributed, in part, to the fact that an educational focus has been utilized rather than a behavioral and motivational focus. Many sedentary individuals are not ready to adopt regular exercise because they are unmotivated. Providing them with advice and a physical activity prescription is unlikely to lead to be-

havior change. Therefore, the traditional physical activity intervention may fail to recruit the vast majority of sedentary individuals because they have no intention of becoming active. This finding reflects an incongruity between what is typically offered (action-oriented programs) and population motivational readiness to change (inactive and not intending to become active). Consequently, it is important that health care professionals customize interventions to meet the specific motivational needs of the majority of individuals who are either inactive or underactive.

A second advantage is that adopting a stages of change approach provides researchers with the opportunity to subdivide the at-risk population into precontemplation, contemplation, and preparation stages. This identification of the three types of people at risk allows health care professionals to proactively try to recruit individuals who are most in need but the least likely to react to a physical activity program (i.e., precontemplators and contemplators). It is important to note that the distribution across these stages varies by age. For example, Nigg and his colleagues (1999) found that for people aged 75 and older, 39% were classified in the precontemplation stage, 5% in the contemplation stage, and 10% in the preparation stage. In comparison, for adults less than 55 years of age, 17% were classified in the precontemplation stage, 14% in the contemplation stage, and 18% in the preparation stage.

A third advantage is associated with recruitment and retention. An individual's readiness to change can predict the likelihood that that person will successfully adopt and maintain a healthy lifestyle. Recruitment of people at an earlier stage can be successful if (a) health professionals proactively target them, and (b) an intervention is used that is matched to the specific stage of change. Proactive recruitment by either telephone or a personal letter coupled with stage-matched interventions have resulted in good participation rates (Reed, 1999). As Marcus and her colleagues (2000) stated, " 'One-size-fits-all' programs are rarely as effective as programs that tailor treatment to at least some aspects of the individual or group" (p. 39).

Research by Lichtenstein and Hollis (1992) serves to illustrate Marcus's point. Lichtenstein and Hollis had little success with an action-oriented approach to smoking cessation. That is, following intensive proactive recruitment, participants spent 5 minutes in a counseling session with the physician. If the participant could not be convinced to sign up for a smoking cessation clinic, the next 10 minutes were spent with a nurse. If the participant was still unwilling to sign up for the program, 12 minutes were spent with a health educator and watching a video. The final push was a follow-up telephone call from a counselor. All this labor produced only a 1% participation rate.

Limitations

Because of the advantages of the transtheoretical model, it is not surprising that the model's framework has been applied frequently to change people's health behaviors. Unfortunately, application has occurred without proper validation of the transtheoretical model. That is, as Culos-Reed and her colleagues (2001) noted, limited evidence exists on the theorizing, testing, and critiquing of the model. Thus, Culos-Reed et al. concluded that "there appears to have been a readiness to accept the TTM [transtheoretical model] for application beyond any reasonable amount of validation evidence that would be expected for theories in the behavioral sciences" (p. 713).

Furthermore, Joseph, Curtis, and Skinner (1997) stated five limitations of the transtheoretical model (see Culos-Reed et al., 2001). First, research

does not support the six stages of change as a robust construct. Second, support for the relationship between the processes of changes and the stages of change is equivocal. Third, the transtheoretical model is mostly descriptive as opposed to explanatory. For example, the characteristics within the stages are described, but causal processes are not tested (Culos-Reed et al.). Fourth, the transtheoretical model fails to include the influence of moderator variables (e.g., gender, age, ethnicity). Finally, the integrating of various theories (e.g., self-efficacy, decisional balance) to develop the transtheoretical model places these theories at odds with each other within the transtheoretical model. For example, Bandura (1997) stated that stages should reflect qualitative change and provide an invariant and nonreversible sequence. However, people's progression through the stages of change of the transtheoretical model is reversible (i.e., people can relapse), and advancement from one stage to the next does not reflect a qualitative change (Weinstein, Rothman, & Sutton, 1998).

PHYSICAL ACTIVITY RESEARCH EXAMINING THE TRANSTHEORETICAL MODEL

The transtheoretical model was first applied to physical activity in the late 1980s by Sonstroem (1987), and since then its popularity has grown. Over the last decade the model has been used to examine physical activity in cross-sectional studies and to a lesser extent in longitudinal and quasi-experimental intervention studies. In fact, a literature search found more than 50 studies from 1987 to 2000 that have validated, expanded, applied, and challenged the transtheoretical model for physical activity behavior. Culos-Reed and her colleagues (2001) noted that research on physical activity that also has used the transtheoretical model as a theoretical framework can be classified into one of the following three categories: (a) studies that combine the stages of change with the variables in other social-cognitive models, (b) cross-sectional studies that examine various transtheoretical model constructs, and (c) interventions to enhance a physically active lifestyle that are based on the constructs of the model. Studies in each of these three areas are highlighted in the following sections.

Stages of Change and Social-Cognitive Models

An important construct in both the health belief model (Rosenstock, 1990) and protection motivation theory (Maddux & Rogers, 1983) is perceived severity—an individual's feelings about the seriousness of a health condition if it is contracted or not treated. Courneya (1995b) noted that previous research has been unable to find that perceived severity is an important construct for motivation to engage in physical activity. People may agree that being physically inactive can contribute to coronary problems, but there is no link between people's perceptions of the severity of the problem and their tendency to adopt a physically active lifestyle.

Courneya (1995b) suggested that the absence of a relationship between perceptions of severity and motivation to change could be due in part to the tendency for researchers to implicitly adopt a two-stage model of exercise behavior change whereby the population is considered to be either inactive or active. Consequently, he compared perceptions of the severity of a sedentary lifestyle among 270 senior citizens who were classified within the various stages of the transtheoretical model. He found that the perceived severity of the consequences of an inactive lifestyle were less for individuals in the precontemplation stage than for those in the contemplation stage. However, the contemplation stage represented a plateau in that it did not differ from any of the active stages (i.e., preparation, action, maintenance). Courneya concluded that the main function of perceived severity of physical inactivity is to motivate people to seriously consider becoming physically active. This perception of severity is then maintained through the active stages.

In a 3-year longitudinal study, Courneya, Nigg, and Estabrooks (1998) examined the relationships among the theory of planned behavior (see

Chapter 14 for a detailed discussion of the theory of planned behavior), stages of change, and physical activity behavior in 131 older adults (aged 60 years and over). Participants completed an initial questionnaire sent by mail that assessed the constructs contained in the theory of planned behavior (i.e., attitude, perceived control, subjective norm, and intention) and the stages of change. Three years later, the participants received a telephone call in which their current exercise stage and behavior were assessed. The researchers found that the theory of planned behavior constructs were significant predictors of exercise change and that exercise behavior was best predicted by intention rather than by stages of change. The authors concluded that their results provided "evidence for the long term predictive validity of the theory of planned behavior in the exercise domain and [question] . . . the necessity of combining both intention and stage in a single predictive model" (p. 355).

Finally, Courneya and Bobick (2000) examined, in a cross-sectional design with 427 college students, the processes and stages of change of the transtheoretical model with the theory of planned behavior constructs. They found that the theory of planned behavior constructs mediated 8 of the 10 relationships between the processes of change and stages of change. Also, perceived behavioral control was predicted by behavioral/environmental processes of changes. In contrast, attitude was predicted by both cognitive/experiential and behavioral processes. The authors concluded that the integrated model produced insights into how (i.e., processes of change) and why (i.e., theory of planned behavior constructs) individuals successfully change their exercise behavior.

Cross-Sectional Studies

Marcus and her colleagues were the first to develop self-report instruments to measure the constructs of the transtheoretical model. Through a series of studies they developed measures for the stages of change, self-efficacy, process of change, and decisional balance (Marcus, Selby, et al., 1992 [self-efficacy and stages of change]; Marcus, Rossi, Selby, Niaura, & Abrams, 1992 [pros and cons]; Marcus, Rakowski, & Rossi, 1992 [decisional balance]). Recently, Hausenblas and her colleagues (2001) developed a measure of temptation to not engage in physical activity. Numerous studies have examined various constructs of the transtheoretical model, particularly the stages of change; however, research examining the complete model for physical activity is limited.

One of the few studies to examine all the components of the transtheoretical model (excluding temptation) was undertaken by Nigg and Courneya (1998) with 819 high school students. The students completed measures of decisional balance, self-efficacy, processes of change, and stages of change. The distribution of the sample across the stages of change was 2.1% in precontemplation, 4.2% in contemplation, 28.7% in preparation, 15.7% in action, and 49.3% in maintenance. The study results generally supported the tenets of the transtheoretical model, with the constructs being significant discriminators of at least one stage of change.

Another comprehensive study examining all the constructs within the transtheoretical model was the Gorely and Gordon (1995) research with older Australian adults. Gorely and Gordon also found general support for the model in that the utility of the various processes of change was shown to fluctuate across the stages, that self-efficacy increased systematically from contemplation through maintenance, and that the balance in the importance of the pros and cons for physical activity changed from precontemplation to maintenance.

Important questions about the transtheoretical model revolve around the validity of the various stages. Do contemplators truly differ from precontemplators? Do the latter differ from preparers? If re-search shows that the answers to these questions are yes, it would provide support for the validity of the transtheoretical model. Measures that have been used to examine differences among individuals classified within the various stages have included objective physical indices (% body fat, VO_2 max) and self-reports of physical activity (e.g., Buxton, Wyse, Mercer, & Hale, 1995; Cardinal, 1997; Hausenblas et al., 1999; Reed et al., 1997). The literature applying the stages of change to exercise behavior does not appear to have achieved consensus on the pattern of stage differences in measures of exercise behavior. The failure to detect common patterns of stage differences may be due to the use of different measures and populations.

For example, in a validation study, Cardinal (1997) examined the validity of the stages of change with 135 adults (M age = 34.7). Participants were classified by stage of change and then compared by their scores on a bicycle submaximal aerobic fitness test, on the Leisure-Time Exercise Questionnaire (see Chapter 2 for a description), and on their body mass index. The results of the study revealed a decrease in body mass index across the stages of change. That is, participants in the precontemplation stage had the highest body mass index scores, and participants in the maintenance stage had the lowest body mass index scores. Also, a linear improvement in submaximal aerobic fitness and self-report of exercise was evidenced across the stages. That is, participants in the precontemplation stage were the least aerobically fit, whereas participants in the maintenance stage were the most aerobically fit. See Figure 15-2 for a graphic display of the results. Cardinal concluded that the study findings offered objective support for the stages of change for exercise behavior.

Intervention Research

Marcus and her colleagues (1992) conducted the first intervention study based on the transtheoretical model. The intervention was designed to increase the adoption of physical activity among 610 community volunteers. At baseline, 39% of the participants were in the contemplation stage, 37% were in the prepara-

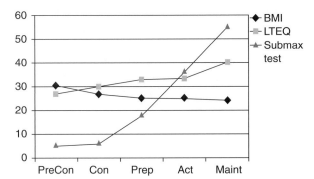

Figure 15-2 Relationship between the stages of change and measures of physical activity.

Note. BMI = body mass index; LTEQ = Leisure-Time Exercise Questionnaire; Submax test = submaximal bicycle test; PreCon = precontemplation; Con = contemplation; Prep = preparation; Act = action; Maint = maintenance. From "Construct Validity of Stages of Change for Exercise Behavior," by B. J. Cardinal, 1997, *American Journal of Health Promotion, 12,* 68–74.

tion stage, and 24% were in the action stage. A 6-week stage-matched intervention consisting of three different sets of self-help materials, a resource manual describing activity options, and weekly fun walks and activity nights were delivered. A subsample of 236 participants were telephoned poststudy to determine the efficacy of the intervention. The results showed that 17% of subjects were in contemplation, 24% were in preparation, and 59% were in action, thus demonstrating that subjects had become significantly more active during the intervention.

In a worksite intervention study, Marcus and her colleagues (1998) used the transtheoretical model constructs to design an intervention to increase the initiation, adoption, and maintenance of physical activity among 1,559 employees. The employees were randomized into either a stage-matched self-help intervention or a standard self-help intervention. Printed physical activity promotion materials were given to subjects at baseline and again 1 month later. The stage-matched group received a motivationally tailored intervention that consisted of five manuals. Each manual focused on one of the stages of change. In comparison, the standard self-help intervention consisted of five manuals on physical activity developed by the American Heart Association. These

manuals were used because they represent typical action-oriented material available to the public. Assessments of motivational readiness for physical activity and time spent in physical activity participation were conducted at the beginning of the program and 3 months later. At the 3-month follow-up, more individuals in the stage-matched group demonstrated positive changes than did individuals in the standard self-help group. Conversely, more individuals in the standard self-help group failed to progress to another stage or even showed regression to an earlier stage compared to the stage-matched group.

Physicians and other health care providers can be important avenues for reaching sedentary individuals and encouraging increases in physical activity levels. Health care providers have the potential to play a vital role in effecting change in the physical activity levels of their patients, with 70% of adults reporting at least one visit to a health care clinic each year (Logsdon, Lazaro, & Meier, 1989). A project called the Provider-Based Assessment and Counseling for Exercise (Calfas et al., 1996; Calfas, Sallis, Oldenburg, & Ffrench, 1997) is one example of a physical activity intervention employing physician counseling that was based on the transtheoretical model and social cognitive theory. In this intervention, 12 primary care physicians provided 3 to 5 minutes of physical activity counseling for their patients. Counseling was tailored to the patients' level of activity and readiness to become active. Evaluation of the Provider-Based Assessment and Counseling for Exercise program at the follow-up assessment of 4 to 6 weeks revealed that patients receiving the counseling increased their duration of walking and demonstrated a greater increase in readiness to become active than did patients not receiving the counseling.

Another physician-based intervention (called the Physically Active for Life intervention; Goldstein et al., 1999) based on the transtheoretical model and social cognitive theory involved 24 physicians who were randomly assigned to either an intervention or control condition. Physicians in the intervention condition provided 3 to 5 minutes of physical activity counseling to their patients. In comparison, physicians in the control condition did not give any physical activity counseling. Results showed that at a 6-week follow-up, individuals in the intervention condition were more likely to be in more advanced stages of motivational readiness for physical activity than were individuals in the control condition. This effect was not maintained at an 8-month follow-up, and the intervention did not produce significant changes in self-reported physical activity. These results suggest that more intensive interventions are needed to promote the adoption of physical activity among sedentary adults in primary care settings.

Summary

This chapter examined the transtheoretical model and its application to physical activity behavior. Over the last decade the transtheoretical model has been increasingly applied to examine physical activity behavior in cross-sectional studies and to a lesser extent in longitudinal and quasi-experimental intervention studies. The core constructs of the model are the stages of change, processes of change, decisional balance, self-efficacy, and temptation. The most frequently examined construct of the transtheoretical model in the exercise domain has been the stages of change construct. The stages of change assesses people's progression and regression through five main stages as they attempt to become physically active: precontemplation (not intending to make changes), contemplation (intending to make changes in the foreseeable future), preparation (immediate intention to change), action (actively engaging in the new behavior), and maintenance (sustaining change over time).

The processes of change are the overt and covert activities that individuals use to alter their experiences and environments to modify behavior change. Decisional balance focuses on the benefits (pros) and costs (cons) of a behavior and is thought to be important in the decision-making process. Self-efficacy is a judgment regarding a person's ability to perform a behavior required to achieve a certain outcome. Finally, temptation is the intensity of a person's urges to engage in a specific habit when in the midst of difficulty.

CHAPTER 16

Motivational Theories of Exercise and Physical Activity

I Know Not the Course Others May Take; But As for Me, Give Me Liberty or Give Me Death.
(Patrick Henry)

CHAPTER OBJECTIVES

After completing this chapter you will be able to

- Define motivation and explain how it is manifested in behavior.

- Differentiate among the various manifestations of motivation that form the basis for self-determination theory.

- Identify the most commonly cited motives for involvement in physical activity.

- Understand how self-determination theory is used to account for involvement in physical activity.

- Explain the main tenets of personal investment theory.

- Understand how personal investment theory is used to account for involvement in physical activity.

M otivation, a derivative of the Latin word *movere* meaning "to move," is the psychological construct used to account for the *why* of behavior. Why do people select certain options over others?

For example, why do you choose to lift weights or run during your free time rather than watch television? Your *selection* of specific activities over others represents your underlying motivation. Motivation-as-reflected-in-selectivity is illustrated by Patrick Henry's famous quote. Henry's sentiments also illustrate the important role that autonomy/self-determination plays in behavior. A motivational theory that is grounded in the concept of self-determination is one of the theories discussed in this chapter.

Why do you expend effort to accomplish an activity? For example, why do you strain to complete that 10th repetition during a set of bench presses? The *effort* you expend on an activity reflects your underlying motivation. Why do you continue to persist in the face of daunting challenges? For example, you may run four to five times a week, week after week. The *persistence* you demonstrate in that activity also reflects your underlying motivation.

Historically, attempting to better understand motivation—the why of behavior—has been the foundation of psychology. The earliest work was characterized by an emphasis on *instincts* (e.g.,

Key terms	
amotivation	incentive congruency
autonomy	measure
competence	intrinsic motivation
external regulation	introjected regulation
identified regulation	relatedness

Freud, 1933) and *drives* (e.g., Hull, 1943). More recently, however, there has been a shift in perspective (or paradigm, as it is also called). Currently, the emphasis is on understanding individual cognitions, perceptions, and emotions. The various theories presented in previous chapters of this book—self-efficacy theory, the health belief model, protection motivation theory, the theories of reasoned action and planned behavior, and the transtheoretical model—all are illustrative of the modern paradigm. Each emphasizes the role that social cognitions, perceptions, and/or emotions play in human behavior. In this chapter, we outline self-determination theory and personal investment theory—two additional approaches that also emphasize social cognitions, perceptions, and emotions.

SELF-DETERMINATION THEORY

Self-determination theory had its origins in the search for understanding the relative influence of intrinsic interest and extrinsic rewards on human behavior. As a consequence, attention was directed toward understanding the function of rewards. A generalization that resulted from the earliest work was that extrinsic rewards can be perceived by a recipient in one of two ways. One way pertains to receiving information about *competence.* Thus, for example, a young child who receives a special treat for playing well in a competition likely would perceive that reward as an affirmation that he or she is competent. Another way pertains to receiving information about *control.* If that same young child is given the special treat as an inducement to participate in the competition, that reward could be perceived to be a bribe to have the child compete. Rewards that convey information to the individual that he or she is highly competent enhance intrinsic motivation. Conversely, however, rewards that convey information that the recipient is no longer fully in control of the reasons for behavior reduce intrinsic motivation.

An anecdote about an old man who lived on a quiet cul-de-sac clearly illustrates the impact of rewards perceived to play a controlling function (Casady, 1974). Unfortunately for the old man, a group of boys began playing games outside his home. The noise became unbearable. So one day, he called them into his house and told them how much he enjoyed their activity. He also indicated that his hearing was failing and, therefore, offered to pay each of them a quarter if they would return the next day and make even more noise. The boys agreed, returned the next day, made a tremendous amount of noise, and were paid. The process was repeated on the second day. The boys returned, made the required amount of noise, and were paid the agreed-upon fee. The third day, however, the old man told the boys he would have to reduce the fee to 20 cents because he was running out of money. Finally, on the fourth day, he informed the boys that he would again have to reduce their fee—this time to 5 cents each. The boys became angry and informed the old man that it wasn't worth their time and effort to make noise for only 5 cents. So, they told him, they wouldn't return. And the cul-de-sac became quiet once again. As the story illustrates, the boys' motivation for an activity that had been highly enjoyable was reduced after rewards were introduced that were perceived to be controlling their behavior.

Sources of Motivation

Early research emphasized the independence of intrinsic and extrinsic motivation; if one was present, it was assumed that the other could not be. However, when research showed that this approach did not adequately explain human behavior, Deci and Ryan (Deci, 1992; Deci & Ryan, 1985, 1991; R. M. Ryan, 1993) developed self-determination theory. Vallerand and his colleagues (Vallerand, 1997; Vallerand, Blais, Brière, & Pelletier, 1989; Vallerand, Deci, & Ryan, 1987; Vallerand et al., 1992, 1993) have carried out a considerable amount of research in the sport sciences with self-determination theory. In self-determination theory, extrinsic and intrinsic motivation are assumed to fall along a continuum (see Figure 16-1). At one end of the continuum is **amotivation**—the absence of motivation toward an activity.

amotivation The absence of motivation toward an activity.

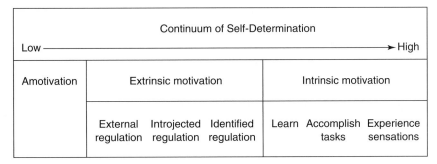

Figure 16-1   A proposed motivational sequence.
Note. Based on Li, 1999, and Vallerand & Losier, 1999.

In the middle of the continuum lies *extrinsic motivation.* According to self-determination theorists, extrinsic motivation is best viewed as multidimensional in nature. One dimension is **external regulation,** the "purest" form of extrinsic motivation. The individual engages in a behavior solely to receive a reward or to avoid punishment. Consider the case of a person who has been told by his or her physician that an immediate consequence of continued inactivity could be hospitalization. So, grudgingly, a program of physical activity is initiated. That person could be considered to be motivated through external regulation.

A dimension of extrinsic motivation that is slightly further along the continuum is **introjected regulation.** It represents the incomplete internalization of a regulation that was previously solely external. To continue our example, our reluctant exerciser might eventually progress to where he or she was no longer at high risk. However, if the person maintained a physical activity program because of a sense of "should" or "must," the source of motivation would be introjected regulation. The distinction between external regulation and introjected regulation lies in the fact that, in the latter case, the individual has begun to internalize the motivation for the behavior.

A third extrinsic motivation dimension that is slightly further along the continuum is **identified regulation.** Here the individual freely chooses to carry out an activity that is not considered to be enjoyable per se but is thought to be important to achieve a personal goal. The individual internalizes

the sentiment "I want to." Identified regulation can be illustrated by an individual who is regularly physically active but does not enjoy the activity in the least; he or she views it as essential for weight control.

At the other extreme on the continuum is **intrinsic motivation,** which is the motivation to do an activity for its own sake or for the pleasure it provides. Vallerand and his colleagues (1989, 1992, 1993) have proposed that intrinsic motivation is also multidimensional in nature. One form is reflected in intrinsic motivation toward *knowledge*—the pleasure of engaging in an activity to learn something new about the activity. An individual who chooses to run a marathon to learn how his or her body will respond under that stress provides an example of this form of intrinsic motivation. For exercise and physical activity contexts, Li (1999) has renamed this dimension of intrinsic motivation *to learn.*

external regulation   A type of extrinsic motivation in which an individual engages in a behavior solely to receive a reward or avoid punishment.

introjected regulation   The incomplete internalization of a regulation that was previously solely external.

identified regulation   A type of extrinsic motivation in which an individual freely chooses to carry out an activity that is not considered to be enjoyable but is thought to be important to achieve a personal goal.

intrinsic motivation   The motivation to do an activity for its own sake or for the pleasure it provides.

A second type is intrinsic motivation toward *accomplishment*. Our would-be marathoner might also want the satisfaction of completing such a long distance. For physical activity and exercise contexts, Li (1999) refers to this dimension as intrinsic motivation *to accomplish tasks*.

Finally, the third type is reflected in intrinsic motivation toward *stimulation*. It represents motivation to experience the pleasant sensations derived from the activity itself. An individual who is physically active because of the bodily sensations accompanying physical activity—sweating, elevated heart rate, muscles responding to the increased load—exemplifies intrinsic motivation toward stimulation. For the context of exercise and physical activity, Li (1999) has renamed this type of intrinsic motivation *to experience sensations*.

The Antecedents of Intrinsic and Extrinsic Motivation

Motives for Physical Activity.   Figure 16-2 provides an overview of self-determination theory. According to Deci and Ryan, the various goals or motives that individuals have for an activity are driven by psychological needs that have as their basis a striving toward growth and the actualization of personal potential. It is useful to examine the typical goals or motives for becoming involved in exercise and physical activity because they could have implications for self-determination. According to Willis and Campbell (1992), the following motives have been identified through research: improve or maintain health and fitness including, for example, the prevention of coronary heart disease; improve physical appearance including, for example, losing body weight; experience a sense of enjoyment, including, for example, obtaining personal satisfaction and fun from an activity; have a social experience such as being in the company of others; and obtain the psychological benefits such as, for example, those documented in Chapters 3 through 6.

Carron and Estabrooks (1999), in their survey of 186 older adults (i.e., >65 years) who were participants at a center devoted to the study of activity and aging, identified four dominant motives. These motives included functional health (e.g., to improve arm strength); psychological well-being (e.g., to feel good); general health (e.g., to stay in shape); and social interactions (e.g., to meet and be with others).

On the basis of other research and a theoretical understanding of incentives for exercise and physical activity, Markland, Hardy, and Ingledew (Markland & Hardy, 1993; Markland & Ingledew, 1997) developed the *Exercise Motivation Inventory* to assess motives for exercise and physical activity. The 14 motives they identified were stress management, revitalization, enjoyment, challenge, social recognition, affiliation, competition, health pressures, ill-health avoidance, positive health, weight management, appearance, strength, and nimbleness.

How do these various motives relate to the self-determination continuum illustrated in Figure 16-1? On the basis of their research, Markland and Ingledew (1997) cautioned that "whilst some motives, such as enjoyment, challenge and appearance im-

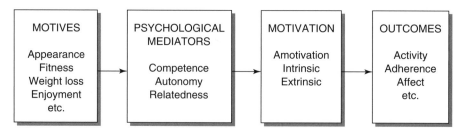

Figure 16-2   The relationships among motives; perceptions of autonomy, competence, and relatedness; intrinsic and extrinsic motivation; and various outcomes. *Note.* Based on Li, 1999, and Vallerand & Losier, 1999.

provement conform reasonably well to conventional definitions of either intrinsic or extrinsic motivation, for others the position is not so obvious" (p. 374). Thus, drawing on self-determination theory, they argued that motives for physical activity "may be better represented by a behavioural regulation continuum ranging from completely non-self-determined to completely self-determined forms of regulation" (p. 374). The relationship between where a motive lies on the behavioral regulation continuum and its implications for affect associated with physical activity as well as adherence is discussed in the following section.

Perceptions of Self-Determination.   As Figure 16-2 shows, the motives and goals that an individual has for physical activity are interpreted by the individual in terms of the degree to which they satisfy three psychological needs: autonomy, competence, and relatedness. The need for **autonomy** refers to the desire to be self-initiating in the regulation of personal behavior. If a sense of autonomy is present, intrinsic motivation is facilitated. Both the anecdote about the old man who lived on a quiet cul-de-sac and the quote by Patrick Henry serve to illustrate the importance of autonomy in human behavior.

The need for **competence** reflects the fact that individuals want to interact effectively within their environment. If an activity provides the individual with a sense of competence, intrinsic motivation is facilitated. Thus, for example, if exercisers begin to attend a step-class and discover that they are never able to coordinate their actions with the rest of their classmates, they are likely to seek out another form of physical activity.

Finally, the need for **relatedness** reflects the fact that individuals want to feel connected to other people. When relatedness is perceived to be present, intrinsic motivation is facilitated. It is not surprising

that social experiences and social interactions were identified as among the most important motives for physical activity by both Willis and Campbell (1992) and Carron and Estabrooks (1999).

According to Deci and Ryan (1985), the various types of motivation are intimately related to perceptions of self-determination (see Figure 16-1). When self-determination is absent, amotivation exists. When an activity is undertaken for extrinsic motives, minimal perceptions of self-determination are present. At the extreme end of the continuum, complete self-determination is associated with the various manifestations of intrinsic motivation.

The schematic illustration of self-determination theory presented in Figure 16-2 is also intended to show that the type of motivation the individual possesses (i.e., extrinsic vs. intrinsic) influences the selection of activities, the effort and persistence devoted to those activities, and the affect experienced. The case of the individual informed by his or her physician to become active or be hospitalized provides a useful example. That person's motive is to follow orders and avoid negative consequences. Thus, perceptions of self-determination would likely be minimal, and his or her motivation could be best described as external regulation. Predictions from self-determination theory would be that persistence and effort could be a problem and that the affect associated with the physical activity would not be highly positive. Conversely, the case of the individual training for a marathon just to accomplish the feat also provides a useful example. That person has freely chosen to attempt the task. Therefore, perceptions of self-determination would be maximal. In this case, a prediction from self-determination theory would be that persistence and effort would be high and the affect associated with the activity would be highly positive.

Implications of Self-Determination Theory for Exercise and Physical Activity.   The recurring motives associated with involvement in physical activity are to improve or maintain health and fitness (e.g., prevention of coronary heart disease), improve physical appearance (e.g., lose weight), experience a sense of enjoyment (e.g., have fun), enjoy a social experience (e.g., meet others), and obtain the psychological

---

autonomy   The desire to be self-initiating in the regulation of personal behavior.

competence   The desire to interact effectively within an environment.

relatedness   The desire to feel connected to other people.

benefits (e.g., reduced anxiety and depression). Many of these motives seem inherently intrinsic in nature including, for example, experiencing a sense of enjoyment, meeting others, and deriving psychological benefits. Thus, it could be predicted from self-determination theory that those individuals for whom these types of motives are particularly salient would not be at risk from an adherence perspective.

Conversely, however, motives such as improving health and/or physical appearance appear to be more extrinsic in nature. That is, individuals who hold these motives might consider exercise as a "must do" or "should do" type of activity. If so, self-determination theory would predict that adherence to programs of physical activity might be a problem. The critical factor, of course, is the individual's perception. Individuals who truly want to improve health and/or physical appearance might be intrinsically motivated toward accomplishment.

Research on Self-Determination Theory in Physical Activity Settings

Much of the earliest research into intrinsic and extrinsic motivation was carried out in laboratory, school, and sport settings. However, researchers have begun to assess the applicability of the theory in physical activity and exercise settings.

Applicability of Self-Determination Theory. In 1999, Li used self-determination as a conceptual framework to develop the *Exercise Motivation Scale*. After confirming the validity of the scale, Li used it to examine 598 male and female college students who varied in their frequency of exercise. Interestingly, Li found differences between males and females in underlying motivations for exercise. Females reported more intrinsic motivation to learn, intrinsic motivation to experience sensations, intrinsic motivation to accomplish tasks, integrated regulation, and identified regulation (see Figure 16-1 again). Frequent exercisers (i.e., individuals who were active 2 or more times per week) also reported higher levels of intrinsic motivation to learn, instrinsic motivaton to experience sensations, integrated regulation, and identified regulation than did infrequent exercisers (i.e., individuals who were active either one or no times per week).

FIT FACTS

Do adverse health behaviors coexist?

It appears so. Smoking, poor diet, low levels of physical activity, and excessive alcohol drinking tend to be related in 18-year-old men and women.

(Burke et al., 2000)

Li (1999) also tested self-determination theory to determine how perceptions of competence, autonomy, and relatedness about physical activity were related to the various forms of motivation illustrated in Figure 16-1. He found that, consistent with what would be predicted from self-determination theory, perceptions of competence, autonomy, and relatedness were positively related to the three types of intrinsic motivation (i.e., to learn, to accomplish tasks, and to experience sensations) and negatively related to amotivation.

The Theories of Reasoned Action and Planned Behavior.   A pivotal construct in the theories of reasoned action and planned behavior is intention (see Chapter 14); it has been found to be a reliable predictor of behavior. Is intention to engage in leisure-time physical activity (and actual leisure-time physical activity) influenced by perceptions of the degree of autonomy present in physical education classes? A sense of minimal personal control in physical education class might transfer to and influence both intention and actual leisure-time physical activity.

Chatzisarantis, Biddle, and Meek (1997) examined this issue with 160 adolescents (average age, 13.5 years). Amotivation was assessed by statements such as "I do not know why I take part in physical education." The researchers assessed the various types of motivation by asking the adolescents to indicate their level of agreement with statements about their participation, such as "because physical education is fun" (intrinsic motivation), "because I will get into trouble if I do not" (external regulation), "because I want to improve in physical education" (identification), and "because I will feel bad about myself if I do not" (introjection).

Chatzisarantis and his colleagues (1997) found that high scores on amotivation were associated with low scores on both intention and leisure-time physical àctivity. Interestingly, contrary to their predictions, they found that both autonomous and controlling forms of behavioral regulation in physical education classes were associated with both intention and leisure-time physical activity. They proposed that one reason for this finding might be that leisure time represents an environment that causes a shift in the perceived locus of causality from external to internal. "Such shifts can occur when important others who are involved with the motivation of behaviour support choice and do not pressure individuals to behave in particular ways" (Chatzisarantis et al., p. 357). It seems that school—including physical education—is a requirement. Therefore, adolescents attend. However, leisure-time activities are chosen on the basis of enjoyment and autonomy (Deci & Ryan, 1985).

As we pointed out in Chapter 14 in our discussion of the theory of planned behavior, attitudes and subjective norm are assumed to influence the individual's intention, and in turn, intention is assumed to influence behavior. Chatzisarantis and Biddle (1998) examined whether the degree to which individual attitude, subjective norm, and perceived behavioral control are perceived to be self-determined moderates in their influence on intention and physical activity behavior. Two groups of adults (mean age of 40 years) were tested: an autonomy group and a controlling group. The autonomy group endorsed the view that they were active more for reasons related to intrinsic motivation to accomplish tasks (e.g., do well in physical exercise) and intrinsic motivation to experience stimulation (e.g., feelings of enjoyment, excitement, fun). The controlling group, on the other hand, endorsed the view that they were active more for reasons related to external regulation (e.g., bad health) and introjected regulation (e.g., worrying about a health condition). Chatzisarantis and Biddle found that the autonomy group reported being involved in more leisure-time physical activities. Also, although there were no differences in perceptions of subjective norm (i.e., the degree to which important others

had an influence on activity), the autonomy group expressed more positive attitudes about physical activity, felt they had more behavioral control, and had stronger intentions to be active.

When the relationships predicted in the theory of planned behavior were tested for the controlling group and the autonomy group, an interesting pattern of results was obtained. For both groups, intention was found to predict leisure-time behavior. Chatzisarantis and Biddle (1998) pointed out that this result

> is expected especially when time [between intention and behavior] is left unspecified. However, only when behavioural regulation is autonomous [would individuals be] expected to keep engaging in tasks, and therefore to display stable motivation. When behavioural regulation is controlling, individuals [would be] expected to keep engaging in tasks as long as external controls are in effect. (p. 318)

Chatzisarantis and Biddle (1998) also found that for both the controlling and autonomous groups, attitude and perceived behavioral control were reliable predictors of intention to engage in leisure-time activity. However, differences were found in the influence of subjective norm. In the theory of planned behavior (and the theory of reasoned action), subjective norm reflects the individual's perception of social pressures to perform or not perform a particular behavior. Those social pressures arise through the influence of important significant others (e.g., family, friends, physician, priest) or groups (e.g., classmates, teammates, church members). For the controlling group tested by Chatzisarantis and Biddle, subjective norms were positively related to intention to engage in leisure-time physical activity. However, for the autonomy group, subjective norms were negatively related to intention.

These findings offer implications for practice and intervention (Chatzisarantis & Biddle, 1998). If people receive the message (implicitly or explicitly) from important others that they must engage in aerobic exercise because it is necessary—to lose weight, to feel good, or to be healthy, for example—the social influence could be viewed as controlling. As such, it would have a negative impact on intention to be physically active (and ultimately on physical activity behavior itself). Conversely, if the message received is that physical activity can take many forms—walking, cycling, jogging, weight lifting, for example—and all are equally beneficial, the recipient is left with a perception of autonomy in terms of the path chosen. This perception of autonomy will have a positive impact on both intention and behavior.

Stages of Change and Self-Determination. Some of the most salient motives for involvement in exercise and physical activity are—at least on surface examination—extrinsic in nature. Thus, for example, improved fitness, health, or weight loss seem to represent motives that have their origin in either external regulation (i.e., the individual considers activity mandatory to avoid negative consequences), introjected regulation (i.e., the individual feels he or she should exercise), or identified regulation (i.e., the individual engages in an activity that is not enjoyable but is considered important). Mullen and Markland (1997) have suggested that although extrinsic motives may be a catalyst for individuals to become involved in activity programs initially, the focus is likely to change between initial adoption and subsequent adherence. This change of focus implies that a shift occurs in regulation over time and exposure from non-self-determination (i.e., external regulation) through limited self-determination (i.e., introjected regulation) to moderate self-determination (i.e., identified regulation) to complete self-determination (i.e., intrinsic motivation to accomplish tasks, experience sensations, and/or learn). Mullen and Markland used the stages of change in the transtheoretical model (see Chapter 15) as a framework to examine this possibility.

Males and females in their mid-30s ($n = 314$) were tested to determine where they fell on the stages of change continuum (see Table 15-1 for a description of each of the five stages). The degree of self-determination was also assessed using the *Behavioral Regulation in Exercise Questionnaire* (Mullen, Markland, & Ingledew, 1997a, 1997b). This questionnaire provides insight into the degree to which an individual is physically active for reasons of external regulation (i.e., I feel pressure from family/ friends to exercise), in-

People can have a number of motives for engaging in physical activity, including weight loss and personal appearance.
©PhotoDisc/Volume 76/Memorable Moments

trojected regulation (i.e., I feel like a failure when I haven't exercised in a while), identified regulation (i.e., I feel it's important to exercise regularly), or intrinsic motivation (i.e., I enjoy exercise sessions).

Mullen and Markland (1997) found that individuals in the first three stages—precontemplation, contemplation, and preparation—indicated less self-determination than did individuals in the action and maintenance stages. In short, as people progress across the stages of change, their behavioral regulation becomes more self-determined. Motives that have their basis in "ought to," "should," or "must" are replaced by motives that have their basis in "like to" and "enjoy." Mullen and Markland did provide a cautionary note, however. Their study involved a cross-sectional design, so it is not possible to determine whether "those in the later stages of change *became* more self-determined in the regulation of their exercise over time as they increased their stage of change, or whether they reached the later stages of change *because* they were more self-determined from the onset" (p. 358).

PERSONAL INVESTMENT THEORY

Researchers have taken a variety of approaches in an attempt to better understand why people are or are not physically active and/or to increase physical activity in the general population. In one general paradigm, the focus has been on the nature of the *situation.* Thus, for example, in Chapter 11 we discussed a study by Brownell, Stunkard, and Albaum (1980) in which the nature of the situation was the principal factor contributing to physical activity involvement. The researchers placed, at a location where people could either take the stairs or ride an escalator, a sign showing a lethargic heavy heart riding up the escalator and a healthy slim heart climbing the stairs. That situational intervention had a substantial effect on the numbers of people choosing to use the stairs.

With another general paradigm, the focus has been on the nature of the *individual.* The stages of change concept that is the foundation of the transtheoretical model focuses on the individual and his or her psychological readiness to engage in physical activity. Thus, for example, in Chapter 15 we discussed a study by Cardinal (1999) that explored individual attitudes and behaviors about physical activity. Specifically, Cardinal investigated whether there are people who reach the termination stage—the final stage in the processes of change. Cardinal found that 16.6% of the 551 adults he examined could be classified within the termination stage—they had been continuously active for five or more years and had 100% self-efficacy in their ability to remain physically active for life.

The theory of personal investment, which was proposed by Maehr (1984; Maehr & Braskamp, 1986), uses a third general paradigm, one that is referred to as an *interaction* approach. In this paradigm, equal emphasis is placed on understanding the individual and understanding the situation. Personal investment theory is an integration of numerous theoretical models and propositions about human behavior.

Five assumptions represent the foundation of personal investment (Maehr & Braskamp, 1986):

- The study of motivation necessarily involves the study of behavior.
- Individual patterns of behavior reflect a personal investment.
- Choice of behavior (i.e., option taken) is important because behavior can take many directions.
- The meaning in a situation determines personal investment.
- The meaning in a situation and its origins can be determined and assessed.

What these five propositions are intended to reflect is that, as humans, we are constantly faced with choices: Take the elevator or use the stairs? Work out or watch television? Go for a run or lift weights? How do you choose to spend your time? What activities do you invest your time and energy in? According to Maehr and Braskamp, people who concentrate on the decisions they make when they are faced with these numerous diverse choices gain insight into the meaning they attach to an activity. In short, people make a personal investment in those options that have more meaning for them.

Components of Meaning

As Figure 16-3 shows, personal investment is influenced by meaning. Figure 16-3 also shows the three interrelated components, or general categories of factors, that in combination determine the meaning attached to various situations or activities. The three components are *sense of self, perceived options,* and *incentives.*

Sense of Self. Maehr and Braskamp (1986) have defined sense of self as the individual's collection of thoughts, perceptions, beliefs, and feelings about who he or she is. Sense of self is considered to be a relatively stable disposition. Thus, for example, in terms of one aspect of your sense of self, you may perceive yourself to be a marathon runner. As part of that belief, you would likely feel that you put a high premium on fitness, that you work hard at it in order to compete periodically. This sense of self could be expected to remain relatively stable over time.

Within personal investment theory, sense of self is assumed to consist of four facets: social identity,

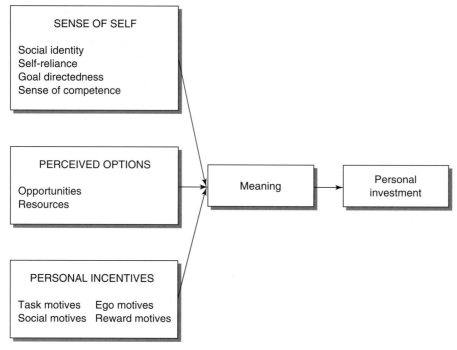

Figure 16-3   Personal investment theory.
Note. Based on Maehr, 1984, and Maehr & Braskamp, 1986.

self-reliance, goal directedness, and sense of competence. Social identity, as the terms suggests, represents the perceptions of the reference groups (i.e., significant others) to which an individual belongs or deems significant. Your sense of self as a marathoner would likely include belonging to that general category of people who place a premium on fitness, train regularly, and compete periodically in distance events.

Self-reliance represents the individual's perceptions of the origins of his or her destiny and degree of personal control present. This concept of self-reliance is similar in nature to the concept of self-determination. Do you as a marathoner perceive that the choice to train and compete periodically is yours to make?

Goal directedness represents an individual's ability to set realistic short- and long-term goals and behave accordingly. Competing periodically in marathons requires goal-directed behavior on your part. The concept of goal directedness is similar to a personality trait referred to as self-motivation that has been linked to adherence in exercise and physical activity programs (Dishman & Gettman, 1980; Dishman & Ickes, 1981).

Finally, sense of competence represents the subjective appraisal of one's ability to be successful in an activity. In our discussion of self-determination theory, we pointed out that individuals seek out activities or make choices or invest their time in those activities in which they exhibit personal competence. Similarly, they avoid activities in which they are incompetent. For you to train and compete in marathons, you would need a sense of competence.

Perceived Options.   A second major contributor to meaning is perceived options (see Figure 16-3). Maehr and Braskamp (1986) have defined perceived options as the behavioral alternatives perceived to be available. In order for an individual to attach meaning to an activity, opportunities must be available to carry it out and resources available to overcome any potential barriers. The concept of perceived options is similar to the concept of perceived behavioral control from the theory of planned behavior (see Chapter 14). Again, the example of you as a marathoner is illustrative. You have many roles—student, family member, friend, competitor, and so on. It requires time and energy to carry out these roles effectively. Occasionally the requirements of one role may be in conflict with the requirements of another; that is, you need to train to be an effective marathoner, but you also need to study to be an effective student. What options are available—study/don't study, short/long/no training run? Any activity carried out because of a sense of necessity and not because it is perceived to be acceptable has minimal meaning and, as a consequence, is done with reduced motivation.

Personal Incentives. Personal incentives represent the motivational focus of the activity. According to Maehr and Braskamp (1986), there are four types of incentives or motivational orientations lying within two categories. Task and ego motives fall within the intrinsic category, whereas social and reward motives fall within the extrinsic category. Task incentives reflect a motivation to become involved in an activity for its own sake and/or to master the task. Maehr and Braskamp pointed out that task orientation could be of two types—task absorption and demonstration of competence. Involvement in exercise and physical activity for the sheer pleasure it provides is an example of the former, and training to accomplish some objective (e.g., run a marathon) would be an example of the latter. The concept of task incentives within personal investment theory is highly similar to the self-determination theory's intrinsic motives to learn, to experience sensations, and to accomplish tasks.

Ego incentives reflect motivation to compete and/or gain power. This motive has, as its basis, social comparison. People have an interest in comparing themselves against other people or against socially defined standards of excellence.

Social incentives are based on an individual's desire to affiliate with others and to enter into meaningful cohesive relationships. The concept of social

incentives is similar to the concept of relatedness within self-determination theory. A common recurring motive cited for involvement in exercise and physical activity is social experiences and social interactions (Carron & Estabrooks, 1999).

The fourth type of incentive listed by Maehr and Braskamp (1986), reward motives, represents a desire to be involved for social approval or financial benefits (in its development, personal investment theory was oriented toward the workplace). The three manifestations of extrinsic motivation within self-determination theory (see Figure 16-1) are closely related to the concept of extrinsic rewards.

Personal Investment in Exercise and Physical Activity

A considerable amount of research has investigated the specific concepts contained in personal investment theory. For example, we addressed questions about perceived motives for physical activity in relation to self-determination theory in this chapter. The relationship between perceived control (a construct similar to perceived options) and physical activity was addressed in Chapter 14. Here, we examine research by Duda and Tappe (1988, 1989a, 1989b, 1989c) that tested the complete theory of personal investment.

In one study, Duda and Tappe (1988) tested the theory with 47 older adults (average age, 65 years). The personal incentives that were measured included mastery, competition, social affiliation, recognition, health, coping with stress, and fitness. Remember the four components that constitute a person's sense of self: competence, self-reliance, goal directedness, and social identity. Perceptions of general physical competence and perceived health status were used to reflect perceived competence. Psychometrically established tests were used to measure self-reliance and goal directedness, whereas social identity was represented through the activity level of close friends and loved ones. Maehr and Braskamp (1986) considered the concept of perceived options to be dependent on the degree to which incentives held to be important can be satisfied. Therefore, Duda and Tappe calculated an **incentive congruency measure,** which they defined as the difference between the emphasis placed on an incentive and the perceived opportunity to satisfy that incentive.

incentive congruency measure   The difference between the emphasis placed on an incentive and the perceived opportunity to satisfy that incentive.

Duda and Tappe (1988) found some support for personal investment theory. Involvement in physical activity was associated with both personal incentives and the degree to which the incentives were considered to be congruent with the focus of the program and sense of self. The incentive found to be most strongly associated with physical activity was recognition.

As Figure 16-3 shows, meaning is assumed to be influenced by sense of self, personal incentives, and social identity. In a second study, Duda and Tappe (1989c) examined whether the personal incentives and sense of self of physically active individuals vary on the basis of differences in age and gender. Male and females classified as young adults (25 to 39 years), middle-aged adults (40 to 60 years), and elderly adults (61 years and older) responded to a set of questions similar to those used in the 1988 Duda and Tappe study. Again, the researchers found support for personal investment theory in that both age and gender influenced the meaning associated with physical activity.

Summary

Motivation is the theoretical construct used to represent the selectivity, intensity, and persistence of behavior. Not surprisingly, therefore, it is a cornerstone of psychological theories of human behavior. Two theories that have been advanced to explain and predict physical activity and exercise behavior are the self-determination theory and the personal investment theory. The former is based on the premise that activities are more likely to be selected and maintained if they satisfy three psychological needs: competence, self-determination, and relatedness. Behavior occurs as a result of either three types of extrinsic motivation (external regulation, introjected regulation, identified regulation) or three types of intrinsic motivation (to learn, to accomplish tasks, and to experience sensations). The various types of motivation are associated with perceptions of self-determination, and perceptions of

self-determination are associated with satisfaction and adherence.

Personal investment theory is based on the premise that people tend to focus their energy (i.e., invest in) those activities high in meaning. The meaning attached to a specific choice or activity is influenced by the individual's sense of self, personal incentives, and perceived options (i.e., the opportunities available to satisfy important incentives). Sense of self is derived from four components: social identity, self-reliance, goal directedness, and sense of competence. Similarly, four main types of incentives are possible: task motives, ego motives, reward motives, and social motives.

Research has shown support for both theories. Thus, both theories offer promise as a means of understanding behavior in the context of exercise and physical activity.

Promoting Physical Activity Involvement

I t's one thing to describe the characteristics of people who do or do not exercise and attempt to explain why, which, of course, is what we have done in earlier chapters. At some point, however, description and explanation have to give way to intervention—programs to change people's behavior. In this section, we provide a summary of intervention programs that have targeted individuals (Chapter 17), groups (Chapter 18), and communities (Chapter 19). In the last chapter (Chapter 20), we discuss the public health impact of physical activity promotion interventions.

CHAPTER 17

Individual Level Intervention Strategies

If the Human Mind Was Simple Enough to Understand, We'd Be Too Simple to Understand It.
(Emerson Pugh)

CHAPTER OBJECTIVES

After completing this chapter you will be able to

- Outline the effectiveness of individual level interventions on increasing physical activity.

- Differentiate among the interventions based on behavior modification, cognitive-behavior modification, health education, health risk appraisal, and exercise.

- Identify the most effective interventions.

- Describe mediation in terms of intervention effectiveness.

- Describe the potential of technology for physical activity promotion.

Key terms

effectiveness trials	interventions
efficacy trials	mediated interventions
expert systems	operant conditioning
face-to-face interventions	

The study of behavior change in individuals is a core area of psychology (Martin & Pear, 1983). Thus, it is not surprising that behavior change interventions that focus on increasing or maintaining regular physical activity reflect the developmental ideas of psychology. Trying to stimulate people, however, to become or stay physically active is not an easy task. Indeed, the majority of the adult population is not active at frequency and intensity levels that are sufficient to result in health benefits or disease prevention. Why? As Emerson Pugh suggests, the human mind (and behavior) is very complex, and thus it is very difficult for researchers and clinicians to understand how to change people's behaviors—including physical activity.

Researchers have come a long way, however, from the early psychologists and psychiatrists who attempted to modify individual behavior. For example, early psychopathologists felt that behavioral anomalies reflected the external manifestation of evil spirits that had entered the victim's body—a physical inactivity demon, if you will. The predominant behavior change strategy consisted of drilling holes in the victim's head so that the evil spirits could fly out: "Hello, Mr. Jones, I think a ½-inch bit should do the trick." Luckily, behavior change interventions have advanced considerably. The purpose of this chapter is to review the research that has examined individual level interventions designed to increase or maintain physical activity.

INTERVENTIONS DEFINED

Interventions can be defined as "health-promoting activities that originate from a health promotion team with the intention of instilling or maintaining health-related attitudes, norms, and behaviors, in a specific target" (Gauvin, Lévesque, & Richard, 2001). As an extension of this definition, interventions can be broken down into efficacy or effectiveness trials. **Efficacy trials** "provide a test of whether a technology, treatment, procedure, or program does more good than harm when delivered under optimum conditions" (Flay, 1986, p. 451). An example of an efficacy trial intervention would be randomly assigning sedentary individuals to either an exercise intervention or a no-exercise control group. In comparison, **effectiveness trials** are "tests of whether a technology, treatment, procedure, intervention, or program does more good than harm when delivered under real-world conditions" (Flay, p. 451). An example of an effectiveness trial would be to introduce a physical activity program into a physical education class and then assess possible changes in physical self-concept over time or in comparison to a similar class without the program. Although effectiveness trials are undoubtedly being done in various physical activity environments, few have been published.

Until around 1990, most exercise intervention studies used one-dimensional approaches with small numbers of people of similar gender, race, ethnicity,

---

interventions   A technology, treatment, procedure, or program developed with the aim of promoting or maintaining specific attitudes, norms, and/or behaviors in a target person or group.

efficacy trials   Tests carried out to establish whether an intervention (a new technology or a treatment, procedure, or program) does more good than harm when it is introduced under ideal conditions.

effectiveness trials   Tests carried out to establish whether an intervention (a new technology or a treatment, procedure, or program) does more good than harm when it is introduced under real-world conditions.

---

education, and economic and health status (Dishman, 1991; Dishman & Sallis, 1994). Subsequently, however, it became increasingly evident that one type of intervention applied to the total population does *not* solve the problem of sedentariness. For example, as Gauvin and her colleagues noted (2001), it is possible that some theories or technologies for increasing physical activity may be more or less effective depending on whether they are targeted to people with a history of sedentariness, a history of infrequent activity, or a history of regular activity. To illustrate their point, Gauvin et al. contrasted the case of a person who regularly jogs over the lunch hour with the case of a sedentary person who attempts to introduce physical activity into his or her lifestyle. Actions required by the former would include bringing jogging clothes to work, leaving the workplace promptly at noon, jogging, quickly showering, and returning to work. Actions by the latter person, however, might include taking the stairs, getting off the bus one stop early, and taking a walk after dinner. Furthermore, the person jogging once a day would need to devote a greater amount of effort in a short period, whereas the individual engaging in lifestyle activity would need smaller amounts of effort over longer periods of time to be involved in moderate-intensity activity. The behaviors undertaken by these two individuals are very different. Therefore, the first challenge faced by researchers examining the promotion of physical activity is to identify the specific behavior pattern that is the focus of the intervention.

OVERVIEW OF THE EFFECTIVENESS OF INDIVIDUAL INTERVENTIONS

A large body of research has examined the effects of a wide variety of individual interventions on physical activity. Fortunately, Dishman and Buckworth (1996) carried out a meta-analysis on this research. They located 127 studies that had approximately 131,000 subjects who had been targeted in community, work site, school, home, and health care settings.

In each of these studies, the independent variable was some type of intervention designed to increase physical activity, and the dependent variable was physical activity.

Dishman and Buckworth (1996) expressed the effect sizes as Pearson correlation coefficients (r). Guidelines established for interpreting effect sizes expressed as correlation coefficients are that correlation values of .10, .30, and .50 are considered small, medium, and large effects, respectively. As the authors pointed out, an effect size of 0 reflects a 50% chance for physical activity adherence in the absence of an intervention. Interestingly, research has typically shown an adherence rate of 50% for supervised or community-based exercise programs in the absence of intervention. So the question of interest is, how much impact will an intervention program have over and above what might be expected normally?

Figure 17-1 provides a schematic illustration of the results reported in the Dishman and Buckworth (1996) meta-analysis. An effect size of .20 is equivalent to an increase in physical activity adherence from 50% to 60%, whereas an effect size of .60 indicates an increase from 50% to 80%. Dishman and Buckworth reported that in the 127 studies a large effect size, .75, was present. This effect size reflects a success rate of 88%. Thus, in general, physical activity interventions have been found to increase adherence rates by 38 percentage points, from 50% to 88%.

Participant Characteristics

Dishman and Buckworth (1996) also examined a variety of moderating variables, including participant characteristics. They found that the beneficial impact of an intervention program was identical for males and females, among individuals of different ages, and between Whites and non-Whites (i.e., African Americans, Mexican Americans, and Native Americans). It was found, however, that the effect among healthy participants was larger when contrasted with all groups of patients (see Figure 17-2). That is, intervention programs produced large ef-

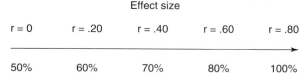

Figure 17-1 Effect sizes in the Dishman and Buckworth (1996) meta-analysis.

Note. From "Increasing Physical Activity: A Quantitative Synthesis," by R. K. Dishman and J. Buckworth, 1996, *Medicine and Science in Sports and Exercise, 28,* 706–719.

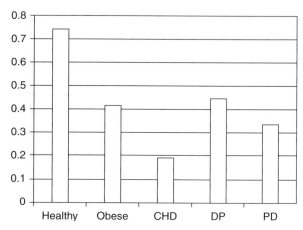

Figure 17-2 Effect sizes for the moderating effect of health status on physical activity interventions.

Note. DP = developmentally disabled; PD = physically disabled or other chronic disease; CHD = coronary heart disease or other chronic disease. From "Increasing Physical Activity: A Quantitative Synthesis," by R. K. Dishman and J. Buckworth, 1996, *Medicine and Science in Sports and Exercise, 28,* 706–719.

fects in terms of increased physical activity for healthy participants. In contrast, only small to moderate effects were observed in studies of people who had cardiovascular disease, were at high risk for cardiovascular disease, were obese, were physically disabled (e.g., arthritis, diabetes), or were developmentally disabled. An important qualifier advanced by Dishman and Buckworth, however, was that only a relatively small number of studies examined interventions with patients.

Types of Intervention

Typically, research has utilized seven different types of interventions: behavior modification (e.g., reinforcement, stimulus control); cognitive behavior modification (e.g., self-monitoring, self-reinforcement); health education; health-risk appraisal (e.g., confronting people with test results showing risk factors for low fitness levels); exercise prescription (e.g., prescribing moderate-intensity exercise); combinations of programs that include two or more distinct interventions; and physical education curriculum (i.e., programs implemented in the schools in place of traditional physical education or health classes). Dishman and Buckworth (1996) found that behavior modification had a very large effect size on increases in physical activity, whereas all the other approaches had small effects (see Table 17-1).

Because behavior modification techniques had the largest impact on physical activity behavior change and maintenance, it might be useful to describe the development of a behavior modification intervention. Behavior modification techniques are based on operant conditioning techniques attributed to B. F. Skinner (1947). **Operant conditioning** proposes that a number of conditions exist within people's environment that cue them to do one behavior or another. A stop sign, for example, provides a cue to stop. These conditions are called antecedents in that they come *before* a behavior occurs. Once cued by an antecedent, a behavior or response will occur. One sees the stop sign and one then stops. This reaction is termed stimulus control. The studies by Brownell et al. (1980) and Estabrooks et al. (1996) both involved interventions based on stimulus control specifically (see Chapter 11). The final component of operant conditioning is the consequence of the response. A response will be repeated if the consequence is reinforcing.

---

operant conditioning The proposal that a number of conditions exist within the human environment that cue people to do one behavior or another.

■ **TABLE 17-1** Effect Sizes (r) for Physical Activity Intervention Type and Setting Characteristics

INTERVENTION CHARACTERISTICS	EFFECT SIZE
Intervention type	
Behavior modification	.92
Cognitive behavior modification	.10
Health education/risk appraisal	.10
Exercise prescription	.21
Physical education curriculum	.21
Combination	.11
Intervention delivery	
Face-to-face	.16
Mediated	.91
Face-to-face and mediated	.10
Setting	
Home	.08
School	.21
Community	.82
Work site	.17
Health care	.24
Social context	
Group	.75
Individual	.16
Family	.05
Level of supervision	
Supervised	.23
Not supervised	.78

Note. Small, medium, and large effect sizes are represented by r = .10, .30, and .50, respectively. From "Increasing Physical Activity: A Quantitative Synthesis," by R. K. Dishman and J. Buckworth, 1996, *Medicine and Science in Sports and Exercise, 28,* 706–719.

Our stop sign example can be used to look at two scenarios. Scenario 1: A driver approaches a stop sign at a new intersection. It is the driver's first experience with this stop sign and so he or she stops. When stopped, the driver notices a heavy flow of traffic on the intersecting street. Avoiding being crushed by oncoming traffic acts as the reinforcing consequence that will ensure that the driver will stop next time he or she encounters this stop sign. Scenario 2: A driver approaches a stop sign on a quiet corner of his or her neighborhood. The driver has seen this stop sign many times before and has never seen traffic on the intersecting street. In this scenario, there is no reinforcing consequence associated with coming to a complete stop (assuming there are no police close by!), but there is a reinforcing consequence to not stopping (saved time). It is likely that the antecedent cue of this stop sign is not enough to elicit the stopping behavior in this scenario.

Katz and Singh (1986) provided a good example of using both stimulus control and reinforcement to increase recess physical activity of children with handicaps. For initial stimulus control, a large colorful poster was placed in a high-profile area of the playground during the two recess periods. The poster showed images of Freddy and Freena Frog playing ball games and climbing on the jungle gym. Prior to the posting of the sign, all the teachers and students were involved in an assembly in which Freddy and Freena were introduced and the activities were explained. Reinforcement was provided in a number of different ways. The children were given verbal praise for being physically active. Active children became members of the Freddy and Freena club. Photographs of active children on the playground were taken daily and placed on the large poster.

INTERVENTION SETTING

The manner in which the intervention is delivered also appears to be important. That is, intervention effects were greater in studies where a mediated approach was used rather than face-to-face delivery. **Mediated interventions** are usually delivered indirectly by mail or telephone, whereas **face-to-face interventions** are delivered directly to the participant. Also, interventions delivered in community

> **mediated interventions**   Interventions delivered indirectly by mail or telephone.
>
> **face-to-face interventions**   Interventions delivered directly to the participant.

settings (see Chapter 19) had a greater impact than those offered in school, home, work site, and health care settings. Interventions delivered in groups (see Chapter 18) had a more beneficial impact than those delivered to individuals, the family, or to an individual combined within a group. Finally, effects were larger in nonsupervised physical activity than in supervised physical activity programs.

The Dose-Response Issue

The beneficial impact of the various interventions were unrelated to the number of weeks they were offered. Thus, for example, it is unimportant whether an intervention is 2 weeks or 4 weeks in duration, because the former has the same effect as the latter on physical activity behavior. Some modes of physical activity are more effective than others. The meta-analysis (Dishman & Buckworth, 1996) showed that the introduction of interventions involving strength activities, aerobic exercises, or aerobic exercises combined with other fitness activities are not as effective in producing changes in physical activity as are interventions that target a more active leisure time (see Table 17-2). Also, effect sizes did not differ according to the weekly frequency or daily duration, but studies that observed low-intensity physical activity reported larger effects compared to studies using physical activities conducted at higher intensities. It would seem that people are more likely to change their physical activity pattern if the behavior is not perceived to be overly stressful.

The Most Effective Aspects of an Intervention

One difficulty in interpreting the results of a meta-analysis is that methodological factors can be confounded with intervention characteristics (Sallis & Owen, 1999). Thus, for example, two studies might use behavior modification as an intervention. In one of those studies, healthy participants might be the target sample and strenuous physical activity the target behavior. In the second study, patients recovering from cardiovascular disease might be the tar-

■ **TABLE 17-2** Effect Sizes (r) for Physical Activity Intervention Features

INTERVENTION CHARACTERISTICS	EFFECT SIZE
Physical activity mode	
Aerobic	.18
Active leisure	.85
Strength	.46
Aerobic and other activities	.15
Physical activity frequency (days per week)	
One or two	.25
Three	.14
Four	.23
Five	.17
Six or seven	.33
Activity duration (minutes)	
Up to 20	.32
20 to 30	.24
30 to 45	.17
45 to 75	.14
Physical activity intensity (% of aerobic capacity)	
Below 50%	.94
Between 50% to 70%	.24
Above 70%	.23
Physical activity measure	
Self-report	.10
Attendance or observation	.88
Physiologic surrogate	.14
Muscular strength	.28

Note. Small, medium, and large effect sizes are represented by $r = .10, .30,$ and $.50$, respectively. From "Increasing Physical Activity: A Quantitative Synthesis," by R. K. Dishman and J. Buckworth, 1996, *Medicine and Science in Sports and Exercise, 28,* 706–719.

get sample and moderate or mild physical activity the target behavior. Both studies might show a positive effect. Furthermore, if the researcher was interested in comparing the impact of different types of interventions (i.e., behavior modification versus other intervention protocols), the effect sizes from those two studies would be combined. What would be lost, however, is whether the effect observed in

the two studies was a product of the intervention program alone (i.e., behavior modification) or the combination of the intervention program with the specific sample (i.e., healthy versus recovering patients) and/or target behavior (i.e., strenuous versus mild physical activity).

The Dishman and Buckworth (1996) meta-analysis shows that physical activity interventions are generally effective, but the specific characteristics of the intervention make a difference. On the basis of their results, Dishman and Buckworth suggested that "interventions based on the principles of behavior modification, delivered to healthy people in a community, are associated with large effects, particularly when the interventions are delivered to groups using mediated approaches or when the physical activity is unsupervised, emphasizing leisure physical activity of low intensity, regardless of the duration or frequency of participation" (p. 712). The researchers also suggested that the design and implementation of future interventions should be based on theories such as those we discussed in Chapters 12 through 16.

INTERVENTIONS BASED ON THEORETICAL MODELS

Subsequent to the Dishman and Buckworth (1996) meta-analysis, Baranowski, Anderson, and Carmack (1998) reviewed the relative effectiveness of various intervention programs that had used a theoretical framework to structure the program. Lewin (1951) has suggested that "there is nothing so practical as a good theory." The Baranowski, Anderson, and Carmack review would seem to confirm Lewin's statement. Interventions based on the types of theoretical models outlined in Chapters 12 to 16 offer a sound foundation for introducing (and evaluating) interventions designed to increase physical activity participation.

Baranowski and his associates (1998) located 25 studies that had employed at least one theory as the guiding framework for the intervention. Social cognitive theory (Bandura, 1986) was most frequently used, and the transtheoretical model (Prochaska &

DiClemente, 1984), social learning theory, decision theory (Janis & Mann, 1977), behavior management, and relapse prevention (Marlett & Gordon, 1986) were used to a much lesser extent. The interventions ranged from 5 weeks to 7 years, and at least one of the behavioral outcomes was physical activity (i.e., walking behavior, leisure-time physical activity, or attendance at a fitness facility).

Baranowski et al. (1998) found that interventions for increasing physical activity were effective primarily when participants were motivated enough to volunteer or when a school-based physical education program changed. The authors noted that even these improvements are important steps in the right direction for increasing physical activity levels. They also noted, however, that the increases in physical activity were modest, and it is not clear what aspects of the programs produced increases in physical activity. That is, programs were not consistently effective in increasing physical activity among the less motivated or unmotivated, and programs did not clarify how to help children increase physical activity outside school. In general the interventions accounted for 30% or less of the variability in physical activity behavior. Baranowski and his associates (1998) suggested that interventions based on a theory are superior to atheoretical interventions.

However, a substantial number of the intervention strategies had little or no effect on physical activity (Baranowski et al., 1998). Why? How can the impact of theory-based interventions for individual behavior change be improved?

When researchers use theory to develop interventions, they target strategies to change certain theoretical variables that are thought to influence physical activity. For example, an intervention based on social cognitive theory may include a strategy based on vicarious experiences (see Chapter 12). The strategy may be aimed at increasing self-efficacy, which in turn is thought to lead to increased physical activity. Interestingly, Baranowski et al. (1998) argued that

> (1) interventions work by means of mediating variables; (2) current theoretical models from which mediating variables are obtained often do not account for substantial variability in the target

outcomes; (3) interventions have not been shown to effect substantial change in the mediating variables; and, together, (4) these factors impose limits on the effectiveness of interventions. (p. 281)

As a result of those limitations, two priorities for physical activity intervention research emerge (Baranowski et al., 1998). First, it is necessary to fully understand the relationships between theoretical mediators and physical activity. Second, the impact of interventions on these mediating variables should be examined. That is, Baranowski et al. recommends that researchers ask, does the intervention change the mediating variables?

Research findings on the interrelationships between an intervention, potential mediating variables, and physical activity are valuable for both researchers and practitioners. For researchers, the efficacy of an intervention should be dependent on the ability of an intervention to change the theoretical mediator. By assessing the theoretical mediators, if an intervention is not efficacious, the researcher can determine whether the problem is with the theory or with the intervention. On the one hand, if the ineffective intervention changes the theoretical mediator but not the physical activity, the theoretical basis of the intervention can be questioned. On the other hand, if the ineffective intervention does not change the theoretical mediator, the strategies used in the intervention can be questioned.

For practitioners, the identification of theoretical mediators allows for less cost-intensive analysis of a physical activity promotion program. Most mediators can be assessed simply through paper and pencil questionnaires. A quick assessment by a fitness professional, rather than frequent and expensive physiological testing, could be used to determine whether an intervention was helping someone become more physically active.

INDIVIDUAL LEVEL INTERVENTIONS AND TECHNOLOGICAL ADVANCES

Physical activity promotion interventions are increasingly impacted by technological developments. Strategic planning of individual level interventions by researchers using technological advances increases their ability to individualize interventions on a large scale and increases the number of channels available for program delivery (Nigg, in press).

One method of individualizing feedback is through the use of **expert systems.** In expert systems, computer technology is used to simulate human experts by providing systematic feedback that is predetermined either by qualified professionals or by statistics (Nigg, Riebe, Rossi, Velicer, & Prochaska, 1999). Expert systems individualize intervention materials through an interactive process. The study participants respond to assessments provided by the expert system, and in return the expert system provides feedback based on the participants' responses.

Interactive technology such as expert systems provides new avenues for intervention delivery

> **expert systems**   Computer technology used to simulate human experts by providing systematic feedback that is predetermined either by qualified professionals or by statistics.

(Nigg, in press). Ideally, expert systems could be completed on a home or community computer via the Internet. The speed of information flow on the Web is currently unrivaled. A participant could complete initial assessments and be provided with the intervention materials immediately. However, access to computers and the Internet can present a barrier for a number of populations. Hence, participant assessment and intervention material distribution can also be handled through a more conventional mailing format. A third avenue for the use of expert systems is through telephone contact.

Marcus and her colleagues (1998) provided an example of the efficacy of an expert system using the transtheoretial model to develop the intervention materials. Participants (N = 1,559) were randomized into either the expert system transtheoretical model intervention or a standard-care American Heart Association physical activity promotion. Compared to the control group, more participants in the expert system condition progressed in stages and fewer regressed.

Summary

Researchers have used a wide variety of interventions in their attempts to stimulate increased involvement in physical activity. These interventions include behavior modification (e.g., reinforcement, stimulus control), cognitive behavior modification (e.g., self-monitoring, self-reinforcement), health education, health risk appraisal (e.g., confronting people with test results showing risk factors for low fitness levels), exercise prescription (e.g., prescribing moderate-intensity exercise), combinations of programs that include two or more distinct interventions, and physical education curriculum (i.e., programs implemented in the schools in place of traditional physical education or health classes). The meta-analysis carried out by Dishman and Buckworth (1996) showed that the most effective interventions are based on behavior modification principles. Also, interventions have a greater impact on healthier

people in a community setting—especially when those interventions are delivered to groups using mediated approaches or when the physical activity is unsupervised and focuses on increasing leisure physical activity of low intensity.

Baranowski and his collaborators (1998) outlined the importance of developing interventions based on good theory. In order to more effectively test the impact of interventions, researchers need to assess the potential mediators that are the focus of the intervention. By identifying and measuring intervention mediators, researchers and practitioners can determine why a given intervention is effective. Finally, technological developments using expert systems, the Internet, and telecommunications offer new and exciting opportunities to implement strong theory-based physical activity interventions.

CHAPTER 18

Group Level Intervention Strategies

*Coming Together Is a Beginning, Staying Together Is Progress,
and Working Together Is Success.*

(Henry Ford)

Henry Ford offered an interesting view on success in the automotive industry. What about physical activity? Does his sentiment apply? On a superficial level, at least, there is some evidence that some of the processes discussed by Ford are in operation in exercise classes. People do come to-

gether and engage in physical activity programs in group settings in private fitness clubs, community centers, universities, and so on. Also, they do stay together and maintain their involvement—or at least some of them do, because the most frequently cited statistic in the physical activity science is that 50% of those people who begin a physical activity regimen drop out within the first 3 to 6 months. So, there is some "staying together" within the physical activity environment—what Ford called progress. But, what about working together—what Ford called success?

Zander (1982) has pointed out that for a collection of individuals to be classified as a group (and, therefore, to be considered working together), they must converse freely; identify the collective as "we" and other collectives as "they"; attend and actively participate in group functions; be primarily interested in group, not personal, accomplishments; and be interested in the progress of the collective. Carron and Spink (1993) noted that

> there is no doubt that fitness classes possess only a
> few of these criteria. Further, even in instances
> where some of these criteria might be present in a
> fitness class (e.g., converse freely, assist others, and
> receive assistance), it seems likely that these group-
> oriented behaviors are only at minimal threshold
> levels. (p. 9)

So, Ford's dictum sounds good—bring people together, keep them together, and get them to cooperate and interact toward a common goal. But can it work in physical activity contexts, or for that matter in other contexts for other health-related behaviors in which individuals are largely concerned with personal accomplishments? Let's take a literary trip to Dyersville, Iowa (Droze, 2000).

THE DYERSVILLE EXPERIENCE

Bobbi Schell and Jane Clemen are community workers in Dyersville. The former is a physical therapist, and the latter is a dietitian. As health professionals within their community, these women began a community service project at the local medical center. The goal of that project was to increase health awareness in Dyersville.

The Beginning

The first step in the project was to bring people together. To do so, Schell and Clemen advertised a program for community members interested in losing weight within a supportive social environment. The response was better than expected—more than 450 participants in a town of 3,800! Ford's *beginning* had been realized—participants had come together.

The Progress

Schell and Clemens also devised a simple strategy to assist the participants in their efforts to maintain involvement in the weekly diet, physical activity, and motivational sessions. Upon entry into the program, participants were assigned to teams. The teams then were instructed to decide on a team name. Those team names—which included, for example, "Lean On Me," "Sisters Plus," and "Melt-Away Mammas"—were then emblazoned on T-shirts for the group members to wear. The participants enjoyed the weekly meetings and were rarely absent. So, Ford's *progress* also had been realized—participants stayed together.

The Success

Success of each of the nutrition and physical activity teams in Dyersville was based on weight loss. How-

ever, individual weight loss was not documented. Each week, entire teams stepped onto a giant truck scale to monitor their progress. The winning teams were those that had lost the most *collective* weight. By providing a venue for common goal attainment, Schell and Clemens helped the participants reach Ford's final step, *success*—the participants worked together. How successful was the Dyersville campaign? The 450 participants lost a combined 7,500 pounds!

THEORETICAL FOUNDATION FOR GROUP ENDEAVORS IN PHYSICAL ACTIVITY SETTINGS

The Dyersville project was not a scientific study into the effectiveness of group interventions to improve individual outcomes. However, it would be difficult to suggest that the program did not work. Adherence to the program was high, and the primary outcome of weight loss was realized. The questions that remain pertain to process and sustainability. Why did the project work? What were the group processes that facilitated behavior change? What components were necessary to ensure sustained participation? Will such a program ensure long-term adherence to healthy eating and/or physical activity?

In an effort to answer these questions in a controlled, scientific context, Carron and Spink (1993) proposed a **conceptual framework** for the application of group dynamics principles in physical activity classes. This conceptual model, which is illustrated in Figure 18-1, was based on the assumption that various inputs and throughputs can lead to desired outputs in group settings. Carron and Spink noted that a fundamental consideration in fitness classes—adherence—is associated with perceptions of cohesiveness. Consequently, in their conceptual model, increased perceptions of cohesion, specifically, increased perceptions of Individual Attractions to the Group—Task, (see Chapter 9 for a full

conceptual framework   Simplified representation of the interrelations between a group of variables.

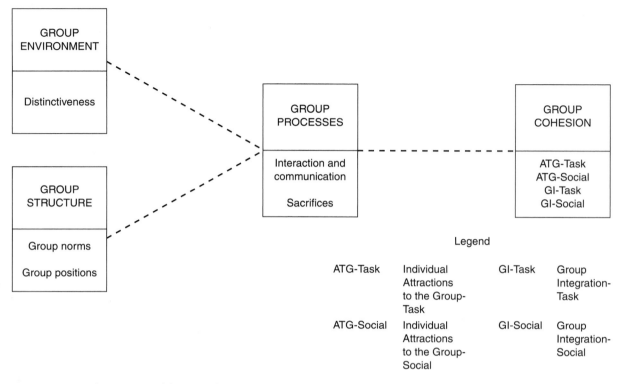

Figure 18-1   The conceptual framework used as a basis for group interventions in fitness classes.
Note. Adapted from "Team Building in an Exercise Setting," by A. V. Carron and K. S. Spink, 1993, *The Sport Psychologist, 7,* 8–18.

discussion on the conception and measurement of cohesion), became the desired *output.* The *inputs* assumed to play a role in the development of Individual Attractions to the Group—Task were the group's environment and its structure. One aspect of the **group environment** that was targeted for attention was class distinctiveness. Two aspects of the **group structure** that were targeted for attention were class norms and individual geographical positions within the class. The *throughputs* assumed to play a role in the development of Individual Attractions to the Group—Task were two **group processes:** interactions and communications among members and sacrifices by members for the collective.

The framework illustrated in Figure 18-1 provides a useful format whereby critical components of group level interventions can be identified and ma-

nipulated. Every physical activity class can be made distinctive from other groups or classes. By having participants develop a group name and wear distinctive apparel (e.g., group T-shirts), a positive and distinct group environment can be developed. The Dyersville weight-loss teams were encouraged to select a catchy name and have T-shirts made. Clearly, that program fostered feelings of distinctiveness within the weight-loss teams.

group environment   The cohesive nature of a group.

group structure   Formal structure which develops when group members assume positions and take on different functions and roles.

group processes   Cooperation, communication, and interactions between group members.

Within group dynamics theory (Carron, 1988), group norms and group positions along with roles and status are elements that contribute to the development of a group's structure. Thus, when members permanently occupy specific positions within a group and develop common expectations about matters of importance to their group (i.e., norms), the group has structure and stability. So, in physical activity classes, individuals can pick their own spot in the class and remain in it for the duration of the program. They can also establish common standards pertaining to the intensity and duration of the workout as well as the goals the class should achieve. In, Dyersville, for example, members developed common expectations around collective goals.

As Figure 18-1 shows, the processes within the class—group interaction and communication and individual sacrifice for the group—contribute directly to class cohesion. Interaction and communication occurs naturally in most group settings. However, it can be directly facilitated by partnering or grouping participants. Also, regular members of a class can be encouraged to spend time helping newer members gain skills and techniques necessary for participation in the class. The latter, of course, would represent a sacrifice for the group. Although there is no documentation of individual sacrifice for the groups in the Dyersville program, the length of the program did provide ample time for the development of group interaction and communication.

TEAM-BUILDING INTERVENTIONS IN PHYSICAL ACTIVITY SETTINGS

Carron and Spink (1993) first applied their group dynamics framework to female participants in 17 university aerobic fitness classes. The classes met 3 times per week for a 13-week period. The 17 classes were randomly assigned to either a team-building or control condition. To introduce the team-building intervention, Carron and Spink used a four-stage process consisting of an introduction, a conceptual stage, a practical stage, and an intervention stage.

Critical to the implementation of any intervention is the assurance that its administrators (i.e., the class instructors) understand the rationale for the strategy. Therefore, the *introductory stage* included a 20-minute presentation (by the principal investigators) to the class instructors. In that presentation, the investigators outlined the importance of having a cohesive physical activity group. The *conceptual stage* provided the class instructors with an understanding of the conceptual framework outlined in Figure 18-1. In the *practical stage,* the class instructors were given the opportunity to become active agents in the development of specific team-building strategies. That is, during this stage, the class instructors and researchers collectively developed the specific intervention strategies associated with the various aspects of the model illustrated in Figure 18-1. Examples of the specific strategies are outlined in Table 18-1.

Finally, the *intervention stage* began in the initial classes of the 13-week program. The specific intervention strategies were introduced and maintained throughout the program. The intervention was successful: Participants in the team-building condition held stronger perceptions of Individual Attractions to the Group—Task than did the participants in the control conditions.

Although the Carron and Spink (1993) study did provide some support for the effectiveness of their team-building intervention, it did not examine the relationship between the intervention and adherence behavior. Therefore, a second study using an identical approach was undertaken by Spink and Carron (1993) to address this issue. Adherence was measured in four ways: attendance, dropout behavior, lateness to class, and early departures from class. Again, the results showed that the team-building intervention enhanced the Individual Attractions to the Group—Task dimension of cohesion. In terms of adherence, individuals in the team-building and control conditions did not differ on attendance. However, there were fewer dropouts from the team-building classes, and participants were less likely to be late.

Any time research is conducted using a sample of university students (or classes), questions of

■ **TABLE 18-1** Examples of Specific Strategies for Group-Based Interventions in Physical Activity Classes

CATEGORY	EXAMPLES OF INTERVENTION STRATEGIES
Group environment Distinctiveness	Have a group name Make up a group T-shirt Hand out neon headbands and/or shoelaces Make up posters/slogans for the class
Group structure Individual positions	Use 3 areas of the class depending on fitness level Have signs to label parts of the group Use specific positions for low-, medium-, & high-impact exercisers
Group norms	Encourage members to become fitness friends Establish a goal to lose weight together Promote a smart work ethic as a group characteristic
Group processes Individual sacrifices	Ask two or three people for a goal for the day Ask regulars to help new people Ask people who are not concerned with weight loss to make a sacrifice for the group on some days (more aerobics)
Interaction and communication	Use partner work and have them introduce themselves Introduce the person on the right and left Work in groups of five and take turns showing a move Use more partner activities

Note. Adapted from "Team Building in an Exercise Setting," by A. V. Carron and K. S. Spink, 1993, *The Sport Psychologist, 7,* 8-18.

generalizability arise. More recently, the model illustrated in Figure 18-1 was used by Estabrooks and Carron (1999a) with physical activity classes for older adults. The researchers extended the previous research by (a) using previously sedentary older adults, (b) facilitating group goals for adherence, and (c) examining both absenteeism and return rates following an extended break in the program. Older adults (> 65 years) who had not previously been involved in a physical activity program or who considered themselves to be sedentary were recruited and assigned to classes experiencing a team-building, placebo, or control condition.

The team-building intervention was implemented during the second week of the program. Attendance at each class was monitored, as was the percentage of participants who returned to the program following a 10-week summer layoff.

Many of the intervention strategies, such as having a class name, were identical to those used by Carron and Spink (1993; Spink & Carron, 1993). However, some of the strategies designed to increase class norms and group processes (see Figure 18-1) were different. To facilitate stronger class norms for adherence behavior, the participants in the team-building condition were asked to set a collective (group) goal for attendance. Also, the group established a collective goal to symbolically walk across the Province of Ontario during the 6-week program. The collective goal was similar in nature to the one established in the Dyersville project. It was decided that 10 minutes of cardiovascular work within the class would constitute 1 kilometer traveled. Because it was a group goal, the probability of attaining the class's goal was directly related to the number of walkers as well as the duration of the cardiovascular component within each class. Also, the more members that attended the class, the more likely it was that the class would achieve its goal.

To facilitate group interaction and communication, each class began and concluded (during the seated warm-up and cooldown) with participant-led discussions on various fitness topics. For example, early in the program, the participants were asked to share their reasons for joining the program. At mid-program, the participants were asked to share progress and report on barriers and motives to participation. Late in the program, participants discussed ways to ensure their continued activity during the 10-week hiatus between the completion of their current program and the beginning of the next.

Class members made sacrifices for the group by providing extra time and service. For example, class members were asked to take regular attendance, to be the class greeter, and so on. Over the 6-week program, each participant fulfilled a group role for at least 2 weeks.

For the class in the placebo condition, a research assistant regularly attended class sessions, expressed interest in individual progress, and participated in the class activities. This protocol ensured that the participants were consistently aware that they were being observed as part of an ongoing evaluation of the program. The class in the control condition received a basic fitness program (i.e., standard care).

Large differences were present in class attendance as well as return rates after the 10-week summer hiatus. The participants in the team-building condition attended, on average, more than 90% of the classes, whereas those in the placebo and control conditions attended only 70% and 65%, respectively. After the 10-week hiatus, more than 90% of the participants in the team-building condition returned to participate in a new class, whereas only 70% and 40% of participants in the placebo and control conditions (respectively) chose to return to the program. Every participant in the team-building condition commented that the best thing about the class was its members. Only one respondent in the other two conditions mentioned others as an important part of the program.

These studies highlight that an intervention targeted at increasing group cohesion will increase physical activity participation of members of traditional physical activity classes. However, Annesi (1999) suggested that the changes in participation rates might be the result of increased leader attention to participants in small groups. This intervention may not be an efficient way to increase participation in larger health facilities. In response, Annesi designed a study to examine the effectiveness of a group cohesion–based intervention with minimal leader contact. To test his intervention, he chose to utilize a large fitness center (i.e., 2,500 members) that had a 500:1 ratio of participants to exercise leaders.

New members of the facility were targeted to participate in the study. Each participant was given the standard orientation and counseling offered at the facility and was prescribed a 3-time-weekly exercise program lasting 15 weeks. The participants were randomly assigned to the intervention arm or to a control group. The intervention participants met in small groups for 5 to 7 minutes before and after each exercise session. During the short sessions an exercise leader led the group through a warm-up and cooldown. The leaders did not provide any motivational strategies, nor did they suggest that the group continue the exercise program together once the warm-up was completed. The results of the study revealed that those participants who received the intervention had higher perceptions of Attractions to the Group—Task. Further, participants in the intervention arm attended more sessions (65% versus 48%) and had fewer dropouts (29% versus 50%). Annesi (1999) concluded that simply having new exercisers warm up and cool down together should increase the probability of program adherence.

CONCERNS ABOUT GROUP-BASED INTERVENTIONS

Even though the findings presented in this chapter appear to show consistent support for group-based interventions, some researchers have expressed concerns about the duration of the impact. In fact, in a

When a group exercise program comes to a conclusion, participants may cease to be physically active.
©PhotoDisc/Volume 103/Senior Lifestyles

recent review focusing on the effectiveness of various interventions, King, Rejeski, and Buchner (1998) questioned the positive impact of group-based approaches. They warned that a group-based intervention might be effective in the short term but counterproductive for long-term participation. Their fundamental point was that when the group is used as a vehicle for intervention, participants could become dependent on the group environment for sustained participation. However, programs invariably end, either for a summer or winter break or because the program's objectives have been met. Consequently, those individuals who depend on the group's support for sustaining physical activity may cease to be physically active if or when the group ceases to exist.

Researchers are correct to be concerned about the long-term impact of group-based interventions, but such interventions are still effective. In the two studies we have described in this chapter (Estabrooks & Carron 1999a; Spink & Carron, 1993), team-building interventions enhanced feelings of cohesion and improved adherence. It is true, however, that none of the studies examined physical activity participation once the program terminated. For example, Estabrooks and Carron successfully increased

return rates to the physical activity program, but did not assess the physical activity behavior between the completion of the first program and the initiation of the second. It is possible that their participants became relatively or completely inactive during the summer hiatus. Additionally, if the program ended, the participants might not have the confidence or skills necessary to complete a similar program at home or on an individual basis. The Spink and Carron and the Estabrooks and Carron group interventions focused on attendance and/or return rates to physical activity classes carried out in a group environment. The question that remains is, can group-based intervention continue to exert an influence on *independent* individual behavior after the group ceases to exist? Some research evidence suggests that it is possible.

GROUP-BASED INTERVENTIONS AS AGENTS FOR CHANGE

Brawley, Rejeski, and Lutes (2000) designed a study to determine if a group-based intervention could be effective for increasing individual participation not only during the life of the intervention program but also when the program was terminated. Their principal objective was to determine if individual skills learned in a group-supported environment would be maintained once the program ceased. Healthy previously sedentary older adults (> 65 years) were recruited and assigned to one of three conditions—a group-motivated cognitive-behavioral condition, a standard physical activity condition, or a wait-list control.

The study was carried out in three periods of 3 months each, and throughout those periods questionnaires were administered to assess participants' levels of physical activity and perceptions about quality of life. During the first 3-month period, the intervention was introduced in the group-motivated cognitive-behavioral condition. Both the group-motivated cognitive-behavioral condition and the standard physical activity condition participated in a structured physical activity program that included physical activities carried out at home. However, individuals in each of these two conditions were exposed to considerably different sets of experiences.

Although not explicitly stated, the intervention used with the group-motivated cognitive-behavioral condition mirrored many components of Carron and Spink's (1993) conceptual model illustrated in Figure 18-1. That is, during the first week of activity, a sense of distinctiveness was generated and group norms were established. To encourage a sense of distinctiveness, the participants selected and adopted a group name. Also, the participants were led to believe that their group was above average in their members' potential to change personal behavior. To generate stronger norms for adherence behavior, the participants were asked to maintain physical activity logs that would be used for group discussion purposes. Also in group-based discussions, individuals were encouraged to establish appropriate norms for both physical activity and inactivity.

During the second week, participant interaction and communication was facilitated. The participants were taught a number of self-regulatory skills associated with self-monitoring of effort, symptoms, and behavior and then were asked to pair up for the purpose of practicing the new skills. During this time, group-relevant goals for monitoring and behavior were also discussed.

In the third week, group communication was enhanced. The group discussed individual and group goals, possible reasons for failure associated with the goals, and group supportive strategies to help individual members overcome any failure. To further instill a sense of distinctiveness, the group was provided with T-shirts bearing a group name.

In Weeks 5 through 11 of the program, emphasis on the group interaction, norms, and support was maintained. The participants were also encouraged to begin discussing how to maintain individual physical activity and to identify and overcome possible cues associated with a relapse into a sedentary lifestyle. In the last week of the intervention period, the group discussed the implications of decreasing contact between the project staff and participants.

In the first 3 months of the study, members of the standard physical activity condition also met regularly. During that time they were instructed on appropriate types of exercise and given information pertaining to duration, frequency, and intensity of involvement. During the initial 3 months, members of the wait-list control condition did simply as the name would suggest—they waited.

During the second 3-month period, the members of both the group-motivated cognitive-behavioral condition and the standard physical activity condition did not meet. They did continue in a home-based program of physical activities, and staff was available for counseling through telephone contacts.

During the final 3-month period, individuals in the wait-list control condition were registered in a physical activity program. The members of both the group-motivated cognitive-behavioral condition and the standard physical activity condition continued in the study by engaging in home-based physical activities with no supportive contact from the program staff.

The results showed that the standard physical activity condition and the group-mediated cognitive-behavioral condition did differ from one another. The participants in the group-mediated cognitive-behavioral condition had a higher average frequency of physical activity as well as a greater total amount of physical activity during the initial 6 months of the intervention. Perhaps more impressive, members of the group-mediated cognitive-behavioral condition were still maintaining a higher rate of activity 9 months after the completion of the program.

Summary

Henry Ford suggested that success comes from groups of people working together. This chapter has highlighted that successful adherence to physical activity programs can also come from groups of people working together. However, simply getting people together as an aggregate does not constitute a group-based intervention.

Carron and Spink (1993) provided an effective framework for the development of group-based interventions for physical activity that includes strategies to improve group perceptions of distinctiveness, goals, norms, and interactions. The Dyersville, Iowa, weight-loss program is a good example of this framework in a real-world setting.

In research, a more systematic manipulation of Carron and Spink's framework showed that group-based interventions are effective for changing the cohesive level of a physical activity class. Group-based interventions are effective for both young and older adults, and success has been documented by improved participant adherence and return rates. Further, group-based interventions with minimal leader contact also have a positive impact on adherence. Finally, the research by Brawley and his associates (2000) provided evidence that group-based interventions are effective for the promotion of in-group and out-group physical activity.

CHAPTER 19

Community Level Intervention Strategies

*In Communities Where Men Build Ships for Their Own Sons to
Fish or Fight from, Quality Is Never a Problem.*

(J.A. Dever)

CHAPTER OBJECTIVES

**After completing this chapter you will
be able to**

- Define the term *community.*

- Describe the impact of school-based
  interventions.

- Describe the impact of work-site-based
  interventions.

- Describe the term *policy.*

- Differentiate between primary and secondary care interventions.

- Describe an effective telephone intervention.

- Outline the Centers for Disease Control
  and Prevention guidelines for community interventions.

Key terms
community
community physical
  activity intervention

primary prevention
secondary prevention

Community physical activity interventions are founded on the premise that population-based prevention strategies assist entire communities to reduce their level of risk factors for cardiovascular disease and, ultimately, will result in a reduction of illness and early death (Rose, 1992). Many of the interventions that we have discussed in this book may also be considered community level interventions, for example, the Dyersville project, a group-based intervention offered to an entire community (see Chapter 18). The primary distinction between individual, group, and community interventions is the level of application and the primary outcome of interest. Community strategies typically include a number of institutions, organizations, and groups who deliver a variety of interventions (Pate et al., 2000). Further, community interventions, when compared to individual or group level interventions, target system change rather than individual behavior change with the assumption that systemic change leads to a behavior change in a large number of individuals.

community physical activity intervention Population-based prevention strategies that assist entire communities to reduce their level of risk factors for cardiovascular disease and that will, ultimately, result in a reduction of illness and early death.

Karen Glanz (1997) provided an outline of the benefit and breadth of community level interventions.

> Community-level models suggest strategies and initiatives that are planned and led by organizations and institutions whose missions are to protect and improve health: schools, worksites, health care settings, community groups, and governmental agencies. Other institutions for whom health enhancement is not a central mission, such as the mass media, also play a critical role. (p. 238)

What is a **community?** A community has been generically defined as an aggregate of people who share common values and institutions (Pate et al., 2000). Shared institutions within a community include, but are not limited to, local hospitals, recreation centers, work sites, faith-based institutions, and schools. Communities also include a spatial component that refers to the locality of an aggregate of people, groups, or institutions. Finally, communities are associated with informal social norms, belief systems, interdependent groups, and attachments (Pate et al.).

J. A. Dever's quote at the beginning of this chapter points out the potential benefit of intervening from the community level. It implies that quality improves when the builders of ships (or interventions) are committed to the future users. Let's modify the wording a little bit: In communities where men and women build strategies for the benefit of their own sons' and daughters' health, quality is never a problem. Intuitively, there is practicality in the development and implementation of physical activity interventions at the community level. A community-based intervention should increase the level of quality and time invested into health promotion because of the intergroup relationships, shared values, and a common attachment within the community. Further, Mittelmark (1996) noted that

> there are additional, seemingly universal, practical reasons to focus on the local community and its settings for health promotion. Many communities are organized as formal administrative units such as

towns, cities, and municipalities. In most of the world, these local political and administrative units have the responsibility, structures, and resources to implement and maintain a wide variety of services for the local population. People tend to identify closely with the district they live in, stimulating citizen involvement in many arenas of community life, including promoting better health in the population. (p. 2)

In this chapter we examine community programs for the promotion of physical activity. The chapter includes four primary sections: site-based interventions; community-wide and policy interventions (i.e., governmental agencies); mass media interventions; and the Centers for Disease Control and Prevention guidelines for community-based physical activity interventions. In the first section, we review physical activity interventions offered in schools, work sites, and health care settings.

SITE-BASED INTERVENTIONS

Schools

The promotion of physical activity in schools has a long history. Elementary, middle, and high schools have traditionally offered physical education classes that entail participation in sport, exercise, and other physical activities. Unfortunately, schools are offering fewer physical education classes, or are offering classes of shorter duration, or have even eliminated classes completely. As a result of this decline in regular physical education courses, two general areas of research targeting physical activity at schools have emerged. One focus of research is on increasing physical activity during physical education classes, and a second is on increasing out-of-school physical activity.

Stone, McKenzie, Welk, and Booth (1998) reviewed and examined the effectiveness of 14 school-based interventions. The review led to three primary findings. First, school-based interventions were typically successful at improving knowledge and attitudes toward physical activity. Second, school-based interventions were typically successful at increasing physical activity during physical education classes. Third, school-based interventions (with some no-

---

community An aggregate of people who share common values and institutions.

table exceptions) were typically unsuccessful at increasing out-of-school physical activity.

A good example of a successful school intervention was the Child and Adolescent Trial for Cardiovascular Health (CATCH; Luepker, Perry, & McKinlay, 1996; McKenzie, Nader, & Strikmiller, 1996). This intervention trial included 96 elementary schools in California, Louisiana, Minnesota, and Texas. About half the schools were assigned to the intervention and half to the control. CATCH targeted intervention strategies at increasing physical activity during physical education classes and outside school time. The intervention was based on social cognitive theory (see Chapter 12) and organizational change strategies. During their third-grade year, students participating in the intervention completed 5 weeks of classroom sessions (15 sessions in all) that targeted important social cognitive variables such as outcome expectations and self-efficacy related to physical activity. During that time CATCH implemented policy interventions such as the provision of space, equipment, and supervision during nonschool hours (i.e., before and after school, lunch, recess). The program also introduced policy and curricula in physical education classes to reduce sedentary behavior or low levels of physical activity.

During their fourth and fifth grade years the students completed 12 weeks of classroom sessions (24 in all) that again highlighted and targeted changes in social cognitive theory variables. The physical activity policy components of the intervention were sustained throughout the fourth and fifth grades. The CATCH project resulted in positive changes in physical activity through the 3 years of the study. During physical education classes and out-of-school hours, students significantly increased their physical activity. Most impressively, the out-of-school increase in physical activity was still present 3 years later (i.e., in eighth grade; Luepker et al., 1996; McKenzie et al., 1996).

Work Sites

Work sites have also been targeted environments for physical activity programs. One motivation behind an increase in physical activity in the workplace is the suspected link between fitness and productivity. A sec-

ond motivation is that work sites have the potential to reach a broad range of adults. Indeed, most adults spend half their waking hours at work. Because of the link between fitness and productivity and because of the public health potential of reaching adults at work, a number of studies have been conducted on work site health promotion programs. However, expert narrative reviews of literature provided no consensus on the effectiveness of these programs (Dishman, Oldenburg, O'Neal, & Shephard, 1998).

In an attempt to reconcile the work site physical activity promotion literature, Dishman and his associates (1998) conducted a meta-analysis on 26 studies examining work site physical activity interventions. Each of the studies was coded on a number of potential moderating variables. Some general moderators examined were intervention type, delivery, location, incentives for participation or achievement, type of work site, and level of supervision. The intervention type was coded as either behavior modification, cognitive-behavior modification, health education, health risk appraisal, exercise prescription, or a combination of strategies. Intervention delivery was coded as face-to-face, mediated (indirectly through print or telephone), or a combination of the two, and location was coded as on-site or off-site. Incentives for participation or achievement were coded as financial, prizes, awards/recognition, or release time. Finally, the type of work site was coded as corporation, university, or public agency, and the level of supervision was coded as supervised or unsupervised.

The results of the meta-analysis revealed a small positive effect for work site physical activity interventions. However, the size of this effect was not significantly different from zero. There were also no significant changes to the size of the effect based on any of the moderators. However, the size of the effect did vary based on the design of the study in that the effects found in quasi-experimental studies were larger than those in randomized experiments. Eight of the 26 studies examined follow-up measures of physical activity. In these studies the effect size was again small; however, there was an intervention effect in that exercise prescription interventions (i.e., specified level of physical activity based on an exercise tolerance test) had larger effects than did other intervention types. This finding should be viewed with caution because one of the eight studies reported eight positive effects and may have biased the results. This meta-analysis indicates that work site physical activity interventions have had little impact to date.

Health Care Settings

The health care system provides many opportunities for community health promotion. On average, adult Americans visit a health care setting two times each year. Recently, Simons-Morton, Calfas, Oldenburg, and Burton (1998) provided a review of physical activity interventions in health care settings. In their review they distinguished between interventions that were targeting **primary prevention,** or physical activity promotion for apparently healthy individuals, and **secondary prevention,** in this case physical activity promotion for individuals with cardiovascular disease.

Twelve primary prevention randomized control trials or quasi-experimental studies were identified. The studies as a whole were based on patient counseling, and none of the interventions included a structured physical activity program. Half the studies were based on an underlying theory; 75% were implemented by doctors, whereas nurses or other health professionals administered the remaining 25%. Although the review did not calculate effect sizes, the study results were generally positive in the short term, but the effect seemed to decrease over time (Simons-Morton et al., 1998).

Project PACE (Provider-Based Assessment and Counseling for Exercise; Calfas et al., 1996) and Project PAL (Physically Active for Life; Goldstein et al., 1999) have recently used similar methodologies to examine the potential of primary care providers as an intervention tool to promote physical activity. In each study, primary care physicians were taught to provide

---

primary prevention   Physical activity promotion for apparently healthy individuals.

secondary prevention   Physical activity promotion for individuals with health problems.

---

counseling based on the stages of change and were directed to distribute stage-matched manuals to patients. In each project, community-based primary care medical practices were assigned to the intervention or to a standard care control.

Project PACE examined the participants at baseline, at 4 weeks, and at 6 weeks following the intervention. Participants in the intervention condition significantly increased their walking and their motivational readiness to change. Project PAL extended the research question to a 6-week and 8-month follow-up. At 6 weeks the participants in the experimental condition had increased in motivational readiness to change. However, the effect had disappeared at the 8-month follow-up. The authors of Project PAL concluded that a more intensive and consistent form of intervention administered by primary care physicians might be necessary for long-term behavior change.

Simons-Morton et al. (1998) identified 24 studies of physical activity interventions for patients with cardiovascular disease. In contrast to the consistent positive findings in primary prevention interventions, only 13 of the 24 studies reported significant changes in physical activity or fitness. In the studies that used an intervention that targeted many risk behaviors (including inactivity), about half were effective in changing physical activity. Based on the review, the most effective interventions (i.e., 75% of the studies) were those that included supervised exercise with behavior modification techniques or the provision of home equipment.

A study from Australia provides a good example of an effective secondary prevention intervention (Oldenburg, Martin, Greenwood, Bernstein, & Allan, 1995). In this study, male patients with cardiovascular disease were provided with structured individual and group exercise sessions for physical activity. The participants met for 30 to 40 minutes of physical activity once a week for 6 weeks. Over that time the participants also attended weekly group sessions in which they were instructed on adherence techniques. Booster sessions were conducted 8 and 12 months after the original intervention was completed. When compared to the control group, the intervention participants had significantly better fitness levels, which indicated that they had been more active during the 12-month period.

COMMUNITY-WIDE AND POLICY INTERVENTIONS

Interventions that have focused on community-wide changes in physical activity have taken a number of different forms: legislative, policy, or environmental. King and her collaborators (1995) provide excellent descriptions of legislative, policy, and environmental approaches to increasing physical activity in communities. Legislation and policy can be distinguished on the basis of legality. Legislation refers to formal legal structures at the local, state, or federal levels of government. Policy, on the other hand, is the formal or informal rules that provide structure to a governing organization. Potential settings for policy approaches include communities, work sites, and schools. King et al. argue that the use of legislation, policy, and environment to change physical activity patterns has a larger public health impact than do individual level interventions. A good example of a passive policy approach is restricting access to urban centers to foot and bicycle traffic. Neighborhood zoning and protection of open spaces for recreational use are good examples of a legislative approach. Both approaches have the potential to influence an entire community in a cost-effective and long-term fashion (King et al.).

One of the initial community-wide interventions that included policy and environmental approaches was the Naval Community Project in California (Linenger, Chesson, & Nice, 1991). Three groups were targeted in the study: the intervention community; a control community; and a Navy-wide sample. The control and intervention communities were matched on size, type of mission, climate, and facilities. Cardiovascular fitness was assessed before and after the 1-year intervention period. Because fitness was the primary outcome of interest in the study, the environmental and policy strategies focused on physical activity and healthy eating.

Policy strategies included extending the hours that the community recreation center was open. Also, communications between superiors and subordinates stressed the expectation that all members of the base should be involved in regular exercise. Further, a policy to include fruits and vegetables at all snack shops on the Naval base was implemented (Linenger et al., 1991).

Environmental changes to promote physical activity represented a large proportion of the intervention. First, bicycle paths were constructed along pre-existing roads. Second, new exercise equipment was purchased for the gymnasiums. Third, a women-only fitness center was opened on the base. Fourth, 1.5-mile running routes were marked out around the base. Other components of the intervention included the organization of athletic events and jogging clubs (Linenger et al., 1991).

The intervention had a number of positive benefits for participants who experienced the environmental change condition. For example, they completed a 1.5-mile run 18 seconds faster following the intervention. They also experienced a reduced failure rate during the physical testing (12.4% pretest, down to 5.1% postintervention). Further, although they did not lose a significant percentage of body fat, on average they did not gain body fat. In contrast, participants in both control conditions showed significant increases in percentage of body fat. Finally, although the number of sedentary individuals (<2,000 kcal of activity) increased in all groups, the increase was at a lower rate in the intervention group when compared to the control conditions (2.7%, 7.9%, and 6.4%, respectively; Linenger et al., 1991).

Perhaps the most important finding of the study was the extent of the intervention's impact. Improvements in fitness occurred in both men and women, in both officers and enlisted personnel, and in each age category. In short, all segments of the population were positively influenced by the intervention strategy, thereby providing support for the King et al. (1995) hypothesis that both environmental and policy approaches are effective for increasing physical activity.

The Stanford Five-City Project provides another example of a successful global community-based intervention (Farquhar et al., 1985). This project utilized a number of strategies to increase knowledge and attitudes toward physical activity and to increase physical activity itself. The researchers used cities as the primary target, and the intervention cities received treatments in two general ways. First, a large media campaign distributed television public service announcements, news stories, and newspaper articles written in both Spanish and English. Second, community programs involved interpersonal contacts, classes, seminars, and other group interventions. Each community program was offered in several settings and delivered through a variety of community agencies (e.g., the health department, colleges, hospitals, nonprofit organizations). The intervention was interactive and combined scientific and community input.

The results of the study revealed that the campaign did not have a consistent impact on physical activity knowledge, attitudes, or self-efficacy in either men or women. However, the physical activity measures indicated a positive treatment effect for men in estimated daily energy expenditure and amount of participation in vigorous activities. Similarly, women in the intervention communities engaged in significantly more moderate physical activities than did those in the control community.

Finally, interventions can also take advantage of the physical activity facilities and programs that already exist within the community. The Community Healthy Activities Model Program for Seniors (CHAMPS) was a community-based intervention that targeted congregate living facilities for older adults (Stewart et al., 1997). CHAMPS was designed to promote physical activity by emphasizing preexisting programs in the community. The researchers chose to direct participants to preexisting programs so that the participants would (a) use resources that are already available, (b) meet new people and have various schedules available, and (c) be more likely to remain active when the intervention was completed. The intervention included a vast array of individual

attention, monthly group meetings, and incentives. The intervention lasted 6 months, and a wait-list control group was used for comparison for the first 4 months of the study.

Surprisingly, at baseline a higher proportion of control participants (37%) than intervention participants (17%) were involved in community programs. However, the results of the study showed that a higher proportion of the intervention participants participated in community activity classes for all subsequent comparisons. At 4 months, 64% of the intervention participants were involved in programs. The authors concluded that the program was effective for the increased participation of older adults in community programs (Stewart et al., 1997).

MASS MEDIA INTERVENTIONS

The term *mass media* is often associated with television, radio, and newspapers. Several mass media campaigns have targeted the reduction of cardiovascular disease generally and targeted physical activity specifically. Mass media campaigns in Canada (PARTICIPACTION), in the United States (Healthstyle), and in Australia (Life—Be in It) have all reported increases in populational awareness (Marcus, Owen, Forsyth, Cavill, & Fridinger, 1998). The lack of assessment of behavior change, however, has led to debate regarding the behavioral impact of mass media interventions. In this section, we discuss the use of telephones, Internet technology, and postal services as components of mass media.

Hellerstedt and Jeffery (1997) examined the potential of a telephone-based intervention to change the physical activity of adults who were between 20 and 80 pounds overweight. The participants were contacted via newspaper advertisements seeking people who wanted to lose weight but did not want to attend an intensive program. All the participants attended two group-based education sessions (1 hour each) in which they were taught the benefits of regular exercise and proper nutrition as well as strategies to stick to a program. After the two sessions, participants were randomly assigned to a minimal contact condition (i.e., no further contact), a weight-focused telephone condition (i.e., a weekly telephone call to assess weight), or a behavior-focused telephone condition (i.e., a weekly telephone call to assess eating and physical activity).

The participants in the study were assessed for weight, nutritional intake, and physical activity at baseline and after 24 weeks of intervention. The researchers hypothesized that the minimal contact group would lose the least weight, eat less healthy, and be less active. Surprisingly, all three groups lost weight. The authors concluded from the study that minimal contact and telephone-based programs for weight loss appear to be attractive to overweight individuals, can be easily administered, and will result in modest weight loss.

Another method of targeting individuals within the community is through the mail. Marcus and her associates (1998) examined the benefits of a mail-based intervention tailored to the individual who received it. The intervention was based on the transtheoretical model (see Chapter 15). The participants for the study were recruited through newspaper advertisements. Those individuals who responded were screened for their current level of physical activity. Only sedentary participants were included for intervention. After the participants were accepted for inclusion, they were randomly assigned to an individually tailored intervention or to a standard intervention.

The individually tailored intervention included the distribution of reports that were based on the participants' completion of an initial battery of surveys that assessed their current stage of change, self-efficacy, decisional balance, use of cognitive and behavioral processes of change, and time spent in physical activity. The participants then received three types of feedback. First, participants were informed of their current stage of change. Second, participants were provided with assessments regarding their personal sense of self-efficacy, decisional balance, and use of the processes of change, and these assessments were compared to those of people who had previously been successful in the program.

Third, participants were given stage-specific motivational manuals developed to move individuals from one stage to the next. All three feedbacks were distributed at baseline and at 1, 3, and 6 months.

The standard intervention that was provided to the comparison group was based on materials developed by the American Heart Association. Four manuals were provided to the participants over the course of the study. The manuals were selected because they provided high-quality information relative to being physically active and took roughly the same amount of time to read as the tailored self-help manuals.

The results of the study were quite impressive. At baseline assessment, both the intervention and comparison groups were physically active for 20 minutes or less per week. Over the course of the study, participants in both groups increased their physical activity significantly. The intervention group increased from 5.5 to 151.4 minutes of physical activity per week at 6 months. The comparison group increased from 20.0 to 97.6 minutes of physical activity per week at 6 months. The analyses showed that although both treatments worked, the tailored model was more effective.

RECOMMENDATIONS FOR COMMUNITY PROGRAMS TO PROMOTE PHYSICAL ACTIVITY

In 1997 the Centers for Disease Control and Prevention (CDC) authored a report that highlighted the potential of community-based interventions aimed at the promotion of lifelong physical activity. This section provides an example of the CDC's recommended strategies for community intervention in the physical activity of school-aged children.

The primary purpose of the CDC report was to summarize 10 recommendations for encouraging physical activity in young people (Table 19-1). The recommendations focused on school and general community programs but most are valuable for, and can be generalized to, any type of community-based intervention.

■ **TABLE 19-1**   Recommendations for School and Community Programs Promoting Lifelong Physical Activity Among Young People

RECOMMENDATION	DESCRIPTION
1. Policy	Establish policies that promote enjoyable, lifelong physical activity for young people.
2. Environment	Provide physical and social environments that encourage and enable safe and enjoyable physical activity.
3. Physical education	Implement physical education curricula and instruction that emphasize enjoyable participation in physical activity and that help students develop the knowledge, attitudes, motor skills, behavioral skills, and confidence needed to adopt and maintain physically active lifestyles.
4. Health education	Implement health education curricula and instruction that help students develop the knowledge, attitudes, behavioral skills, and confidence needed to adopt and maintain physically active lifestyles.
5. Extracurricular activities	Provide extracurricular physical activity programs that meet the needs and interests of all students.
6. Parental involvement	Include parents and guardians in physical activity instruction and in extracurricular and community physical activity programs and encourage them to support their children's participation in enjoyable physical activities.
7. Personnel training	Provide training for education, coaching, recreation, health care, and other school and community personnel that imparts the knowledge and skills needed to effectively promote enjoyable, lifelong physical activity among young people.
8. Health services	Assess physical activity patterns among young people, counsel them about physical activity, refer them to appropriate programs, and advocate for physical activity instruction and programs for young people.
9. Community programs	Provide a range of developmentally appropriate community sports and recreation programs that are attractive to all young people.
10. Evaluation	Regularly evaluate school and community physical activity instruction, programs, and facilities.

Note. Adapted from "Guidelines for School and Community Programs to Promote Lifelong Physical Activity Among Young People," by Centers for Disease Control and Prevention, 1997, *Morbidity and Mortality Weekly Report, 46,* (no. RR-6), 1-37.

Policy

The CDC defined policies as the provision of "formal and informal rules that guide schools and communities in planning, implementing, and evaluating physical activity for young people" (CDC, 1997, p. 7). A policy should follow state and local laws and be written with input from administrators, teachers, coaches, athletic trainers, parents, students, and other community personnel. The CDC also advised that the written statement should include five basic requirements: comprehensive daily physical education for students in kindergarten through 12th grade; comprehensive health education for students in kindergarten through 12th grade; adequate resources, including funding and facilities, for physical activity instruction and programs; physical education specialists, health education specialists, and qualified people to direct school and community physical activity programs; and physical activity instruction and programs that meet the needs and interests of all students.

Environment

Chapter 11 discussed a number of environmental correlates of physical activity participation. Based on the findings mentioned in Chapter 11 and other findings, the CDC (1997) recommended that physical and social environments should encourage and enable safe and enjoyable physical activity. Five guidelines were provided for the provision of safe and enjoyable environments.

First, communities should provide safe places and facilities for physical activity. School gymnasiums, hallways, and facilities are key community spaces that can be used before and after school as well as on the weekends and vacation days. Other community facilities include parks, fitness trails, and swimming pools. Integral to the fulfillment of this guideline is the development of community coalitions to coordinate the availability of these spaces for physical activity programs.

Second, communities should provide and enforce measures to prevent physical activity injuries and illnesses (CDC, 1997). Administrators, facility personnel, teachers, coaches, and participants share in the responsibility to reduce the occurrence of injury and illness occasionally associated with physical activity. Explicit safety rules are required, and often the awareness of potential injuries will reduce participant risk (CDC, 1997).

Third, for school-based initiatives, students should be given time to participate in unstructured physical activity during the school day (CDC, 1997). In the United States, students in Grades 1 through 4 have an average recess period of 30 minutes. Students should be encouraged to use this time for active forms of socialization and play. Explicit within this guideline is that this time should be provided *in addition* to physical activity classes. The fourth and somewhat related guideline is to ensure that physical activity is not used as a form of punishment. Such punishments include forcing participation, offering unenjoyable activities, and withholding physical activity. Using physical activity as a punishment has the potential to create negative feelings toward, and thus decrease, physical activity (CDC, 1997).

The fifth environmental guideline is to provide physical activity programs that include school and community staff (CDC, 1997). Involving school and community staff provides other participants with healthy role models for physical activity. It also has been shown to improve the fitness of teachers and reduce the number of work days absent (CDC, 1997).

Physical and Health Education

The CDC (1997) recommended that physical education be provided through a curriculum that focuses on the enjoyment of physical activity and provides opportunities for students to develop the knowledge, skills, and confidence to initiate and maintain an active lifestyle (CDC, 1997). One guideline to achieving an enjoyable curriculum is to use active learning strategies, which provide the students with opportunities for input and choice regarding what physical activity will be done within the class. A second guideline is to ensure that a large proportion of each student's recommended weekly amount of physical activity is achieved during physical education classes. Finally, the physical education curriculum should promote physical activity not only in school but at home and in the community as well. One potential mechanism for transferring school-based physical activity to the home environment is to provide homework for children to do with their families (CDC, 1997).

The health education curriculum should complement the physical education curriculum by reinforcing the students' knowledge, attitudes, and skills necessary for lifelong physical activity. Health education classes can provide information regarding the national standards for physical activity. For optimal physical activity promotion the CDC suggested that physical and health education teachers collaborate with each other and with other teachers and administrators to provide multiple programs and opportunities for physical activity.

Extracurricular Activities and Community Programs

Unfortunately, physical education classes cannot be all things for all students all the time. Providing a variety of extracurricular physical activity options increases the likelihood that children will be active.

The CDC (1997) provided two guidelines for the optimal development of extracurricular activities. First, programs should offer activities that provide a range of both competitive and noncompetitive physical activities. Typically, extracurricular activities are highly competitive interscholastic athletic programs or competition-based intramural programs. Extramural walking, cycling, swimming, or running clubs can be used as noncompetitive alternatives.

One potential barrier to increased noncompetitive extracurricular activities is a lack of personnel. This problem is addressed in the second guideline: Connect students with physical activity programs that are offered in the community, and use community resources to support school programs. Students can then go to other community facilities for extracurricular activities, or community organizations can provide the personnel to conduct programs at the school facilities.

Parental Involvement

Simply put, parental involvement is critical in the development of a sustained environment that promotes physical activity (CDC, 1997). Three primary guidelines include parental advocacy, support, and role modeling. Parents are encouraged to be advocates for comprehensive daily physical education in schools. The CDC also suggested that parents take an active role in identifying or developing other community physical activity programs. Parental support and role modeling can improve children's perceptions of physical activity. However, because peers and friends can also influence children's physical activity, parents should offer their children physical activity options that allow them to be active with their friends (CDC, 1997).

Personnel Training and Health Services

One barrier to providing physical activity programs is a lack of trained personnel. Teachers should be trained to deliver programs that provide a large proportion of each student's necessary weekly physical activity as well as incorporate knowledge and skill building for lifelong participation. Community personnel should be trained on the development of positive physical activity environments. Finally, school and community personnel should be trained on how best to collaborate and include parents in physical activity promotion initiatives.

Physicians, school nurses, and other health care professionals are encouraged to ensure that the physical activity patterns of those in their care are monitored. Health care professionals can assess physical activity patterns and fitness and can become advocates for individual and program level physical activity.

Evaluation

Evaluation is the cornerstone to the improvement of any program, policy, or initiative. The final recommendation provided by the CDC (1997) was to regularly evaluate school and community physical activity instruction, programs, and facilities. The CDC suggested that paper and pencil tests may be the most appropriate evaluation for student feedback. Although fitness testing is regularly done in schools, it should not be used as a method of student feedback. Fitness testing, however, is useful to determine if a physical activity program is having a physical impact on the students in general.

Summary

Community-based interventions have a strong potential for physical activity promotion. This chapter has highlighted physical activity interventions that can be administered through specific settings, across community organizations and environments, and through mass media techniques. School-based physical activity interventions hold a great deal of promise for promoting sustained behavior change. Similarly, physician-administered physical activity interventions have been successful in primary prevention environments. Unfortunately, a recent meta-analysis on work site physical activity interventions suggests that the overall impact is not significantly different from no intervention at all.

Community-wide and policy-based interventions can increase physical activity within the community as a whole. Strategies that include targeted messages can be implemented by a number of avenues. Research has shown that telephone, mail, and primary care physicians are all viable mechanisms for intervention. Further, mass media messages combined with a system of community organizations and programs aimed at improving physical activity can also effect change in a neighborhood or city. Finally, the CDC (1997) provided important recommendations that point toward specific strategies for intervention.

CHAPTER 20

A Framework for Evaluating the Public Health Impact of Physical Activity Promotion Interventions

In Theory, There Is No Difference Between Theory and Practice. In Practice There Is.

(Yogi Berra)

CHAPTER OBJECTIVES

After completing this chapter you will be able to

- Outline the importance of assessing the public health impact of interventions.

- Describe the dimensions of the RE-AIM framework.

- Differentiate among the terms *reach, efficacy, adoption, implementation,* and *maintenance.*

- Describe the strengths of the RE-AIM framework.

- Describe the limitations of the RE-AIM framework.

Yogi Berra is perhaps one of the most quoted personalities of our time, which is not surprising because he is a funny guy. However, the humor associated with his quote about theory and practice epitomizes a concern of many health care professionals. Let's take some editorial license and change Yogi's quote a little: In research, there is no difference between research and practice; in practice there is. Many health care professionals are concerned about the external validity of interventions developed and tested in very controlled environments (i.e., randomized controlled trials). That is, those interventions that work in the environment of the randomized clinical control trial are often ineffective in real-world settings. Why? It could be because the resources within real-world settings are different from those in the control trial. It could be because the trained professionals who offered the intervention in the controlled trial were more qualified than those who offered it in a real-world setting. So, in randomized control trials there is no difference between *research* and practice, but in the real world there is. In this final chapter we outline the RE-AIM framework developed by Glasgow, Vogt, and Boles (1999). The **RE-AIM framework** was developed to

Key terms

adoption

implementation

maintenance

reach

RE-AIM framework

RE-AIM framework A method to evaluate the public health impact of a health promotion intervention and dealing with issues related to impact in real-world settings and the translation of research to practice.

■ **TABLE 20-1**   The RE-AIM Framework Dimensions

DIMENSION	LEVEL OF ANALYSIS	QUESTIONS ANSWERED
1. Reach	Individual	What proportion of the target audience participated?
		Do the participants have the same characteristics as the target audience?
2. Efficacy	Individual	Did the intervention work?
3. Adoption	Organizational	What proportion of similar organizations participated?
4. Implementation	Organizational	Did the organization ensure that every aspect of the intervention was administered as intended?
5. Maintenance	Individual/Organizational	Did the participants maintain the healthy behavior after the intervention was completed?
		Did the organization continue to offer the intervention?

determine the public health impact of health promotion intervention and "is concerned with issues related to impact in real-world settings and the translation of research to practice" (Glasgow, McKay, Piette, & Reynolds, in press, p. 3).

The RE-AIM framework proposes the following five dimensions necessary to examine the impact of a given intervention: a) reach, the proportion of the target population that participated in the intervention, b) efficacy, the success in promoting physical activity, c) adoption, the proportion of settings that subsequently uses the intervention, d) implementation, practitioner's fidelity to the intervention's protocol, and e) maintenance, the level of sustained use of the intervention over time. Together these five dimensions provide an indication of an intervention's public health impact (Glasgow, Vogt, & Boles, 1999).

Integral to the RE-AIM framework is the assumption that a public health framework must acknowledge the existence of both individual and organizational levels of impact. Reach and efficacy are measured at the level of the individual. Reach reflects the number of individuals, whereas efficacy reflects the degree to which people's behavior changes at an individual level. Adoption and implementation are organizational levels; adoption is the number of organizations that begin the intervention, and im-

plementation is how well the protocol of the intervention is adhered to at an organizational level. Finally, maintenance reflects both an individual and organizational level in that the sustained behavior of individuals and organizational use of an intervention can be documented. Table 20-1 highlights the RE-AIM dimensions, level of analysis, and basic questions that can be answered when the model is used as a tool to assess programs or interventions.

REACH

Reach is a public health outcome that is measured at the level of the individual and simply reflects the percentage of those individuals from a targeted population who actually participate in a given health promotion initiative (Glasgow et al., 1999). Oftentimes the reach of a randomized controlled trial can be determined by the participation rate of those contacted, but this calculation would tend to overestimate the

> **reach**   A public health outcome that is measured at the level of the individual and reflects the percentage of those individuals from a targeted population who actually participate in a given health promotion initiative.

reach of a given intervention. Typically, reach should be documented by using census information. Take, for example, an intervention aimed at individuals between 20 and 30 years old in a given community. The number of participants in the intervention should be divided by the total number of individuals between 20 and 30 years old within the community (Glasgow et al., 1999).

To identify the level of reach into a target population, let's look at an example based on research on the use of reinforcement to improve attendance at a fitness facility (Courneya, Estabrooks, & Nigg, 1997). The study was designed to examine the effects of a simple reinforcement strategy (a 1-month free membership) on improving attendance at a university facility. The selection criteria identified paying members of the facility who had attended between 4 and 11 times during a random 4-week period. One hundred randomly selected individuals were then offered a 1-month extension to their membership if they attended the facility 12 times over a given 4-week period. The intervention was described to the participants in a short form letter, and the postal service acted as the intervention delivery system. Follow-up telephone calls confirmed that all participants received the intervention letter. As we have already stated, the reach of a randomized control trial such as this one could be computed as 100%. That is, 100 participants were targeted, and subsequently all 100 participants received the intervention. However, a more appropriate calculation of reach would include the entire population of members at the fitness facility, in this case approximately 2,000 members, who had attended the facility the appropriate number of times over the 4-week selection period. This new information results in a reach of 5%, and this percentage would be smaller still if considered relative to the paying members of all similar facilities within the community. Therefore, the reach of this study—although high in terms of a research objective—was low in terms of the actual population.

The setting of an intervention is an important consideration when the intervention is aimed at management of chronic illnesses (Glasgow et al., in press). Glasgow and his associates categorized 13 specific intervention types into high, medium, or low reach. One-on-one in-person counseling was rated as a low-reach intervention when it was only offered to individuals with a professional referral. However, if the one-on-one counseling was delivered as part of a clinic's regular check-up, the reach was considered to be high (Glasgow et al., in press). For example, Albright and her collaborators (2000) examined the potential of physical activity promotion by primary care physicians. In their study, 54 physicians were trained to provide sedentary patients with advice on physical activity. Those 54 physicians in turn had contact with 874 sedentary adults.

Glasgow and his associates (in press) provide a general rating for reach for a number of intervention delivery methods. Telephone calls and mailed print messages are considered high-reach delivery systems, whereas hospital-based group counseling and call-in telephone interventions are considered to have low reach. Finally, interactive computer and community-based group counseling sessions are considered to have medium reach.

EFFICACY

Within the Glasgow et al. (1999) framework, efficacy is examined at the level of individual behavior change. Efficacy is determined by examining the effect size associated with a given intervention. A higher effect size indicates a more efficacious intervention. In terms of physical activity promotion, the efficacy issue is at the forefront of research. Indeed, if a public health intervention is not efficacious, then the issue of reach becomes irrelevant.

Much of this book focuses on the determination of efficacious physical activity promotion interventions. Chapters 17 and 18 provided a review of the efficacy of individual level and group level interventions. Recall Dishman and Buckworth's (1996) conclusion that strategies that used behavior modification and that were provided to healthy individuals at the community level are associated with large effects. The efficacy of interventions also seems to improve when the interventions are delivered to groups through mediated strategies. Further, Baranowski and his colleagues (1998) concluded that interventions based on theoretical mediators are more efficacious than those that are not.

ADOPTION

Adoption in the RE-AIM framework may best be conceptualized as the assessment of reach at the organizational level. Adoption is defined as the proportion and representativeness of settings that begin to use the intervention protocol. Let's look again at the reinforcement study example we used in the previous section (Courneya et al., 1997). Adoption would be measured by the number of fitness facilities that began to offer a 1-month membership extension to members who attended 12 times over a given 4-week period. Adoption is the missing link between research and practice. Unfortunately, research that has examined physical activity promotion has failed to document the success of interventions based on the adoption of these interventions into mainstream settings.

Although the literature on adoption of physical activity promotion interventions is sparse, Pate and his associates (2000) have suggested that effective community-based interventions must include mechanisms to ensure adoption of the intervention to various community settings (see Chapter 19). Pate et al. provide a number of mechanisms to increase adoption. First, when designing a community physical activity promotion intervention, consult and inform individuals from all major community groups and institutions. Second, integrate activities with existing community activities. Third, create a systematic plan to constantly identify, recruit, and involve new people and organizations in the project. Finally, summarize and disseminate the results of intervention programs to the participants, community leaders, and important organizations within the community (Pate et al., 2000).

> **adoption**   The proportion and representativeness of settings that begin to use the intervention protocol.

These mechanisms should increase the potential adoption of a given intervention to other settings and organizations. Integrating community groups and using existing resources will improve the chances that an intervention will be adopted. If program organizers do not communicate and coordinate with other community organizations, those organizations may be forced to increase the number of employees or the number of hours worked by their employees, which will discourage the organization from adopting the intervention. Finally, the dissemination of intervention results is tantamount to marketing a product. The better the marketing strategy, the more likely it is that the intervention protocol will be adopted.

IMPLEMENTATION

One concern of physical activity promotion researchers is the extent to which an intervention will be delivered as it was intended (Glasgow et al., 1999). **Implementation** is an organizational level variable and reflects the fidelity of practitioners or researchers to the intended intervention protocol. The primary importance of implementation is that the degree of adherence to an intervention protocol has a potential moderating effect on the efficacy of the intervention. The interaction between implementation and efficacy is often described as the *effectiveness* of the intervention in real-world settings. Implementation can be measured as treatment fidelity through systematic manipulation checks. As with reach and adoption, few studies have examined the implementation of interventions at an organizational level.

Studies that have assessed the implementation of physical activity interventions typically do so by determining which participants actually completed the intervention as intended. Turner and her associates (1997) provided an example of implementation

> **implementation**   The reflection of the fidelity of practitioners or researchers to the intended intervention protocol.

assessment. In this study, the behavior of a physical activity group leader was manipulated to include socially enriched behaviors or socially bland behaviors. The socially enriched condition included the use of participant names, frequent individual attention, positive reinforcement, and performance feedback. To ensure that the intervention was delivered as intended, a videotaped analysis was completed in each of the two conditions. The analysis confirmed that the leader was implementing the intervention as intended.

Implementation is also dependent on the delivery personnel used. In the smoking cessation literature, it has been shown that a brief hospital-based intervention was more successful when implemented by the research staff than when implemented by the hospital staff (Glasgow et al., 1999). This finding emphasizes that research is needed to examine the training necessary for appropriate implementation. Also of interest is why a research staff is more effective than a hospital or community staff. Research is needed to determine if differences are due to inadequate technical training or to staff unwillingness because of the increased workload that the intervention creates.

MAINTENANCE

Maintenance refers to the long-term participation in behavior change and is assessed at both the individual and organizational level. Typical relapse rates show the need to document the length of adherence to a given positive health behavior. In terms of individual level maintenance, research in physical activity promotion has been promising. Many intervention studies include 6-month and 12-month follow-up data points to assess the maintenance of participants' physical activity (e.g., Brawley et al., 2000). This type of follow-up is necessary to determine the longevity of an intervention's impact. This variable also has an interactive role with the efficacy of an intervention and

---

maintenance   The long-term participation in behavior change.

---

could potentially provide information on dose-response effectiveness. Although follow-up data is available, more work is needed to examine the necessity of repeated or singular interventions.

Maintenance can also be examined at the organizational level. Once a program is started, its length of existence is seldom reported. Anecdotally, while conducting research at the Canadian Centre of Activity and Ageing in London, Ontario, researchers have initiated 14 physical activity programs over a 15-year period, all to fulfill a brief (i.e., 6 to 12 months) research need. However, all 14 classes have remained operational indefinitely.

USING THE RE-AIM MODEL AS A PRACTICAL EVALUATION

In our descriptions of the RE-AIM framework thus far, our examples have all been related to research. The basis of the RE-AIM framework is to begin with research and to then evaluate how well that research translates to the real world. This valuable information can identify gaps in research, such as limited examination of adoption and maintenance at the organizational level.

The underlying importance of the RE-AIM framework is the necessity to find interventions that are efficacious and then integrate those interventions across organizational structures (i.e., adoption, implementation) to increase the reach to individuals over an extended period of time (i.e., maintenance). How can this information be used to help a physical activity promotion professional? Take, for example, Jennie, a fictitious director of health promotion for her community. Using the RE-AIM framework, Jennie systematically evaluates the programs that are being offered through her community. Let's focus on a program that Jennie developed for older adults to become more physically active. The program was implemented at a test facility.

First, Jennie assesses the reach of her program for older adults. Her research tells her that within the community 600 individuals are over the age of 65. Currently in her program Jennie has 15 members. Hence, the program's reach is very low (2.5%). Second, Jennie examines the efficacy of her program. She examines the program records and discovers that all the participants have tripled their weekly minutes of regular physical activity since joining the program. Now Jennie knows that her program is working and is very efficacious. Third, Jennie assesses the number of fitness centers that have implemented the intervention. Currently only one program is being offered. Hence, the organizational adoption of the intervention is low. Fourth, after viewing some videotaped sessions of the intervention, Jennie concludes that the instructor is implementing the intervention as was initially intended. Hence, the implementation of the intervention is good. Finally, both the program and the individuals within the program are still ongoing, which reflects good maintenance both at the individual and organizational level.

By using her evaluation Jennie can identify major areas in need of attention for her program for older adults. First, she has a program that works very well but she is reaching only a small percentage of the program's target audience. She needs to place more emphasis on increasing the reach of the program. Increased marketing targeted at older adults within the community could be a potential option. Second, Jennie determined that there has been no additional organizational adoption of the program. She now knows to target her efforts at marketing the intervention to other communities or organizations.

LIMITATIONS OF THE RE-AIM FRAMEWORK

Although the RE-AIM framework offers an important value to the evaluation of physical activity interventions, it has some limitations that should be addressed. First, the framework is a descriptive model, and it provides a very logical way to evaluate programs. What it does not provide are the processes through which to change the evaluated outcomes. For example, the model describes different avenues for reach and even identifies avenues that are better than others. However, it offers no underlying theory that describes how to increase reach within a given avenue. Therefore, the RE-AIM framework should be used in conjunction with a mediational model that describes how to impact within a dimension (see Chapter 17 for a description of theory-based interventions).

A second limitation of the RE-AIM model is that relatively little data support the claim that each level of the model is equally important. Without efficacy, all other components of the model are irrelevant. Further, the multiplicative structure for computing the public health impact has not been fully tested. There is no doubt that each dimension is important; however, the interactive nature of the dimensions is still in question.

Summary

This chapter provides a description of the RE-AIM framework for the evaluation of health promotion intervention. The framework proposes five dimensions necessary to examine the impact of a given intervention: (a) Reach, the proportion of the target population who participated in the intervention; (b) Efficacy, the intervention's success in promoting physical activity; (c) Adoption, the proportion of settings that subsequently use the intervention; (d) Implementation, the practitioners' fidelity to the intervention's protocol; and (e) Maintenance, the level of sustained use of the intervention over time. Therefore, the RE-AIM framework should be used in conjunction with a theoretical model that describes how to impact a given RE-AIM dimension (i.e., reach, efficacy, adoption, implementation, and maintenance).

Glossary

A

accelerometer An objective instrument for measuring acceleration.

action A stage of the transtheoretical model in which a person is actively engaging in the new behavior for less than six months.

active living A way of life in which physical activity is valued and integrated into daily life.

adoption The proportion and representativeness of settings that begin to use the intervention protocol.

affective body image measures Assessment of an individual's level of anxiety or discomfort about his or her body.

affective regulation explanation An explanation of exercise dependence that suggests that physical activity leads to positive psychological states, whereas the cessation of exercise results in negative psychological states.

amotivation The absence of motivation toward an activity.

anorexia analogue hypothesis A type of personality trait explanation of exercise dependence that argues that male obligatory runners resemble anorexia nervosa patients on personality traits.

attachment Emotional support.

attitude Individual's positive or negative evaluation of performing a behavior (theory of planned behavior).

autonomy The desire to be self-initiating in the regulation of personal behavior.

B

barriers efficacy Beliefs about possessing the capability to overcome obstacles to physical activity.

behavior Activities that are performed or avoided as a result of the perception of pain; the fourth component of pain.

behavioral beliefs Perceived consequences of carrying out an action and a personal evaluation of each of these consequences (theory of planned behavior).

behavioral body image measures Determination of the degree to which an individual engages in activities designed to avoid intimacy, hide his or her body, or avoid situations where his or her body might be the object of scrutiny by other people.

β-endorphins Endogenous compounds that decrease sensitivity to pain, which results in euphoric effects and addictive behavioral tendencies.

β-endorphin explanation An explanation of exercise dependence that is based on the premise that β-endorphin levels in the blood rise with exercise because of an increased need for blood to be transported to the working muscles.

body image A subjective perception of how one's body appears.

C

clinical depression A lowered mood or loss of interest/pleasure for a minimum of two weeks and accompanied by at least five of the following symptoms: loss of appetite, weight loss/gain, sleep disturbance, psychomotor agitation or retardation, energy decrease, sense of worthlessness, guilt, difficulty in concentrating, thoughts of suicide.

cognition Pertaining to the mental processes of comprehension, judgment, memory, and reasoning, as contrasted with emotional and volitional processes.

219

cognitive body image measures Assessment of the individual's general attitude about his or her body.

community An aggregate of people who share common values and institutions.

community physical activity intervention Population-based prevention strategies that assist entire communities to reduce their level of risk factors for cardiovascular disease and that will, ultimately, result in a reduction of illness and early death.

competence The desire to interact effectively within one's environment.

concurrent validity Type of validity involving the correlation of a measure with a criterion or gold standard measure.

contemplation A stage of the transtheoretical model at which a person intends to make changes within the foreseeable future, which is defined as the next 6 months.

continuance A criterion of exercise dependence in which physical activity is maintained despite the awareness of a persistent physical or psychological problem.

control beliefs The perceived presence or absence of required resources and opportunities, the anticipated obstacles or impediments to behavior, and the perceived power of a particular control factor to facilitate or inhibit performance of the behavior (theory of planned behavior).

coping appraisal An evaluation of the factors that influence the likelihood of engaging in a recommended preventive response (protection motivation theory).

cues to action Strategies to activate readiness (health belief model).

D

decisional balance The balance between the potential advantages and disadvantages of a behavior.

description The first stage of science, which informs about "what is."

determinants Individual characteristics that influence exercise behavior.

disease-specific efficacy Beliefs about self-efficacy in specific populations engaged in the secondary prevention of disease through exercise rehabilitation.

dose-response issue How much of the dose is necessary to obtain the desired response.

duration The length of time that an activity lasts.

E

effect size The result from an individual study converted to a standard score.

effectiveness trials Tests of whether a technology, treatment, procedure, intervention, or program does more good than harm when delivered under real-world conditions.

efficacy trials Tests of whether a technology, treatment, procedure, or program does more good than harm when delivered under optimum conditions.

electroencephalography (EEG) The process of recording brain wave activity.

electromyography (EMG) The process of electrically recording muscle action potentials.

enacted support Support offered by the provider in a social support exchange.

endogenous pain Naturally occurring pain.

energy expenditure A consequence of body movement related to body size.

environment All of the many factors, physical and psychological, that influence or affect the life and survival of a person.

evaluation The degree to which people possess positive and/or negative self-perceptions.

exercise A specific form of physical activity in which the individual engages for the specific purpose of improving fitness, physical performance, or health.

exercise dependence A craving for leisure-time physical activity that results in uncontrollable excessive exercise behavior and that manifests in physiological and/or psychological symptoms.

exercise deprivation sensations The psychological and physiological effects that occur during periods of no physical activity.

expert systems Computer technology used to simulate human experts by providing systematic feedback that is predetermined either by qualified professionals or by statistics.

explanation The second stage of science, which involves theory development.

external regulation A type of extrinsic motivation in which an individual engages in a behavior solely to receive a reward or avoid punishment (self-determination theory).

F

face-to-face interventions Interventions delivered directly to the participant.

feasibility The practicality of administering a measure to a certain population.

frequency The number of times a person engages in an activity over a predetermined period.

G

generality of self-efficacy Degree to which efficacy beliefs transfer to related tasks.

group cohesion A dynamic process that is reflected in the tendency for a group to stick together and remain united in pursuit of its instrumental objectives and/or for the satisfaction of member affective needs.

Group Environment Questionnaire (GEQ) Inventory used to assess cohesiveness.

H

health A human condition with physical, social, and psychological dimensions, each characterized by a continuum varying from positive to negative poles.

health behavior efficacy Beliefs about the capability of engaging in health-promoting behaviors.

heart rate monitor An objective physical activity measure that utilizes the linear relationship between heart rate and energy expenditure during steady-state exercise.

I

identified regulation A type of extrinsic motivation in which an individual freely chooses to carry out an activity that is not considered to be enjoyable but is thought to be important to achieve a personal goal (self-determination theory).

imagery experience The use of visualization to repeatedly and successfully confront and master challenging situations.

implementation The reflection of the fidelity of practitioners or researchers to the intended intervention protocol.

incentive congruency measure The difference between the emphasis placed on an incentive and the perceived opportunity to satisfy that incentive.

instructor efficacy A measure of participants' confidence in their activity leader's abilities.

intensity The degree of overload an activity imposes on physiological systems compared to resting states.

intention Person's willingness and how much effort he or she is planning to exert to perform the behavior (theory of planned behavior).

intervention The fourth stage of science (also called control), which involves application of what has been learned from the previous three stages.

interventions Health-promoting activities that originate from a health promotion team with the intention of instilling or maintaining health-related attitudes, norms, and behaviors, in a specific target.

intrinsic motivation The motivation to do an activity for its own sake or for the pleasure it provides.

introjected regulation A type of extrinsic motivation which is manifested as the incomplete internalization of a regulation that was previously solely external (self-determination theory).

L

lack of control A criterion of exercise dependence in which physical activity is maintained despite a persistent desire to cut down or control it.

large effect Any effect size that is over .80.

level of self-efficacy Belief in personal ability to accomplish a particular task or component of a task.

M

maintenance A stage of the transtheoretical model at which a person has been engaging in the new behavior for longer than six months.

mastery experience The experience of carrying out a task successfully.

mediated interventions Interventions usually delivered indirectly by mail or telephone.

meta-analysis The statistical analysis of the summary findings of many empirical studies.

metabolic equivalents (METs) Multiples of the resting rate of oxygen consumption during physical activity.

moderate effect Any effect size within the range of .40 to .70.

moderator variables Variables that have a direct influence on the relationship of an individual variable, making it a dependent variable.

momentary time sampling Observation method in which activity level is coded at the moment the observation interval ends.

muscle dysmorphia A form of body image distortion in which the individual perceives himself or herself as unacceptably small.

N

negative affect Feelings such as anxiety, depression, fatigue, anger, and confusion.

nocioception The detection of tissue damage by sensory receptors known as nociceptors; the first component of pain.

nonclinical depression A mental state characterized by feelings of gloom and listlessness.

nonrapid eye movement sleep (NREM) A state of sleep characterized by four stages.

normative beliefs Perceived expectation of important significant others or groups and an individual's motivation to comply with the expectations of these important significant others (theory of planned behavior).

O

objectivity (interrater reliability) The ability of different testers or scorers to provide similar results for a given individual.

obtaining of guidance Information support.

operant conditioning The proposal that a number of conditions exist within the human environment that cue people to do one behavior or another.

opportunity for nurturance Increased self-worth from assisting others.

outcome expectation The belief about the effects of a behavior.

overtraining A short period of training, usually lasting a few days to a few weeks, during which training increases to near or at maximal capacity.

P

pain An unpleasant sensory and emotional experience associated with actual or potential tissue damage, or described in terms of such damage.

partial time sampling Observation method in which observers code all activities that occur during a short interval, usually 5 to 20 seconds.

participant reactivity The tendency for subjects to alter their usual activity when they know they are being watched.

pedometer Instrument that can either count steps or estimate distance walked.

per sonae Latin for "to speak through."

perceived barriers Person's opinion of the physical and psychological costs of the advised action.

perceived behavioral control Beliefs about the degree of personal control in the decision to engage in physical activity; the perceived ease or difficulty of performing a behavior (theory of planned behavior).

perceived benefits Person's opinion of the efficacy of the advised action to reduce risk or seriousness of impact (health belief model).

perceived severity Person's opinion of the seriousness of a condition and its consequences (health belief model).

perceived support The individual's cognitive appraisal of his or her social network.

perceived susceptibility Person's opinion of his or her chances of getting a disease (health belief model).

perceived vulnerability Person's estimate of the degree of personal risk for a specific health hazard if a current unhealthy behavior is continued.

perception of pain The second component of pain.

perceptual body image measures Assessment of the accuracy of an individual's perceptions about his or her body size.

personality trait explanation An explanation of exercise dependence that states that exercise dependent individuals have specific personality characteristics such as perfectionism, obsessive-compulsiveness, neuroticism, low self-esteem, and high trait anxiety.

physical activity Any body movement produced by skeletal muscles and resulting in a substantial increase over the resting energy expenditure.

Physical Activity Group Environment Questionnaire (PAGEQ) Inventory developed specifically for use in older adult samples to measure cohesion.

POMS Profile of Mood States.

positive affect Feelings such as vigor, pleasantness, and euphoria.

precaution strategy Person's intention to adopt exercise even though he or she holds weak beliefs about its effectiveness and is not convinced of his or her at-risk status.

precontemplation A stage of the transtheoretical model at which a person does not intend to make changes within the next six months.

precontemplation believer A person who believes that physical activity is a worthwhile behavior but cannot seem to start participating in it.

precontemplation nonbeliever A person who either does not believe in regular physical activity or does not see the value of engaging in it.

prediction The third stage of science, which involves theory testing.

predisposition A state of being particularly susceptible.

preparation A stage of the transtheoretical model at which a person intends to change in the immediate future, which is defined as within 1 month.

primary exercise dependence Exercise dependence in which the physical activity is an end in itself.

primary prevention Physical activity promotion for apparently healthy individuals.

psychology of physical activity The area of science devoted to an understanding of individual attitudes, cognitions, and behaviors in the context of physical activity and exercise and of the social factors that influence those attitudes, cognitions, and behaviors.

psychophysiological reactivity The influence of acute and chronic physical activity on modulating psychological and physiological responses to social stressors.

R

rapid eye movement sleep (REM) A state of sleep characterized by rapid eye movements, increased frequency and reduced amplitude of EEG recordings, and a reduction in EMG activity.

reach A public health outcome that is measured at the level of the individual and simply reflects the percentage of those individuals from a targeted population who actually participate in a given health promotion initiative.

RE-AIM framework A method for determining the public health impact of health promotion intervention and dealing with issues related to impact in real-world settings and the translation of research to practice.

reassurance of worth Esteem support.

received support Support received by the recipient in a social support exchange.

recency effect The phenomenon by which people can more accurately recall what physical activity they engaged in in the immediate past (e.g., last 7 days).

relatedness The desire to feel connected to other people.

reliability The ability of a test to yield consistent and stable scores.

reliable alliance Tangible aid.

response efficacy Person's expectancy that complying with recommendations will remove the threat (protection motivation theory).

S

scheduling efficacy Confidence that physical activity can be scheduled into a daily or weekly routine.

secondary exercise dependence Exercise dependence in which the motivation for physical activity is the control and manipulation of body composition.

secondary prevention Physical activity promotion for individuals with health problems.

self-concept The multitude of attributes and roles through which individuals evaluate themselves to establish self-esteem judgments.

self-efficacy The belief that one has the personal capability to carry out the actions required to produce a given outcome; confidence in one's ability to take action.

self-esteem A global and relatively stable evaluative construct reflecting the degree to which an individual feels positive about himself or herself.

self-presentation The attempts by an individual to selectively present aspects of the self and to omit self-relevant information to maximize the likelihood that a positive social impression will be generated and an undesired impression will be avoided.

slow wave sleep (SWS) Stages 3 and 4 of nonrapid eye movement sleep.

small effect Any effect size within the range of .10 to .30.

social integration The degree to which the individual participates in family life, the social life of the community, church, and so on and has access to resources and support systems; also known as social embedment.

social physique anxiety Social anxiety that arises as a result of concerns about the self-presentation of the body.

social support A wide cross section of concepts that includes belonging, bonding, and binding; attributes of groups, relationships, and persons; and processes that are social, behavioral, and affective in nature.

staleness A psychological state of overtraining that manifests as deteriorated readiness.

state anxiety The level of anxiety that an individual experiences at any given point in time.

strength of self-efficacy Degree of conviction that a particular task or component of a task can be carried out successfully.

subjective aversion An excessively depressed or excited resting physiological state.

subjective norm The perceived social pressure to perform or not perform the behavior (theory of planned behavior).

support appraisal The satisfaction expressed with positive social interactions.

support behavior Frequency of occurrence or the likelihood that others will provide the behavior.

support networks The individual's social network from a functional perspective; also known as network resources.

supportive climates The quality of social relationships and systems; also known as supportive environments.

sympathetic arousal explanation An explanation of exercise dependence that states that excessive exercise produces an increase in fitness level and in energy use efficiency.

T

task exercise self-efficacy Beliefs about the capability of successfully engaging in incremental bouts of physical activity.

termination A stage of the transtheoretical model at which a person has 0% temptation to engage in old behavior and 100% self-efficacy in all previously tempting situations.

test-retest reliability Measure of reliability that assesses stability over time.

threat appraisal An evaluation of the factors that influence the likelihood of engaging in an unhealthy behavior.

time A criterion of exercise dependence in which considerable time is spent in activities essential to physical activity maintenance.

tolerance A criterion of exercise dependence in which increased physical activity levels are needed to achieve the desired effect, or in which the same physical activity level produces markedly diminished effects.

tomato effect A phenomenon whereby highly efficacious therapies are ignored or rejected because the therapies do not seem to make sense in light of popular beliefs or common understandings, or because the available evidence is simply ignored.

tracking The phenomenon of children maintaining their relative ranking on a variable over time.

trait anxiety The predisposition to perceive certain environmental stimuli as threatening or nonthreatening and to respond to these stimuli with varying levels of state anxiety.

triadic reciprocal causation The theory that behavior is influenced by and influences internal personal factors and external situational factors.

type A reference to the main physiological systems that are activated during activity.

V

validity The ability of a test to accurately assess what it is supposed to measure.

verbal persuasion The act of providing participants with considerable information about the why, what, and where of physical activity.

W

withdrawal A criterion of exercise dependence in which the cessation of physical activity produces negative symptoms, or in which physical activity is used to relieve or forestall the onset of these symptoms.

vicarious experience The act of observing the successes and failures of other, similar people.

vicarious learning The act of learning through watching other people successfully engaged in the target activity.

References

Aarnio, M., Winter, T., Kujala, U. M., & Kaprio, J. (1997). Familial aggregation of leisure time physical activity: A three generation study. *International Journal of Sport Medicine, 18,* 549–556.

ACSM (2000). *ACSM's guidelines for exercise testing and prescription* (6th ed.). Baltimore, MD: Lippincott, Williams, & Wilkins.

Adams, J., & Kirkby, R. (1997). Exercise dependence: A problem for sports physiotherapists. *Australian Journal of Physiotherapy, 43,* 53–58.

Adams, J., & Kirkby, R. J. (1998). Exercise dependence: A review of its manifestation, theory, and measurement. *Sports Medicine Training and Rehabilitation, 8,* 265–276.

Aho, W. R. (1979). Smoking, dieting, and exercise: Age differences in attitudes and behavior to selected health belief model variables. *Rhode Island Medical Journal, 62,* 85–92.

Ainsworth, B. E., Haskell, W. L., Leon, A. S., Jacobs, D. R., Montoye, H. J., Sallis, J. F., & Paffenbaarger, R. S. (1993). Compendium of physical activities: Classification of energy costs of human physical activities. *Medicine and Science in Sports and Exercise, 25,* 71–80.

Ainsworth, B. E., Haskell, W. L., Whitt, M. C., Irwin, M. L., Swartz, A. M., Strath, S. J., O'Brien, W. L., Bassett, D. R., Jr., Schmitz, K. H., Emplaincourt, P. O., Jacobs, D. R., Jr., & Leon, A. S. (2000). Compendium of physical activities: An update of activity codes and MET intensities. *Medicine and Science in Sports and Exercise, 32,* S498–S516.

Ajzen, I. (1985). *From intentions to actions: A theory of planned behavior.* In J. Kuhl and J. Beckman (Eds.), *Action control: From cognition to behavior* (pp. 11–39). Heidelberg: Springer.

Ajzen, I. (1987). Attitudes, traits, and actions: Dispositional prediction of behavior in personality and social psychology. In L. Berkowitz (Ed.), *Advances in experimental and social psychology* (Vol. 20, pp. 1–63). New York: Academic Press.

Ajzen, I. (1988). *Attitudes, personality, and behavior.* Chicago: Nasey.

Ajzen, I. (1991). The theory of planned behavior. *Organizational Behavior and Human Decision Processes, 50,* 179–211.

Ajzen, I. (in press). Perceived behavioral control, self-efficacy, locus of control, and the theory of planned behavior. *Journal of Applied Social Psychology.*

Ajzen, I., & Driver, B. L. (1992). Application of the theory of planned behavior to leisure choice. *Journal of Leisure Research, 24,* 207–224.

Ajzen, I., & Fishbein, M. (1980). *Understanding attitudes and predicting social behavior.* Englewood Cliffs, NJ: Prentice Hall.

Albright, C. L., Cohen, S., Gibbons, L., Miller, S., Marcus, B., Sallis, J. F., Imai, K., Jernick, J., & Simons-Morton, D. G. (2000). Incorporating physical activity advice into primary care: Physician-delivered advice within the activity counseling trial. *American Journal of Preventive Medicine, 18*(3), 225–234.

Aldana, S. G., Sutton, L. D., Jacobson, B. H., & Quirk, M. G. (1996). Relationships between leisure time physical activity and perceived stress. *Perceptual and Motor Skills, 82,* 315–321.

American Psychiatric Association. (1987). *Diagnostic and statistical manual of mental disorders* (3rd ed.). Washington, DC: Author.

American Psychiatric Association. (1994). *Diagnostic and statistical manual of mental disorders* (4th ed.). Washington, DC: Author.

Andersson, H. I. (1994). The epidemiology of chronic pain in a Swedish rural sample. *Quality of Life Research, 3,* S19–S26.

Annesi, J. J. (1999). Effects of minimal group promotion on cohesion and exercise adherence. *Small Group Research, 30*(5), 542–557.

Anshel, M. H. (1991). A psycho-behavioral analysis of addicted versus non-addicted male and female exercisers. *Journal of Sport Behavior, 14,* 145–154.

Appenzeller, O., Standefer, J., Appenzeller, J., & Atkinson, R. (1980). Neurology of endurance training V: Endorphins. *Neurology, 30,* 418–419.

Arent, S. M., Landers, D. M., & Etnier, J. L. (in press). The effects of exercise on mood in older adults: A meta-analytic review. *Journal of Aging and Physical Activity.*

Argyle, M. (1992). Benefits produced by supportive social relationships. In H. O. F. Veiel & U. Baumann (Eds.), *The meaning and measurement of social support* (pp. 13–32). New York: Hemisphere.

Armstrong, C. A., Sallis, J. F., Hovell, M. F., & Hofstetter, C. R. (1993). Stages of change, self-efficacy, and the adoption of vigorous exercise: A prospective analysis. *Journal of Sport and Exercise Psychology, 15,* 390–402.

Artal, R. (1992). Exercise and pregnancy. *Clinics in Sports Medicine, 11,* 363–377.

Baekeland, F. (1970). Exercise deprivation: Sleep and psychological reactions. *Archives of General Psychiatry, 22,* 365–369.

Bahrke, M. S., & Morgan, W. P. (1978). Anxiety reduction following exercise and meditation. *Cognitive Therapy and Research, 2,* 323–333.

Bain, L. L., Wilson, T., & Chaikind, E. (1989). Participant perceptions of exercise programs for overweight women. *Research Quarterly for Exercise and Sport, 60,* 134–143.

Bandura, A. (1977). Self-efficacy: Toward a unifying theory of behavioral change. *Psychological Review, 84,* 191–215.

Bandura, A. (1986). Social foundations of thought and action: A social-cognitive theory. Englewood Cliffs, NJ: Prentice Hall.

Bandura, A. (1992). Exercise of personal agency through the self-efficacy mechanism. In R. Schwarzer (Ed.), *Self-efficacy: Thought, control, and action* (pp. 3–38). Washington, DC: Hemisphere.

Bandura, A. (1997). *Self-efficacy: The exercise of control.* New York: W. H. Freeman.

Bane, S., & McAuley, E. (1996). The role of efficacy cognitions in reducing physique anxiety in college females. *Medicine and Science in Sport and Exercise, 28,* S85.

Bane, S., & McAuley, E. (1998). Body image and exercise. In J. L. Duda (Ed.), *Advances in sport and exercise psychology measurement* (pp. 311–322). Morgantown, WV: Fitness Information Technology.

Baranowski, T., Anderson, C., & Carmack, C. (1998). Mediating variable frameworks in physical activity interventions: How are we doing? How might we do better? *American Journal of Preventive Medicine, 15,* 266–297.

Baranowski, T., Thompson, W. O., DuRant, R. H., Baranowski, J., & Puhl, J. (1993). Observations on physical activity in physical locations: Age, gender, ethnicity, and month effects. *Research Quarterly for Exercise and Sports, 64,* 127–133.

Barrera, M., Jr., Sandler, I. N., & Ramsay, T. B. (1981). Preliminary development of a scale of social support: Studies on college students. *American Journal of Community Psychology, 9,* 435–447.

Bassett, D. R., Ainsworth, B. E., Leggett, S. R., Mathien, C. A., Main, J. A., Junter, D. C., & Duncan, G. E. (1996). Accuracy of five electronic pedometers for measuring distance walked. *Medicine and Science in Sports and Exercise, 28,* 1071–1077.

Baumeister, R. F., & Leary, M. R. (1995). The need to belong: Desire for interpersonal attachment as a fundamental human motivation. *Psychological Bulletin, 117,* 497–529.

Becker, M. H. (1974). The health belief model and sick role behavior. *Health Education Monograph, 2,* 409–419.

Becker, M. H., Kaback, M., Rosenstock, I. M., & Ruth, M. (1975). Some influences on public participation in a genetic screening program. *Journal of Community Health, 1,* 3–14.

Beh, H. C., Mathers, S., & Holden, J. (1996). EEG correlates of exercise dependency. *International Journal of Psychophysiology, 23,* 121–128.

Berscheid, E., Walster, E., & Bohrnstedt, G. (1973). The happy American body: A survey report. *Psychology Today, 7,* 119–131.

Biddle, S. (1995). Exercise motivation across the lifespan. In S. J. H. Biddle (Ed.), *European perspectives on exercise and sport psychology* (pp. 3–25). Leeds, UK: Human Kinetics.

Biddle, S., Goudas, M., & Page, A. (1994). Social-psychological predictors of self-reported actual and intended physical activity in a university workforce sample. *British Journal of Sport Medicine, 28,* 160–163.

Biddle, S., Sallis, J. F., & Cavill, N. A. (Eds.). (1998). *Young and active? Young people and health enhancing physical activity: Evidence and implications.* London: Health Education Authority.

Blair, S. N., Haskell, W. L., Ho, P., Paffenbarger, R. S., Jr., Vranizan, K. M., Farquhar, J. W., & Wood, P. D. (1985). Assessment of habitual physical activity by a seven-day recall in a community survey and controlled experiments. *American Journal of Epidemiology, 122*, 794–804.

Blair, S. N., Jacobs, D. R., Jr., & Powell, K. E. (1985). Relationships between exercise or physical activity and other health behaviors. *Public Health Reports, 100*, 172–180.

Blamey, A., Mutrie, N., & Aitchison, T. (1995). Health promotion by encouraged use of stairs. *The British Medical Journal, 311*, 289–290.

Blanchard, C., Poon, P., Rodgers, W., & Pinel, B. (2000). Group environment questionnaire and its applicability in an exercise setting. *Small Group Research, 31*, 210–224.

Blue, C. L. (1995). The predictive capacity of the theory of reasoned action and the theory of planned behavior in exercise research: An integrated literature review. *Research Nursing and Health, 18*, 105–121.

Blumenthal, D. (1984, February 5). Body image. *New York Times Magazine*, p. 54.

Blumenthal, J. A., O'Toole, L. C., & Chang, J. L. (1984). Is running an analogue of anorexia nervosa? An empirical study of obligatory running and anorexia nervosa. *JAMA, 27*, 520–523.

Bond, G. G., Aiken, L. S., & Somerville, S. C. (1992). The health belief model and adolescents with insulin-dependent diabetes mellitus. *Health Psychology, 11*, 190–198.

Booth, M. L., Owen, N., Bauman, A., Clavisi, O., & Leslie, E. (2000). Social-cognitive and perceived environment influences associated with physical activity in older Australians. *Preventive Medicine, 31*, 15–22.

Borg, G. (1971). The perception of physical performance. In R. J. Shephard (Ed.), *Frontiers of fitness* (pp. 280–294). Springfield, IL: Charles C. Thomas.

Borg, G. (1998). *Borg's perceived exertion and pain scales.* Champaign, IL: Human Kinetics.

Bouchard, C. (1994). Physical activity, fitness, and health: Overview of the consensus symposium. In H. A. Quinney, L. Gauvin, & A. E. T. Wall (Eds.), *Toward active living* (pp. 7–14). Champaign, IL: Human Kinetics.

Bouchard, C., & Shephard, R. J. (1991, August 22). *Physical activity, fitness, and health: A model and key concepts* (Consensus Doc-017). Document prepared for the International Consensus Symposium on Physical Activity, Fitness, and Health. Toronto, ON.

Boutcher, S. H., & Landers, D. M. (1988). The effects of vigorous exercise on anxiety, heart rate, and alpha level of runners and nonrunners. *Psychophysiology, 25*, 696–702.

Bouten, C. V., Van Marken Lichtenbelt, W. D., & Westerderp, K. R. (1996). Body mass index and daily physical activity in anorexia nervosa. *Medicine and Science in Sports and Exercise, 28*, 967–973.

Bozionelos, G., & Bennett, P. (1999). The theory of planned behavior as predictor of exercise: The moderating influence of beliefs and personality variables. *Journal of Health Psychology, 4*, 517–529.

Bravo, G., Gauthier, P., Roy, P. M., Payette, H., Dubois, M., Harvey, M., & Gaulin, P. (1996). Comparison of a group versus a home-based exercise program in osteopenic women. *Journal of Aging and Physical Activity, 4*, 151–164.

Brawley, L. R., Carron, A. V., & Widmeyer, W. N. (1988). Exploring the relationship between cohesion and group resistance to disruption. *Journal of Sport and Exercise Psychology, 10*, 199–213.

Brawley, L. R., Rejeski, W. J., & Lutes, L. (2000). A group-mediated cognitive-behavioral intervention for increasing adherence to physical activity in older adults. *Journal of Applied Biobehavioral Research, 5*, 47–65.

Brehm, B. J., & Steffen, J. J. (1998). Relation between obligatory exercise and eating disorders. *American Journal of Health Behavior, 22*, 108–119.

Brenes, G. A., Strube, M. J., & Storandt, M. (1998). An application of the theory of planned behavior to exercise among older adults. *Journal of Applied Social Psychology, 28*, 2274–2290.

Brewer, B. W., & Karoly, P. (1992). Recurrent pain in college students. *Journal of American College Health, 41*, 67–69.

Brown, B. S., Payne, T., Kin, C., Moore, P., & Martin, W. (1979). Chronic response of rat brain norepinephrine and serotonin levels of endurance training. *Journal of Applied Physiology, 46*, 19–23.

Brown, D. R., Croft, J. B., Anda, R. F., Barrett, D. H., & Escobedo, L. G. (1996). Evaluation of smoking on the physical activity and depressive symptoms relationship. *Medicine and Science in Sport and Exercise, 21*, 233–240.

Brown, S. W., Welsh, M. C., Labbe, E. E., Vitulli, W. F., & Kulkarnie, P. (1992). Aerobic exercise in the psychological treatment of adolescents. *Perceptual and Motor Skills, 74,* 555–560.

Brownell, K. D. (1991). Dieting and the search for the perfect body: Where physiology and culture collide. *Behavior Therapy, 22,* 1–12.

Brownell, K. D., Stunkard, A. J., & Albaum, J. M. (1980). Evaluation and modification of exercise patterns in the natural environment. *American Journal of Psychiatry, 137,* 1540–1545.

Buckley, W. A., Yesalis, C. E., Friedle, C. E., Anderson, W., Streit, A., & Wright, J. (1988). Estimated prevalence of anabolic steroid use among male high school seniors. *JAMA, 260,* 3341–3445.

Bull, F. C., & Jamrozik, K. (1998). Advice on exercise from a family physician can help sedentary patients to become active. *American Journal of Preventive Medicine, 15,* 85–94.

Burke, V., Richards, J., Milligan, R. A. K., Beilin, L. J., Dunbar, D., & Gracey, M. P. (2000). Stages of change for health-related behaviors in 18-year-old Australians. *Psychology and Health, 14,* 1061–1075.

Buxton, K. E., Wyse, J. P., Mercer, T. H., & Hale, B. (1995). Assessing the stages of exercise behaviour change and the stages of physical activity behavior change. *Journal of Sport Sciences, 13,* 50–51.

Calfas, K. J., Long, B. J., Sallis, J. F., Wooten, W. J., Pratt, M., & Patrick, K. (1996). A controlled trial of physical counseling to promote the adoption of physical activity. *Preventive Medicine, 25,* 225–233.

Calfas, K. J., Sallis, J. F., Oldenburg, B., & French, M. (1997). Mediators of change in physical activity following an intervention in primary care: PACE. *Preventive Medicine, 26,* 297–304.

Calfas, K. J., & Taylor, W. C. (1994). Effects of physical activity on psychological variables in adolescents. *Pediatric Exercise Science, 6,* 406–423.

Canadian Fitness and Lifestyle Research Institute. (1996a). Barriers to physical activity. *Progress in Prevention, 4.*

Canadian Fitness and Lifestyle Research Institute (1996b). How active are Canadians? *Progress in Prevention, 1.*

Cardinal, B. J. (1997). Construct validity of stages of change for exercise behavior. *American Journal of Health Promotion, 12,* 68–74.

Cardinal, B. J. (1999). Extended stage model for physical activity behavior. *Journal of Human Movement Sciences, 37,* 37–54.

Cardinal, B. J. (2000). Are sedentary behaviors terminable? *Journal of Human Movement Studies, 38,* 137–150.

Carlsson, D., Dencker, S. J., Grimby, G., & Heggendal, J. (1967). Circulatory studies during physical exercise in mentally disordered patients: Effects of physical training with and without administration of Chlorpromazine. *Acta Medica Scandinavica, 184,* 511–516.

Carron, A. V. (1990). Group size in sport and physical activity: Social psychological and performance consequences. *International Journal of Sport Psychology, 21,* 286–304.

Carron, A. V., Brawley, L. R., & Widmeyer, W. N. (1990). The impact of group size in an exercise setting. *Journal of Sport and Exercise Psychology, 12,* 376–387.

Carron, A. V., Brawley, L. R., & Widmeyer, W. N. (1998). The measurement of cohesiveness in sport groups. In J. L. Duda (Ed.), *Advances in sport and exercise psychology measurement* (pp. 213–226). Morgantown, WV: Fitness Information Technology.

Carron, A. V., & Estabrooks, P. A. (1999, May). *The role that social variables play in exercise in older adults.* Paper presented at ALCOA National Forum on Older Adults and Active Living, Center for Activity and Aging, University of Western Ontario, London, Ontario.

Carron, A. V., Estabrooks, P. A., Horton, H., Prapavessis, H., & Hausenblas, H. A. (1999). Reductions in social anxiety of women associated with group membership: Distraction, anonymity, security, or diffusion of evaluation? *Group Dynamics, 3,* 1–9.

Carron, A. V., & Hausenblas, H. A. (1998). *Group Dynamics in Sport* (2nd ed.). Morgantown, WV: Fitness Information Technology.

Carron, A. V., Hausenblas, H. A., & Estabrooks, P. A. (1999). Social influence and exercise involvement. In S. Bull (Ed.), *Adherence issues in sport and exercise* (pp. 1–17). New York: Wiley.

Carron, A. V., Hausenblas, H., & Mack, D. A. (1996). Social influence and exercise: A meta analysis. *Journal of Sport and Exercise Psychology, 18,* 1–16.

Carron, A. V., & Prapavessis, H. (1977). Self-presentation and group influence. *Small Group Research, 28,* 500–516.

Carron, A. V., & Spink, K. S. (1993). Team building in an exercise setting. *The Sport Psychologist, 7,* 8–18.

Carron, A. V., & Spink, K. S. (1995). The group size-cohesion relationship in minimal groups. *Small Group Research, 26,* 85–105.

Carron, A. V., Widmeyer, W. N., & Brawley, L. R. (1985). The development of an instrument to assess cohesion in sport teams: The group environment questionnaire. *Journal of Sport Psychology, 7,* 244–266.

Carron, A. V., Widmeyer, W. N., & Brawley, L. R. (1988). Group cohesion and individual adherence to physical activity. *Journal of Sport and Exercise Psychology, 10,* 127–138.

Casady, M. (1974). The tricky business of giving rewards. *Psychology Today, 8,* 52.

Cash, T. F., & Brown, T. A. (1989). Gender and body image: Stereotypes and realities. *Sex Roles, 21,* 361–373.

Cash, T. F., & Deagle, E. A. (1997). The nature and extent of body-image disturbance in anorexia nervosa and bulimia nervosa: A meta-analysis. *International Journal of Eating Disorders, 22,* 107–125.

Cash, T. F., & Henry, P. E. (1995). Women's body images: The results of a national survey in the U.S.A. *Sex Roles, 33,* 19–28.

Cash, T. F., & Pruzinsky, T. (1990). *Body images: Development, deviance, and change.* New York: Guilford.

Cash, T. F., Winstedt, B. A., & Janda, L. H. (1986). The great American shape-up. *Psychology Today, 20,* 30–37.

Caspersen, C. J., Merritt, R. K., & Stephens, T. (1994). International physical activity patterns: A methodological perspective (pp. 73–110). In R. K. Dishman (Ed.), *Advances in exercise adherence.* Champaign, IL: Human Kinetics.

Cassel, J. (1976). The contributions of the social environment to host resistance. *American Journal of Epidemiology, 104,* 107–123.

Centers for Disease Control and Prevention. (1997). Guidelines for school and community programs to promote lifelong physical activity among young people. *Morbidity and Mortality Weekly Report, 46* (no. RR-6), 1–37.

Chapman, C. L., & DeCastro, J. M. (1990). Running addiction: Measurement and associated psychological characteristics. *The Journal of Sports Medicine and Physical Fitness, 30,* 283–290.

Chatzisarantis, N. L. D., & Biddle, S. J. H. (1998). Functional significance of psychological variables that are included in the theory of planned behaviour: A self-determination theory approach to the study of attitudes, subjective norms, perceptions of control and intentions. *European Journal of Social Psychology, 28,* 303–322.

Chatzisarantis, N. L. D., Biddle, S. J. H., & Meek, G. A. (1997). A self-determination theory approach to the study of intentions and the intention-behaviour relationship in children's physical activity. *British Journal of Health Psychology, 2,* 343–360.

Chemers, M. M. (2000). Leadership research and theory: A functional integration. *Group Dynamics: Theory, Research and Practice, 4,* 27–43.

Chen, C., Strecker Neufeld, P., Feely, C. A., & Sugg Skinner, C. (1998). Factors influencing compliance with home exercise programs among patients with upper-extremity impairment. *The American Journal of Occupational Therapy, 153,* 171–180.

Chirico, A. M., & Stunkard, A. J. (1960). Physical activity and human obesity. *New England Journal of Medicine, 263,* 935–940.

Chodzko-Zajko, W. J. (1991). Physical fitness, cognitive functioning, and aging. *Medicine and Science in Sports and Exercise, 23,* 868–872.

Chogahara, M., O'Brien Cousins, S., & Wankel, L. M. (1998). Social influence on physical activity in older adults: A review. *Journal of Aging and Physical Activity, 6,* 1–17.

Choma, C., Sfora, G., & Keller, B. (1998). Impact of rapid weight loss on cognitive function in collegiate wrestlers. *Medicine and Science in Sports and Exercise, 30,* 746–749.

Christie, M. J., & Chesher, G. B. (1982). Physical dependence on physiologically released endogenous opiates. *Life Science, 30,* 1173–1177.

Cobb, S. (1976). Social support as a moderator of life stress. *Psychosomatic Medicine, 3B,* 300–314.

Cockerill, I. M., Nevill, A. M., & Byrne, B. A. (1992). Mood, mileage, and the menstrual cycle. *British Journal of Sports Medicine, 26,* 145–150.

Coen, S. P., & Ogles, B. M. (1993). Psychological characteristics of the obligatory runner: A critical examination of the anorexia analogue hypothesis. *Journal of Sport and Exercise Psychology, 15,* 338–354.

Cohen, J. (1969). *Statistical power analysis for the behavioral sciences.* New York: Academic Press.

Cohen, J. (1992). A power primer. *Psychological Bulletin, 112,* 155–159.

Cohn, P. F. (1985). Silent myocardial ischemia: Classification, prevalence, and prognosis. *American Journal of Medicine, 79,* 2–6.

Coleman, K. J., Saelens, B. E., Wiedrich-Smith, M. D., Finn, J. D., & Epstein, L. H. (1997). Relationships between TriTrac-R3D vectors, heart rate, and self-report in obese children. *Medicine and Science in Sport and Exercise, 29,* 1535–1542.

Costa, P. T., Jr., & McCrae, R. R. (1992). *The NEO Personality Inventory-R: Professional manual.* Odessa, FL: Psychological Assessment Resources.

Courneya, K. S. (1994). Predicting repeated behavior from intention: The issue of scale correspondence. *Journal of Applied Social Psychology, 24,* 580–594.

Courneya, K. S. (1995a). Cohesion correlates with affect in structured exercise classes. *Perceptual and Motor Skills, 81,* 1021–1022.

Courneya, K. S. (1995b). Perceived severity of the consequences of physical inactivity across the stages of change in older adults. *Journal of Sport and Exercise Psychology, 17,* 447–457.

Courneya, K. S., & Bobick, T. M. (2000). Integrating the theory of planned behavior with the processes and stages of change in the exercise domain. *Psychology of Sport and Exercise, 1,* 41–56.

Courneya, K. S., Estabrooks, P. A., & Nigg, C. R. (1997). A simple reinforcement strategy for increasing attendance at a fitness facility. *Health Education and Behavior, 24*(6), 708–715.

Courneya, K. S., & Friedenreich, C. M. (1997). Determinants of exercise during colorectal cancer treatment: An application of the theory of planned behavior. *Oncology Nursing Forum, 24,* 1715–1723.

Courneya, K. S., & Friedenreich, C. M. (1999). Utility of the theory of planned behavior for understanding exercise during breast cancer treatment. *Psycho-Oncology, 8,* 112–122.

Courneya, K. S., Friedenreich, C. M., Arthur, K., & Bobick, T. M. (1999). Understanding exercise motivation in colorectal cancer patients: A prospective study using the theory of planned behavior. *Rehabilitation Psychology, 44,* 68–84.

Courneya, K. S., & Hellsten, L. M. (1998). Personality correlates of exercise behavior, motives, barriers, and preferences: An application of the five-factor model. *Personality and Individual Differences, 24,* 625–633.

Courneya, K. S., & McAuley, E. (1993). Can short-range intentions predict physical activity participation? *Perceptual and Motor Skills, 77,* 115–122.

Courneya, K. S., & McAuley, E. (1994). Are there different determinants of the frequency, intensity, and duration of physical activity? *Behavioral Medicine, 20,* 84–90.

Courneya, K. S., & McAuley, E. (1995a). Cognitive mediators of the social influence–exercise adherence relationship: A test of the theory of planned behavior. *Journal of Behavioral Medicine, 18*(5), 499–515.

Courneya, K. S., & McAuley, E. (1995b). Reliability and discriminant validity of subjective norm, social support, and cohesion in an exercise setting. *Journal of Sport and Exercise Psychology, 17,* 325–337.

Courneya, K. S., Nigg, C. R., & Estabrooks, P. A. (1998). Relationships among the theory of planned behavior, stages of change, and exercise behavior in older persons over a three year period. *Psychology and Health, 13,* 355–367.

Courneya, K. S., Plotnikoff, R. C., Hotz, S. B., & Birkett, N. J. (2000). Social support and the theory of planned behavior in the exercise domain. *American Journal of Health Promotion, 24,* 300–308.

Craft, L. L., & Landers, D. M. (1998). The effects of exercise on clinical depression and depression resulting from mental illness: A meta-analysis. *Journal of Sport and Exercise Psychology, 20,* 339–357.

Craig, S., Goldberg, J., & Dietz, W. H. (1996). Psychosocial correlates of physical activity among fifth and eighth graders. *Preventive Medicine, 25,* 506–513.

Crawford, S., & Eklund, R. C. (1994). Social physique anxiety, reasons for exercise, and attitudes toward exercise settings. *Journal of Sport and Exercise Psychology, 16,* 70–82.

Crews, D. J., & Landers, D. M. (1987). A meta-analytic review of aerobic fitness and reactivity to psychosocial stressors. *Medicine and Science in Sports and Exercise, 19* (Suppl. 5), S114–S120.

Crossman, J., Jamieson, J., & Henderson, L. (1987). Responses of competitive athletes to lay-offs in training: Exercise addiction or psychological relief? *Journal of Sport Behavior, 10,* 28–38.

Culos-Reed, S. N., Gyurcsik, N. C., & Brawley, L. R. (2001). Using theories of motivated behavior to understand physical activity: Perspectives on their influence. In R. N. Singer, H. A. Hausenblas, & C. M. Janelle (Eds.), *Handbook of research on sport psychology* (2nd ed., pp. 695–717). New York: Wiley.

Cummings, K. M., Jette, A. M., Brock, B. M., & Haefner, D. P. (1979). Psychological determinants of immunization behavior in a swine influenza campaign. *Medical Care, 17,* 639–649.

Curtis, J., White, P., & McPherson, B. (2000). Age and physical activity among Canadian women and men: Findings from longitudinal national survey data. *Journal of Aging and Physical Activity, 8,* 1–19.

Dannenberg, A. L., Keller, J. B., Wilson, P. W. F., & Castelli, W. P. (1989). Leisure-time physical activity in the Framingham Offspring Study: Description, seasonal variation, and risk factor correlates. *American Journal of Epidemiology, 129,* 76–88.

Davis, C. (2000). Exercise abuse. *International Journal of Sport Psychology, 31,* 278–289.

Davis, C., Elliott, S., Dionne, M., & Mitchell, I. (1991). The relationship of personality factors and physical activity to body satisfaction in men. *Personality and Individual Differences, 12,* 689–694.

Davis, C., & Fox, J. (1993). Excessive exercise and weight preoccupation in women. *Addictive Behaviors, 18,* 201–211.

Davis, C., Kennedy, S. H., Ravelski, E., & Dionne, M. (1994). The role of physical activity in the development and maintenance of eating disorders. *Psychological Medicine, 24,* 957–967.

Davis, C., Kennedy, S. H., Ralevski, E., Dionne, M., Brewer, H., Neitzert, C., & Ratusny, D. (1995). Obsessive compulsiveness and physical activity in anorexia nervosa and high-level exercising. *Journal of Psychosomatic Research, 39,* 967–976.

Deci, E. L. (1992). On the nature and functions of motivation theories. *Psychological Science, 3,* 167–171.

Deci, E. L., & Ryan, R. M. (1985). *Intrinsic motivation and self-determination in human behavior.* New York: Plenum.

Deci, E. L., & Ryan, R. M. (1991). A motivational approach to self: Integration in personality. In R. A. Dienstbier (Ed.), *Nebraska symposium on motivation: Vol. 38. Perspectives on motivation* (pp. 237–288). Lincoln: University of Nebraska Press.

Dennison, B. A., Straus, J. H., Mellits, D., & Charney, E. (1988). Childhood physical fitness tests: Predictor of adult physical activity levels? *Pediatrics, 82,* 324–330.

Desharnais, R., Jobin, J., Cote, C., Levesque, L., & Godin, G. (1993). Aerobic exercise and the placebo effect: A controlled study. *Psychosomatic Medicine, 55,* 149–154.

deVries, H. A., Beckman, P., Huber, H., & Dieckmeir, L. (1968). Electromyographic evaluation of the effects of sauna on the neuromuscular system. *Journal of Sports Medicine and Physical Fitness, 8,* 1–11.

Dew, M. A., Roth, L. H., Thompson, M. E., & Kormos, R. L. (1996). Medical compliance and its predictors in the first year after heart transplantation. *Journal of Heart and Lung Transplantation, 15,* 631–645.

DiClemente, C. C., Prochaska, J. O., Velicer, W. F., Fairhurst, S., Rossi, J. S., & Velasquez, M. (1991). The process of smoking cessation: An analysis of precontemplation, contemplation, and preparation states of change. *Journal of Consulting and Clinical Psychology, 9,* 295–304.

Diekhoff, G. M. (1984). Running amok: Injuries in compulsive runners. *Journal of Sport Behavior, 7,* 120–129.

Dietz, W. H., & Gortmaker, S. L. (1985). Do we fatten our children at the television set? Obesity and television viewing in children and adolescents. *Pediatrics, 75,* 807–812.

Dion, K. L. (2000). Group cohesion: From "Field of Forces" to multidimensional construct. *Group Dynamics: Theory, Research, and Practice, 4,* 7–26.

Dishman, R. K. (1986). Mental health. In V. Seefeldt (Ed.), *Physical activity and well-being.* Reston, VA: American Association for Health, Physical Education, and Dance.

Dishman, R. K. (1991). Increasing and maintaining exercise and physical activity. *Behavior Therapy, 22,* 345–378.

Dishman, R. K. (1993). Exercise adherence. In R. N. Singer, M. Murphey, & L. K. Tennant (Eds.), *Handbook of research on sport psychology* (pp. 779–798). New York: Macmillan.

Dishman, R. K. (Ed.). (1994). *Exercise adherence: Its impact on public health.* Champaign, IL: Human Kinetics.

Dishman, R. K., & Buckworth, J. (1996). Increasing physical activity: A quantitative synthesis. *Medicine and Science in Sports and Exercise, 28,* 706–719.

Dishman, R. K., & Buckworth, J. (1997). Adherence to physical activity. In W. P. Morgan (Ed.), *Physical activity and mental health* (pp. 63–80). Washington, DC: Taylor & Francis.

Dishman, R. K., & Gettman, L. R. (1980). Psychobiologic influence on exercise adherence. *Journal of Sport Psychology, 2,* 295–310.

Dishman, R. K., & Ickes, W. (1981). Self-motivation and adherence to therapeutic exercise. *Journal of Behavioral Medicine, 4,* 421–438.

Dishman, R. K., Oldenburg, B., O'Neal, H., & Shephard, R. J. (1998). Worksite physical activity interventions. *American Journal of Preventive Medicine, 15,* 344–361.

Dishman, R. K., & Sallis, J. F. (1994). Determinants and interventions for physical activity and exercise. In C. Bouchard, R. J. Shephard, & T. Stephens (Eds.), *Physical activity, fitness, and health: International proceedings and consensus statement* (pp. 214–238). Champaign, IL: Human Kinetics.

Dishman, R. K., Sallis, J. F., & Orenstein, D. M. (1985). The determinants of physical activity and exercise. *Public Health Reports, 100,* 158–171.

Dishman, R. K., Washburn, R. A., & Schoeller, D. A. (2001). Measurement of physical activity. *Quest, 53,* 295–309.

Doyle, A. C. (1998). Adventure I. A scandal in Bohemia. In *The original illustrated "Strand" Sherlock Holmes* (pp. 117–131). Wordsworth: Ware, Hertfordshire, UK.

Drewnowski, A., & Yee, D. K. (1987). Men and body image: Are males satisfied with their body weight? *Psychosomatic Medicine, 49,* 626–634.

Driver, H. S., Roger, G. G., Mitchell, D., Borrow, S. J., Allen, M., Luus, H. G., & Shapiro, C. M. (1994). Prolonged endurance exercise and sleep disruption. *Medicine and Science in Sports and Exercise, 26,* 903–907.

Droze, K. (2000). *How Dyersville became dietsville.* Retrieved from September 5, 2000, from http:/www.ediets.com/news/article.cfm/article_id= 1593.

Ducharme, K. A., & Brawley, L. R. (1995). Predicting the intensity and duration of exercise initiates using two forms of self-efficacy. *Journal of Behavioral Medicine, 18,* 479–497.

Duda, J. L., & Tappe, M. K. (1988). Predictions of personal investment in physical activity among middle-aged and older adults. *Perceptual and Motor Skills, 66,* 543–549.

Duda, J. L., & Tappe, M. K. (1989a). The personal incentives for exercise questionnaire: Preliminary development. *Perceptual and Motor Skills, 68,* 1122.

Duda, J. L., & Tappe, M. K. (1989b). Personal investment in exercise among middle-aged and older adults. In A. C. Ostrow (Ed.), *Aging and motor behavior* (pp. 219–238). Indianapolis, IN: Benchmark.

Duda, J. L., & Tappe, M. K. (1989c). Personal investment in exercise among adults: An examination of age and gender-related differences in motivational orientation. In A. C. Ostrow (Ed.), *Aging and motor behavior* (pp. 239–256). Indianapolis, IN: Benchmark.

Duncan, T. E., Duncan, S. C., & McAuley, E. (1993). The role of domain and gender-specific provisions of social relations in adherence to a prescribed exercise program. *Journal of Sport and Exercise Psychology, 15,* 220–231.

Duncan, T. E., & McAuley, E. (1993). Social support and efficacy cognitions in exercise adherence: A latent growth curve analysis. *Journal of Behavioral Medicine, 16,* 199–218.

Duncan, T. E., McAuley, E., Stoolmiller, M., & Duncan, S. C. (1993). Serial fluctuations in exercise behavior as a function of social support and efficacy cognitions. *Journal of Applied Social Psychology, 64,* 1–16.

Duncan, T. E., & Stoolmiller, M. (1993). Modeling social and psychological determinants of exercise behaviors via structural equation systems, *Research Quarterly for Exercise and Sport, 64,* 1–16.

Dunn, A. L., Anderson, R. E., & Jakicic, J. M. (1998). Lifestyle physical activity interventions: History, short- and long-term effects, and recommendations. *American Journal of Preventive Medicine, 15,* 398–412.

Dunn, A. L., Marcus, B. H., Kampert, J. B., Garcia, M. E., Kohl, H. W., & Blair, S. N. (1997). Reduction in cardiovascular disease risk factors: 6-month results from Project Active. *Preventive Medicine, 26,* 883–892.

Dzewaltowski, D. A., Johnston, J. A., Estabrooks, P. A., & Johannes, E. (2000, October). *Healthy Places.* Paper presented at the Governors Conference on the Prevention of Child Abuse and Neglect, Topeka, KS.

Eaton, W. O., & Enns, L. R. (1986). Sex differences in human motor activity level. *Psychological Bulletin, 100,* 19–28.

Eimer, M., Cable, T., Gal, P., Rothenberg, L. A., & McCue, J. D. (1985). The effect of clorazepate on breathlessness and exercise tolerance in patients with chronic airflow obstruction. *Journal of Family Practice, 21,* 359–362.

Ekelund, U., Sjostrom, M., Yngve, A., Poortvliet, E., Nilsson, A., Frobert, K., Wedderkopp, N., & Westerterp, K. (2000). Physical activity assessed by activity monitor and doubly labeled water in children. *Medicine and Science in Sports and Exercise, 33,* 275–281.

Ekkekakis, P., & Petruzzello, S. J. (1999). Acute aerobic exercise and affect: Current status, problems, and prospects regarding dose-response. *Sports Medicine, 28,* 337–374.

Ekkekakis, P., & Petruzzello, S. J. (2000). Analysis of the affect measurement conundrum in exercise psychology: 1. Fundamental issues. *Psychology of Sport and Exercise, 1,* 71–88.

Epling, W. F., & Pierce, W. D. (1988). Activity-based anorexia: A biobehavioral perspective. *International Journal of Eating Disorders, 7,* 475–485.

Estabrooks, P. A. (2000). Sustaining exercise participation through group cohesion. *Exercise and Sport Sciences Reviews, 28,* 63–67.

Estabrooks, P. A., & Carron, A. V. (1997). The association among social support, subjective norm, and cohesion in elderly exercisers. *Journal of Applied Sport Psychology, 9,* S90.

Estabrooks, P. A., & Carron, A. V. (1998). The conceptualization and effect of control beliefs on exercise attendance in the elderly. *Journal of Aging and Health, 10,* 441–457.

Estabrooks, P. A., & Carron, A. V. (1999a). Group cohesion in older adult exercisers: Prediction and intervention effects. *Journal of Behavioral Medicine, 22*(6), 575–588.

Estabrooks, P. A., & Carron, A. V. (1999b). The influence of the group with elderly exercisers. *Small Group Research, 30*(4), 438–452.

Estabrooks, P. A., & Carron, A. V. (2000). Predicting scheduling self-efficacy in older adult exercisers: The role of task cohesion. *Journal of Aging and Physical Activity, 8,* 41–50.

Estabrooks, P. A., & Carron, A. V. (2000). The Physical Activity Group Environment Questionnaire: An instrument for the assessment of cohesion in exercise classes. *Group Dynamics: Theory, Research, and Practice, 4,* 230–243.

Estabrooks, P. A., Courneya, K. S., & Nigg, C. R. (1996). Effect of a stimulus control intervention on attendance at a university fitness center. *Behavior Modification, 20,* 202–215.

Estabrooks, P. A., & Gyurcsik, N. C. (2000). Resources for physical activity participation: A metropolitan analysis. *Annals of Behavioral Medicine, 23,* S118.

Eston, R. G., Rowlands, A. V., & Ingledew D. K. (1998). Validity of heart rate, pedometry, and accelerometry for predicting the energy cost of children's activity. *Journal of Applied Physiology, 84,* 362–371.

Etnier, J. L., Salazar, W., Landers, D. M., Petruzzello, S. J., Han, M., & Nowell, P. (1997). The influence of physical fitness and exercise upon cognition functioning: A meta-analysis. *Journal of Sport and Exercise Psychology, 19,* 249–277.

Eyler, A. A., Baker, E., Cromer, L., King, A. C., Brownson, R. C., & Donatelle, R. J. (1998). Physical activity and minority women: A qualitative study. *Health Education and Behavior, 25,* 640–652.

Eysenck, H. J., & Eysenck, S. B. G. (1964). *The Eysenck Personality Inventory.* London: University of London Press.

Fallon, E. A., & Hausenblas, H. A. (2001). Transtheoretical model of behavior change: Does the termination stage really exist? *Journal of Human Movement Studies, 40,* 465–479.

Farauhar, J. W., Fortman, S. P., MacCoby, N., Haskell, W. L., Williams, P. T., Flora, J. A., Barr Taylor, C., Brown, B. W., Solomon, D. S., & Hulley, S. B. (1985). The Stanford Five-City Project: Design and methods. *American Journal of Epidemiology, 122,* 323–334.

Faulkner, G., & Sparkes, A. (1999). Exercise as therapy for schizophrenia: An ethnographic study. *Journal of Sport and Exercise Psychology, 21,* 52–69.

Fehling, P. C., Smith, D. L., Warner, S. E., & Dalsky, G. P. (1999). Comparison of accelerometers with oxygen consumption in older adults during exercise. *Medicine and Science in Sports and Exercise, 31,* 171–175.

Fishbein, M., & Ajzen, I. (1975). *Belief, attitude, intention, and behavior.* Don Mills, NY: Addison-Wesley.

Fisher, E., & Thompson, J. K. (1994). A comparative evaluation of cognitive-behavioral therapy (CBT) versus exercise therapy (ET) for the treatment of body image disturbance. *Behavior Modification, 18,* 171–185.

Fitness Canada. (1991). *Active living: A conceptual overview.* Ottawa: Government of Canada.

Flay, B. R. (1986). Efficacy and effectiveness trials (and other phases of research) in the development of health promotion programs. *Preventive Medicine, 15,* 451–474.

Floyd, D. L., Prentice-Dunn, S., & Rogers, R. W. (2000). A meta-analysis of research on protection motivation theory. *Journal of Applied Social Psychology, 30,* 407–429.

Forsyth, D. R. (2000). One hundred years of group research: Introduction to the special issue. *Group Dynamics: Theory, Research, and Practice, 4,* 3–6.

Fox, K. R. (1998). Advances in the measurement of the physical self. In J. L. Duda (Ed.), *Advances in sport and exercise psychology measurement* (pp. 295–310). Morgantown, WV: Fitness Information Technology.

Fox, K. R. (2000). Self-esteem, self-perceptions, and exercise. *International Journal of Sport Psychology, 31,* 228–240.

Fox, K. R. (in press). The effects of exercise on self-perceptions and self-esteem. In S. J. H. Biddle, K. R. Fox, & S. H. Boutcher (Eds.), *Physical activity and psychological well-being.* London: Routledge.

Fox, L. D., Rejeski, W. J., & Gauvin, L. (2000). Effects of leadership style and group dynamics on enjoyment of physical activity. *American Journal of Health Promotion, 14,* 277–283.

Franklin, B. (1984). Exercise program compliance: Improvement strategies. In J. Storlie & H. Jordan (Eds.), *Behavioral management of obesity* (pp. 105–135). New York: Spectrum.

Franklin, B. (1988). Program factors that influence exercise adherence: Practical adherence skills for the clinical staff. In R. K. Dishman (Ed.), *Exercise adherence* (pp. 237–258). Champaign, IL: Human Kinetics.

Franz, S. I., & Hamilton, G. V. (1905). The effects of exercise upon retardation in conditions of depression. *American Journal of Insanity, 62,* 239–256.

Freedson, P. S., & Miller, K. (2000). Objective monitoring of physical activity using motion sensors and heart rate. *Research Quarterly for Exercise and Sport, 71,* S21–S29.

Freud, S. (1933). *New introductory lectures on psychoanalysis (1932).* (W. J. H. Sprott, Trans.). New York: Norton.

Frewen, S., Schomer, H., & Dunne, T. (1994). Health belief model interpretation of compliance factors in a weight loss and cardiac rehabilitation programme. *South African Journal of Psychology, 24,* 39–43.

Friedenreich, C. M., Courneya, K. S., & Bryant, H. A. (1998). The Lifetime Total Physical Activity Questionnaire: Development and reliability. *Medicine and Science in Sports and Exercise, 30,* 266–274.

Fruin, D. J., Pratt, C., & Owen, N. (1991). Protection motivation theory and adolescents' perceptions of exercise. *Journal of Applied Social Psychology, 22,* 55–69.

Fuchs, R., Powell, K. E., Semmer, N. K., Dwyer, J. H., Lippert, O., & Hoffmeister, H. (1988). Patterns of physical activity among German adolescents: The Berlin-Bremen study. *Preventive Medicine, 17,* 756–763.

Fuller, A. K., & Robinson, M. E. (1995). Perceptual differences between patients with chronic low back pain and healthy volunteers using magnitude matching and clinically relevant stimuli. *Behavior Therapy, 26,* 241–253.

Furst, D. M., & Germone, K. (1993). Negative addiction in male and female runners and exercisers. *Perceptual and Motor Skills, 77,* 192–194.

Gardner, A. W., & Poehlman, E. T. (1995). Exercise rehabilitation programs for the treatment of claudication pain: A meta-analysis. *JAMA, 274,* 975–980.

Garner, D. M. (1997, January/February). The body image survey. *Psychology Today,* 32–84.

Gauvin, L., Lévesque, L., & Richard, L. (2001). Helping people initiate and maintain a more active lifestyle: A public health framework for physical activity promotion research. In R. N. Singer, H. A. Hausenblas, & C. M. Janelle (Eds.), *Handbook of sport psychology* (2nd ed., pp. 718–739). New York: Wiley.

Gauvin, L., Rejeski, W. J., & Norris, J. L. (1996). A naturalistic study of the impact of acute physical activity on feeling states and affect in women. *Health Psychology, 15,* 391–397.

Gauvin, L., Wall, A. E. T., & Quinney, H. A. (1994). Physical activity, fitness, and health: Research and practice. In H. A. Quinney, L. Gauvin, & A. E. T. Wall (Eds.), *Toward active living* (pp. 1–5). Champaign, IL: Human Kinetics.

Gillett, P. A., Johnson, M., Juretich, M., Richardson, N., Slagle, L., & Farikoff, K. (1993). The nurse as exercise leader. *Geriatric Nursing, 14,* 133–137.

Glanz, K. (1997). Community and group intervention models of health behavior change. In K. Glanz, F. Marcus Lewis, & B. K. Rimer (Eds.), *Health behavior and health education: Theory, research, and practice* (2nd ed., pp. 237–286). San Francisco: Jossey-Bass.

Glasgow, R. E., McKay, H. G., Piette, J. D., & Reynolds, K. D. (in press). The RE-AIM framework for evaluating interventions: What can it tell us about approaches to chronic illness management? *Patient Education and Counseling.*

Glasgow, R. E., Vogt, T. M., & Boles, S. M. (1999). Evaluating the public health impact of health promotion interventions: The RE-AIM framework. *American Journal of Public Health, 89,* 1322–1327.

Glass, G. V. (1976). Primary, secondary, and meta-analysis of research. *Education Research, 5,* 3–8.

Glass, G. V., McGaw, B., & Smith, M. L. (1981). *Meta-analysis in social research.* Beverly Hills, CA: Sage.

Glasser, W. (1976). *Positive addiction.* New York: Harper & Row.

Glassman, A. H., & Bigger, J. T. (1981). Cardiovascular effects of therapeutic doses of tricyclic antidepressants: A review. *Archives of General Psychiatry, 38,* 815–820.

Godin, G. (1993). The theories of reasoned action and planned behavior: Overview of findings, emerging problems, and usefulness for exercise promotion. *Journal of Applied Sport Psychology, 5,* 141–157.

Godin, G. (1994). Theories of reasoned action and planned behavior: Usefulness for exercise promotion. *Medicine and Science in Sports and Exercise, 26,* 1391–1394.

Godin, G., Cox, M. H., & Shephard, R. J. (1983). The impact of physical fitness evaluation on behavioral intentions toward regular exercise. *Canadian Journal of Applied Sport Sciences, 8,* 240–245.

Godin, G., Jobin, J., & Bouillon, J. (1986). Assessment of leisure time exercise behavior by self-report: A concurrent validity study. *Canadian Journal of Public Health, 77,* 359–361.

Godin, G., & Kok, G. (1996). The theory of planned behavior: A review of its applications to health-related behaviors. *Science and Health Promotion, 11,* 87–98.

Godin, G., & Shephard, R. J. (1985). A simple method to assess exercise behavior in the community. *Canadian Journal of Applied Sport Science, 10,* 141–146.

Goldstien, M. G., Pinto, B. M., Marcus, B. H., Lynn, H., Jette, A. M., Rakowski, W., McDermott, S., DePue, J. D., Milan, F. B., Dube, C., & Tennstedt, S. (1999). Physician-based physical activity counseling for middle-aged and older adults: A randomized trial. *Annals of Behavioral Medicine, 21,* 40–47.

Goodwin, J. S., & Goodwin, J. M. (1984). The tomato effect: Rejection of highly efficacious therapies. *Journal of the American Medical Association, 251,* 2387–2390.

Gorely, T., & Gordon, S. (1995). An examination of the transtheoretical model and exercise behavior in older adults. *Journal of Sport and Exercise Psychology, 17,* 312–324.

Graham, F. (1981). The anxiety of the runner: Terminal helplessness. In M. H. Sachs & M. L. Sachs (Eds.), *Psychology of running.* Champaign, IL: Human Kinetics.

Grahame-Smith, D. G., Green, A. R., & Costain, D. W. (1978). Mechanisms of anti-depressant action of ECT therapy. *Lancet, 1,* 254–257.

Gray, S. H. (1977). Social aspects of body image: Perceptions of normalcy of weight and affect of college undergraduates. *Perceptual and Motor Skills, 45,* 1035–1040.

Grimley, D., Prochaska, J. O., Velicer, W. F., Blais, W. F., & DiClemente, C. C. (1994). The transtheoretical model of change. In T. M. Brinthaupt & R. P. Lipka (Eds.), *Changing the sell: Philosophies, techniques, and experiences* (pp. 201–227). Albany: State University of New York.

Grove, J. R., & Lewis, M. A. E. (1996). Hypnotic susceptibility and the attainment of flowlike states during exercise. *Journal of Sport and Exercise Psychology, 18,* 380–391.

Gruber, A. J., & Pope, H. G. (1998). Ephedrine abuse among 36 female weightlifters. *American Journal on Addictions, 7,* 256–261.

Gruber, J. J. (1986). Physical activity and self-esteem development in children: A meta-analysis. In G. A. Stull & H. M. Eckert (Eds.), *Effects of physical activity on children: A special tribute to Mabel Lee* (pp. 30–48). Champaign, IL: Human Kinetics.

Gulanick, M. (1991). Is phase 2 cardiac rehabilitation necessary for early recovery of patients with cardiac disease? A randomized, controlled study. *Heart Lung, 20,* 9–15.

Gyurcsik, N. C., Culos, S. N., Bray, S. R., & DuCharme, K. A. (1998). Instructor efficacy: Third-party influence of exercise adherence. *Journal of Sport and Exercise Psychology, (Suppl.) 20,* S9.

Haefner, P., & Kirscht, J. P. (1970). Motivational and behavioral effects of modifying health beliefs. *Public Health Reports, 85,* 478–484.

Hailey, B. J., & Bailey, L. A. (1982). Negative addiction in runners: A quantitative approach. *Journal of Sport Behavior, 5,* 150–154.

Hammermeister, J., & Burton, D. (1995). Anxiety and the ironman: Investigating the antecedents and consequences of endurance athletes' state anxiety. *The Sport Psychologist, 9,* 29–40.

Harda, N. D., Chiu, V., King, A. C., & Stewart, A. L. (2001). An evaluation of three self-report physical activity instruments for older adults. *Medicine and Science in Sports and Exercise, 33,* 962–970.

Hart, E. A., Leary, M. R., & Rejeski, W. J. (1989). The measurement of social physique anxiety. *Journal of Sport and Exercise Psychology, 11,* 94–104.

Haskell, W. L. (1994). Physical/physiological/biological outcomes of physical activity. In H. A. Quinney,

L. Gauvin, & A. E. T. Wall (Eds.), *Toward active living* (pp. 17–23). Champaign, IL: Human Kinetics.

Hausenblas, H. A., & Carron, A. V. (1999). Eating disorder indices and athletes: An integration. *Journal of Sport and Exercise Psychology 21*, 230–258.

Hausenblas, H. A., Carron, A. V., & Mack, D. A. (1997). The theories of reasoned action and planned behavior: A meta analysis. *Journal of Sport and Exercise Psychology, 19*, 47–62.

Hausenblas, H. A., Dannecker, E. A., Connaughton, D. P., & Lovins, T. R. (1999). Examining the validity of the stages of exercise change algorithm. *American Journal of Health Studies, 15*, 94–99.

Hausenblas, H. A., & Fallon, E. A. (2001, October). *Body image and physical activity: A meta-analysis.* Paper presented at the annual conference of the Association for the Advancement of Applied Sport Psychology, Orlando, FL.

Hausenblas, H. A., & Martin, K. A. (2000). Bodies on display. Predictors of social physique anxiety in female aerobic instructors. *Women in Sport and Physical Activity Journal, 9*, 1–14.

Hausenblas, H. A., Nigg, C. R., Dannecker, E. A., Symons, D. A., Ellis, S. R., Fallon, E. A., Focht, B. C., & Loving, M. G. (2001). A missing piece of the transtheoretical model applied to exercise: Development and validation of the Exercise Temptation Scale. *Psychology and Health: An International Journal, 16*, 381–390.

Hausenblas, H. A., & Symons Downs, N. (2001a). A comparison of body image between athletes and nonathletes: A meta-analytic review. *Journal of Applied Sport Psychology, 13*, 323–333.

Hausenblas, H. A., & Symons Downs, N. (in press). Exercise dependence: A systematic review. *Psychology of Sport and Exercise.*

Hausenblas, H. A., & Symons Downs, N. (in press). How much is too much? The development and validation of the Exercise Dependence Scale. *Psychology and Health: An International Journal.*

Hayslick, B., Weigand, D., Weinberg, R., Richardson, P., & Jackson, A. (1996). The development of new scales for assessing health belief model constructs in adulthood. *Journal of Aging and Physical Activity, 4*, 307–323.

Hellerstedt, W. L., & Jeffery, R. W. (1997). The effect of a telephone-based intervention on weight loss. *American Journal of Health Promotion, 11*, 177–182.

Heroltz, K., Buskies, W., Rist, M., Pawlik, G., Hollman, W., & Heiss, W. D. (1987). Regional cerebral blood flow in man at rest and during exercise. *Journal of Neurology, 234*, 9–13.

Higgins, L. C., & Oldenburg, B. (1999). Desire as a determinant of physical activity: Evidence from a sample of young adult females. *Psychology and Health, 14*, 309–321.

Hightower, M. (1997). Effects of exercise participation on menstrual pain and symptoms. *Women and Health, 26*, 15–27.

Hill, J. L., & Estabrooks, P. A. (2000, September). *The relationships between group interaction and cohesion in exercise classes for older adults.* Paper presented at the meeting of the Association for the Advancement of Applied Sport Psychology, Nashville, TN.

Hogg, M. A., & Williams, K. D. (2000). From I to we: Social identity and the collective self. *Group Dynamics: Theory, Research, and Practice, 4*, 81–97.

Hull, C. L. (1943). *Principles of behavior.* New York: Appleton-Century-Crofts.

Isreal, B. A. (1982). Social networks and health status: Linking theory, research, and practice. *Patient Counseling and Health Education, 4*, 65–69.

Issacs, K. R., Anderson, B. J., Alcantara, A. A., Black, J. E., & Greenough, W. T. (1992). Exercise and the brain: Angiogenesis in the adult rat cerebellum after vigorous physical activity and motor skill learning. *Journal of Cerebral Blood Flow and Metabolism, 12*, 110–119.

Iverson, D. C., Fielding, J. E., Crow, R. S., & Christenson, G. M. (1985). The promotion of physical activity in the United States population: The status of programs in medical, worksite, community, and school settings. *Public Health Reports, 100*, 212–224.

Jacobs, D. (1986). A general theory of addictions. A new theoretical model. *Journal of Gambling Behavior, 2*, 15–31.

Jacobs, D., Ainsworth, B., Hartman, T., & Leon, A. (1993). A simultaneous evaluation of 10 commonly used physical activity questionnaires. *Medicine and Science in Sports and Exercise, 25*, 81–91.

Jakicic, J. M., Polley, B. A., & Wing, R. R. (1998). Accuracy of self-reported exercise and the relationship with weight loss in overweight women. *Medicine and Science in Sports and Exercise, 30*, 634–638.

Jakicic, J. M., Wing, R. R., Butler, B. A., & Robertson, R. J. (1995). Prescribing exercise in multiple short bouts versus one continuous bout: Effects on adherence, cardiorespiratory fitness, and weight loss in overweight women. *International Journal of Obesity, 19*, 893–901.

Janal, M. N. (1996). Pain sensitivity, exercise, and stoicism. *Journal of the Royal Society of Medicine, 89,* 376–381.

Janis, I. L., & Mann, L. (1977). *Decision-making: A psychological analysis of conflict, choice, and commitment.* New York: Free Press.

Janson, C., Giaslason, T., De Backer, W., Plaschke, P., Bjoarnsson, E., Hetta, J., Kristbjarnason, H., Vermeire, P., & Boman, G. (1995). Insomnia and sleep: Prevalence of sleep disturbances among young adults in three European countries. *Sleep, 18,* 589–597.

Janz, K. F., Dawson, J. D., & Mahoney, L. T. (2000). Tracking physical fitness and physical activity from childhood to adolescence: The Muscatine study. *Medicine and Science in Sports and Exercise, 32,* 1250–1257.

Janz, N., & Becker, M. (1984). The health belief model: A decade later. *Health Education Quarterly, 11,* 1–47.

Jibaja-Rusth, M. L. (1989). *The development of a psychosocial risk profile for becoming an obligatory runner.* Unpublished doctoral dissertation, University of Houston, Houston, TX.

Johnson, M. D. (1994). Disordered eating in active and athletic women. *Clinics in Sports Medicine, 13,* 355–369.

Johnson, R. (1995). Exercise dependence: When runners don't know when to quit. *Sports Medicine and Arthroscopy Review, 3,* 267–273.

Jones, D. A., Ainsworth, B. E., Croft, J. B., Macera, C. A., Lloyd, E. E., & Yusuf, H. R. (1998). Moderate leisure-time physical activity: Who is meeting the public health recommendations? A national cross-sectional study. *Archives of Family Medicine, 7,* 285–289.

Joseph, J., Curtis, B., & Skinner, H. (1997). *Critical perspectives on the transtheoretical model and the stages of change* (Ontario Tobacco Research Unit: Working Papers Series No. 30). Toronto, Canada: Ontario Tobacco Research Unit.

Kagan, D. M. (1987). Addictive personality factors. *The Journal of Psychology, 121,* 533–538.

Kandel, E. R., Schwartz, J. H., & Jessell, T. M. (2000). *Principles of neural science* (4th ed.). New York: McGraw-Hill.

Katz, R. C., & Singh, N. N. (1986). Increasing recreational behavior in mentally retarded children. *Behavior Modification, 10,* 508–519.

Kavussanu, M., & McAuley, E. (1995). Exercise and optimism: Are highly active individuals more optimistic? *Journal of Sport and Exercise Psychology, 17,* 246–258.

Keefe, F. J., & Williams, D. A. (Eds.). (1992). *Assessment of pain behaviors.* New York: Guilford Press.

Kemper, H. C. G., Verschuur, R., Ras, K. G. A., Snel, J., Splinter, P. G., & Tavecchio, L. W. C. (1976). Effect of 5- versus 3-lessons-a-week physical education program upon the physical development of 12 and 13 year old school boys. *Journal of Sports Medicine and Physical Fitness, 16,* 319–326.

Kendzierski, E. D., Furr, R. M., Jr., & Schiavoni, J. (1998). Physical activity self definitions: Correlates and perceived criteria. *Journal of Sport and Exercise Psychology, 20,* 176–193.

Kerlinger, F. N. (1973). *Foundations of behavioral research* (2nd ed.). New York: Holt, Rinehart, & Winston.

King, A. C., Blair, S. N., Bild, D. E., Dishman, R. K., Dubbert, P. M., Marcus, B. H., Oldridge, N. B., Paffenbarger, R. S., Powell, K. E., & Yeager, K. K. (1994). Determinants of physical activity and interventions in adults. *Medicine and Science in Sports and Exercise, 24,* S221–S236.

King, A. C., Castro, C., Eyler, A. A., Wilcox, S., Sallis, J. F., & Brownson, R. C. (2000). Personal and environmental factors associated with physical inactivity among different racial-ethnic groups of U.S. middle-aged and older-aged women. *Health Psychology, 19,* 354–364.

King, A. C., Jeffery, R. W., Fridinger, F., Dusenbury, L., Provence, S., Hedlund, S. A., & Spangler, K. (1995). Environmental and policy approaches to cardiovascular disease prevention through physical activity: Issues and opportunities. *Health Education Quarterly, 22,* 499–511.

King, A. C., Oka, R., Pruitt, L., Phillips, W., & Haskell, W. L. (1997). Developing optimal exercise regimens for seniors: A clinical trial. *Annals of Behavioral Medicine, 19,* S056.

King, A. C., Rejeski, W. J., & Buchner, D. M. (1998). Physical activity interventions targeting older adults: A critical review and recommendations. *American Journal of Preventive Medicine, 15,* 316–333.

Kirscht, J. P. (1974). The health belief model and illness behavior. *Health Education Monograph, 2,* 387–408.

Klein, A. M. (1995). Life's too short to die small. In D. Sabo & F. D. Gordon (Eds.), *Men's health and illness* (pp. 105–120). London: Sage.

Klesges, R. C., Eck, L. H., Hanson, C. L., Haddock, C. K., & Klesges, L. M. (1990). Effects of obesity, social interactions, and physical environment on physical activity in preschoolers. *Health Psychology, 9,* 435–449.

Knapp, D. A., & Koch, H. (1984). *The management of new pain in office-based ambulatory care: National Ambulatory Medical Care Survey* (No. 97 DHHS Publication No. PHS 84-1250). Hyattsville, MD: Public Health Service.

Koltyn, K. F. (2000). Analgesia following exercise: A review. *Sports Medicine and Physical Fitness, 29,* 85–98.

Koltyn, K. F., Garvin, A. W., Gardiner, G. R., & Nelson, T. F. (1996). Perception of pain following aerobic exercise. *Medicine and Science in Sports and Exercise, 28,* 1418–1421.

Kouyanou, K., Pither, C. E., & Wessely, S. (1997). Medication misuse, abuse, and dependence in chronic pain patients. *Journal of Psychosomatic Research, 43,* 497–504.

Krelstein, M. (1983). Is running an analogue of anorexia nervosa? *New England Journal of Medicine, 309,* 48.

Kressler, D. N. (1997). *Megorexia nervosa: Using eating disorders as a model for obligatory bodybuilding.* Unpublished dissertation, University of Missouri–Kansas City.

Kucera, M. (1985). Spontaneous physical activity in preschool children. In R. A. Binkhorst & H. C. G. Kemper (Eds.), *Children and exercise: XI.* Proceedings of the XIth International Congress on Pediatric Work Physiology (pp. 175–182). Champaign, IL: Human Kinetics.

Kugler, J., Seelback, H., & Krüskemper, G. M. (1994). Effects of rehabilitative exercise programmes on anxiety and depression in coronary patients: A meta-analysis. *British Journal of Clinical Psychology, 33,* 401–410.

Kujala, U. M., Taimela, S., & Viljanen, T. (1999). Leisure physical activity and various pain symptoms among adolescents. *British Journal of Sports Medicine, 33,* 325–328.

Lahad, A., Malter, A. D., Berg, A. O., & Deoy, R. A. (1994). The effectiveness of four interventions for the prevention of low back pain. *JAMA, 272,* 1286–1291.

Laireiter, A., & Baumann, U. (1992). Network structures and support functions—theoretical and empirical analyses. In H. O. F. Veiel & U. Baumann (Eds.), *The meaning and measurement of social support* (pp. 33–55). New York: Hemisphere.

Lampinen, P., Heikkinen, R., & Ruoppila, I. (2000). Changes in intensity of physical exercise as predictors of depressive symptoms among older adults: An eight-year follow-up. *Preventive Medicine: An International Journal Devoted to Practice and Theory, 30,* 371–380.

Landers, D. M., & Arent, S. M. (2001). Physical activity and mental health. In R. N. Singer, H. A. Hausenblas, & C. M. Janelle (Eds.), *Handbook of research on sport psychology* (2nd ed., pp. 740–765). New York: Wiley.

Landers, D. M., & Petruzzello, S. J. (1994). The effectiveness of exercise and physical activity in reducing anxiety and reactivity to psychosocial stressors. In H. A. Quinney, L. Gauvin, & A. E. T. Wall (Eds.), *Toward active living* (pp. 77–82). Champaign, IL: Human Kinetics.

Larsen, K. D. (1983). Is running an analogue of anorexia nervosa? *New England Journal of Medicine, 309,* 47.

Lazarus, R. S., & Cohen, J. P. (1977). Environmental stress. In I. Altman & J. F. Wohlwill (Eds.), *Human behavior and the environment: Current theory and research.* New York: Plenum.

Leary, M. J. (1992a). Self-presentation in exercise and sport. *Journal of Sport and Exercise Psychology, 14,* 339–351.

Leary, M. J. (1992b). *Understanding social anxiety.* Newbury Park, CA: Sage.

Leary, M. J., & Kowalski, R. M. (1990). Impression management: A literature review and two-component model. *Psychological Bulletin, 107,* 34–47.

Lee, C. (1993). Attitudes, knowledge, and stage of change: A survey of exercise patterns in older Australian women. *Health Psychology, 12,* 476–480.

le Grange, D., & Eisler, I. (1993). The link between anorexia nervosa and excessive exercise: A review. *European Eating Disorders Review, 1,* 100–109.

Leighton, D., & Swerissen, H. (1995). Correlates of physical activity in young adults during school transition. *Australian Psychologist, 30,* 113–118.

Leppin, A., & Schwartzer, R. (1990). Social support and physical health: An updated meta-analysis. In L. R. Schmidt, P. Schwenkmezger, J. Weinman, & S. Maes (Eds.), *Health psychology: Theoretical and applied aspects* (pp. 185–202). London: Harwood.

Leslie, E., Fotheringham, M. J., Owen, N., & Bauman, A. (2001). Age-related differences in physical activity levels of young adults. *Medicine and Science in Sports and Exercise, 33,* 255–258.

Leslie, E., Owen, N., Salmon, J., Bauman, A., Sallis, J. F., & Lo, S. K. (1999). Insufficiently active Australian college students: Perceived personal, social, and environmental influences. *Preventive Medicine, 28,* 20–27.

Lewin, K. (1951). *Field theory in social science.* New York: Harper.

Li, F. (1999). The Exercise Motivation Scale: Its multifaceted structure and construct validity. *Journal of Applied Sport Psychology, 11,* 97–115.

Lichtenstien, E., & Hollis, J. (1992). Patient referral to smoking cessation programs: Who will follow through? *The Journal of Family Practice, 34,* 739–744.

Linenger, J. M., Chesson, C. V., & Nice, D. S. (1991). Physical fitness gains following simple environmental change. *American Journal of Preventive Medicine, 7,* 298–310.

Little, J. C. (1979). Neurotic illness in fitness fanatics. *Psychiatric Aspects of Sports, 9,* 148–156.

Lobstein, D., & Rasmussen, C. (1991). Decreases in resting plasma beta-endorphine and depression scores after endurance training. *Journal of Sports Medicine and Physical Fitness, 31,* 543–551.

Loeser, J. D., & Melzack, R. (1999). Pain: An overview. *Lancet, 353,* 1607–1609.

Logsdon, D. N., Lazaro, C. M., & Meier, R. V. (1989). The feasibility of behavioral risk reduction in primary care medical care. *American Journal of Preventive Medicine, 5,* 249–256.

Long, B. C., & van Stavel, R. (1995). Effects of exercise training on anxiety: A meta-analysis. *Journal of Applied Sport Psychology, 7,* 167–189.

Lox, C. L., McAuley, E., & Tucker, R. S. (1995). Exercise as an intervention for enhancing subjective well-being in an HIV-1 population. *Journal of Sport and Exercise Psychology, 17,* 345–362.

Luepker, R. V., Perry, C. L., & McKinlay, S. M. (1996). Outcomes of a field trial to improve children's dietary patterns and physical activity: The child and adolescent trial for cardiovascular health (CATCH). *JAMA, 275,* 768–776.

Maddux, J., (1995). Looking for common ground: A comment on Bandura and Kirsch. In J. Maddux (Ed.), *Self-efficacy, adaptation, and adjustment: Theory, research, and application* (pp. 377–385). New York: Plenum Press.

Maddux, J., & Rogers, R. W. (1983). Protection motivation and self-efficacy: A revised theory of fear appeals and attitude change. *Journal of Experimental Social Psychology, 19,* 469–479.

Maehr, M. L. (1984). Meaning and motivation. In R. Ames & C. Ames (Eds.), *Research on motivation in education* (Vol. 1, pp. 115–144). New York: Academic Press.

Maehr, M. L., & Braskamp, L. A. (1986). *The motivation factor: A theory of personal investment.* Lexington, MA: Lexington Press.

Maganaris, C. N., Collins, C., & Martin, S. (2000). Expectancy effects and strength training: Do steroids make a difference? *The Sport Psychologist, 14,* 272–278.

Malina, R. M. (2001). Adherence to physical activity from childhood to adulthood: A perspective from tracking studies. *Quest, 53,* 346–355.

Manley, A. F. (1996). Preface. In U.S. Department of Health and Human Services, *Physical activity and health: A report of the Surgeon General executive summary.* Pittsburgh: Author.

Marcus, B. H., Banspach, S. W., Lefebvre, J. S., Rossi, R., Carleton, R. A., & Abrams, D. B. (1992). Using the stages of change model to increase the adoption of physical activity among community participants. *American Journal of Health Promotion, 6,* 424–429.

Marcus, B. H., Bock, B. C., Pinto, B. M., Forsyth, L. H., Roberts, M. B., & Traficante, R. M. (1998). Efficacy of an individualized, motivationally tailored physical activity intervention. *Annals of Behavioral Medicine, 20,* 174–180.

Marcus, B. H., Dubbert, P. M., Forsyth, L. H., McKenzie, T. L., Stone, E. J., Dunn, A. L., & Blair, S. N. (2000). Physical activity behavior change: Issues in adoption and maintenance. *Health Psychology, 19,* 32–41.

Marcus, B. H., Emmons, K. M., Simkin-Silverman, L. R., Linnan, L. A., Taylor, E. R., Bock, B. C., Roberts, M. B., Rossi, J. S., & Abrams, D. B. (1998). Evaluation of motivationally tailored vs. standard self-help physical activity interventions at the workplace. *American Journal of Health Promotion, 12,* 246–253.

Marcus, B. H., & Owen, N. (1992). Motivational readiness, self-efficacy, and decision-making for exercise. *Journal of Applied Social Psychology, 22,* 3–16.

Marcus, B. H., Owen, N., Forsyth, L. H., Cavill, N. A., & Fridinger, F. (1998). Physical activity interventions using mass media, print media, and information technology. *American Journal of Preventive Medicine, 15,* 362–378.

Marcus, B. H., Pinto, B. M., Simkin, L. R., Audrain, J. E., & Taylor, E. R. (1994). Application of theoretical models to exercise behavior among employed women. *American Journal of Health Promotion, 9,* 49–55.

Marcus, B. H., Rakowski, W., & Rossi, J. S. (1992). Assessing motivational readiness and decision making for exercise. *Health Psychology, 11,* 257–261.

Marcus, B. H., Rossi, J. S., Selby, V. C., Niaura R. S., & Abrams, D. B. (1992). The stages and processes of exercise adoption and maintenance in a worksite sample. *Health Psychology, 11*, 386–395.

Marcus, B. H., Selby, V. C., Niaura, R. S., & Rossi, J. S. (1992). Self-efficacy and the stages of exercise behavior change. *Research Quarterly for Exercise and Sport, 63*, 60–66.

Markland, D., & Hardy, L. (1993). The Exercise Motivation Inventory: Preliminary development and validity of a measure of individuals' reasons for participation in regular physical exercise. *Personality and Individual Differences, 15*, 289–296.

Markland, D., & Ingledew, D. K. (1997). The measurement of exercise motives: Factorial validity and invariance across gender of a revised Exercise Motivation Inventory. *British Journal of Health Psychology, 2*, 361–376.

Martens, R., Vealey, R. S., & Burton, D. (1990). *Competitive anxiety in sport.* Champaign, IL: Human Kinetics.

Martinsen, E. W. (1987). The role of aerobic exercise in the treatment of depression. *Stress Medicine, 3*, 93–100.

Martinsen, E. W., Hoffart, A., & Solberg, O. (1989). Comparing aerobic and nonaerobic exercise in the treatment of clinical depression: A randomized trial. *Comprehensive Psychiatry, 30*, 324–331.

Martinsen, E. W., & Morgan, W. P. (1997). Antidepressant effects of physical anxiety. In W. P. Morgan (Ed.), *Physical activity and mental health* (pp. 93–106). Washington, DC: Taylor & Francis.

Martinsen, E. W., & Stanghelle, J. K. (1997). Drug therapy and physical activity. In W. P. Morgan (Ed.), *Physical activity and mental health* (pp. 81–90). Philadelphia, PA: Taylor & Francis.

McArthur, R. D., Levine, S. D., & Berk, T. J. (1993). Supervised exercise training improves cardiopulmonary fitness in HIV infected persons. *Medicine and Science in Sports and Exercise, 25*, 648–688.

McAuley, E. (1993). Self-efficacy and the maintenance of exercise participation in older adults. *Journal of Behavioral Medicine, 16*, 103–113.

McAuley, E. (1994). Enhancing psychological health through physical activity. In H. A. Quinney, L. Gauvin, & A. E. T. Wall (Eds.), *Toward active living: Proceedings of the International Conference on Physical Activity, Fitness, and Health* (pp. 83–90). Champaign, IL: Human Kinetics.

McAuley, E., Bane, S. M., & Mihalko, S. L. (1995). Exercise in middle-aged adults: Self-efficacy and self-presentation outcomes. *Preventive Medicine, 24*, 319–328.

McAuley, E., Bane, S. M., Rudolph, D., & Lox, C. (1995). Physique anxiety and exercise in middle-aged adults. *Journal of Gerontology, 50B*, 229–235.

McAuley, E., & Jacobson, L. (1991). Self-efficacy and exercise participation in sedentary adult females. *American Journal of Health Promotion, 5*, 185–191.

McAuley, E., & Mihalko, S. L. (1998). Measuring exercise-related self-efficacy. In J. L. Duda (Ed.), *Advances in sport and exercise psychology measurement* (pp. 371–390). Morgantown, WV: Fitness Information Technology.

McAuley, E., Mihalko, S. L., & Bane, S. M. (1996). Acute exercise and anxiety reduction: Does the environment matter? *Journal of Sport and Exercise Psychology, 18*, 408–419.

McAuley, E., Mihalko, S. L., & Rosengren, K. (1997). Self-efficacy and balance correlates of fear of falling in the elderly. *Journal of Aging and Physical Activity, 5*, 329–340.

McAuley, E., & Rowney, T. (1990). Exercise behavior and intentions: The mediating role of self-efficacy cognitions. In L. V. Velden & J. H. Humphrey (Eds.), *Psychology and sociology of sport* (pp. 3–15). New York: AMS Press.

McAuley, E., Shaffer, S. M., & Rudolph, D. (1995). Affective responses to acute exercise in elderly impaired males: The moderating effects of self-efficacy and age. *International Journal of Aging and Human Development, 41*, 13–27.

McAuley, E., Wraith, S., & Duncan, T. E. (1991). Self-efficacy, perceptions of success, and intrinsic motivation for exercise. *Journal of Applied Social Psychology, 21*, 139–155.

McCain, G. A., Bell, D. A., Mai, F. M., & Halliday, P. D. (1988). A controlled study of the effects of a supervised cardiovascular fitness training program on the manifestations of primary fibromyalgia. *Arthritis and Rheumatism, 31*, 1135–1141.

McCann, I., & Holmes, D. (1984). The influence of aerobic exercise on depression. *Journal of Personality and Social Psychology, 46*, 1142–1147.

McDonald, D. G., & Hodgdon, J. A. (1991). *The psychological effects of aerobic fitness training: Research and theory.* New York: Springer-Verlag.

McDonald, K., & Thomson, J. K. (1992). Eating disturbance, body image dissatisfaction, and reasons for exercising: Gender differences and correlational findings. *International Journal of Eating Disorders, 11*, 289–292.

McGrath, J. E. (1970). Major methodological issues. In J. E. McGrath (Ed.), *Social and psychological factors in stress* (pp. 19–49). New York: Holt, Rinehart, & Winston.

McKenzie, T. L. (1991). Observational measures of children's physical activity. *Journal of School Health, 61,* 224–227.

McKenzie, T. L., Marshall, S. J., Sallis, J. F., & Conway, T. L. (2000). Leisure-time physical activity in school environments: An observational study using SOPLAY. *Preventive Medicine, 30,* 70–77.

McKenzie, T. L., Nader, P. R., & Strikmiller, P. K. (1996). School physical education: Effect of the child and adolescent trial for cardiovascular health. *Preventive Medicine, 25,* 423–431.

McKenzie, T. L., Sallis, J. F., Nader, P. R., Patterson, T. L. K., Elder, J. P., Berry, C. C., Rupp, J. W., Atkins, C. J., Buono, M. J., & Nelson, J. A. (1991). BEACHES: An observational system for assessing children's eating and physical activity behaviors and associated events. *Journal of Applied Behavior Analysis, 24,* 141–151.

McNair, D. M., Lorr, M., & Droppleman, L. F. (1971). *EDITS manual for POMS.* San Diego, CA: Educational and Industrial Testing Service.

Mellinger, G. D., Balter, M. B., & Uhlenhuth, E. H. (1985). Insomnia and its treatment: Prevalence and correlates. *Archives of General Psychiatry, 42,* 225–232.

Milne, S., Sheeran, P., & Orbell, S. (2000). Prediction and intervention in health-related behavior: A meta-analytic review of protection motivation theory. *Journal of Applied Social Psychology, 30,* 106–143.

Minor, M. A., & Brown, J. D. (1993). Exercise maintenance of persons with arthritis after participation in a class experience. *Health Education Quarterly, 20,* 83–95.

Mischel, W., Shoda, Y., & Rodriguez, M. L. (1989). Delay of gratification in children. *Science, 244,* 933–938.

Mittelmark, M. (1996). Centrally initiated health promotion: Getting on the agenda of a community and transforming a project to local ownership. *Internet Journal of Health Promotion.* Retrieved from http://www.monash.edu.au/health/IJHP/1996/6.

Mondin, G. W., Morgan, W. P., Piering, P. N., Stegner, A. J., Stotesbery, C. L., Trine, M. R., & Wu, M. (1996). Psychological consequences of exercise deprivation in habitual exercisers. *Medicine and Science in Sports and Exercise, 28,* 1199–1203.

Montoye, H. J., Kemper, H. C. G., Saris, W. H. M., & Washburn, R. A. (1996). *Measuring physical activity and energy expenditure.* Champaign, IL: Human Kinetics.

Morgan, W. P. (1979). Negative addiction in runners. *The Physician and Sports Medicine, 7,* 57–77.

Morgan, W. P. (1985). Affective beneficence of vigorous physical activity. *Medicine and Science in Sports and Exercise, 17,* 94–100.

Morgan, W. P. (1988). Exercise and mental health. In R. K. Dishman (Ed.), *Exercise adherence: Its impact on public health* (pp. 91–121). Champaign, IL: Human Kinetics.

Morgan, W. P. (1994). Psychological components of effort sense. *Medicine and Science in Sports and Exercise, 26,* 1071–1077.

Morgan, W. P. (1997). *Physical activity and mental health.* Washington, DC: Taylor & Francis.

Morgan, W. P., Brown, J. S., Raglin, J. S., O'Connor, P. J., & Ellickson, K. A. (1987). Psychological monitoring of overtraining and staleness. *British Journal of Sports Medicine, 21,* 107–114.

Morgan, W. P., & Goldston, S. E. (1987). *Exercise and mental health.* Washington, DC: Hemisphere.

Morgan, W. P., & O'Connor, P. J. (1989). Psychological effects of exercise and sports. In E. Ryan & R. Allman (Eds.), *Sports medicine* (pp. 671–689). New York: Academic Press.

Morrow, J., & Harvey, P. (1990, November). Exermania! *American Health, 9,* 31–32.

Mota, J. (1998). Parents' physical activity behaviors and children's physical activity. *Journal of Human Movement Studies, 35,* 89–100.

Mullen, E., & Markland, D. (1997). Variations in self-determination across the stages of change for exercise in adults. *Motivation and Emotion, 21,* 349–363.

Mullen, E., Markland, D., & Ingledew, D. K. (1997a). A graded conceptualization of self-determination in the regulation of exercise behaviour: Development of a measure using confirmatory factor analytic procedures. *Personality and Individual Differences, 23,* 745–752.

Mullen, E., Markland, D., & Ingledew, D. K. (1997b). Motivation for exercise: Development of a measure of behavioural regulation. *Journal of Sport Sciences, 15,* 98–99.

National Commission on Sleep Disorders Research. (1993). *Wake up America: A national sleep alert.* Executive Summary and Executive Report. National Heart, Blood, and Lung Institute, Bethesda, Maryland.

National Institute of Dental and Craniofacial Research. (1995). Biobehavioral pain research. *NIH Guide, 24*(15).

Nichols, J. F., Patterson, P., & Early, T. (1992). A validation of a physical activity monitor for young and older adults. *Canadian Journal of Sport Science, 17,* 299–303.

Nigg, C. R. (in press). Technology's influence on physical activity and exercise science and application: The present and the future. *Psychology of Sport and Exercise.*

Nigg, C. R., Burbank, P. M., Padula, C., Dufresne, R., Rossi, J. S., Velicer, W. F., Laforge, R. G., & Prochaska, J. O. (1999). Stages of change across ten health risk behaviors for older adults. *The Gerontologist, 39,* 473–482.

Nigg, C. R., & Courneya, K. S. (1998). Transtheoretical model: Examining adolescent exercise behavior. *Journal of Adolescent Health, 22,* 214–224.

Nigg, C. R., Riebe, D., Rossi, J. S., Velicer, W. F., & Prochaska, J. O. (1999, June). *Individualized expert system interventions for adopting and maintaining physical activity.* Presentation at ACSM Special Event: Demonstrations of New Information Technology to Promote Physical Activity, Seattle, WA.

Noble, B. J., & Noble, J. M. (1998). Perceived exertion: The measurement. In J. L. Duda (1998), *Advances in sport and exercise psychology measurement* (pp. 351–360). Morgantwon, WV: Fitness Information Technology.

Noble, B. J., & Robertson, R. J. (1996). *Perceived exertion.* Champaign, IL: Human Kinetics.

Norman, P., & Smith, L. (1995). The theory of planned behaviour and exercise: An investigation into the role of prior behavior, behavioral intentions, and attitude variability. *European Journal of Social Psychology, 25,* 403–415.

North, T. C., McCullagh, P., & Tran, Z. V. (1990). Effect of exercise on depression. *Exercise and Sport Science Reviews, 18,* 379–415.

Nuckolls, K. B., Cassel, J., & Kaplan, B. H. (1972). Psychosocial assets, life crisis, and the prognosis of pregnancy. *American Journal of Epidemiology, 95,* 431–441.

O'Connell, J. K., Price, J. H., Roberts, S. M., Jurs, S. G., & McKinely, R. (1985). Utilizing the health belief model to predict dieting and exercising behavior of obese and nonobese adolescents. *Health Education Quarterly, 12,* 343–351.

O'Connor, P. J. (1997). *Overtraining and staleness.* In W. P. Morgan (Ed.), *Physical activity and mental health* (pp. 145–160). Washington, DC: Taylor & Francis.

O'Connor, P. J., & Cook, D. B. (1999). Exercise and pain: The neurobiology, measurement, and laboratory study of pain in relation to exercise in humans. *Exercise and Sport Sciences Reviews, 27,* 119–165.

O'Connor, P. J., Morgan, W. P., & Raglin, J. S. (1991). Psychobiologic effects of 3 d of increased training in female and male swimmers. *Medicine and Science in Sports and Exercise, 23,* 1055–1061.

O'Connor, P. J., & Smith, J. C. (1999). Physical activity and eating disorders. In J. M. Rippe (Ed.), *Lifestyle medicine* (pp. 1005–1015). Cambridge, MA: Blackwell Science.

Oldenburg, B., Martin, A., Greenwood, J., Bernstein, L., & Allan, R. (1995). A controlled trial of a behavioral and educational intervention following coronary artery bypass surgery. *Journal of Cardiopulmonary Rehabilitation, 15,* 39–46.

Oldridge, N. B. (1977). What to look for in an exercise class leader. *The Physician and Sport Medicine, 5,* 85–88.

Oldridge N. B., & Rogowski, B. L. (1990). Self-efficacy and in-patient cardiac rehabilitation. *The American Journal of Cardiology, 66,* 362–365.

Oldridge, N. B., & Streiner, D. L. (1990). The health belief model: Predicting compliance and dropout in cardiac rehabilitation. *Medicine and Science in Sports and Exercise, 22,* 678–683.

Olivardia, R., Pope, H. G., & Hudson, J. I. (2000). Muscle dysmorphia in male weight lifters: A case-control study. *American Journal of Psychiatry, 157,* 1291–1296.

O'Loughlin, J., Paradis, G., Meshefedjian, G., & Kishchuk, N. (1998). Evaluation of an 8-week mailed healthy-weight intervention. *Preventive Medicine, 27,* 288–295.

Orleans, C. T. (2000). Promoting the maintenance of health behavior change: Recommendations for the next generation of research and practice. *Health Psychology, 19,* 76–83.

Orwell, G. (1949). *1984.* San Diego: Harcourt, Brace, Jovanovich.

Ossip-Klein, D. J., Doyne, E. J., Bowman, E. D., Osborn, K. M., McDougall-Wilson, I. B., & Neimeyer, R. A. (1989). Effects of running or weight lifting on self-concept in clinically depressed women. *Journal of Consulting and Clinical Psychology, 57,* 158–161.

Pageot, J. C. (1987). Obstacles to participation in physical activities of the Canadian elderly population. In M. E. Berridge and G. R. Ward (Eds.), *International perspectives on adapted physical activity.* Champaign, IL: Human Kinetics.

Paskevich, D. M., Estabrooks, P. A., Brawley, L. R., & Carron, A. V. (2001). Group cohesion in sport and exercise. In R. N. Singer, H. A. Hausenblas, & C. M. Janelle (Eds.), *Handbook of research on sport psychology* (2nd ed., pp. 472–494). New York: Wiley.

Patala, E., & Shumway-Cook, A. (1999). Dimensions of mobility: Defining the complexity and difficulty associated with community mobility. *Journal of Aging and Physical Activity, 7,* 7–19.

Pate, R. R., Baranowski, T., Dowda, M., & Trost, S. G. (1996). Tracking of physical activity in young children. *Medicine and Science in Sports and Exercise, 28,* 92–96.

Pate, R. R., Long, B. J., & Heath, G. (1994). Descriptive epidemiology of physical activity in adolescents. *Pediatric Exercise Science, 6,* 434–447.

Pate, R. R., Pratt, M., Blair, S. N., Haskell, W. L., Macera, C. A., Bouchard, C., Buchner, D., Ettinger, W., Heath, G. W., King, A. C., Kriska, A., Leon, A. S., Marcus, B. H., Morris, J., Paffenbarger, R. S., Patrick, K., Pollock, M. L., Rippe, J. M., Sallis, J. F., & Wilmore, J. H. (1995). Physical activity and public health: A recommendation from the Centers for Disease Control and Prevention and the American College of Sports Medicine. *JAMA, 273,* 402–407.

Pate, R. R., Trost, S. G., Mullis, R., Sallis, J. F., Wechsler, H., & Brown, D. R. (2000). Community interventions to promote proper nutrition and physical activity among youth. *Preventive Medicine, 31,* S138–S149.

Peterson, S. L. (1993, December). Qualities to look for in an exercise leader. *Fitness Management, 52,* 32–33.

Petruzzello, S. J. (1997). Anxiety reduction following exercise: Methodological artifact or "real" phenomenon? *Journal of Sport and Exercise Psychology, 17,* 105–111.

Petruzzello, S. J., Landers, D. M., Hatfield, B. D., Kubitz, K. A., & Salazar, W. (1991). A meta-analysis on the anxiety-reducing effects of acute and chronic exercise. *Sports Medicine, 11,* 143–182.

Pierce, E. F., Eastman, N. W., Tripathi, H. L., Olson, K. G., & Dewey, W. L. (1993). β-endorphin response to endurance exercise: Relationship to exercise dependence. *Perceptual and Motor Skills, 77,* 767–770.

Plotnikoff, R. C., & Higginbotham, N. (1988). Protection motivation theory and the prediction of exercise and low-fat diet behaviours among Australian cardiac patients. *Psychology and Health, 13,* 411–429.

Poag, K., & McAuley, E. (1992). Goal setting, self-efficacy, and exercise behavior. *Journal of Sport and Exercise Psychology, 14,* 352–360.

Poag-Ducharme, K. A., & Brawley, L. R. (1993). Self-efficacy theory: Use in the prediction of exercise behavior in the community setting. *Journal of Applied Sport Psychology, 5,* 178–194.

Pope, H. G., Gruber, A. J., Choi, P., Olivardia, R., & Phillips, K. A. (1997). Muscle dysmorphia: An underrecognized form of body dysmorphic disorder. *Psychosomatics, 38,* 548–557.

Pope, H. G., & Katz, D. L. (1994). Psychiatric and medical effects of anabolic steroid use. *Archives of General Psychiatry, 51,* 375–382.

Pope, H. G., Katz, D. L., & Hudson, J. I. (1993). Anorexia nervosa and "reverse anorexia" among 108 male bodybuilders. *Comprehensive Psychiatry, 34,* 406–409.

Powers, P. S., Schocken, D. D., & Boyd, F. R. (1998). Comparison of habitual runners and anorexia nervosa patients. *International Journal of Eating Disorders, 23,* 133–143.

Price, D. D., & Harkins, S. W. (Eds.). (1992). *Psychophysical approaches to pain measurement and assessment.* New York: Guilford Press.

Prochaska, J. O., & DiClemente, C. C. (1984). *The transtheoretical approach: Crossing traditional boundaries of change.* Homewood, IL: Dorsey.

Prochaska, J. O., & DiClemente, C. C. (1986). Toward a comprehensive model of change. In W. R. Miller & N. Heather (Eds.), *Treating addictive behaviors: Processes of change* (pp. 3–27). New York: Plenum.

Prochaska, J. O., & Marcus, B. H. (1994). The transtheoretical model: Applications to exercise. In R. K. Dishman (Ed.), *Advances in exercise adherence* (pp. 161–180). Champaign, IL: Human Kinetics.

Prochaska, J. O., & Velicer, W. F. (1997). The transtheoretical model of health behavior change. *American Journal of Health Promotion, 12,* 38–48.

Pucher, J., & Lefevre, C. (1996). *The urban transportation crisis in Europe and North America.* London: Macmillan.

Racette, S. B., Schoeller, D. A., & Kushner, R. F. (1995). Comparison of heart rate and physical activity recall with doubly labeled water in obese women. *Medicine and Science in Sports and Exercise, 27,* 126–133.

Raglin, J. S. (1997). The anxiolytic effect of physical activity. In W. P. Morgan (Ed.), *Physical activity and mental health* (pp. 107–126). Philadelphia, PA: Taylor & Francis.

Raglin, J. S., & Morgan, W. P. (1985). Influence of vigorous exercise on mood state. *Behavior Therapist, 8,* 179–183.

Rauck, R. L. (1996). Cost-effectiveness and cost/benefit ratio of acute pain management. *Regional Anesthesia, 21,* 139–143.

Reboussin, B., Rejeski, W., Martin, K., Callahan, K., Dunn, A., & Sallis, J. (2000). Correlates of satisfaction with body function and body appearance in middle and older aged adults: The Activity Counseling Trial (ACT). *Psychology and Health, 15,* 239–254.

Redding, C. A., & Rossi, J. S. (1999). Testing a model of situational self-efficacy for safer sex among college students: Stage of change and gender-based differences. *Psychology and Health, 14,* 467–486.

Redding, C. A., Rossi, J. S., Fava, J. L., Rossi, S. R., Prochaska, J. O., Velicer, W. F., & DiClemente, C. C. (1989). *Dynamic factors in the maintenance of smoking cessation: A naturalistic study.* Paper presented at the 10th annual meeting of the Society of Behavioral Medicine, San Francisco, CA.

Reed, G. R. (1999). Adherence to exercise and the transtheoretical model of behavior change. In S. Bull (Ed.), *Adherence issues in sport and exercise* (pp. 19–46). New York: Wiley.

Reed, G. R., Velicer, W. F., Prochaska, J. O., Rossi, J. S., & Marcus, B. H. (1997). What makes a good algorithm: Examples from regular exercise. *American Journal of Health Promotion, 12,* 57–66.

Regier, D. A., Myers, J. K., Kramer, M., Robins, L. N., Blazer, D. G., Hough, R. L., Eaton, W. W., & Locke, B. Z. (1984). The NIMH epidemiologic catchment area program. *Archives of General Psychiatry, 41,* 934–941.

Rejeski, W. J., & Brawely, L. R. (1988). Defining the boundaries of sport psychology. *The Sport Psychologist, 2,* 231–242.

Rejeski, W. J., & Thompson, A. (1993). Historical and conceptual roots of exercise psychology. In P. Seraganian (Ed.), *Exercise psychology: The influence of physical exercise on psychological processes* (p. 3–38). New York: Wiley.

Remers, L., Widmeyer, W. N., Williams, J. M., & Myers, L. (1995). Possible mediators and moderators of the class size–member adherence relationship in exercise. *Journal of Applied Sport Psychology, 7,* 38–49.

Riumallo, J. A., Schoeller, D., Barrera, G., Gattas, V., & Vauy, R. (1989). Energy expenditure in underweight free-living adults: Impact of energy supplementation as determined by doubly labeled water and indirect calorimetry. *American Journal of Clinical Nutrition, 49,* 239–246.

Rogers, R. W. (1975). A protection motivation theory of fear appeals and attitude change. *Journal of Psychology, 91,* 93–114.

Rogers, R. W. (1983). Cognitive and physiological processes in fear appeals and attitude change: A revised theory of protection motivation. In J. R. Cacioppo & R. E. Petty (Eds.), *Social psychology: A source book* (pp. 153–176). New York: Guilford Press.

Rohm Young, D., Haskell, W. L., Barr Taylor, C., & Fortmann, S. P. (1996). Effect of community health education on physical activity knowledge, attitudes, and behavior: The Stanford Five-City Project. *American Journal of Epidemiology, 144,* 264–274.

Rook, K. S. (1992). Detrimental aspects of social relationships: Taking stock of an emerging literature. In H. O. F. Veiel & U. Baumann (Eds.), *The meaning and measurement of social support* (pp. 157–169). New York: Hemisphere.

Rosenstock, I. M. (1974). Historical origins of the health belief model. *Health Education Monographs, 2,* 1–9.

Rosenstock, I. M. (1990). The health belief model: Explaining health behavior through expectancies. In K. Glanz, F. Lewis, & B. Rimer (Eds.), *Health behavior and health education* (pp. 39–62). San Fancisco: Jossey-Bass.

Rosenstock, I. M., Stretcher, V. J., & Becker, M. (1988). Social learning theory and the health belief model. *Health Education Quarterly, 15,* 175–183.

Ross, C. E. (2000). Walking, exercising, and smoking: Does neighborhood matter? *Social Science and Medicine, 51,* 265–274.

Ross, J. C., Dotson, C. O., Gilbert, G. G., & Katz, S. J. (1985). After physical education: Physical activity outside of school physical education programs. *Journal of Physical Education, Recreation, and Dance, 56,* 35–39.

Ross, J. G., & Pate, R. R. (1987). The national children and youth fitness study II: A summary of findings. *Journal of Physical Education, Recreation, and Dance, 58,* 51–56.

Roth, D. L. (1989). Acute emotional and psychophysiological effects of aerobic exercise. *Psychophysiology, 26,* 593–602.

Roth, D. L., Bachtler, S. D., & Fillingam, R. (1990). Acute emotional and cardiovascular effects of stressful mental work during aerobic exercise. *Psychophysiology, 27,* 694–701.

Rowland, T. W. (1990). *Exercise and children's health.* Champaign, IL: Human Kinetics.

Rudolph, D. L., & McAuley, E. (1995). Self-efficacy and salivary cortisol responses to acute exercise in physically active and less active adults. *Journal of Sport and Exercise Psychology, 17,* 206–213.

Rudolph, D. L., & McAuley, E. (1996). Self-efficacy and perceptions of effort: A reciprocal relationship. *Journal of Sport and Exercise Psychology, 18,* 216–223.

Rudy, E. B., & Estok, P. J. (1989). Measurement and significance of negative addiction in runners. *Western Journal of Nursing Research, 11,* 548–558.

Russell, D., & Cutrona, C. (1984, August). *The provisions of social relationships and adaptation to stress.* Paper presented at the annual meeting of the American Psychological Association, Toronto, Ontario, Canada.

Ruuskanen, J., & Puoppila, I. (1995). Physical activity and psychological well-being among people aged 65–84 years. *Age and Aging, 24,* 292–296.

Ryan, A. J. (1983). Exercise is medicine. *Physician and Sportsmedicine, 11,* 10–15.

Ryan, A. J. (1984). Exercise and health: Lessons from the past. *Exercise and Health: American Academy of Physical Education Papers, 17,* 3–13.

Ryan, R. M. (1993). Agency and organization: Intrinsic motivation, autonomy, and the self in psychological development. In J. E. Jacobs (Ed.), *Nebraska Symposium on Motivation: Vol. 40. Developmental perspectives on motivation* (pp. 1–56). Lincoln: University of Nebraska Press.

Sachs, M. L. (1981). Running addiction. In M. H. Sachs & M. L. Sacks (Eds.), *Psychology of running* (pp. 116–126). Champaign, IL: Human Kinetics.

Sallis, J. F., Buono, M. J., Roby, J. J., Micale, F. G., & Nelson, J. A. (1993). Seven-day recall and other physical activity self-reports in children and adolescents. *Medicine and Science in Sports and Exercise, 25,* 99–108.

Sallis, J. F., Haskell, W. L., Fortman, S. P., Vranizan, K. M., Taylor, C. B., & Solomon, D. S. (1986). Predictors of adoption and maintenance of physical activity in a community sample. *Preventive Medicine, 15,* 331–341.

Sallis, J. F., Haskell, W. L., Wood, P. D., Fortmann, S. P., Rogers, T., Blair, S. N., & Paffenbarger, R. S. (1985). Physical activity assessment methodology in the Five-City Project. *American Journal of Epidemiology, 121,* 91–106.

Sallis, J. F., Hovell, M. F., Hofstetter, C. R., & Barrington, E. (1992). Explanation of vigorous physical activity during two years using social learning variables. *Social Science and Medicine, 34,* 25–32.

Sallis, J. F., Hovell, M. F., Hofstetter, C. R., Elder, J. P., Faucher, P., Spry, V. M., Barrington, E., & Hackley, M. (1990). Lifetime history of relapse from exercise. *Addictive Behaviors, 15,* 573–579.

Sallis, J. F., Hovell, M. F., Hofstetter, C. R., Elder, J. P., Hackley, M., Caspersen, C. J., & Powell, K. E. (1990). Distance between homes and exercise facilities related to frequency of exercise among San Diego residents. *Public Health Reports, 105,* 179–185.

Sallis, J. F., Johnson, M. F., Calfas, K. J., Caparosa, S., & Nichols, J. F. (1997). Assessing perceived physical environmental variables that may influence physical activity. *Research Quarterly for Exercise and Sport, 68,* 345–351.

Sallis, J. F., Nader, P. R., Broyles, S. L., Berry, C. C., Elder, J. P., McKenzie, T. L., & Nelson, J. A. (1993). Correlates of physical activity at home in Mexican-American and Anglo-American preschool children. *Health Psychology, 12,* 390–398.

Sallis, J. F., & Owen, N. (1999). *Physical activity and behavioral medicine.* Thousand Oaks, CA: Sage.

Sallis, J. F., Prochaska, J. J., Taylor, W. C., Hill, J. O., & Geraci, J. C. (1999). Correlates of physical activity in a national sample of girls and boys in grades 4 through 12. *Health Psychology, 18,* 410–415.

Sallis, J. F., Strikmiller, P. K., Harsha, D. W., Feldman, H. A., Ehlinger, S., Stone, E. J., Williston, B. J., & Woods, S. (1996). Validation of interviewer and self-administered physical activity checklists for fifth grade students. *Medicine and Science in Sports and Exercise, 28,* 840–851.

Salmon, P. (2001). Effects of physical exercise on anxiety, depression, and sensitivity to stress: A unifying theory. *Clinical Psychology Review, 21,* 33–61.

Sarason, B. R., Pierce, G. R., & Sarason, I. G. (1990). Social support: The sense of acceptance and the role of relationships. In Sarason, B. R., Sarason, I. G., & Pierce, G. R. (Eds.), *Social support: An interactional view* (pp. 97–128). New York: Wiley.

Sarason, B. R., Pierce, G. R., Shearin, E. N., Sarason, I. G., Waltz, J. A., & Poppe, L. (1991). Perceived social support and working models of self and actual others. *Journal of Personality and Social Psychology, 60,* 273–287.

Sarason, I. G., Levine, H. M., Basham, R. B., & Sarason, B. R. (1983). Assessing social support: The Social Support Questionnaire. *Journal of Personality and Social Psychology, 44,* 127–139.

Sarason, I. G., Sarason, B. R., & Pierce, G. R. (1992). Three contexts of social support. In H. O. F. Veiel & U. Baumann (Eds.), *The meaning and measurement of social support* (pp. 143–154). New York: Hemisphere.

Sardoni, C., & Carron, A. V. (2000, October). *Social anxiety, self-presentation, and group membership.* Paper presented at the Canadian Psychomotor Learning and Sport Psychology Meeting, Waterloo, Ontario.

Sarkin, J. A., Nichols, J. F., Sallis, J. F., & Calfas, K. J. (1998). Self-report measures and scoring protocols affect prevalence estimates of meeting physical activity guidelines. *Medicine and Science in Sports and Exercise, 32,* 149–156.

Schacht, S. P., & Unnithan, N. P. (1991). Mall walking and urban sociability. *Sociological Spectrum, 11,* 351–367.

Scheier, M. F., Matthews, K. A., Owens, J. F., Magovern, G. J., Sr., Lefebvre, R. C., Abbott, R. A., & Carver, C. S. (1989). Dispositional optimism and recovery from coronary bypass surgery: The beneficial effects of physical and psychological well-being. *Journal of Personality and Social Psychology, 57,* 1024–1040.

Schoeller, D. A., & Racete, S. B. (1990). A review of filed techniques for the assessment of energy expenditure. *Journal of Nutrition, 120,* 1492–1495.

Schlicht, W. (1994). Does physical exercise reduce anxious emotions? A meta-analysis. *Anxiety, Stress, and Coping, 6,* 275–288.

Schwartzer, R., & Leppin, A. (1989). Social support and health: A meta-analysis. *Psychology and Health: An International Journal, 3,* 1–15.

Schwartzer, R., & Leppin, A. (1992). Possible impact of social ties and support on morbidity and mortality. In H. O. F. Veiel & U. Baumann (Eds.), *The meaning and measurement of social support* (pp. 65–83). New York: Hemisphere.

Scully, D., Kremer, J., Meade, M. M., Graham, R., & Dudgeon, K. (1998). Physical exercise and psychological well being: A critical review. *British Journal of Sports Medicine, 32,* 111–120.

Shavelson, R. J., Hubner, J. J., & Stanton, G. C. (1976). Self-concept: Validation of construct interpretations. *Review of Educational Research, 46,* 407–411.

Shepard, R. J., Jequier, J. C., Lavallee, H., LaBarre, R., & Rajic, M. (1980). Habitual physical activity. Effects of sex, milieu, season, and required activity. *Journal of Sports Medicine and Physical Fitness, 20,* 55–66.

Siff, M. (1992, August). Bodybuilding anorexia? *Fitness and Sports Review International,* 119.

Simons-Morton, B. G., Taylor, W. C., & Huang, I. W. (1994). Validity of the physical activity interview and caltrac with preadolescent children. *Research Quarterly for Exercise and Sport, 65,* 84–88.

Simons-Morton, D. G., Calfas, K. J., Oldenburg, B., & Burton, N. W. (1998). Effects of interventions in health care settings on physical activity or cardiorespiratory fitness. *American Journal of Preventive Medicine, 15,* 413–430

Sirard, J. R., & Pate, R. R. (2001). Physical activity assessment in children and adolescents. *Sports Medicine, 31,* 439–454.

Skinner, B. F. (1947). Superstition in the pigeon. *American Psychologist, 2,* 426.

Slenker, S. E., Price, J. H., Roberts, S. M., & Jurs, S. G. (1984). Joggers versus nonexercisers: An analysis of knowledge, attitudes, and beliefs about jogging. *Research Quarterly for Exercise and Sport, 55,* 371–378.

Solomon, R. L. (1980). The opponent-process theory of acquired motivation: The costs of pleasure and the benefits of pain. *American Psychologist, 35,* 691–712.

Sommers, J. M., Andres, F. F., & Price, J. H. (1995). Perceptions of exercise of mall walkers utilizing the health belief model. *Journal of Health Education, 26,* 158–166.

Sonstroem, R. J. (1987, August). *Stage model of exercise adoption.* Paper presented at the meeting of the American Psychological Association, New York.

Sonstroem, R. J., Harlow, L. L., & Josephs, L. (1994). Exercise and self-esteem: Validity of model expansion and exercise associations. *Journal of Sport and Exercise Psychology, 16,* 29–42.

Spano, L. (2001). The relationship between exercise and anxiety, obsessive-compulsiveness, and narcissism. *Personality and Individual Differences, 30,* 87–93.

Spence, J. C. (1999). When a note of caution is not enough: A comment on Hausenblas, Carron, and Mack. *Journal of Sport and Exercise Psychology, 21,* 376–381.

Spink, K. S. (1992). Relation of anxiety about social physique to location of participation in physical activity. *Perceptual and Motor Skills, 74,* 1075–1078.

Spink, K. S., & Carron, A. V. (1992). Group cohesion and adherence in exercise class. *Journal of Sport and Exercise Psychology, 14,* 78–86.

Spink, K. S., & Carron, A. V. (1993). The effects of team building on the adherence patterns of female exercise participants. *Journal of Sport and Exercise Psychology, 15,* 39–49.

Spink, K. S., & Carron, A. V. (1994). Group cohesion effects in exercise classes. *Small Group Research, 25,* 26–42.

Starling, R. D., Matthew, D. E., Ades, P. A., & Poehlman, E. T. (1999). Assessment of physical activity in older individuals: A doubly labeled water study. *Journal of Applied Physiology, 86,* 2090–2096.

Stephens, T., & Caspersen, C. J. (1994). The demography of physical activity. In C. Bouchard & R. J. Shephard (Eds.), *Physical activity, fitness, and health: International proceedings and consensus statement* (pp. 204–213). Champaign IL: Human Kinetics.

Stephens, T., Jacobs, & White, C. C. (1985). A descriptive epidemiology of leisure-time physical activity. *Public Health Reports, 100,* 147–158.

Stetson, B. A., Rahn, J. M., Dubbert, P. M., Wilner, B. I., & Mercury, M. G. (1997). Prospective evaluation of the effects of stress on exercise adherence in community-residing women. *Health Psychology, 16,* 515–520.

Stewart, A. L., Mills, K. M., King, A. C., Haskell, W. L., Gillis, D., & Ritter, P. L. (2001). CHAMPS Physical Activity Questionnaire for older adults: Outcomes for intervention. *Medicine and Science in Sports and Exercise, 33,* 1126–1141.

Stewart, A. L., Mills, K. M., Sepsis, P. G., King, A. C., McLellan, B. Y., Roitz, K., & Ritter, P. L. (1997). Evaluation of CHAMPS, a physical activity promotion program for older adults. *Annals of Behavioral Medicine, 19,* 353–361.

Stone, E. J., McKenzie, T. L., Welk, G. J., & Booth, M. J. (1998). Effects of physical activity interventions in youth: Review and synthesis. *American Journal of Preventive Medicine, 15,* 298–315.

Strath, S. J., Swartz, A. M., Bassett, D. R., Jr., O'Brien, W. L., King, G. A., & Ainsworth, B. E. (2000). Evaluation of heart rate as a method for assessing moderate intensity physical activity. *Medicine and Science in Sports and Exercise, 32,* S465–S470.

Stratton, J. R., & Halter, J. B. (1985). Effect of benzodiazapine on plasma epinephrine and norepinephrine levels during exercise stress. *Cardiovascular Pharmocology, 56,* 136–139.

Sullum, J., Clark, M. M., & King, T. K. (2000). Predictors of exercise relapse in a college population. *Journal of American College Health, 48,* 175–180.

Szabo, A. (1995). The impact of exercise deprivation on well-being of habitual exercisers. *The Australian Journal of Science and Medicine in Sport, 27,* 68–75.

Szabo, A., Frenkl, R., & Caputo, A. (1997). Relationship between addiction to running, commitment, and deprivation from running: A study on the Internet. *European Yearbook of Sport Psychology, 1,* 130–147.

Taggart, H. M., & Connor, S. E. (1995). The relation of exercise habits to health beliefs and knowledge about osteoporosis. *Journal of American College Health, 44,* 127–130.

Tappe, M. K., Duda, J. L., & Ehrnwald, P. M. (1989). Perceived barriers to exercise among adolescents. *Journal of School Health 59,* 153–155.

Taras, H. F., Sallis, J. F., Patterson, T. L., Nader, P. R., & Nelson, J. A. (1989). Television's influence on children's diet and physical activity. *Deviant Behaviors in Pediatrics, 10,* 176–180.

Taylor, W. C., Baranowski, T., & Sallis, J. F. (1994). Family determinants of childhood physical activity: A social cognitive model. In R. K. Dishman (Ed.), *Advances in exercise adherence* (pp. 319–360). Champaign, IL: Human Kinetics.

Taylor, W. C., Blair, S. N., Cummings, S. S., Wun, C. C., & Malina, R. M. (1999). Childhood and adolescent physical activity patterns and adult physical activity. *Medicine and Science in Sports and Exercise, 31,* 118–123.

Taylor, W. N. (1985). *Hormonal manipulation: A new era of monstrous athletes.* Jefferson, NC: McFarland.

Terry, D. J., & O'Leary, J. E. (1995). The theory of planned behaviour: The effects of perceived behavioural control and self-efficacy. *British Journal of Social Psychology, 34,* 199–220.

Theberge, N. (1991). A content analysis of print media coverage of gender, women, and physical activity. *Journal of Applied Sport Psychology, 3,* 36–48.

Thomas, T. R., Lawson, B. R., Ziogas, G., & Cox, R. H. (1994). Physiological and psychological responses to eccentric exercise. *Canadian Journal of Applied Physiology, 19,* 91–100.

Thompson, J. K., & Blanton, P. (1987). Energy conservation and exercise dependence: A sympathetic arousal hypothesis. *Medicine and Science in Sports and Exercise, 19,* 91–99.

Thompson, J. K. (1986). Larger than life. *Psychology Today, 24,* 38–44.

Thornton, E. W., & Scott, S. E. (1995). Motivation in the committed runner: Correlations between self-report scales and behaviour. *Health Promotion International, 10,* 177–184.

Tirrell, B. E., & Hart, L. K. (1980). The relationship of health beliefs and knowledge to exercise compliance in patients after coronary bypass. *Heart Lung, 9,* 487–493.

Treasure, D. C., Lox, C. L., & Lawton, B. R. (1998). Determinants of physical activity in a sedentary obese female population. *Journal of Sport and Exercise Psychology, 20,* 218–224.

Trinder, J., Montgomery, I., & Paxton, S. (1988). Effects of exercise on sleep: The negative view. *Acta Physiologica Scandinavica, 133(S574),* 14–20.

Trost, S. G. (2001). Objective measurement of physical activity in youth: Current issues, future directions. *Exercise and Sport Sciences Reviews, 29,* 32–36.

Trost, S. G., Pate, R. R., Dowda, M., Saunders, R., Ward, D. S., & Felton, G. (1996). Gender differences in physical activity and determinants of physical activity in rural fifth grade children. *Journal of School Health, 66,* 145–150.

Trost, S. G., Pate, R. R., Saunders, R., Ward, D., Dowda, M., & Felton, G. (1997). A prospective study of the determinants of physical activity in rural fifth-grade children. *Preventive Medicine, 26,* 257–263.

Tsuang, M., Perkins, K., & Simpson, J. C. (1983). Physical diseases in schizophrenia and affective disorder. *Journal of Clinical Psychiatry, 44,* 42–46.

Tucker, L. A. (1987). Effect of weight training on body attitudes: Who benefits most? *Journal of Sports Medicine, 27,* 70–77.

Tucker, L. A., & Hager, R. L. (1996). Television viewing and muscular fitness of children. *Perceptual and Motor Skills, 82,* 1316–1318.

Turner, E. E., Rejeski, W. J., & Brawley, L. R. (1997). Psychological benefits of physical activity are influenced by the social environment. *Journal of Sport and Exercise Psychology, 19,* 119–130.

U.S. Department of Health and Human Services. (1996). *Physical activity and health: A report of the Surgeon General.* Atlanta: U.S. Department of Health and Human Services, Centers for Disease Control and Prevention, National Center for Chronic Disease Prevention and Health Promotion.

U.S. Department of Health and Human Services. (1999). *Promoting physical activity at the community level: A guide for action.* Champaign, IL: Human Kinetics.

U.S. Department of Health and Human Services. (2000). Physical activity and fitness. In *Healthy People 2010.* Retrieved from www.health.gov/healthypeople/document/html/volume2/22physical.htm

Vallerand, R. J. (1997). Toward a hierarchical model of intrinsic and extrinsic motivation. *Advances in Experimental and Social Psychology, 29,* 271–360.

Vallerand, R. J., Blais, M. R., Brière, N. M., & Pelletier, L. G. (1989). Construction et validation de l'Échelle Motivation en Éducation (ÉMÉ) [Development and validation of the Academic Motivation Scale]. *Canadian Journal of Behavioural Science, 21,* 323–349.

Vallerand, R. J., Deci, E. L., & Ryan, R. M. (1987). Intrinsic motivation in sport. *Exercise and Sport Science Reviews, 15,* 389–425.

Vallerand, R. J., Pelletier, L. G., Blais, M. R., Brière, N. M., Senécal, C. B., & Vallières, E. F. (1992). The Academic Motivation Scale: A measure of intrinsic, extrinsic, and amotivation in education. *Educational and Psychological Measurement, 52,* 1003–1019.

Vallerand, R. J., Pelletier, L. G., Blais, M. R., Brière, N. M., Senécal, C. B., & Vallières, E. F. (1993). On the assessment of intrinsic, extrinsic, and amotivation in education: Evidence on the concurrent and construct validity of the Academic Motivation Scale. *Educational and Psychological Measurement, 53,* 159–172.

Vanden Auweele, Y., Rzewnicki, R., & Van Mele, V. (1997). Reasons for not exercising and exercise intentions: A study of middle-aged sedentary adults. *Journal of Sport Sciences, 15,* 151–165.

Vara, L., & Agras, W. S. (1989). Caloric intake and activity levels are related in young children. *International Journal of Obesity, 13,* 613–617.

Vaux, A. (1988). *Social support: Theory, research, and intervention.* New York: Praeger.

Vaux, A. (1992). Assessment of social support. In H. O. F. Veiel & U. Baumann (Eds.), *The meaning and measurement of social support* (pp. 193–216). New York: Hemisphere.

Veale, D. (1987). Exercise dependence. *British Journal of Addiction, 82,* 735–740.

Veale, D. (1995). Does primary exercise dependence really exist? In J. Annett, B. Cripps, & H. Steinberg (Eds.), *Exercise addiction: Motivation for participation in sport and exercise* (pp. 1–5). Leicester, UK: British Psychological Society.

Veiel, H. O. F., & Baumann, U. (1992). The many meanings of social support. In H. O. F. Veiel & U. Baumann (Eds.), *The meaning and measurement of social support* (pp. 1–9). New York: Hemisphere.

Veith, R. C., Raskind, M. A., Claswell, J. H., Barnes, R. F., Gumbrecht, G., & Rithie, J. L. (1982). Cardiovascular effects of tricyclic anti-depressants in depressed patients with chronic heart disease. *New England Journal of Medicine, 306*, 954–959.

Vohra, J., Burrows, J. D., & Sloma, J. (1975). Assessment of cardiovascular side effects of therapeutic doses of tricyclic anti-depressants. *Australian and New Zealand Journal of Medicine, 5*, 7–11.

Von Korff, M., Dworkin, S. F., & Le Resche, L. (1990). Graded chronic pain status: An epidemiological evaluation. *Pain, 40*, 279–291.

Vuori, I., Urponen, H., Hasan, J., & Partinen, M. (1988). Epidemiology of exercise effects on sleep. *Acta Physiologica Scandinavica, 133(S574)*, 3–7.

Waaler Loland, N. (1998). Body image and physical activity: A survey among Norwegian men and women. *International Journal of Sport Psychology, 29*, 339–365.

Wankel, L. M., Mummery, K., Stephens, T., & Craig, C. L. (1994). Prediction of physical activity intention from social psychological variables: Results from the Campbell's Survey of Well-Being. *Journal of Sport and Exercise Psychology, 16*, 56–69.

Wareham, N. J., & Rennie, K. L. (1998). The assessment of physical activity in individuals and populations: Why try to be more precise about how physical activity is assessed? *International Journal of Obesity, 22*, S30–S38.

Washburn, R. A., Smith, K. W., Jetter, A. M., & Janney, C. A. (1993). The physical activity scale for the elderly (PASE): Development and evaluation. *Journal of Clinical Epidemiology, 46*, 153–162.

Waters, B. (1981). Defining the runner's personality. *Runner's World, 16*, 48–51.

Weinstein, N. D., Rothman, A. J., & Sutton, S. R. (1998). Stage theories of health behavior: Conceptual and methodological issues. *Health Psychology, 17*, 290–299.

Weiss, J. M. (1982). *A model of neurochemical study of depression.* Paper presented at the annual convention of the American Psychological Association, Washington, DC.

Weiss, M. R., McCullagh, P., Smith, A. L., & Berlant, A. R. (1998). Observational learning and the fearful child: Influence of peer models on swimming skill performance and psychological response. *Research Quarterly for Exercise and Sport, 69*, 380–394.

Weiss, R. S. (1974). The provisions of social relationships. In Z. Rubin (Ed.), *Doing unto others* (pp. 17–26). Englewood Cliffs, NJ: Prentice Hall.

Welk, G. J., Differding, J. A., Thompson, R. W., Blair, S. N., Dziura, J., & Hart, P. (2000). The utility of the Digi-Walker step counter to assess daily physical activity patterns. *Medicine and Science in Sports and Exercise, 32*, S481–S488.

Wells, R. J. (1983). Is running an analogue of anorexia nervosa? *New England Journal of Medicine, 309*, 47.

Wier, L. T., Jackson, A. S., & Pinkerton, M. B. (1989). Evaluation of the NASA/JSC health related fitness program. *Aviation Space Environment Medicine, 60*, 438–444.

Wilcox, S., & Storandt, M. (1996). Relations among age, exercise, and psychological variables in a community sample of women. *Health Psychology, 15*, 110–113.

Willis, J. D., & Campbell, L. F. (1992). *Exercise psychology.* Champaign, IL: Human Kinetics.

Wood, T. M. (2000). Issues and future directions in assessing physical activity: An introduction to the conference proceedings. *Research Quarterly for Exercise and Sport, 71*, ii–vii.

World Health Organization. (1985). *Targets for Health for All.* Copenhagen: Author. Cited in Biddle, S. J. H. (1995). Exercise motivation across the lifespan. In S. J. H. Biddle (Ed.), *European perspectives on exercise and sport psychology* (pp. 3–25). Leeds, UK: Human Kinetics.

Wurtele, S. K., & Maddux, J. E. (1987). Relative contributions of protection motivation theory components in predicting exercise intentions and behavior. *Health Psychology, 6*, 453–466.

Yates, A., Leehey, K., & Shisslak, C. M. (1983). Running—An analogue of anorexia? *New England Journal of Medicine, 308*, 251–255.

Yesalis, C. E., & Cowart, V. S. (1998). *The steroids game: An expert's inside look at anabolic steroid use in sports.* Champaign, IL: Human Kinetics.

Yeung, R. R., & Hemsley, D. R. (1997). Personality, exercise, and psychological well-being: Static relationships in the community. *Personality and Individual Differences, 22*, 47–53.

Youngstedt, S. D. (1997). Does exercise truly enhance sleep? *The Physician and Sportsmedicine, 25*, 72–82.

Youngstedt, S. D. (2000). The exercise-sleep mystery. *International Journal of Sport Psychology, 31,* 241–255.

Youngstedt, S. D., O'Connor, P. J., Crabbe, J. B., & Dishman, R. K. (1998). Acute exercise reduces caffeine-induced anxiogenesis. *Medicine and Science in Sports and Exercise, 30,* 740–745.

Youngstedt, S. D., O'Connor, P. J., & Dishman, R. K. (1997). The effects of acute exercise on sleep: A quantitative synthesis. *Sleep, 20,* 203–214.

Youngsedt, S. D., Kripke, D., & Elliot, J. (1999). Is sleep disturbed by vigorous late-night exercise? *Medicine and Science in Sports and Exercise, 31,* 864–868.

Zander, A. (1982). *Making groups effective.* San Francisco: Jossey-Bass.

Zornetzer, S. F. (1985). Catecholamine system involvement in age-related memory dysfunction. *Annals of the New York Academy of Sciences, 444,* 242–254.

End of Book Credits

Note that credits preceded by two stars (**) are copyrighted material and the credit listed is the copyright holder's preference.

Chapter 1

Table 1-1 — Caspersen, et al. (1994). International physical activity patterns: A methodological perspective (Chapter 3, pp. 73-110). In R. K. Dishman (Ed.), *Advances in exercise adherence*. Champaign, IL: Human Kinetics. Used with permission.

Table 1-2. — ACSM (1978). ACSM's guidelines for exercise testing and prescription. Baltimore, MD: Lipincott, Williams & Wilkins; and Pate, et al. (1995). Physical activity and public health: A recommendation from the Centers for Disease Control and Prevention and the American College of Sports Medicine. *JAMA, 273*, 402-407.

Table 1-3 — Godin et al. (1983). The impact of physical fitness evaluation on behavioral intentions toward regular exercise. *Canadian Journal of Applied Sport Sciences, 8*, 240-245.

Table 1-4 — Gauvin et al. (1994). Physical activity, fitness, and health: Research and practice. In H. A. Quinney, L. Gauvin, & A. E. T. Wall (Eds.), *Toward active living* (Chapter 1, pp. 1-5). Champaign, IL: Human Kinetics.

Chapter 2

Table 2-1 — Sirard & Pate (2001). Physical activity assessment in children and adolescents. *Sports Medicine, 31*, 413-430.

Table 2-2 — Ainsworth et al. (1993). Compendium of physical activities: Classification of energy costs of human physical activities. *Medicine and Science in Sports and Exercise, 25*, 71-80; and Ainsworth et al. (2000). Compendium of physical activities: An update of activity codes and MET intensities *Medicine and Science in Sports and Exercise, 32*, S498-S516.

Figure 2-1 — Borg (1998). *Borg's perceived exertion and pain scales*. Champaign, IL: Human Kinetics.

**Figure 2-2 — "The utility of the Digi-Walker step counter to assess daily physical activity patterns." By G. J. Welk et al., 2000, *Medicine and Science in Sports and Exercise, 32*, S481-S488. Reprinted with permission.

Figure 2-3 — Jakicic et al. Accuracy of self-reported exercise and the relationship with weight loss in overweight women. *Medicine and Science in Sports and Exercise, 30*, 634-638.

Chapter 3

Table 3-1 — Etnier et al. (1997). The influence of physical fitness and exercise upon cognition functioning: A meta-analysis. *Journal of Sport and Exercise Psychology, 19*, 249-277.

Chapter 4

Table 4-1 — North et al. (1990). Effect of exercise on depression. *Exercise and Sport Science Reviews, 18*, 379-415.

Table 4-2 — North et al. (1990). Effect of exercise on depression. *Exercise and Sport Science Reviews, 18*, 379-415; and Craft & Landers (1998). The effects of exercise on clinical depression and depression resulting from mental illness: A meta-analysis. *Journal of Sport and Exercise Psychology, 20*, 339-357.

Table 4-3 — McDonald & Hodgdon (1991). *The psychological effects of aerobic fitness training: Research and theory*. New York: Springer-Verlag.

Chapter 5

Table 5-1 — Petruzzello et al. (1991). A meta-analysis on the anxiety-reducing effects of acute and chronic exercise. *Sports Medicine, 11*, 143-182; and Gruber (1986). Physical activity and self-esteem development in children: A meta-analysis. In G. A. Stull & H. M. Eckert (Eds.), *Effects of physical activity on children: A special tribute to Mabel Lee* (pp. 30-48). Champaign, IL: Human Kinetics; and McDonald & Hodgdon (1991). *The psychological effects of aerobic fitness training: Research and theory*. New York: Springer-Verlag.

Figure 5-1 — Petruzzello, S. J., Landers, D. M., Hatfield, B. D., Kubitz, K. A., & Salazar, W. (1991). A meta-analysis on the anxiety-reducing effects of acute and chronic exercise. *Sports Medicine, 11*, 143-182.

Figure 5-2 — Fox, K. R. (1998). Advances in the measurement of the physical self. In J. L. Duda (Ed.), *Advances in sport and exercise psychology measurement* (pp. 295-310). Morgantown, WV: Fitness Information Technology; and Shavelson, R. J., Hubner, J. J., & Stanton, G. C. (1976). Self-concept: Validation of construct interpretations. *Review of Educational Research, 46*, 407-411; and Sonstroem, R. J., Harlow, L. L., & Josephs, L. (1994). Exercise and self-esteem: Validity of model expansion and exercise associations. *Journal of Sport and Exercise Psychology, 16*, 29-42.

Figure 5-3 — Berscheid, E., Walster, E., & Bohrnstedt, G. (1973). The happy American body: A survey report. *Psychology Today, 7*, 119-131; and Cash, T. F., Winstedt, B. A., & Janda, L. H. (1986). The great American shape-up. *Psychology Today, 20*, 30-37; and Cash, T. F., & Henry, P. E. (1995). Women's body images: The results of a national survey in the U.S.A. *Sex Roles, 33*, 19-28.

Chapter 6

Table 6-1 — Youngstedt et al. (1997). The effects of acute exercise on sleep: A quantitative synthesis. *Sleep, 20*, 203-214.

Table 6-2 — Crews and Landers (1987). A meta-analytic review of aerobic fitness and reactivity to psychosocial stressors. *Medicine and Science in Sports and Exercise, 19 (Suppl. 5)*, S114-S120.

Figure 6-1 — Koltyn, K. F., Garvin, A. W., Gardiner, G. R., & Nelson, T. F. (1996). Perception of pain following aerobic exercise. *Medicine and Science in Sports and Exercise, 28*, 1418-1421.

Chapter 7

Table 7-3 — American Psychiatric Association. *Diagnostic and Statistical Manual for Mental Disorders* (4th ed.). Washington, DC: Author.

Figure 7-1 — Mondin, G. W., Morgan, W. P., Piering, P. N., Stegner, A. J., Stotesbery, C. L., Trine, M. R., & Wu, M. (1996). Psychological consequences of exercise deprivation in habitual exercisers. *Medicine and Science in Sports and Exercise, 28*, 1199-1203.

Figure 7-2 — O'Connor, P. J., Morgan, W. P., & Raglin, J. S. (1991). Psychobiologic effects of 3 d of increased training in female and male swimmers. *Medicine and Science in Sports and Exercise, 23*, 1055-1061.

**Figure 7-3 — "Estimated prevalence of anabolic steriod use among male high school seniors." By W. A. Buckley et al., 1988, *JAMA, 260*, 3441-3445. Reprinted with permission.

Chapter 8

Figure 8-1 — United States Department of Health and Human Services (2000). Physical activity and fitness. In *Healthy People 2010* [Online]. Available: www.health.gov/healthypeople/document/html/volume2/22physical.htm

Figure 8-2 — United States Department of Health and Human Services (2000). Physical activity and fitness. In *Healthy People 2010* [Online]. Available: www.health.gov/healthypeople/document/html/volume2/22physical.htm

Figure 8-3 — United States Department of Health and Human Services (2000). Physical activity and fitness. In *Healthy People 2010* [Online]. Available: www.health.gov/healthypeople/document/html/volume2/22physical.htm

Chapter 9

Table 9-1 — Carron et al. (1985). The development of an instrument to assess cohesion in sport teams: The group environment questionnaire. *Journal of Sport Psychology, 7*, 244-266; and Estabrooks & Carron (2000). The Physical Activity Group Environment Questionnaire: An instrument for the assessment of cohesion in exercise classes. *Group Dynamics: Theory, Research, and Practice, 4*, 230-243.

Table 9-2 — Fox et al. (2000). Effects of leadership style and group dynamics on enjoyment of physical activity. *American Journal of Health Promotion, 14*, 277-283.

Figure 9-1 — Carron, A. V., Widmeyer, W. N., & Brawley, L. R. (1985). The development of an instrument to assess cohesion in sport teams: The group environment questionnaire. *Journal of Sport Psychology, 7*, 244-266.

Chapter 10

Table 10-1 — Vaux (1992). Assessment of social support. In H. O. F. Veiel & U. Baumann (Eds.), *The meaning and measurement of social support* (pp. 193-216). New York: Hemisphere Publishing.

Table 10-2 — Carron, Hausenblas, & Mack (1996). Social influence and exercise: A meta-analysis. *Journal of Sport and Exercise Psychology, 18*, 1-16.

Table 10-3 — Carron, Hausenblas, & Mack (1996). Social influence and exercise: A meta-analysis. *Journal of Sport and Exercise Psychology, 18*, 1-16.

Chapter 11

**Figure 11-1 — Evaluation and modification of exercise patterns in the natural environment. *American Journal of Psychiatry, 137*, 1540-1545, 1980. Copyright, the American Psychiatric Association. Reprinted by permission.

Chapter 12

Table 12-1 — McAuley (1994). Enhancing psychological health through physical activity. In H. A. Quinney, L. Gauvin, & A. E. T. Wall (Eds.), *Toward active living: Proceedings of the International Conference on Physical Activity, Fitness, and Health* (pp. 83-90). Champaign, IL: Human Kinetics. Used with permission.

Figure 12-1 — Bandura, A. (1997). *Self-efficacy: The exercise of control.* New York: W. H. Freeman & Co.

Figure 12-2 — Bandura, A. (1997). *Self-efficacy: The exercise of control.* New York: W. H. Freeman & Co.

Chapter 13

Table 13-2 — Wurtele & Maddux (1987). Relative contributions of protection motivation theory components in predicting exercise intentions and behavior. *Health Psychology, 6*, 453-466.

Figure 13-1 — Janz, N., & Becker, M. (1984). The health belief model: A decade later. *Health Education Quarterly, 11*, 1-47.

Figure 13-2 — Rogers, R. W. (1983). Cognitive and physiological processes in fear appeals and attitude change: A revised theory of protection motivation. In J. R. Cacioppo & R. E. Petty (Eds.), *Social psychology: A source book* (pp. 153-176). New York: Guilford Press.

Figure 13-3 — Courneya (1995). Perceived severity of the consequences of physical inactivity across the stages of change in older adults. *Journal of Sport & Exercise Psychology, 17*, 447-457.

Chapter 14

Table 14-1 — Hausenblas et al. (1997). The theories of reasoned action and planned behavior: A meta-analysis. *Journal of Sport and Exercise Psychology, 19*, 47-62.

Figure 14-1 — From intentions to actions: A theory of planned behavior. In J. Kuhl and J. Beckman (Eds.), *Action control: From cognition to behavior* (pp. 11-39). Heidelberg: Springer.

Chapter 15

Table 15-1 — Reed et al. (1997). What makes a good algorithm: Examples from regular exercise. *American Journal of Health Promotion, 12*, 57-66.

Table 15-2 — Reed (1999). Adherence to exercise and the transtheoretical model of behavior change. In S. Bull (Ed.), *Adherence issues in sport & exercise* (pp. 19-46). New York: John Wiley & Sons.

Figure 15-2 — Cardinal, B. J. (1997). Construct validity of stages of change for exercise behavior. *American Journal of Health Promotion, 12*, 68-74.

Chapter 16

Figure 16-1 — Li, F. (1999). The Exercise Motivation Scale: Its multifaceted structure and construct validity. *Journal of Applied Sport Psychology, 11*, 97-115.

Figure 16-2 — Li, F. (1999). The Exercise Motivation Scale: Its multifaceted structure and construct validity. *Journal of Applied Sport Psychology, 11*, 97-115.

Figure 16-3 — Maehr, M. L. (1984). Meaning and motivation. In R. Ames & C. Ames (Eds.), *Research on motivation in education (Vol. 1),* (pp. 115-144). New York: Academic Press; and Maehr, M. L., & Braskamp, L. A. (1986). *The motivation factor: A theory of personal investment.* Lexington, MA: Lexington Press.

Chapter 17

Table 17-1 — Dishman & Buckworth (1996). Increasing physical activity: A quantitative synthesis. *Medicine and Science in Sports and Exercise, 28*, 706-719.

Table 17-2 — Dishman & Buckworth (1996). Increasing physical activity: A quantitative synthesis. *Medicine and Science in Sports and Exercise, 28*, 706-719.

Figure 17-1 — Dishman, R. K., & Buckworth, J. (1996). Increasing physical activity: A quantitative synthesis. *Medicine and Science in Sports and Exercise, 28*, 706-719.

Figure 17-2 — Dishman, R. K., & Buckworth, J. (1996). Increasing physical activity: A quantitative synthesis. *Medicine and Science in Sports and Exercise, 28*, 706-719.

Chapter 18

**Table 18-1 — Adapted by permission from A. V. Carron & K. S. Spink, 1993. "Team building in an exercise setting," *The Sport Psychologist, 7*, 8-18.

**Figure 18-1 — Adapted by permission from A. V. Carron & K. S. Spink, 1993. "Team building in an exercise setting," *The Sport Psychologist, 7*, 8-18.

Chapter 19

Table 19-1 — Centers for Disease Control and Prevention (1997). Guidelines for school and community programs to promote lifelong physical activity among young people. *Morbidity and Mortality Weekly Report, 46* (no. rr-6), 1-37.

Name Index

Subject Index

Note: Page numbers followed by f indicate figures; those followed by t indicate tables.